WJEC/EDUQAS
Religious Studies for AS & A Level
Philosophy of Religion

Revised Edition

Karl Lawson
Series editor: Richard Gray

WJEC Eduqas bears no responsibility for the sample answer provided, any commentary or marks awarded.

The teaching content of this resource is endorsed by WJEC Eduqas to support AS and A Level Religious Studies.

This resource has been reviewed against WJEC Eduqas' endorsement criteria. As this resource belongs to a third party, there may be occasions where a specification may be updated and that update will not be reflected in the third party resource. Users should always refer to WJEC Eduqas' specification and Sample Assessment Materials to ensure that learners are studying the most up to date course.

It is recommended that teachers use a range of resources to fully prepare their learners for the exam and not rely solely on one textbook or digital resource.

WJEC, nor anyone employed by WJEC has been paid for the endorsement of this resource, nor does WJEC receive any royalties from its sale.

WJEC Eduqas bears no responsibility for the sample answers provided, any commentary or marks awarded.

Although every effort has been made to ensure that website addresses are correct at time of going to press, Hachette Learning cannot be held responsible for the content of any website mentioned in this book. It is sometimes possible to find a relocated web page by typing in the address of the home page for a website in the URL window of your browser.

Hachette UK's policy is to use papers that are natural, renewable and recyclable products and made from wood grown in well-managed forests and other controlled sources. The logging and manufacturing processes are expected to conform to the environmental regulations of the country of origin.

To order, please visit www.HachetteLearning.com or contact Customer Service at education@hachette.co.uk / +44 (0)1235 827827.

ISBN: 978 1 0360 0492 7

© Richard Gray and Karl Lawson 2025

First published in 2020

This edition published in 2025 by

Hachette Learning,

An Hachette UK Company

Carmelite House

50 Victoria Embankment

London EC4Y 0DZ

www.HachetteLearning.com

The authorised representative in the EEA is Hachette Ireland, 8 Castlecourt Centre, Castleknock Road, Castleknock, Dublin 15, D15 YF6A, Ireland

Impression number   5 4 3 2 1

Year   2029 2028 2027 2026 2025

All rights reserved. Apart from any use permitted under UK copyright law, no part of this publication may be reproduced or transmitted in any form or by any means, electronic or mechanical, including photocopying and recording, or held within any information storage and retrieval system, without permission in writing from the publisher or under licence from the Copyright Licensing Agency Limited. Further details of such licences (for reprographic reproduction) may be obtained from the Copyright Licensing Agency Limited, www.cla.co.uk

Cover photo © sborisov – stock.adobe.com

Illustrations by Integra Software Services

Typeset in India

Printed in the UK by Bell and Bain Ltd, Glasgow

A catalogue record for this title is available from the British Library.

CONTENTS

About this book 4

Theme 1: Arguments for the existence of God – inductive 8
A: Inductive arguments – cosmological — 8
B: Inductive arguments – teleological — 16
C: Challenges to inductive arguments — 23

Theme 1: Arguments for the existence of God – deductive 30
D: Deductive arguments – origins of the ontological argument — 30
E: Deductive arguments – developments of the ontological argument — 37
F: Challenges to the ontological argument — 44

Theme 2: Challenges to religious belief – the problem of evil and suffering 50
A: The problem of evil and suffering — 50
B: Religious responses to the problem of evil: Augustinian-type theodicy — 58
C: Religious responses to the problem of evil: Irenaean-type theodicy — 66

Theme 2: Challenges to religious belief – religious belief as a product of the human mind 73
D: Religious belief as a product of the human mind: Sigmund Freud — 73
E: Religious belief as a product of the human mind: Carl Jung — 86
F: Issues relating to rejection of religion: atheism — 99

Theme 3: Religious experience (1) 113
A: The nature of religious experience — 113
B: Mystical experience — 125
C: Challenges to the objectivity and authenticity of religious experience — 132

Theme 3: Religious experience (2) 140
D: The influence of religious experience on religious practice and faith — 140
E: Different definitions of miracles — 153
F: Contrasting views on the possibility of miracles: David Hume and Richard Swinburne — 164

Theme 4: Religious language (1) 172
A: Inherent problems of religious language — 172
B: Religious language as cognitive, but meaningless — 182
C: Religious language as non-cognitive and analogical — 195

Theme 4: Religious language (2) 205
D: Religious language as non-cognitive and symbolic — 205
E: Religious language as non-cognitive and mythical — 220
F: Religious language as a language game — 238

Glossary 250

Index 253

About this book

With the A Level in Religious Studies, there is a lot to cover in preparation for the examinations at the end of the course. The aim of these books is to provide enough support for you to achieve success at A Level, whether as a teacher or a learner.

This series of books is skills-based in its approach to learning, which means it aims to combine covering the content of the specification with examination preparation from the start. In other words, it aims to help you get through the course while at the same time developing some important skills needed for the examinations.

To help you study, there are clearly defined sections for each of the AO1 and AO2 areas of the specification. These are arranged according to the specification themes and use, as far as is possible, specification headings to help you see that the content has been covered.

The AO1 content is detailed but precise, with the benefit of providing you with references to both religious/philosophical works and to the views of scholars. The AO2 responds to the issues raised in the specification and provides you with ideas for further debate, to help you develop your own evaluation skills.

Ways to use this book

In considering the different ways in which you may teach or learn, it was decided that the books needed to have an inbuilt flexibility to adapt. As a result, they can be used for classroom learning, for independent work by individuals, as homework, and they are even suitable for the purposes of 'flip learning' if your school or college does this.

You may be well aware that learning time is so valuable at A Level and so we have also taken this into consideration by creating flexible features and activities, again to save you the time of painstaking research and preparation, either as teacher or learner.

Features of the books

The books all contain the following features that appear in the margins, or are highlighted in the main body of the text, in order to support teaching and learning.

Key terms of technical, religious and philosophical words or phrases.

> **Key terms**
>
> **Holy Spirit:** God as spiritually active in the world

Key quotes either from religious and philosophical works and/or the works of scholars.

> **Key quote**
>
> I ... decided, after investigating everything carefully from the very first, to write an orderly account.
>
> (Luke 1:3)

Key person boxes summarise essential figures.

> **Key person**
>
> **Rudolf Bultmann (1884–1976):** a German theologian who called for the 'demythologisation' of the New Testament

AO1 activities that serve the purpose of focusing on identification, presentation and explanation, and developing the skills of knowledge and understanding required for the examination.

> **AO1 Activity**
>
> a   Using bullet points, outline the key ideas in both the classical and modern forms of the problem of evil.
>
> This helps with presenting a thorough and extensive knowledge and understanding of the topic area.

AO2 activities that serve the purpose of focusing on conclusions, as a basis for thinking about the issues, developing critical analysis and the evaluation skills required for the examination.

> **AO2 Activity** *Possible lines of argument*
>
> Listed below are some conclusions that could be drawn from the AO2 reasoning in the accompanying text:

Specification content boxes highlight exactly what is being covered in each section and how it connects to the specification.

> **Specification content**
>
> The extent to which the classical form of the problem of evil is a problem.

Glossary of all the key terms for quick reference.

AO2 skills: critical analysis and evaluation

A good way to prepare yourself for an AO2 part (b) evaluation answer is to consider the different ways to approach this. Sometimes writing frames or anacronyms may be suggested. Whilst these are useful, they are meant as 'scaffolding' or support for an answer, but the danger is that they end up restricting more natural and personal evaluation.

One useful approach is to think about some different styles of writing and relate these to 'characters' that are easily remembered.

Strong evaluative characters

We can look at what are considered **strong evaluative character styles** that display all the qualities that avoid the pitfalls above. By this we mean different aspects, elements or ingredients of an effective critical analysis and evaluation.

If we look at the table below, we can see 7 characters, each of which has a specific strength and quality that display skills of critical analysis and/ or evaluation. The strength of each character forms a **part** of a strong evaluation. In a full AO2 answer it may be useful to vary the characters in terms of depth and breadth.

The characters can be used as a checklist not a structured plan or rigid writing frame. The best way to use them is to consider the different styles and skills **before** writing an answer and then measure your answer by checking that the critical analysis and evaluation elements are there.

Examples of this can be seen in the sample answer we provide. In these sample answers you may notice that not all the character styles have been used in the same order, detail or combination; however, generally, most are often covered.

In the table below, we have attempted to demonstrate how each character may fulfil the criteria for a band 5 evaluation using the descriptors it presents. These are highlighted in blue in the third column.

Character	Strength	Application and AO2 Band descriptor link
Tennis player	<ul><li>The tennis player deals with specific lines of arguments (often from either named scholars or schools of thought) and returns counter arguments.</li><li>The tennis player manages arguments and counter arguments, making sure there is consideration of several lines of argument in response to the statement in the question.</li><li>This is sometimes understood as 'for' or in support of an argument and 'against'; however, this does not necessarily always have to be done in an even or balanced way since some answers may wish to argue effectively towards a conclusion that is supported by several lines of reasoning, evidence and argument that support each other.</li></ul>	<ul><li>The tennis player ensures that **thorough, sustained and clear views are given** in an answer.</li><li>The tennis player also ensures that the **views of scholars/schools of thought are used extensively**.</li></ul>
Detective	<ul><li>The detective has a forensic ability to examine, collate and clarify evidence and provide examples. The detective makes sure that the argument presented is substantial in that it is based in evidence and examples to support the reasoning presented.</li><li>The detective selects details that are accurate and relevant in a thorough way. They make sure that there is correct reference to specialist language in the correct context.</li></ul>	<ul><li>The **views of scholars/schools of thought are used appropriately and in context**.</li><li>There is a **thorough and accurate use of specialist language and vocabulary in context**.</li></ul>
Philosopher	<ul><li>The philosopher likes to raise and ask interesting and relevant questions.</li><li>The philosopher often indicates that there may be problems or challenges to a specific approach and likes to suggest a solution.</li><li>When an argument or analysis is in 'full flow' we may think of questions that we would like to raise in response to views analysed. The philosopher loves to do this.</li></ul>	<ul><li>The philosopher character is typical of **perceptive evaluation**.</li><li>The philosopher successfully **identifies the issues raised by the question set**.</li></ul>
News reporter	<ul><li>The news reporter provides perspective, clarity, an overview of the debate. Commentary is vital in an AO2 answer as it demonstrates that the student is engaging with the debate that the statement presents. It is an easy way to demonstrate that you are thinking about the issues.</li><li>The best way to provide yourself with an opportunity to develop a more personalised approach is to practice pausing and reflecting upon points made, developing them with evidence and examples and commenting on the qualities a line of argument possesses.</li></ul>	<ul><li>Using a news reporter style ensures that a response **thoroughly addresses the issues raised by the question set**.</li></ul>

Explorer	• The explorer likes to suggest some alternative ways of answering a question. Sometimes it feels as though a debate needs a different angle, approach or perspective. The explorer often suggests new ways of attempting to arrive at a solution to the debate. • This can often be your own response in considering a given statement including a new suggestion or perhaps a question you would like to raise. • You can even try to bring in other strands and evidence beyond the immediate topic from other areas of the course.	• This ensures that there is **confident and perceptive analysis of the nature of connections between the various elements of the approaches studied**.
Critical thinker	• The critical thinker points out more technical aspects of an argument. The critical thinker is often concerned with how an argument 'works' and 'flows'. • The critical thinker sometimes challenges more forensic aspects of an argument. • The critical thinker checks for coherence and consistency. Does the evidence support the conclusion? Is there a counter argument?	• The critical thinker ensures that there is **extensive, detailed reasoning** in an answer.
Judge	Makes an overall ruling and concludes matters. The judge in some ways is the most vital character. They cannot stand alone and rely upon others and their contributions to make a final decision. This can be in favour or against the statement, or, it may be that the statement itself is questionable. Often an overall judgement ends an answer; however, sometimes an overall conclusion may start the answer and then discuss, analyse and reason why this may be the case. Strong evaluative answers often have several judgments or mini-conclusions throughout the answer.	• The judge is the final voice of an answer. They may appear anywhere in an answer but usually summarises at the end. The judge should be clear evidence of **confident critical analysis**.

Summary of a strong evaluative answer

- Offers clear, sustained and varied lines of argument (view) like the exchanges of a tennis player.
- The varied evidence of scholarly views and schools of thought are precisely examined and coherently presented like the report of a detective.
- Issues are identified to focus on, and questions may be raised like a philosopher.
- Engages with a debate by offering commentary and reflection upon the points presented like a news reporter.
- May explore some new ways of answering the question and possible refer to other elements of the course like an explorer.
- Contains reasoning that is detailed, ordered, coherent and effective like a critical thinker.
- Ensures there is an overall judgment made that clearly links to the reasoning and evidence contained in the answer like a judge.

Arguments for the existence of God – inductive

This section covers AO1 content and skills

Specification content
Inductive proofs; the concept of *a posteriori*

A: Inductive arguments – cosmological

Imagine that you are trying to solve a murder mystery. You know where the crime took place, you know roughly when it took place and you think you know who was at the scene of the crime. However, you did not actually witness it first-hand, so how can you prove what happened? How do you solve the crime?

The only way to do so is to gather evidence. So, you begin your search for clues. After some time, you have managed to gather witness statements, you have photographs of the murder scene, you have examined the body, you have had forensics experts reporting back to you and, finally, you are ready to reveal who the murderer is and why he or she committed the crime.

Looking for clues

Inductive proofs

What you have just done is to induct a judgement, based on evidence and experience that has led to a possible conclusion. In philosophical terms, you have reached your conclusion via **inductive proof**. Such proof is the only type available to us in many circumstances – particularly when we are not available to gather direct proof: that is, we were not present at the time of the event to witness it **empirically**. Equally, we cannot use pure logical reasoning to come up with a conclusion because neither the circumstances nor the events allow this to happen.

Key terms

inductive proof: argument constructed on evidence and/or experience that puts forward a possible conclusion based on these

empirically: using knowledge gained through the experiences of any of the five senses

The concept of *a posteriori*

Inductive proofs are **a posteriori** because they need evidence and/or experience for them to make sense. In the philosophy of religion, any argument that is constructed on evidence and/or experience is an *a posteriori*, inductive, argument.

Cosmological argument: St Thomas Aquinas' first Three Ways

First Way

St Thomas Aquinas' First Way is often referred to as 'motion' or 'change'. Essentially, Aquinas says that when we observe the universe, we notice that things tend to be in a state of change or motion. From this observation, Aquinas notes that things do not do this of their own accord, but are instead 'moved' (or 'changed') by something else (here Aquinas is restating what Aristotle said).

> **Key quote**
>
> It is certain, and evident to our senses, that in the world some things are in motion. Now whatever is in motion is put in motion by another, for nothing can be in motion except it is in potentiality to that towards which it is in motion; whereas a thing moves inasmuch as it is in act. For motion is nothing else than the reduction of something from potentiality to actuality. But nothing can be reduced from potentiality to actuality, except by something in a state of actuality.
>
> (Aquinas, *Summa Theologica*)

The Unmoved Mover

Aquinas says that if we look back down this sequence of movements or changes, we will eventually have to come to something that started off the whole sequence. Now, as all things in the universe (that are observable) are either moving or movers, we need to find a point that started these things. That has to mean looking outside of the universe: that is, to something that has not been moved by anything else and is, in fact, incapable of being moved or changed by anything else, but is responsible for starting the whole sequence of movement or change.

The Ancient Greek philosopher Aristotle named this the *Prime Mover*, and Aquinas developed this into the *Unmoved Mover*: 'that which all men call God'.

The efficient cause

To illustrate this point further, Aquinas builds on Aristotle's examples and explanations. Aristotle speaks of things moving from a state of **potentiality** (that is, a situation where it has a possibility of moving or changing into something else) towards a state of **actuality** (where it actually achieves or reaches its potential).

> **Key term**
>
> *a posteriori*: based on actual observation, evidence, experimental data or experience – relates to *inductive reasoning*

> **Specification content**
>
> Cosmological argument; St Thomas Aquinas' first Three Ways (motion or change; cause and effect; contingency and necessity)

> **Key terms**
>
> **potentiality**: the ability to become something else
> **actuality**: when something is in its fully realised state

> **Key terms**
>
> **efficient cause:** the 'third party' that moves potentiality to actuality

However, both Aristotle and Aquinas note that this change could happen only if something that already possessed a state of actuality acted on something that was in its state of potentiality. This third party is known as the **efficient cause**.

Aquinas uses the example of wood becoming hot, via fire, to illustrate this point.

Fire is the efficient cause that makes wood hot

> **Key quote**
>
> Thus that which is actually hot, as fire, makes wood, which is potentially hot, to be actually hot, and thereby moves and changes it. Now it is not possible that the same thing should be at once in actuality and potentiality in the same respect, but only in different respects. For what is actually hot cannot simultaneously be potentially hot; but it is simultaneously potentially cold. It is therefore impossible that in the same respect and in the same way a thing should be both mover and moved, i.e. that it should move itself.
>
> (Aquinas, *Summa Theologica*)

Aquinas is stating that the fire that makes wood hot must already have the property of hotness to make the wood hot. If it had any other state (e.g., coldness), then it would be impossible to make the wood hot.

Second Way

> **Key quote**
>
> Now in efficient causes it is not possible to go on to infinity, because in all efficient causes following in order, the first is the cause of the intermediate cause, and the intermediate is the cause of the ultimate cause, whether the intermediate cause be several, or only one. Now to take away the cause is to take away the effect. Therefore, if there be no first cause among efficient causes, there will be no ultimate, nor any intermediate cause.
>
> (Aquinas, *Summa Theologica*)

Aquinas' Second Way deals with the concept of cause and effect. Aquinas believed that everything observable in nature is subject to this law. He also believed that it was impossible for this chain of cause and effect to go back infinitely. This led Aquinas to ask the question: 'What was the first cause?' and, for him, the answer was 'God'.

Aquinas states here not only the idea that cause and effect is a simple, undeniable law of the universe, but also that it is impossible for anything within the universe to cause itself. (It would be like you being your own parent – you cannot exist before you exist; you need something else to bring you into existence.)

Cause and effect

Third Way

Aquinas' Third Way deals with the concept of contingency and necessity. Again, Aquinas notes that everything that exists has the possibility of not existing (that is, it is **contingent**). He concludes that if this is true of everything in existence, then nothing would ever have come into existence. This is because for contingent beings to exist, there has to be a non-contingent (that is, **necessary**) **being** that brought everything else into existence. For Aquinas, this necessary being is 'God'.

> **Key quote**
>
> The third way is taken from possibility and necessity, and runs thus. We find in nature things that are possible to be and not to be, since they are found to be generated, and to corrupt, and consequently, they are possible to be and not to be. But it is impossible for these always to exist, for that which is possible not to be at some time is not. Therefore, if everything is possible not to be, then at one time there could have been nothing in existence … it would have been impossible for anything to have begun to exist; and thus even now nothing would be in existence … which is absurd.
>
> (Aquinas, *Summa Theologica*)

Aquinas states that all things in nature are limited in their existence. They all have beginnings and endings. Following this idea to its logical conclusion, Aquinas notes that this means at one point in history nothing existed and that without a necessary being, even now, nothing would exist – which is plainly not the case.

A way of thinking of this idea is to consider the relationship of the parent and the child. Without the existence of the parent, the child cannot come into existence. Or, to put it another way, the child is contingent on the parent for its existence.

The Kalam cosmological argument

From the Arabic word *Kalam*, meaning 'to argue or discuss', the Kalam cosmological argument traces its origins to the work of Islamic scholars in the ninth and eleventh centuries AD. It has been modernised and championed by Christian **apologist** William Lane Craig.

Craig outlined his argument as follows:

1. Everything that begins to exist has a cause of its existence.
2. The universe began to exist.
3. Therefore, the universe has a cause of its existence.
4. Since no scientific explanation (in terms of physical laws) can provide a causal account of the origin of the universe, the cause must be personal (explanation is given in terms of a personal agent).

Key terms

contingent: anything that depends on something else; in the case of a contingent being, it is contingent upon another being for its existence (e.g. a child is contingent upon its parent)

necessary being: Aquinas' contention that a non-contingent being is necessary for contingent beings to exist; it is this necessary being that is the source of all existence for all other contingent beings

Specification content

The Kalam cosmological argument with reference to William Lane Craig (rejection of actual infinities and concept of a personal creator)

Key term

apologist: a person who promotes and explains a specific point of view or cause, often in the context of responding to opposition to that view or cause

Key term

actual infinite: a concept that suggests things can exist in time and space yet be never ending; this idea was classically rejected by Aristotle and is also rejected by Craig in his Kalam argument

Key term

potential infinite: the potential infinite is something that could continue, were effort to be applied (e.g. it would be possible always to continue a number line if we wanted to, as we could always come up with a bigger number)

Summary

- Inductive arguments use evidence or experience as their basis.
- The cosmological argument is an *a posteriori* inductive argument for the existence of God.
- Aquinas supports this argument with the first three of his Five Ways: change, cause and contingency.
- William Lane Craig has developed the argument in recent times; it is known as the *Kalam cosmological argument*.

This is a (relatively) straightforward and easy-to-follow argument. However, to answer challenges to the idea that the universe might be considered infinite, Craig developed the following defence to his second point:

a An **actual infinite** cannot exist.
b A beginningless temporal series of events is an actual infinite.
c Therefore, a beginningless temporal series of events cannot exist.

The example of the infinite library

The example of a library is often used to explain an actual infinite. Imagine a library with an actually infinite number of books. Suppose that the library also contains an infinite number of red and an infinite number of black books. You would have to conclude logically that the infinite number of red books was equal to the total number of books in the library (that is, both red and black books), but that conclusion makes no sense. This conclusion shows that infinities make no sense either, and so can't exist in the physical universe.

Potential v. actual infinity

However, critics point out that this is ignoring that there are two types of infinity recognised in standard mathematics: *actual* and *potential*. Craig refers only to the impossibility of the first, not the second, in his initial argument. Craig's response to this criticism forms the second part of his argument: if an actual infinite is recognised as impossible, a **potential infinite** confirms that the universe had a beginning.

The influence of Craig's Kalam cosmological argument

Craig's Kalam cosmological argument is often seen as very confusing, not least because it depends on an understanding of the concepts of infinity, which are, in themselves, difficult to grasp. However, in its simplest form, it is straightforward and appealing; to such a degree that it has had significant influence in philosophical debates against atheism. This is especially true in the fundamentalist Christian churches of the USA.

AO1 Activity

a Explain Craig's Kalam argument as two separate arguments:
  i   that the universe had a beginning
  ii that the beginning of the universe was due to the deliberate choice of a personal creator.

  This helps with presenting a thorough and extensive knowledge and understanding of the topic area.

b Select the five most important ideas presented by Aquinas and Craig, and explain why they are important to our understanding of the cosmological argument.

  This helps develop skills of organisation by selecting and ordering evidence and examples.

> **Specification content**
> The extent to which the Kalam cosmological argument is convincing

> This section covers AO2 content and skills

Issues for analysis and evaluation

The extent to which the Kalam cosmological argument is convincing

Possible line of argument	Critical analysis and evaluation
Craig's Kalam cosmological argument benefits from being able to draw on the widely accepted scientific view that the universe had a beginning	Craig's Kalam cosmological argument would seem to benefit from being written in the modern scientific age. He has access to contemporary scientific information about the universe: the Big Bang theory, cosmological background radiation, etc. These all provide straightforward, scientifically validated evidence that the universe is finite and thus had a beginning. This provides an extremely useful evidence base for any argument attempting to demonstrate that a beginning of the universe is required.
The first part of Craig's Kalam cosmological argument is scientifically valid and therefore convincing	In a sense, this renders the need for Craig to prove the universe is finite as meaningless. Why argue for something that most of the scientific world supports? The concept that all things in our experience – including the universe itself – have beginnings, lends itself nicely to the first part of Craig's argument. Craig's work here, it would seem, is done – the Kalam cosmological argument for God's existence appears to be entirely convincing.
Craig's Kalam cosmological argument is potentially weakened when he suggests the universe has a specific cause	However, Craig's argument moves from demonstrating that the universe had a beginning to the suggestion that this beginning had a cause, external to the universe – which Craig eventually asserts as being God. The question of how convincing the argument is now rests on how far the individual is willing to accept the next steps in Craig's argument.
The universe cannot be explained in terms of physical laws	Effectively, Craig suggests that the cause of the universe must be through the deliberate choice of a personal being, as the physical laws of the universe, which cause everything within the universe to work, did not themselves exist until the universe existed. Therefore, the cause of the universe could not be explained in terms of them.
The cause of the universe must be personal	The only other viable explanation for Craig is that the cause is personal. For Craig, the only viable personal agent capable of existing outside of the universe and having the will, power and ability to create the universe is God.
The appeal for theists of the argument	For the theist, there is much that is attractive about this argument. It involves modern cosmology, appears entirely rational and fits with traditional theistic interpretations regarding creation. In this sense, it is a convincing argument.
The issue for non-theists	For those not predisposed to the position of the theist, however, the argument does not have the same power to convince. Why should God be the answer? Why not something else entirely?
The Kalam cosmological argument is not convincing because it contradicts itself	Craig states in his Kalam cosmological argument that infinity is impossible, which is why the universe must have a beginning. However, later in the argument, he refers to a personal creator that is infinite. As an argument, this is self-contradictory and is one of the key reasons for non-theists to reject the Kalam cosmological argument for God's existence.

T1 Arguments for the existence of God – inductive

> **AO2 Activity**
>
> **a** Analyse three possible conclusions that could be drawn from the critical analysis and evaluation of the cosmological argument. What are their strengths and weaknesses? Which conclusion is strongest?
>
> **b** Using the strongest conclusion, select three lines of argument that you would use to support this conclusion. Try to explain why you have selected these three lines.

Specification content

Whether inductive arguments for God's existence are persuasive

Exam practice

Sample question

Evaluate whether inductive arguments for God's existence are persuasive.

Sample answer

One of the key strengths of inductive arguments for God's existence lies in its ability to establish probability – gathering evidence, such as the existence of the universe, and suggesting the most likely conclusion, i.e. that it was deliberately created by an all-powerful being, based on this evidence. Evidence-based arguments are often more persuasive than arguments not based on evidence. Inductive arguments are *a posteriori* and synthetic (true in relation to how they relate to the world) as they depend on experience and/or evidence. This provides them with credibility and makes them more likely to be persuasive. Inductive arguments rely on experience that may be universal and testable – allowing them to be widely used. For many people, this is extremely important as it makes the argument more understandable and accessible and, therefore, persuasive. This is particularly relevant for the theist, in showing that, based on inductive criteria, God's existence can be proved.

A good introduction that outlines how inductive arguments work and also indicates how the evaluation may proceed, in respect to the existence of God – a good overview. It is also grounded in accurate terminology that the writer correctly understands.

Another key strength is that the argument recognises there may be more than one correct answer – the evidence used can support more than one probable conclusion, which is particularly useful if an individual is not entirely certain what the conclusion should be. This means the argument can be persuasive precisely because it has flexibility. This also allows for the possibility of error, which means changes can be made to elements of the reasoning without undermining the process (or conclusion) as a whole. This provides the theist with a suitable response should God not be the conclusion reached by other forms of inductive reasoning.

This response highlights one of the main reasons that inductive arguments can be effective and points out that it's the very flexibility of this approach that gives it its strength.

Furthermore, inductive arguments are the basis of the vast majority of scientifically accepted theories, and these have a wide appeal in the twenty-first-century world. People readily accept such theories as valid precisely because of the inductive and evidence-based approaches that led to these theories being formed. Does this mean that any philosophical or theological reasoning that mirrors the work of science must surely have a similar claim to both validity and persuasiveness – unlike any reasoning that has not been based on such foundations?

The answer explores the impact that inductive-based theories have in the contemporary world in their scientific context. It then raises interesting questions as to possible use as a reason to confirm validity in both a philosophical and theological context.

However, some may argue that inductive arguments are not persuasive – often for the same reasons as others would claim they are. For instance, one of the significant weaknesses of inductive arguments is that we can accuse them of having limited effectiveness as 'undeniable proofs'. Their very flexibility means that we could consider them weak arguments and, because of this, not persuasive.

It is also true to state that we can readily challenge inductive arguments if alternative evidence, which is equally likely to be true, is provided – thereby undermining the persuasiveness of the argument. An extension to this is that it is also equally possible to accept all the evidence but to deny the conclusion without contradiction. If we accept this, then it suggests that there can be no persuasiveness in the argument as this limits its effectiveness, particularly in terms of attempting to establish the existence of a divine being with specific characteristics: for example, the God of classical theism as the designer of the universe.

Perhaps most important to consider is that the premises, while supporting the conclusion, do not make it definite – for many, this means that inductive arguments are not persuasive enough to support a basis for a belief in the existence of God.

Tennis player
This argument delivers a direct counterpoint to the previous one, demonstrating that the greatest strength of inductive arguments may also be their greatest weakness.

News reporter
Critical thinker
The answer revisits the theme of flexibility and provides an overview of the debate. It then develops the reasoning in the argument to show the key flaw in this approach as one of trying to 'prove' definitively the existence of God.

Judge
The conclusion the candidate draws follows the inevitable line of reasoning in the second part of the answer and points out the mechanics of inductive arguments as fundamentally undermining the power of a persuasive argument.

Evaluation

This is a very good answer. There is a clear and well-developed line of reasoning, considering the strengths and then the weaknesses within the argument, leading to a clear conclusion. The candidate shows how the same characteristic of inductive arguments can be used both for and against it and acknowledges that, while flexibility of approach is useful in a scientific context, it provides a challenge when attempting to reach a definitive conclusion.

Over to you

For this first task, try using the framework/writing frame provided to help you practise the AO2 skills needed to answer the question below.

As the units in each section of the book develop, the amount of support will gradually reduce to encourage you to be independent and to perfect your AO2 skills.

Question

'Inductive arguments for God's existence are persuasive.' Evaluate this view.

(Q3b, Component 2: Philosophy of Religion, WJEC, Summer 2024)

Writing frame

The issue for debate here is whether arguments such as the cosmological and teleological arguments can show that God exists, which they attempt to do by …

The following evidence supports the contention …

We could, however, reject the contention by considering the following points …

It is my view that … and I base this argument on the following reasons: …

> This section covers AO1 content and skills

Specification content

St Thomas Aquinas' Fifth Way – concept of governance; archer and arrow analogy

B: Inductive arguments – teleological

St Thomas Aquinas' Fifth Way

Aquinas' teleological argument can be found in the fifth of his Five Ways in the *Summa Theologica*. Here, in explaining the concept of governance (how God 'governs' the universe), Aquinas states that something that lacks intelligence cannot move towards fulfilling a useful end, unless something with intelligence moves it.

> **Key quote**
>
> The Fifth Way is taken from the governance of the world. We see that things which lack knowledge, such as natural bodies, act for an end, and this is evident from their acting always, or nearly always, in the same way, so as to obtain the best result. Hence it is plain that they achieve their end, not fortuitously, but designedly.
>
> Now whatever lacks knowledge cannot move towards an end, unless it be directed by some being endowed with knowledge and intelligence; as the arrow is directed by the archer. Therefore, some intelligent being exists by whom all natural things are directed to their end; and this being we call God.
>
> (Aquinas, *Summa Theologica*)

Imagine, for example, that you need to write your essay with a pen. The pen itself is non-intelligent and cannot (however much you may wish it!) write your essay for you. The only way that it will do this is if you (as an intelligent being) pick up the pen; hold it in a way that is appropriate for writing; and then apply it to the paper, moving it to make the shapes (writing) to communicate your ideas.

Aquinas' own example was that of the arrow and the archer. Archery was a well-known activity in his day, both as a sport and as a way of killing other people in war; therefore, his analogy would have made sense to his audience.

Aquinas' Fifth Way uses the example of the arrow and archer to demonstrate guiding intelligence

Guiding intelligence

Aquinas stated that the arrow cannot, by itself, reach the target. The archer needs to fire it for this to happen. He then relates this to how the universe works. He states that everything in the universe follows natural laws, even if it possesses no intelligence: for example, the regular movement of the stars in the sky – for which, in Aquinas' time, people had no rational 'scientific' explanation.

That these things also tend to follow natural laws and, in doing so, fulfil some purpose or end goal (their **telos**), yet don't have the ability to 'think' for themselves, suggests that (like the arrow) they have been 'guided' by something else. For Aquinas, the only possible explanation was that this something else, this 'guiding intelligence', was God.

● **Key term**

telos: this term can have a number of meanings, but it generally refers to the 'end' (as in the final destination), 'goal' or 'purpose' of something – the term is frequently found in Aristotle's philosophy

Paley's watchmaker

Analogy of complex design

William Paley, the eighteenth-century Archdeacon of Carlisle, is widely credited with proposing the design argument in its popular modern form. He proposed his version in his *Natural Theology*, which was published at the beginning of the nineteenth century. His basic argument is that, if we discovered a stone while out walking, we might ask how it came to be. By considering natural events, we might conclude how it was formed. However, if we discovered a watch, we would not come to the same conclusions. Paley was interested in pointing out why this was the case.

> **Specification content**
> Paley's watchmaker – analogy of complex design

" Key quote

In crossing a heath, suppose I pitched my foot against a stone, and were asked how the stone came to be there; I might possibly answer, that, for anything I knew to the contrary, it had lain there forever: nor would it perhaps be very easy to show the absurdity of this answer. But suppose I had found a watch upon the ground, and it should be inquired how the watch happened to be in that place; I should hardly think of the answer I had before given, that for anything I knew, the watch might have always been there. ... There must have existed, at some time, and at some place or other, an artificer or artificers, who formed [the watch] for the purpose which we find it actually to answer; who comprehended its construction, and designed its use. ... Every indication of contrivance, every manifestation of design, which existed in the watch, exists in the works of nature; with the difference, on the side of nature, of being greater or more, and that in a degree which exceeds all computation.

William Paley, *Natural Theology* (1802)

Workings of a watch

Paley's watch/watchmaker analogy

Watches in the 1800s consisted of a watch-face with numerals on it and hands that pointed towards the time. The inner workings of the watch would reveal a very complicated system of cogs, springs and gears that enabled the hands to move in a way that measured the passage of time. The very complexity of these mechanisms would lead to a conclusion that this watch had been designed by a being of intelligence, and was not the result of random chance.

Paley states that we could draw this conclusion even if we were unaware of the purpose of the watch, if the watch went wrong, or even if we didn't understand what some of the parts of the watch actually did. In summary, the watch, with all its complexities, needs an intelligent watchmaker to explain how it came into being. Paley then states that the universe (and using the natural world as evidence) is likewise complex and therefore also points towards a designer. For Paley this was a divine designer, i.e. God.

Paley's examples from nature (showing complex design)

In his writing, Paley spends a large amount of time detailing the workings of the human eye – from the way that it sees objects, to the function of the secretions that keep the eyeball moving, as well as the eyelids that protect the eye. He suggests that the incredible complexity of this unit within the human body alone is evidence for a designing intelligence.

Paley also details how other examples in nature seem to point towards the same conclusion:

- The instincts of birds ensure that they sit on their eggs while the young are growing inside them, thereby providing the perfect incubating environment.
- Moths and butterflies lay their eggs on precisely the sort of plant that their larvae need to feed on to survive and grow to maturity.
- The structure of a beetle's exoskeleton allows the beetle to squeeze through narrow holes, while also having sufficient protection to prevent its wings from damage.

F.R. Tennant's anthropic and aesthetic arguments

The anthropic principle

The anthropic principle (literally the 'humankind principle') suggests that there is strong evidence within the universe that it was deliberately designed for human life. In other words, this argument tries to show that God must exist and has deliberately gone about designing a universe that would eventually lead to the creation of his ultimate creation – human beings.

One of the more famous philosophers that developed this idea was F.R. Tennant. While not using the specific term *anthropic principle*, in his 1928 work *Philosophical Theology*, Tennant developed a set of evidences that are widely recognised as **anthropic** principles today.

Tennant's evidence for the anthropic principle

- The **natural world** where we live provides precisely the things that are necessary to sustain life: for example, air to breathe, water to drink and so on.
- We can analyse the natural world where we live so that we know how it works: for example, the water cycle, photosynthesis and so on.
- The process of evolution, through natural selection, has led to the development of intelligent human life – to the degree that this intelligent life can observe and analyse the universe that it exists in.

Specification content

F.R. Tennant's anthropic and aesthetic arguments – the universe specifically designed for intelligent human life

Key terms

anthropic: related to being human

natural world: the world of nature, comprising all objects (organic and inorganic)

Tennant stated that the theory of evolution supported the idea of an intelligent designer

The aesthetic argument

Tennant's **aesthetic** argument relates to the natural appreciation that human beings have for things that are 'beautiful', and asks why we have such an appreciation as part of our nature. When looking at the rest of the natural world, there appears to be no other species that reacts to its surroundings in this way.

In fact, this can be extended to the appreciation that humans have for music, art, poetry and other forms of literature, as well as an appreciation for such areas as fashion and cosmetics, which are said to enhance human beauty.

If a purely rational approach is taken towards human beings as a species, then only those things that are essential for our survival are necessary for us to have in the world around us. Our scientific understanding of the natural world tells us that living organisms operate on a 'survival of the fittest' mechanism, and that a species quickly rejects anything that does not aid its evolution as it develops over time. Why then do we, as human beings, have an appreciation of beauty? Why are aesthetics so important to us?

Tennant's response was to claim that this appreciation of beauty (*aesthetics*) is a direct result of a loving God, who not only wants his human creation to live in the world, but also to enjoy living in it. For Tennant, it was through this appreciation of beauty that human beings would be led, by way of revelation, to discovering the fact of God's existence for themselves.

> ### AO1 Activity
> a   Explain what is meant by a *divine designer*. Choose one example of this from each of Aquinas, Paley and Tennant.
> This helps consolidate your learning by developing the skill of selecting relevant examples and explaining how they illustrate the question focus.
> b   Draw a table of two columns and four rows. List Aquinas, Paley, Anthropic and Aesthetic in the left-hand column and then write two or three bullet points for each in the right-hand column.
> This helps develop skills of organisation by selecting and ordering evidence and examples.

 **Key term**

aesthetic: related to the concept and appreciation of beauty

Summary

★   The teleological argument is an *a posteriori* inductive argument for the existence of God.

★   Aquinas supported this argument with the fifth of his Five Ways.

★   William Paley and his watch/watchmaker analogy also support this argument.

★   In the twentieth century, Frederick Tennant further developed the argument with what has become known as his *anthropic principle* and *aesthetic* argument.

T1 Arguments for the existence of God – inductive

This section covers AO2 content and skills

> **Specification content**
> The effectiveness of the teleological argument for God's existence

Issues for analysis and evaluation

The effectiveness of the teleological argument for God's existence

Possible line of argument	Critical analysis and evaluation
The concept of a divine designer was rooted in widely respected classical Greek philosophy	When Plato spoke of a 'craftsman' over 2500 years ago, it makes us wonder why he would come to such a conclusion when considering why the world we live in is the way that it is. His ideas laid the foundations for Judeo-Christian philosophy to claim that the world we live in is the result of a divine designer.
The argument's effectiveness is directly related to the evidence of complexity in the universe	The effectiveness of the argument is said to be in its *a posteriori*, inductive form. Based on evidence of design obvious to the casual observer, the sheer complexity of our universe, with its many life forms and complex, interconnected systems that support life on the planet, point clearly towards deliberate design from some almighty mind.
Paley's proposal that complexity was not down to random chance strengthens the effectiveness of the argument	The analogical evidence Paley provides is effective in pointing out that, just like a complex machine, our complex universe could not be the result of chance. It is down to an intelligent designing creator.
Tennant's evidence further supports the effectiveness of the argument	Furthermore, the contribution of Tennant, with both his anthropic and aesthetic arguments, surely proves beyond reasonable doubt that this is a universe deliberately designed for intelligent human life. We live in a world that provides everything we need – not only for our survival, but also for our enjoyment.
However, the analogies used to support the argument are weak	However, when we look at the teleological argument more closely, it starts to show signs of weakness. The use of analogy is suspect at best as no human machine can ever adequately compare to the complex universe we inhabit. Therefore, how could we put forward the idea of an intelligent designer based purely on this?
There are too many unanswered questions about the design of the universe, even if we accept that it was designed	Even if we did accept the analogy as valid, what about the times when things go wrong in the universe? Is the designer therefore inept? Or, as is the case for many machines, is it the case that there was more than one designer? Did they leave when they had finished putting our universe together? How do we even know that this is a good universe? What have we got to compare it to?
The evidence from science offers a more rational and understandable view of how the universe, and all its complexities, came to be	There are those who suggest that to assert a divine designer that fits into the theistic model of religion is an arrogant claim. Proposing such an idea and asking others to accept it as true flies in the face of the evidence of the scientific age – modern-day evolutionary scientists such as Richard Dawkins point out that to hold such a view of a divine designer is 'unhelpful', 'childish' and 'superstitious nonsense' – in that it prevents people from properly engaging with a 'grown-up' view of the world as a place governed by the laws of nature, not the laws of some god.
The teleological argument is not effective because there are too many evidence-based criticisms	Despite the initial attractiveness of the teleological argument, the criticisms of it are simply too devastating and too wide ranging ever to accept that it is an effective argument for God's existence.

> **AO2 Activity**
>
> a Select three lines of argument from the critical analysis and evaluation of the effectiveness of the teleological argument. Find three references from scholars, schools of thought or religious and philosophical texts that would support those arguments.
>
> b Using the strongest line of argument, try to identify three key quotations that might be used – they could be from scholars, religious texts or schools of thought.

Exam practice

Sample question

Evaluate whether cosmological arguments for God's existence are persuasive in the twenty-first century.

Sample answer

The twenty-first century is home to the modern scientific age. With computing technology and the ability to communicate via the internet, human beings are able to share information like never before. In doing so, we have access to all sorts of information about ourselves and the universe we live in. This includes ideas such as the Big Bang theory, oscillating universe, multi-verses and quantum mechanics. These ideas are fascinating and, for many, persuasive, in terms of providing an answer to the age-old question of 'How did the universe begin?'

Equally, detractors of traditional theistic arguments, such as the cosmological argument, considerably undermine its claims to persuasiveness by pointing out that Aquinas' arguments are flawed by an incorrect understanding of agreed scientific principle. Newton's First Law of Motion, for example, points out that the idea that nothing can move unless moved by another ignores the principle of inertia and is therefore wrong – things *can* move themselves. Anthony Kenny famously declared this observation as 'wrecking the First Way'.

With all this in mind, it would seem that the cosmological arguments, first put forward over 2500 years ago by Ancient Greek philosophers, and then developed by medieval Christian monks, have little relevance in today's scientific world. As such, we can consider them to lack any power to persuade people.

However, we should bear in mind that the cosmological argument is based on the fact that there is a universe. This is an *a posteriori* observation: that is, a scientific method. In which case, the fundamentals of the argument are based on the same assumptions as that of scientific theories. This would suggest that the cosmological arguments are persuasive in the twenty-first century.

We should also consider that, while science can quite effectively explain how the universe works and the way it works (and therefore how it started), what it can't do is answer *why* the universe started. The cosmological argument can. In fact, Craig's Kalam cosmological argument convincingly demonstrates that the universe was the result of a deliberate choice from a personal creator.

> **Specification content**
> Whether cosmological arguments for God's existence are persuasive in the twenty-first century

News reporter

This is a good introduction that explains that people turn to scientific explanations to understand the workings of the universe and the origins of humankind.

Critical thinker

This response provides additional information, from a different perspective, to develop the opening argument further.

Judge

The information here presents an early summary of the evidence and forms a conclusion in relation to the question.

Tennis player

This argument delivers a direct counterpoint to the previous ones, highlighting the shared methodology of science and the cosmological argument in adopting an inductive approach.

Explorer

The candidate develops the argument further and suggests that Craig's form of the argument demonstrates a superior approach to that of science.

Judge — The conclusion the candidate draws follows the inevitable line of reasoning in the second part of the answer and shows how theistic arguments can still offer valid and persuasive views even in the face of supposed scientific 'fact'.

The cosmological arguments are clearly based on cause-and-effect arguments; and so is science. For this reason alone, we should not discount them. For the religious believer, the additional faith dimension provides the important element of hope and comfort, rather than just cold, hard scientific fact. The twenty-first century, with all its modern-day wonders, still has room in it to accept that the cosmological arguments for God's existence are persuasive.

Evaluation

This is a very good answer. There is a clear and well-developed line of reasoning, where the points that are often used to discredit the cosmological argument are first presented and then undermined by the evidence from the theistic arguments. The candidate even makes an appeal to emotion, contrasting science as 'hard and cold' whereas religion provides 'hope and comfort' – an effective tool when trying to 'persuade' others to your point of view.

Over to you

For this task, select six key points from the ten listed, which are relevant to the evaluation question below. Put your selection into the order that you would use to address the question.

If you explain why you have chosen these six to answer the question, you will find that you are developing a process of reasoning. This helps you to develop an argument to decide whether or not scientific arguments are more persuasive than teleological arguments in explaining the universe.

Question

'Scientific arguments are more persuasive than teleological arguments in explaining the universe.' Evaluate this view.

(Q4b, Component 2: Philosophy of Religion, WJEC, Summer 2018)

Evaluation statements

1. Scientifically evidenced arguments will always be more effective than philosophical religious arguments.
2. Religion relies too heavily on a 'God of the gaps' approach to explaining the universe's existence – scientific explanations are far more persuasive.
3. The lack of clear evidence from science undermines how persuasive scientific explanations for the universe's existence are in the face of philosophical explanations from religion.
4. Science is based on empiricism and rational knowledge acquired through the use of the five senses.
5. The philosophical arguments for God as the starting point of the universe are much older than the scientific ones.
6. Science uses evidence-based rational thought to demonstrate how the universe works: that is, why things are the way that they are.
7. Paley's watchmaker analogy is too simplistic to be effective.
8. It is our interpretation of patterns in the workings of the universe that makes us see design – in other words, design is only apparent, not real.
9. If a complex machine requires an intelligent designer, then surely it is entirely rational to suggest that a complex universe also implies an intelligent designer.
10. Inductive arguments only offer possibilities, not conclusive proofs.

C: Challenges to inductive arguments

Overview: challenges to the cosmological argument

Having existed for over 2500 years, the cosmological argument has attracted not only supporters but also critics. Scientific developments, particularly in the last hundred years, have taken our traditional understanding of a cause-and-effect universe and turned it on its head. Quantum physics, chaos theory and similar radical progressions in our understanding of the workings of the universe have all played a role in weakening the claims of supporters of the cosmological argument. However, these criticisms are not always wholly successful. Indeed, some scientific theories, including most notably the Big Bang theory, have even been used to support parts of the cosmological argument – not least in demonstrating that the universe had a starting point.

> This section covers AO1 content and skills

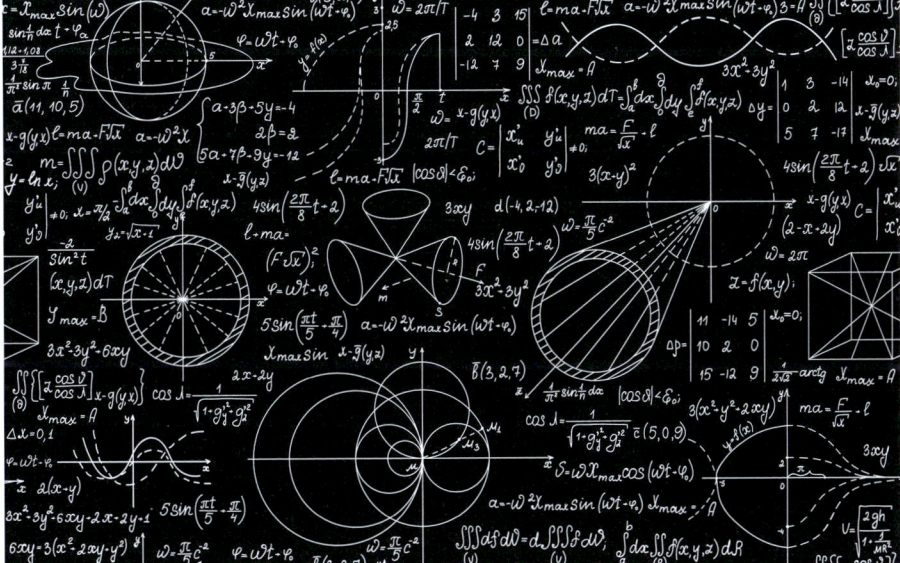

Scientific developments in the last hundred years have taken our traditional understanding of a cause-and-effect universe and turned it on its head

Specification content
David Hume – empirical objections and critique of causes (cosmological)

Key person
David Hume (1711–76): Scottish enlightenment philosopher who, as an empiricist, demonstrated a number of the flaws in the main theistic arguments for God's existence; the most significant work in relation to this is his *Dialogues Concerning Natural Religion*

David Hume: challenges to the cosmological argument

The empirical philosopher **David Hume** was uncomfortable with the reasoning behind the cosmological argument. He had particular issues with its arguments about causes.

Hume presents four major challenges:

1. Just because we observe cause and effect *in* the universe does not mean that this rule applies to the universe itself. (Russell used the example 'Just because every human has a mother does not mean the whole of humanity has a mother.') This is often called the **fallacy of composition**.
2. While we can talk about things that we have experience of with some certainty, we have no experience of creating a universe and therefore cannot talk meaningfully about that.
3. There is not enough evidence to say whether the universe had a cause, and definitely not enough to conclude what the cause might have been.
4. Even if 'God' could be accepted as the cause of the universe, there is no way to determine what sort of God this would be and certainly no way of determining whether it was the God of classical theism.

Key term
fallacy of composition: philosophical notion that what is true of the parts is not necessarily true of the whole (i.e. atoms are colourless but this does not mean that a cat, which is made of atoms, is colourless)

Specification content
David Hume – problems with analogies; rejection of traditional theistic claims; designer not necessarily God of classical theism; apprentice god; plurality of gods; absent god (teleological)

T1 Arguments for the existence of God – inductive

Overview: challenges to the teleological argument

Tracing its origins to the earliest of Western civilisation's greatest thinkers, the design or teleological argument represents one of the most commonly called-upon defences for those who believe in God. The idea that the universe is far too complex, contains purpose for all things within it and has produced a life-form capable of observing, analysing and even philosophising about it, and that none of these things seems likely to have happened by chance, all point towards the existence of God; or so religious believers would like to claim. However, like the cosmological argument, this too has those who claim it is not an effective argument. The counterarguments all need serious consideration:

- We lack sufficient experience to make such claims about a grand design.
- The analogies do not hold up to scrutiny.
- If the universe is designed, why does it have so many flaws?
- Scientific enquiry proposes alternative solutions.

Hume's house and universe example

Hume criticises human analogies to demonstrate that the universe is designed. He used the example of a house and an architect or builder and said that, just because we know how a house is designed or built, it does not mean that we can infer from this how the universe is designed or built. The house and the universe are just too different to draw that comparison, no matter the other ways they may be similar.

Problem with analogies

Analogies normally work on the following basis:

1. X and Y are similar.
2. X has the characteristic Z.
3. Therefore, Y has the characteristic Z.

However, to claim what is true of Y based purely on a similarity to X is only as strong as the point at which X and Y are similar. If the similarity between them is weak, then the conclusion the analogy draws is likewise weak.

Hume concludes that, as the universe is unique, no analogy is sufficient to explain its origins. This would be used to devastating effect as a criticism when, years later, Paley constructed his analogy of the watchmaker.

Limitations of human experience

Any analogy human beings make is necessarily based on the experience that human beings have. If we lack experience of the thing that the analogy is being used to 'prove', then how can we be certain that the analogy is sound? As human beings have no experience of how the universe was designed, any analogy put forward to try to prove this matter is ultimately futile.

The universe as organic construct

The suggestion that the universe is comparable to some artificial construct, such as a house or a machine, is also rejected. The universe demonstrates greater similarities to the living organisms within the natural world than it does to a static artificial construct.

> And does not a plant or animal, which springs from vegetation or generation, bear a stronger resemblance to the world, than does any artificial machine, which arises from reason and design? (Hume, *Dialogues Concerning Natural Religion*)

Fallacy of apparent design (the Epicurean hypothesis)

In his *Dialogues Concerning Natural Religion*, Hume suggests there is fallacy (false belief) in assuming that the universe is designed just because it seems so. He makes the distinction between what is deliberately designed and apparent design. Deliberate design is the classical theist's claim – that God is responsible for the design of the universe. However, in apparent design, what we have is an appearance of design where none actually exists.

Apparent design is a belief, which Epicurus stated, that the current so-called order in the universe that exists is nothing more than the random association of atoms that had previously been in a chaotic state but, through the principal nature of the universe (which is change), these atoms reorganise themselves infinitely, and occasionally do so in a way that resembles order (and, thereby, design).

Problems of comparison

Even if we assume that the universe has a designer, as we have no universes to compare this one to, how do we know that it has been designed well? It may be that, if we were able to make such a comparison, we would find the designer of this one to be lacking in skill. Hume makes the comparison with a shipbuilder. If we saw a ship for the first time, we might assume that the shipbuilder was a genius to have made such a thing. However, if we were to investigate further, we might find that the ship we are observing is nothing more than an imitation of other ships and, in comparison, it's not even that good.

Rejection of traditional theistic claims

(i) Designer not necessarily God of classical theism

Even were we to accept the idea that the universe had a designer, there exists no proof of who or what was responsible for designing it. Therefore, drawing a conclusion that the designer was the God of classical theism is suspect at best, not least because any number of other suggestions as to the identity of a designer could be put forward with equal validity.

(ii) The apprentice god

If we saw a ship for the first time, we would not take into account the various other ships that this shipbuilder might have tried to make along the way, in perfecting their art. Relating this to the work of a god in designing the universe, Hume observes that there may be better universes out there and that, in practising their art, the apprentice god has produced a series of worlds and universes that have been 'botched and bungled, throughout an eternity, ere this system was struck out' (Hume, *Dialogues*).

(iii) Plurality of gods

After referring to the ship/shipbuilder analogy, Hume suggests that, as a house or ship has many builders, surely it makes sense to say that there were many builders involved in constructing the universe. In making this argument, Hume is demonstrating that using human analogies is a double-edged sword for those theists who rely on them to show the likelihood of the existence of a designing creator God.

(iv) The absent god (teleological)

Furthermore, after shipbuilders or housebuilders have completed their task, they move on. Perhaps this is also true of the supposed designer of the universe? This designer may well have left the universe to its own devices or perhaps may even have died. There is no necessity for such a designer to have to exist for eternity, just because the design does.

Hume uses the example of a shipbuilder to strengthen his argument

> **Specification content**
>
> Alternative scientific explanations including the Big Bang theory and Charles Darwin's theory of evolution by natural selection

Alternative scientific explanations

The Big Bang theory

The Big Bang theory is often used as a 'proof' that it was a random action that caused the beginning of the universe, not God. (However, many theists suggest that this action was not random but caused by God.) The Big Bang theory can be summarised by referring to an event that happened nearly 14 billion years ago, when a singularity appeared. A *singularity* is a scientific concept referring to a point in space–time that defies our current understanding of the laws of physics, but where infinity exists. This singularity inflated, expanded and cooled to give us the universe we have today.

Charles Darwin's theory of evolution by natural selection

In his *On the Origin of Species*, **Charles Darwin** notes that it was random chance that organised life in the universe, according to the principles of evolution and natural selection. The reason for species being so well suited to their environment is not, as had been previously thought, due to a benevolent designer. It is because of their ability to adapt to their surroundings and to pass on the favourable characteristics that allow this adaptation to be successful.

This is the concept of 'natural selection' and demonstrates that what happens in the universe, in terms of life, is down to what Herbert Spencer, the 19th century philosopher and biologist, termed 'the survival of the fittest'. Following his reading of Darwin's work he pointed out that there was no overall purpose to the way in which life was organised itself other than that the strongest tended to survive.

> **Key person**
>
> **Charles Darwin (1809–82):** English naturalist who revolutionised the Western world's understanding of how life developed; his most famous work, *On the Origin of Species*, published in 1859, put forward the idea that life on Earth had developed through processes of natural selection and evolution

Charles Darwin's theory of evolution challenged traditional understandings of the development of human life

> **Summary**
>
> * There are several philosophical and scientific challenges to both the cosmological and teleological arguments.
> * Many of these arguments are based on our lack of direct experience of how the universe came to be.
> * Hume critiques the teleological argument based on issues with analogy and experience.
> * Modern scientific theories challenge the cosmological and teleological arguments based on empirically verifiable evidence.

> **AO1 Activity**
>
> a Outline each of Hume's specific challenges to the teleological argument.
>
>   This helps consolidate your learning by developing the skill of selecting relevant examples and explaining how they illustrate the question focus.
>
> b Draw a two-column table. In the right-hand column, write a one- or two-sentence summary of each of Hume's challenges. In the left-hand column, further summarise the challenge in one or two words.
>
>   This helps with presenting a thorough and extensive knowledge and understanding of the topic area.

> **Specification content**
> The effectiveness of the challenges to the teleological argument for God's existence

This section covers AO2 content and skills

Issues for analysis and evaluation

The effectiveness of the challenges to the teleological argument for God's existence

Possible line of argument	Critical analysis and evaluation
Hume believed that no analogy or empirical evidence could be used to support the existence of God	Hume was adamant that the teleological argument for the existence of a designing God is at best flawed and at worst entirely ineffective. Hume considers it implausible to use human experience to conjure up analogies relating to a cosmic entity beyond human experience – there is no empirical evidence that can conclusively point towards the existence of such a being.
The universe is not designed – it only appears that way	The argument that design is only apparent is an effective challenge. The order that we can see in the universe is not evidence of intention. To suggest otherwise is illogical.
Scientific ideas around evolution undermine the concept of a designed universe	Scientific evidence proves time and again an effective challenge to the teleological argument. Based on evidence from nineteenth-century scientist Charles Darwin and his work on natural selection and evolution, the teleological argument seems not to hold up under scrutiny. Genetic research adds considerable weight to Darwin's original theories.
A 'God of the gaps' argument is not rational	In fact, the suggestion is that the teleological argument is more of a 'God of gaps' argument, rather than based on empirical evidential claims. As such, it is outdated and unnecessary in a rational scientific age.
However, like science, the teleological argument is based on inductive proofs	However, we should bear in mind that the teleological argument is based on observation of apparent design, order and purpose in the universe (*a posteriori*) – i.e. a scientific method. In which case, the fundamentals of the argument are based on the same assumptions as scientific theories. Surely this proves that not all the challenges to the argument are effective.
Science is not infallible and scientific ideas can change	Equally, scientific theories are often in need of updating or are proved to be false – there have been plenty of examples over the centuries where what was once accepted as effective scientific 'fact' has instead been overturned as new evidence has come to light. Therefore, scientific evidence against the teleological argument does not necessarily prove an effective challenge. To develop this point further, contemporary scientists such as Polkinghorne, Behe and Davies all support the design concept. Why would they risk their reputations as scientific professionals, were there not something to it?
The argument is preference, rather than evidence, based	This shows that scientific evidence can be used to support as well as challenge the teleological argument. In which case, the strength of the argument may come down to a personal preference, negating the effectiveness of the challenges.

T1 Arguments for the existence of God – inductive

> **AO2 Activity**
> a Evaluate three lines of argument from the critical analysis and evaluation of the effectiveness of the challenges to the teleological argument. What are their strengths and weaknesses? Which line of argument is strongest?
> b Using the strongest line of argument, try to identify three key questions that might be asked – they could be critical, challenge, hypothetical or direct questions.

Specification content
Whether scientific explanations are more persuasive than philosophical explanations for the universe's existence

Exam practice

Sample question
Evaluate whether scientific explanations are more persuasive than philosophical explanations for the universe's existence.

Sample answer

The introduction sets the scene for the evaluation, citing the variety of scientific explanations that could potentially be called upon to explain the universe's existence. It also makes correct use of relevant terminology.

The consideration of whether scientific explanations are more persuasive than philosophical explanations for the universe's existence can encompass a variety of explanations. Scientific discovery in the last hundred years has occurred at a pace previously unknown in the history of the human race. Science is based on empiricism and rational knowledge acquired through the use of the five senses – it is easily and widely accepted.

The answer reflects on a key scientific explanation and shows how the commonality that it provides to both science and philosophy naturally leads on to a question that neither has a definitive response to.

Interestingly, the widely accepted Big Bang theory indicates a starting point of the universe. The majority of the scientific community accepts that the universe definitely had a beginning, which the first parts of all cosmological arguments always attempt to prove. This is a point of agreement between science and philosophy. The contention then becomes 'What caused the starting point?'

Detective

Tennis player

The answer considers potential reasons why science may be preferred over philosophy. The candidate selects and uses specialist language accurately, making a counterpoint that demonstrates another commonality between science and philosophy, and providing a line of reasoning to support this.

Developing this point further, it is true to say that science uses evidence-based rational thought to demonstrate how the universe began. Such thought underpins much of the workings of contemporary society. This is at odds with the suggestion of a divine being as the first cause of the universe. However, science works on assumptions that like causes produce like effects, and this deterministic view of the universe lends itself to the model used to determine God as the first cause for the universe.

The answer draws a conclusion based on the evidence presented so far. It also raises a pertinent question.

We should take into account that, as there is no definitive answer as to how the universe began, then it is entirely rational to accept certain religious and philosophical arguments as having persuasive power. For instance, have scientific observers proven beyond reasonable doubt that God is not the first cause of the universe?

News reporter

The answer develops a line of reasoning based on the 'fact' of the Big Bang, and the lack of knowledge of what happened prior to it, to support the potential primacy of philosophical explanations in this instance.

Scientific evidence can talk meaningfully about time only after the Big Bang – not the moments before. This allows for the possibility of a divine being as the cause of the Big Bang, thus demonstrating that philosophical explanations for the universe's existence may be considered persuasive.

Additionally, scientific explanations can often be extremely complex. For many people listening to contemporary scientific conversation about sub-quantum realities, multi-dimensional universes and other seemingly fantastical ideas, these explanations may in themselves seem so far-fetched that a commonsense philosophical explanation, taking an 'Ockham's razor'-type approach of not multiplying the difficulty for an explanation, seems to make more sense. It could therefore be argued as being, ultimately, more persuasive – in that it can be more easily understood.

The conclusion relates back to the introduction by referring to a variety of explanations – yet explores the idea, in this context, that they may lead to confusion rather than clarification. The response then draws on material outside of the specification (e.g. Ockham's razor) to suggest that a simpler philosophical explanation may prove more persuasive.

Evaluation

This is a very good answer. There is a clear and well-developed line of reasoning, which considers both sides of the argument before putting forward a conclusion. The candidate shows how the explanations from science (which sometimes have commonality with those of philosophy) do not always have universal support due to their complexity, and that sometimes it's the simpler answer that is preferred.

Over to you

For this task, develop each of the evaluation statements below by adding evidence and examples to evaluate fully the argument presented in each statement. The first one is done for you.

This helps you to answer examination questions for AO2 by ensuring that 'sustained and clear views are given, supported by extensive, detailed reasoning and/or evidence' (Level 5 AO2 band descriptor).

Evaluation statements

The following evaluation statements deal with the effectiveness of the challenges to the inductive arguments for God's existence.

1. Some argue that arguments based on analogies are not convincing.
   Development: The teleological argument is based on analogies and Hume's challenge to this, where he points out that the effectiveness of an analogy depends on how strong the connection is at the point of comparison. It is particularly effective because any artificial construct (such as the watch in Paley's analogy) cannot reliably compare to the vastly more complex universe – they're simply too different.
2. The challenges are effective as the argument has no sound empirical basis.
3. Relying on scientific evidence to challenge the teleological argument is ineffective as it can also be used to support the argument.
4. Quantum physics suggests that, at the sub-atomic level, our traditional understanding of a cause-and-effect universe is not necessarily relevant.
5. Both scientific and philosophical arguments agree that the universe had a starting point.

T1 Arguments for the existence of God – deductive

This section covers AO1 content and skills

Specification content
Deductive proofs; the concept of *a priori*

 Key terms

a priori: without or prior to evidence or experience
deductive proof: a proof where, if the premises are true, then the conclusion must be true
premises: statements or propositions used to construct an argument

D: Deductive arguments – origins of the ontological argument

Deductive proofs – the concept of *a priori*

In part A, we looked at the concept of inductive proofs. These are useful when basing an argument on evidence or experience. However, not all philosophical arguments can be based on these two useful sources. Occasionally, it is necessary to argue based on no prior experience or evidence – and this is where the term **a priori** comes from.

If an argument or proof is *a priori*, it literally means it is an argument or proof that has no experience or evidence as its starting point. Instead, logic or reasoning are used to put forward an argument or proof. Philosophical arguments and proofs can be made *a priori*, and it is often useful to do so.

When we use such steps in logic or reasoning to put forward a conclusion, we call this process *deductive reasoning* or **deductive proof**.

Deductive argument – premises and conclusion

Deductive proofs are often composed of a series of **premises** or statements that, when stacked together, point towards a conclusion that is usually logically inescapable. For instance, look at the following:

[Premise 1]   All oceans contain water.
[Premise 2]   The Atlantic is an ocean.
[Conclusion]   Therefore the Atlantic contains water.

Premise 1 is followed by premise 2, and these lead to a conclusion that is both logically sound and factually accurate.

Deductive argument – the importance of accurate premises

This is all very well and good when the premises that point towards the conclusion are both accurate and true, but occasionally this is not the case. However, the conclusion that is drawn is still inescapable.

[Premise 1]   All birds can fly.
[Premise 2]   Penguins are birds.
[Conclusion]   Therefore penguins can fly.

In this case, the deductive proof leads to a conclusion that, while logically sound, is factually inaccurate. Why? Well, the reason is that at least one of the premises is suspect (or wrong!). In this case, the premise 'All birds can fly' is not factually accurate and, because of this, the conclusion is not accurate either.

Penguins can't fly – be careful with deductive reasoning!

Deductive argument – an argument fit for God?

St Anselm of Canterbury

Deductive proofs are incredibly powerful pieces of logical reasoning that, when well constructed, are virtually impossible to contradict. Deductive proof is the basis for the **ontological argument** for the existence of God. This is why, for its supporters, it is the most persuasive form of philosophical argument that there is when arguing for the existence of a divine being.

St Anselm

In the eleventh century, St Anselm of Bec, later to be Archbishop of Canterbury as part of the Norman invasion of England, composed the **Proslogion**. It is sometimes referred to by its original title *Fides Quaerens Intellectum*, which, when translated, means 'faith seeking understanding' as this was the purpose of Anselm writing the *Proslogion*. Within this book, which is written as a prayer or meditation, St Anselm attempts to offer a single logical proof for the existence of God. This single argument was expressed in a deductive form.

It's helpful for us to note here that, for St Anselm, the relationship between **faith** and **reason** differs from some of the key thinkers that you may study elsewhere in the course. For St Anselm, faith comes first. His faith was that God exists; that God is the source of all being and the ultimate good. He employs reason to deepen his understanding of what his faith told him:

> For I do not seek to understand that I may believe, but I believe in order to understand. For this also I believe, that unless I believed, I should not understand. (St Anselm, *Proslogion* 1)

This leads the reader into the second chapter of his work, referred to as *Proslogion* 2. Opening with a reference to Psalm 14:1, he states 'Truly there is a God, although the fool has said in his heart, "There is no God".'

Proslogion 2 – God as the greatest possible being

St Anselm places the fool onto the losing side of the argument. As we shall see from both *Proslogion* 2 and *Proslogion* 3, St Anselm shows, by clear deductive argument, that to say 'there is no God' makes no rational sense.

To start with, *Proslogion* 2 invites the reader to consider God as 'a being than which nothing greater can be conceived'. While we need to accept that St Anselm's definition is a little vague, it states the rational position that God is the greatest possible thing that can be thought of by the human mind.

 Key term

ontological argument: argument for the existence of God based on the concept of the nature of being

 Key terms

Proslogion: a work written by St Anselm, used as a meditation, but including within it the classical form of the ontological argument

faith: a strong belief or trust in something or someone

reason: the use of logic in thought processes or in an argument

Specification content

St Anselm – God as the greatest possible being (*Proslogion* 2)

T1 Arguments for the existence of God – deductive

St Anselm develops this argument by stating that it is possible to exist in the mind and to exist in reality, but that the two ideas are not mutually inclusive. That is, they don't both have to be true at the same time – just because something exists in the mind does not mean it has to exist in reality. However, as God is considered to be the 'being than which nothing greater can be conceived', then, as a result, he exists both in the mind and in reality. Otherwise, he is not the greatest possible being.

Summarising *Proslogion* 2

This is quite a confusing idea at first sight. It may be better to consider it as:

[Premise 1]   Beings exists both in the mind and in reality.
[Premise 2]   God is the greatest possible being that can be thought of.
[Conclusion] To be the greatest thing that can be thought of, God must exist both in the mind and in reality.

The conclusion would be true if you accepted the idea that it is 'greater' (or 'better') to exist in reality than just in the mind.

In essence, this remains a difficult idea. In fact, initially it seems logically weak in terms of its premises. It certainly attracted criticism, as we shall see later.

St Anselm uses the example of a painter and a painting – pointing out that, before it exists in reality, a painting needs to exist in the mind of the painter.

Proslogion 3 – God has necessary existence

'God cannot be conceived not to exist.' St Anselm starts Chapter 3 of his *Proslogion* by developing his theme from Chapter 2 of God as the greatest possible being. He widens his definition to include the idea that, once you have understood what it means for God to be the greatest possible being, then the next logical step is to conclude that God has necessary existence: that is, that God cannot be thought not to exist.

St Anselm's reasoning goes something like this:

1   It is possible to think of a being who has the property of having to exist (i.e. that can be thought of as existing and not being able not to exist).
2   It is also possible to think of something that does not have to exist.
3   When thinking of the two, side by side, the one that cannot not exist is clearly greater than the one that does not have to exist.

Working out *Proslogion* 3

Put another way: God, if he exists, is either a being that cannot be thought of as not existing (i.e. he is necessary) or a being that can be thought of as not existing (i.e. he is contingent).

If the definition we use for God is that he is 'that than which nothing greater can be conceived' (as is the case from *Proslogion* 2), then God's existence must be necessary – as this is clearly greater than being contingent. Here, St Anselm presents us with the idea that God's existence is necessary and that this is an integral part of what it means to be God – a unique feature above that of all existent beings (i.e. necessary existence).

So, in summary, St Anselm's idea of God as having necessary existence demonstrates that God is the greatest possible being that can be thought of, as anything that exists is greater than anything that does not.

> **Specification content**
>
> St Anselm – God has necessary existence (*Proslogion* 3)

Therefore, if God is the greatest possible thing that there is, then he must, necessarily, exist in reality – not just as an idea. This is because, otherwise, anything that existed in reality would be greater than God (if he was only an idea). Our definition of God 'as the greatest possible being' means that he must necessarily exist.

> **Summary**
> - Deductive arguments are based on a series of premises that point towards a conclusion that is usually logically inescapable.
> - The ontological argument, which St Anselm of Canterbury proposed in his *Proslogion*, is an *a priori* deductive argument for the existence of God.
> - *Proslogion* 2 states via deductive argument that God is the greatest possible being.
> - *Proslogion* 3 states via deductive argument that God has necessary existence.

AO1 Activity

a Explain what we mean when we use the phrase *deductive arguments*. Provide an example from the ontological argument that illustrates how deductive arguments work.

This helps with presenting a thorough and extensive knowledge and understanding of the topic area.

b Draw a two-column table. In the left-hand column, write 'Proslogion 2'. In the right-hand column, write a bullet point summary of the main features of *Proslogion* 2. Then repeat this for *Proslogion* 3.

This helps develop skills of organisation by selecting and ordering evidence and examples.

> **This section covers AO2 content and skills**

> **Specification content**
> The extent to which *a priori* arguments for God's existence are persuasive

Issues for analysis and evaluation

The extent to which *a priori* arguments for God's existence are persuasive

Possible line of argument	Critical analysis and evaluation
A priori arguments are useful	*A priori* arguments for God's existence are useful because they are independent of our experience or any evidence that may present itself to us. In general terms, the only thing needed for an *a priori* argument is an understanding of the language it is expressed in.
A priori arguments are intrinsically persuasive	In this sense, it could be argued that this very independence from experience means that they are intrinsically persuasive, as they are not tainted by the experience of an individual or group; neither do they rely on evidence (which can often be found to be unreliable).
However, in the twenty-first century, evidence-based approaches are often preferred	On the other hand, in general terms, *a posteriori* arguments – those based on evidence and experience – give us an empirical basis to prove, with scientific method, how reliable a particular claim or argument may be. This seems far more sensible to the twenty-first-century mind! We accept arguments about the reliability of medicines, technology and even educational systems based on empirical research, i.e. *a posteriori* research. We would not accept *a priori* that any of these things could be claimed as reliable, which proves that *a posteriori* arguments are more persuasive than *a priori* ones.
However, *a priori* conclusions, by their nature, are more persuasive	Countering this is that *a priori* arguments tend to lead to inescapable conclusions – they state what is known and it is accepted as such. This could lead to a consideration that *a priori* arguments are more persuasive – particularly when dealing with subject matter such as the possible existence of God.
However, the premises in *a priori* arguments can be flawed, which means the conclusion is flawed too	However, we should bear in mind that *a priori* deductive proofs depend heavily on their premises in terms of providing sound arguments. If the premises are suspect, inaccurate or wrong, then the conclusion that they lead to inevitably also suffers from these defects. This considerably undermines the persuasiveness of an *a priori* argument for God's existence.
The ontological argument, if the premises are accepted, is highly persuasive	The ontological argument, as an *a priori* form, depends on the understanding of what it means to be God. We accept certain facts about God, purely based on the definition of the word. This makes the highly persuasive assertion that God necessarily exists because he is the greatest possible being that can be thought of and must possess all perfections, including that of existence.
However, *a posteriori* arguments are considered to be more persuasive	Countering this is the existence of *a posteriori* arguments for God's existence, such as the cosmological and teleological forms. Both of these are long-lived as possible arguments for God's existence, and philosophers and theologians use them even today in the twenty-first century, accepting them as more persuasive forms or proofs for the existence of God.

> **AO2 Activity**
> a Evaluate three possible conclusions that could be drawn from the critical analysis and evaluation of the extent to which *a priori* arguments for God's existence are persuasive. What are their strengths and weaknesses? Which conclusion is strongest?
> b Using the strongest conclusion, select three lines of argument that you would use to support this conclusion. Try to explain why you have selected these.

Exam practice

Sample question

Evaluate the extent to which different religious views on the nature of God impact on arguments for the existence of God.

Sample answer

According to the traditional concept of God in classical theism, God is omnipotent, omniscient and omnipresent. In other words, God can do all things, knows all things and is everywhere. This is a view upheld by Christianity, Islam and Judaism.

When considering the theistic proofs considered so far (i.e. cosmological, teleological and ontological), it is worth reflecting on how much each of these is based on an understanding of God's nature as presented by these faiths. For example, is not God's omnipotence a key feature of both cosmological and teleological arguments, which describe a being capable of creating a universe and designing a universe respectively? Were God not attributed with this power, then how could we attribute either of these feats to him? It must be considered vital to these arguments that God has these abilities (creator/designer) as an essential part of whom we consider him to be.

Equally, the ontological argument describes God as possessing 'all perfections'. Indeed, this definition of God is the crux of the argument. Were it not so, then the ontological argument would be a non-starter. The very idea of God is a God whose nature includes the idea of these perfections as a necessary part of who he is.

We can then ask 'What about other considerations about the nature of God?' Would these arguments still work if God is described in any other form, for example impersonal, limited to a specific sphere of nature, entirely transcendent (i.e. beyond our physical world and incapable of interacting with it) and so on? Certainly, this would seem to undermine the validity of all three arguments, at least as we traditionally understand them.

However, concepts of God beyond those recognised above do not necessarily entail such characteristics. In such cases, the nature of God – which might contain characteristics of limited power or malevolent intent – do not impede traditional questions regarding the existence of God in the face of the issues regarding evil and suffering, for instance. (We could include polytheistic or dualist faith traditions in this.) While the traditional theistic arguments as outlined above do not usually promote an understanding of the nature of God in this way, they certainly raise interesting questions about attempting to explain God's nature, and ask why we accept the characteristics attributed to the God of classical theism.

Specification content

The extent to which different religious views on the nature of God impact on arguments for the existence of God

News reporter

The introduction sets the scene for the evaluation, citing a variety of characteristics of God's nature. It uses relevant terminology accurately.

Philosopher

By linking the traditional characteristics of God to the creation and design of the universe, the response directly addresses the issue the question raises, and poses two pertinent questions as a response to this.

Detective

The answer provides further clarification based on the nature of God – this time from the ontological argument. This is effective use of relevant evidence to support the reasoning of the argument.

Tennis player

The answer then raises a question as a counterpoint; the answer to this question potentially undermines the previous line of argument.

Explorer

This paragraph explores alternative ways of looking at the debate, with reference to religious traditions outside of the classical theistic traditions.

The candidate draws a simple conclusion based on the lines of reasoning.

In conclusion, traditional arguments for God's existence tend to arise out of specific faith traditions and, consequently, are intimately associated with the specific nature of God as described in that tradition. As such, it would appear that different religious views about the nature of God do indeed impact on arguments for the existence of God.

Evaluation

This is a very good answer. There is a clear and well-developed line of reasoning that considers different perspectives of the debate before putting forward a conclusion. There is good use of questions that emerge from the material presented.

Over to you

Below is a summary of two different points of view concerning the persuasiveness of *a priori* arguments for God's existence. It is around 150 words long.

Use these two views and lines of argument to answer the evaluation question below. Remember, just listing them is not really evaluating them. So, present the two views in a more evaluative style, firstly by condensing each argument and then, secondly, by commenting on how effective each one is (*weak* or *strong* are good terms to start with). Write about 200 words in total.

When you have completed the task, refer to the band descriptors for A2 (WJEC) or A Level (Eduqas) and, in particular, look at the demands described in the higher band descriptors, which you should be aspiring towards. Ask yourself:

- Is my answer a confident critical analysis and perceptive evaluation of the issue?
- Is my answer a response that successfully identifies and thoroughly addresses the issues the question raises?

Question

'A *priori* arguments for God's existence are very persuasive.' Evaluate this view.

(Q4b, Component 2: Philosophy of Religion, WJEC, Summer 2022)

Summary

We can categorise arguments for God's existence into *a priori* and *a posteriori* arguments. A *priori* arguments are arguments that are independent of our experience or any evidence that may present itself to us. A *priori* arguments tend to lead to logically inescapable conclusions, so we should consider them persuasive when dealing with subject matter such as the possible existence of God. However, we should bear in mind that *a priori* deductive proofs depend heavily on their premises; if these are suspect, inaccurate or wrong, then the conclusion that they lead to also suffers from these defects. On the other hand, *a posteriori* arguments – those based on evidence and experience – give us an empirical basis to prove how reliable a particular claim or argument may be. We accept arguments about the reliability of medicines, technology and even educational systems based on empirical research: that is, *a posteriori* research.

E: Deductive arguments – developments of the ontological argument

René Descartes

Concept of God as supremely perfect being

For Descartes, the definition of God is that God is the most perfect being – or, to put it another way, a being that possesses all **perfections**. While Descartes is a little vague on precisely what he means by the concept of 'perfection', the implication is that he means God possesses the very best form of all possible **attributes**.

When talking of the God of classical theism, the attributes of power, knowledge and love are magnified so that he is all-powerful (*omnipotent*), all-knowing (*omniscient*) and all-loving (*omnibenevolent*). That is to say, God possesses each of those attributes in their perfect state.

René Descartes

For Descartes, God as the supremely perfect being possesses all perfections, and he includes within this the idea of existence that God possesses as an attribute. Were he not to possess the perfection of each and every positive attribute that it is possible to possess, then God would not be the supremely perfect being. Thus, the definition of God, for Descartes, is phrased in positive terms – unlike St Anselm's negative 'God is that than which nothing greater can be conceived'.

To help us understand this concept further, Descartes uses two analogies.

Analogy of a triangle

Descartes points out that to think of a triangle is necessarily to think of a shape that has both three sides and interior angles that add up to 180°.

It does not mean that this shape necessarily exists in any external reality: that is, it's not something you can go and visit in our physical world. However, to be able to think about the idea of a triangle, there needs to be a set of criteria that everyone can understand and that forms part of the definition of what a triangle is. This is why when you've read the word *triangle* on this page, you have already got a picture of one in your head!

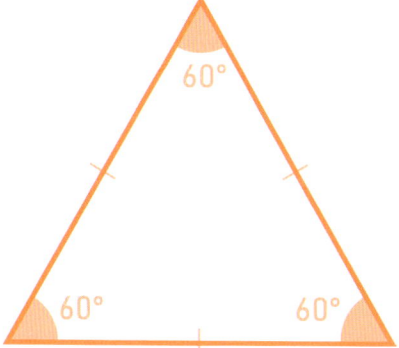

Triangles necessarily have three sides and interior angles that add up to 180

This section covers AO1 content and skills

Specification content

René Descartes – concept of God as supremely perfect being; analogies of triangles and mountains/valleys

Key terms

perfection: the complete absence of flaws; also the ultimate state of a positive trait

attributes: descriptive characteristics that someone or something possesses

T1 Arguments for the existence of God – deductive

It is similar with God: according to Descartes, it is equally impossible to think of God unless we consider the attribute of existence as a necessary part of the definition of what God is. In other words, Descartes says the concept of God contains the idea of his existence as a necessary perfection that he possesses, in the same way that the concept of a triangle refers to a shape with three sides and interior angles that add up to 180°. The attributes and the idea are completely and totally linked in both cases.

Analogy of mountains and valleys

The second analogy that Descartes uses is the idea that we cannot think of a mountain without thinking of the corresponding valley – for wherever there is one, there is always, by definition, the other. Descartes uses this analogy to reinforce the idea that it is impossible to separate the idea of God and the idea of his existence:

> ... for from the fact that I cannot conceive a mountain without a valley, it does not follow that there is any mountain or any valley in existence, but only that the mountain and the valley, whether they exist or do not exist, cannot in any way be separated one from the other.

> While from the fact that I cannot conceive God without existence, it follows that existence is inseparable from Him, and hence that He really exists; not that my thought can bring this to pass, or impose any necessity on things, but, on the contrary, because the necessity which lies in the thing itself, i.e. the necessity of the existence of God, determines me to think in this way.
>
> For it is not within my power to think of God without existence (that is, of a supremely perfect Being devoid of a supreme perfection).
> (Descartes, *Meditations*)

Descartes is stating that God alone possesses this perfection (that is, of necessary existence) as the supremely perfect being. In making this statement, Descartes is deductively pointing to the conclusion that God, necessarily, exists.

Norman Malcolm

God as unlimited being: God's existence as necessary rather than just possible

In *The Philosophical Review* (1960), Norman Malcolm revisits the ontological argument and presents it in a form that responds to its previous critics and develops the argument further from St Anselm's and Descartes' arguments, centuries earlier.

> **Specification content**
> Norman Malcolm – God as unlimited being: God's existence as necessary rather than just possible

Rejection of *Proslogion* 2

Malcolm rejects both St Anselm's argument stated in *Proslogion* 2, and that proposed by Descartes. Malcolm agrees with both Gaunilo's and Kant's objections. He says that to state that something exists either because it is greater to exist in reality, or because existence is a perfection and God possesses all perfections, is a false argument. You cannot merely add the concept of existence to a list of qualities that something has and then claim that it therefore exists!

Extending *Proslogion* 3

However, Malcolm does sympathise with the argument that St Anselm puts forward in *Proslogion* 3: that is, St Anselm's conclusion (following his proof in *Proslogion* 2) that because God is the greatest possible being that can be thought of, then he must have necessary existence.

This is, as seen earlier, a necessary consequence of being the greatest possible being that can be thought of – quite simply because a being that did not have necessary existence would be inferior to one that did have necessary existence.

As both can be conceived, then it is the being with necessary existence that is the greater – and, as the greatest possible being, must exist.

God as an unlimited being

For Malcolm, the very fact that God is the greatest possible being that can be thought of necessarily means that God should equally be described as an unlimited being: that is, as a being that has no limits, possesses all perfections to the greatest possible degree, and (because God is considered as an unlimited being), for the religious believer, is worthy of worship. If God were not a being that is unlimited, then that would mean there are limits to some, if not all, aspects of his being. This, in turn, would mean he is not the greatest thing that can be thought of, would not fit our understanding of what it means to be 'God' (as defined by St Anselm), and therefore would not be worthy of worship. Therefore by definition, God must be an unlimited being.

Summary of Malcolm's argument

Malcolm summarises in the following steps how the ontological argument shows God's existence to be necessary.

Step 1 of Malcolm's argument

- If God, as an unlimited being, does not exist, then he cannot come into existence.
- This is because he would either have been caused to come into existence, or just randomly come into existence. This would mean he had a starting point – a beginning – and this would make him a limited being. However, this would be to disagree with our definition of what God is.
- Therefore, since God cannot come into existence, if God does not already exist, then we have to conclude deductively that his existence is impossible.

Step 2 of Malcolm's argument

- However, if God does exist, then (for the reasons given above) he cannot have come into existence, nor can he cease to exist (because if he ceased to exist, then that would also be a limit because it would mean he had come to an end, which, if he is an unlimited being, makes no sense).
- Therefore, the only conclusion that we can deductively reach is that, if God exists, his existence is necessary.

Concluding Malcolm's argument

- Thus God's existence is either impossible (step 1) or necessary (step 2).
- It can be impossible only if the concept of an unlimited being is self-contradictory or in some way logically ridiculous.
- If we do not think that it is either of these things, the only possible conclusion we can reach is that God necessarily exists.

Summary

- ★ René Descartes developed the ontological argument and defined God as the supremely perfect being.
- ★ He used the examples of mountains and valleys as well as the features of a triangle to support his deductive argument.
- ★ In the twentieth century, Norman Malcolm developed the argument and defined God as an unlimited being.
- ★ He stated that unless the idea of God was somehow self-contradictory or logically ridiculous, God's existence must be necessary.

AO1 Activity

a   Explain how Descartes uses his examples to support his ontological argument.
    This helps with presenting a thorough and extensive knowledge and understanding of the topic area.

b   On revision cards, summarise the key features of Norman Malcolm's ontological argument.
    This helps with prioritising and selecting a core set of points to develop an answer and ensure that you are making accurate use of specialist language and vocabulary in context.

> **Specification content**
> The effectiveness of the ontological argument for God's existence

> This section covers AO2 content and skills

Issues for analysis and evaluation

The effectiveness of the ontological argument for God's existence

Possible line of argument	Critical analysis and evaluation
The ontological argument's longevity and logical basis make it an effective argument	The ontological argument for God's existence has a thousand-year history in the annals of religious philosophy and deserves respect. As an *a priori* argument, it is a rational proof the logic of which is inescapable when the deductive form of its premises is accepted. For St Anselm, this argument was entirely effective in confirming his own theistic beliefs – that God's existence is both obvious and necessary.
The basis of St Anselm's ontological argument is confirmed in the classical theistic traditions	Theistic religions from the Abrahamic tradition, such as Christianity, Judaism and Islam, all accept the definition of God as proposed by St Anselm and therefore they also consider this to be an effective form of argument as it confirms their own faith views: that God is the greatest possible being; one that nothing greater can be thought of in the entire realm of reality.
Contemporary philosophical forms support the ontological argument	What further demonstrates the effectiveness of the ontological argument is that it fits contemporary forms of philosophy and logic, such as the modal systems that modern-day ontological-argument philosophers, such as Malcolm, adopt.
The ontological argument makes logical sense and is therefore effective	The ontological argument, as an *a priori* form, depends on the understanding of what it means to be God. We accept certain facts about God, purely based on the definition of the word. The assertion that God necessarily exists, because he is the greatest possible being that can be thought of and must possess all perfections, including that of existence, shows how effective the argument is.
Deductive proofs lead to logically definitive conclusions	We should also bear in mind that the ontological argument, as a deductive, *a priori* argument, leads to an inescapable conclusion – that God exists. This makes it highly effective – as long as we accept the reasoning put forward in the argument!
The ontological argument can be challenged based on the use and interpretation of the language used	However, not all philosophers or religious believers accept that the ontological argument is an effective proof for God's existence. Indeed, one of its earliest critics was St Anselm's contemporary, Gaunilo, who rejected the idea that it was possible to define anything into existence. Equally, Immanuel Kant, centuries later, also rejected the argument, suggesting that Descartes was misusing the word *exist*. It is not possible, in his view, simply to add the word *exist* to a list of perfections that something does or doesn't have – thereby showing the argument to be ineffective.
Flawed premises lead to flawed conclusions	We should also appreciate, in line with these critiques, that whenever we can show any of the premises of an *a priori* argument to be weak or inaccurate, then the conclusion that is produced by virtue of the reasoning is also either weak or inaccurate. This links strongly to the views Kant put forward.
Robust counterarguments render the ontological argument ineffective	In conclusion, the arguments against the ontological argument are sufficiently robust to undermine any reasonable claim that it is an effective argument in proving the existence of God.

T1 Arguments for the existence of God – deductive

> **AO2 Activity**
>
> a Evaluate three lines of argument from the critical analysis and evaluation of the effectiveness of the ontological argument for God's existence. What are their strengths and weaknesses? Which line of argument is strongest?
>
> b Using the strongest line of argument, try to identify three key questions that might be asked – they could be critical, challenge, hypothetical or direct questions.

Specification content

Whether the ontological argument is more persuasive than the cosmological/teleological arguments for God's existence

Exam practice

Sample question

Evaluate whether the ontological argument is more persuasive than the cosmological/teleological arguments for God's existence.

Sample answer

A good introduction that provides a helpful overview of the key areas for focus in the evaluation to come.

God's existence or non-existence has long been a debate for philosophers. Strong views are formed on both sides of the debate. To support this debate, a number of different forms of 'proof' have been offered. These proofs exist in both *a priori* and *a posteriori* forms. The ontological argument is an *a priori* argument for the existence of God, while both the cosmological and teleological arguments are *a posteriori* forms.

The argument presents significant evidence via a line of reasoning that shows the grounds on which the ontological argument can be considered effective and therefore persuasive.

The persuasiveness of the ontological argument depends, as is so often the case, on the willingness of the individual to accept the deductive premises upon which it is based. If these premises are accepted – that is, the idea that the definition of God is 'that than which nothing greater can be conceived', and the associated argument that this proves God has necessary existence (otherwise God cannot be the greatest possible thing that can be thought of) – then it is very difficult to deny the conclusion that God necessarily exists. This would make the ontological argument entirely persuasive.

This paragraph makes a counterpoint to show the 'flaw' in deductive reasoning that the ontological argument rests on.

However, if the premises are rejected – as Gaunilo, Kant and others did – then the ontological argument fails entirely. It is never accepted because the idea of existence following on from definition is seen as entirely fallacious and is not at all persuasive.

This paragraph explores an alternative line of reasoning, drawing on relevant evidence, to show how the traditional inductive theistic proofs work.

The cosmological argument is based on the empirical fact that there is a universe, and poses the question 'What started the universe?' The reasoning of philosophers such as Aquinas, Leibniz and Craig proposes the answer as God. The teleological argument starts from the philosophical observation that the universe contains evidence of design and that things within the universe appear to work towards an end or purpose, even when there is no obvious reason for this to happen. The conclusion philosophers such as Aquinas, Paley and Tennant draw inductively is that the reason for this is God.

This paragraph develops a line of reasoning based on the preference for empirical evidence in the contemporary, scientific world, and draws a conclusion relating to their relative persuasiveness due to this.

Both of the latter arguments use empirical evidence. In a scientific age, empirical evidence is always valued as a starting point for any persuasive argument, and, therefore, it could be argued, these arguments are both more persuasive than the ontological argument in proving the existence of God.

However, both of these inductive arguments are subject to a number of criticisms, not least that even if we accept all other ideas within the line of inductive reasoning, why does the ultimate conclusion for this inductive reasoning have to be God? Neither argument gives a definitive or persuasive answer to this question.

This paragraph makes another counterpoint, this time attacking the flaw in inductive reasoning – namely, that the conclusion is not definitive.

It then becomes a matter of preference which type of reasoning we adopt as providing a more persuasive form of argument for the existence of God. Might it be the case that those who prefer an experience or evidence base will prefer the inductive arguments from cosmology or design, whereas those who prefer logical reasoning will prefer the deductive form of the ontological argument? We can therefore conclude that the relative persuasiveness of the arguments becomes a subjective matter – much like the acceptance or denial of belief in a divine being.

The response then considers the evidence presented so far, and draws the conclusion, based on a pertinent question, that the persuasiveness of each form of argument may be an entirely subjective matter, based on preference.

Evaluation

This is an effective and balanced response. It considers both sides of the argument, and raises questions before putting forward a conclusion. The candidate makes accurate use both of terminology and of the views of different philosophers.

Over to you

Below are some conclusions that could be drawn in relation to a question that asks you to evaluate whether ontological arguments for God's existence are completely ineffective.

Consider each of the conclusions and collect evidence and examples to support each argument from the AO1 and AO2 material you have studied in relation to ontological arguments for God's existence.

Select the conclusion that you think is most convincing and explain why it is so. Now contrast this with the weakest conclusion in the list, justifying your argument with clear reasoning and evidence.

Question

'The ontological arguments for God's existence are completely ineffective.' Evaluate this view.

(Q3b, Component 2: Philosophy of Religion, WJEC, Summer 2018)

Conclusions

1. The ontological argument effectively proves God's existence beyond any reasonable doubt.
2. Only later forms of the ontological argument are acceptable; the classical form from St Anselm is entirely ineffective.
3. Using the ontological argument to prove God's existence is philosophically futile.
4. The ontological argument's effectiveness depends on your religious beliefs.
5. Modern scientific thought undermines the effectiveness of the ontological argument.

This section covers AO1 content and skills

F: Challenges to the ontological argument

Gaunilo's reply to St Anselm

St Anselm's ontological argument was met with criticism by a monk, who lived at the same time as St Anselm, by the name of Gaunilo of Marmoutier. In a work titled *On Behalf of the Fool*, Gaunilo replied to St Anselm's proof by using an argument structure known as **reductio ad absurdum**.

He makes a claim that if St Anselm can 'prove' the existence of God through the definition 'that than which nothing greater can be conceived', then Gaunilo argued that he could prove the existence of a perfect island by the same method. Gaunilo wants to show how you cannot move from an idea of something to that idea being a reality, no matter how you define it – he regarded this thinking as flawed.

Gaunilo's analogy as ridicule of St Anselm's logic

Gaunilo argues that if you can have an idea of such an island, then, following St Anselm argument, that island must exist. Gaunilo recognised that arguing for the existence of a 'perfect' island in such way was an absurd idea:

> If a man should try to prove to me by such reasoning that this island truly exists, and that its existence should no longer be doubted, either I should believe that he was jesting, or I know not which I ought to regard as the greater fool: myself, supposing that I should allow this proof; or him, if he should suppose that he had established with any certainty the existence of this island. (Gaunilo, *On Behalf of the Fool*)

In other words, Gaunilo is stating that the idea of a something that can be thought of as existing separately outside of our minds, just because it is the greatest thing we can think of, is a logical nonsense. Just because you can define the greatest possible being does not automatically lead to the fact that one actually exists. It's here that Gaunilo makes use of his island analogy to underline the absurdity of St Anselm's argument.

Specification content

Gaunilo, his reply to St Anselm; his rejection of the idea of a greatest possible being that can be thought of as having separate existence outside of our minds; his analogy of the idea of the greatest island as a ridicule of St Anselm's logic

Key term

reductio ad absurdum: an argument that shows a statement to be false or absurd if its logical conclusions were to be accepted

The perfect island?

Immanuel Kant's objection

In the eighteenth century, Prussian philosopher Immanuel Kant put forward a criticism of Descartes' form of the ontological argument. Descartes had claimed that God possessed all perfections, and that existence was one of those. However, Kant objected to this claim, stating that it is inaccurate to describe existence as a perfection.

The reasons for this are that the perfections that Descartes was referring to are attributes or **predicates**. Existence, says Kant, cannot not be a predicate simply because existence can be a thing that an object can possess or lack. Predicates do not describe anything about the nature of an object. For example, if we describe God as all-loving, then we are describing a predicate that God has – it is a predicate (or attribute or characteristic) that tells us something about God's nature.

Existence is not a determining predicate

The same is true when we describe God as omnipresent or omniscient. If we say 'God exists', what does that tell us about his nature? For Kant, it is for this reason that Descartes is mistaken in suggesting that God's existence is a determining predicate that he possesses.

To make this clearer, let us consider again what we mean by a *predicate*. If I say 'my car is blue', then I am describing something about my car that allows others to know something about it. I could go further and say that 'my car has four wheels', 'my car has five doors', 'my car has windscreen wipers' and so on. All these things are predicates of my car – they explain things about my car; things that it possesses and things that help others to understand something about the nature of my car. However, if I say 'my car exists', I am saying nothing about its nature – I am just making the point that my car is in existence, as opposed to my car not being in existence.

Kant's thalers example

Kant further elaborates on his denial of existence as a predicate by providing the example of 100 **thalers**. He asks the reader to consider what difference is held in the understanding of thalers by adding the phrase 'it exists' to the list of other predicates: for example, that they are round, made of gold and so on. He states that, as nothing changes in our minds by adding this phrase, it shows how existence is not a real predicate – despite 100 thalers in reality being preferable to 100 thalers in the mind alone!

Immanuel Kant (1724–1804)

The word *exists* adds nothing to our idea of God. This suggests that Descartes' (and, by association, St Anselm's) ontological arguments fail *a priori* (that is, they fail as a deductive argument) to prove the existence of God.

> **Specification content**
>
> Immanuel Kant's objection – existence is not a determining predicate: it cannot be a property that an object can either possess or lack

> **Key term**
>
> **predicate:** a defining characteristic or attribute

> **Key term**
>
> **thaler:** currency used in eighteenth-century Prussia

Summary

★ St Anselm's contemporary, Gaunilo, challenged St Anselm's ontological argument, saying it is not possible to define something into existence.

★ Gaunilo uses the example of the perfect island to support his challenge.

★ Immanuel Kant challenged Descartes' ontological argument by challenging his use of perfections and predicates.

★ Kant rejects the idea that existence can be a defining predicate, and therefore claims Descartes' argument fails.

AO1 Activity

a   Explain the key arguments of both Gaunilo and Kant. Show how they counter the arguments of St Anselm and Descartes respectively.

This helps with presenting a thorough and extensive knowledge and understanding of the topic area.

b   On revision cards, create a summary of the key points in Gaunilo's objections. Support the explanations with relevant quotations from Gaunilo.

This helps develop skills of organisation by selecting and ordering evidence and examples.

> **Specification content**
> The effectiveness of the challenges to the ontological argument for God's existence

This section covers AO2 content and skills

Issues for analysis and evaluation

The effectiveness of the challenges to the ontological argument for God's existence

Possible line of argument	Critical analysis and evaluation
Gaunilo demonstrated that St Anselm's argument is absurd	Gaunilo's challenge to the ontological argument is that he felt that St Anselm used an absurd argument. Using the philosophical argument *reductio ad absurdum*, Gaunilo shows that trying to define something into existence merely by definition is a ridiculous idea.
The concept of a perfect island shows the absurdity of St Anselm's reasoning	Gaunilo's presentation of the perfect island is in response to St Anselm's definition of God as a being greater than which cannot be conceived. Gaunilo stated that he could think of an island of which none greater could be conceived, but that did not mean that it actually existed – indeed, such a claim clearly made no sense. Gaunilo's challenge here appears particularly effective, as it attacks the core of St Anselm's argument.
Gaunilo misunderstood St Anselm's position	However, Gaunilo did not appreciate that St Anselm's claim is uniquely about God – and as God is that than which nothing greater can be conceived, then that definition applies to him alone. Gaunilo's concept of a perfect island could not work, as an island can always be added to or improved. Complete perfection (in the sense that nothing could ever be improved upon it) makes no sense when talking about a contingent reality such as an island. God is necessary – an island is not. This leads to Gaunilo's attack on St Anselm's argument being considered ineffective as it does not make use of valid reasoning.
Kant rejected Descartes' claim that existence is a predicate	Kant challenged Descartes' assertion that existence is a predicate of God. Descartes stated that, as the supremely perfect being, God possesses all perfections. Included in this is the 'perfection' of existence. However, Kant rejected this, as he felt that Descartes' use of the word *existence* is incorrect. *Predicates* tells us something about the nature of the reality they are trying to describe. The concept of existence tells us nothing about the nature of a reality. Therefore, according to Kant, the ontological argument fails – and his challenge to the ontological argument is considered effective.
Kant may have misunderstood what St Anselm said and therefore his challenge is not valid	Some have questioned whether Kant's understanding of St Anselm's original argument is fully accurate. They observe that Kant was talking about St Anselm adding the concept of existence to the concept of God to make his argument work. However, other scholars have suggested that this misunderstands St Anselm, who they say was instead asking his readers to compare something existing merely in the understanding with something existing in reality as well.

T1 Arguments for the existence of God – deductive

> **AO2 Activity**
>
> a Select three lines of argument from the critical analysis and evaluation of the effectiveness of the challenges to the ontological argument for God's existence. Find three references from scholars, schools of thought or religious and philosophical texts that would support those arguments.
>
> b Using the strongest line of argument, try to identify three key quotations that might be used – they could be from scholars, religious texts or schools of thought.

Specification content

The extent to which objections to the ontological argument are persuasive

Exam practice

Sample question

Evaluate the extent to which objections to the ontological argument are persuasive.

Sample answer

The relative persuasiveness of the objections to the ontological argument depends on how far the individual considers these objections to be valid, as well as how far they accept the original arguments as sound.

The introduction focuses on the key area for debate and indicates how the evaluation may proceed.

Gaunilo's objections centre on the claim that, in the same way that St Anselm argues it is possible to argue the existence of God through the definition of God as 'that than which nothing greater can be conceived', it must therefore be possible to have the idea of a perfect island and, because of this idea, this island must exist. Gaunilo says 'If a man should try to prove to me by such reasoning that this island truly exists … I know not which I ought to regard as the greater fool: myself, supposing that I should allow this proof, or him, if he should suppose that he had established with any certainty the existence of this island.' How persuasive is this as an argument? Should we reflect on Gaunilo's stance that, just because you can define a greatest possible being, this does not automatically lead to one actually existing?

The answer provides an accurate summary of Gaunilo's response to St Anselm's *Proslogion* 2. It then poses questions regarding the nature of Gaunilo's response, implying that it may be problematic.

Reflections from critics of Gaunilo state that he misunderstood the ontological argument and is applying his criticism incorrectly. Gaunilo does not seem to understand that, because of God's uniqueness, the ontological argument applies only to him – not to any other being. This is because only God is necessary (non-contingent). All other beings are contingent, and so cannot apply the same definition to themselves. This counterargument, if accepted, considerably undermines any persuasiveness that Gaunilo may have had with his objection.

This paragraph presents and considers relevant details regarding the perceived weakness in Gaunilo's response.

Contrary to the relative non-persuasiveness of Gaunilo's objections, Kant's objections appear far more persuasive. This is because Kant does not attempt to undermine St Anselm's argument directly by virtue of his definition, but instead challenges Descartes' position. This, in turn, affects St Anselm's position on the nature of God. Kant shows Descartes' reasoning (in defining God's existence through a consideration of his perfections) as invalid. Kant explains that existence, which was considered a perfection possessed by God, is not a determining predicate – as existence cannot add anything to the idea of something. Only those qualities that add to the nature of God (e.g. omnipotence, omniscience, omnipresence and so on) can be called *predicates*. Existence adds nothing new to our understanding of the nature of God, and so cannot be called a predicate. This therefore undermines Descartes' position and strengthens the persuasiveness of Kant's objection.

This paragraph presents a very thorough analysis of Kant's position, and compares it to the positions of St Anselm and Descartes. The information is highly accurate and relevant, and this enables, through counterpoint to the suggestion that the ontological argument is persuasive, the debate to be further examined and clarified.

WJEC/Eduqas Religious Studies for A Level Philosophy of Religion

However, has Kant misunderstood St Anselm? Perhaps the idea of adding the concept of existence to the concept of God was not what St Anselm was suggesting? If we accept this as true, then the strength of Kant's objections are somewhat undermined. This would therefore demonstrate that Kant's objections are not as persuasive as first thought.

The persuasiveness of the challenges to the ontological argument rests entirely on whether the objections both Gaunilo and Kant raise are considered valid. If they are accepted, then the ontological argument must be considered fundamentally flawed and the challenges to it as entirely persuasive. If not, then the challenges fail and the victory of persuasiveness belongs to the ontological argument and its supporters.

This paragraph raises a simple counterpoint through questioning, leading to a conclusion regarding Kant's point of view.

Judge

The conclusion presents the final line of reasoning, which highlights the crux of the debate – namely, the philosophical validity of the challenges – and then draws an appropriate conclusion based on this.

Evaluation

This is a good answer. There is a clear and well-developed line of reasoning that considers both sides of the argument before putting forwards a conclusion. The response shows that, while the challenges raise several important philosophical points regarding the way the ontological argument works (namely, the premises it rests on as a form of deductive reasoning), they themselves are not immune from criticism.

Over to you

Below is an argument concerning the persuasiveness of the challenges of Gaunilo and Kant to the ontological argument.

Respond to this argument by thinking of three key questions you could ask the writer that would challenge their view and force them to defend their argument.

When you have completed the task, refer to the band descriptors for A2 (WJEC) or A Level (Eduqas) and, in particular, look at the demands described in the higher band descriptors, which you should be aspiring towards. Ask yourself:

- Is my answer a confident critical analysis and perceptive evaluation of the issue?
- Is my answer a response that successfully identifies and thoroughly addresses the issues the question raises?

Argument

Gaunilo's objections centre on the claim that, in the same way that St Anselm argues it is possible to argue the existence of God through the definition of God as 'that than which nothing greater can be conceived', it must be possible to have the idea of a perfect island and, because of this idea, this island must exist. To demonstrate how persuasive an argument we could consider this to be, we should reflect on Gaunilo's stance that, just because you can define a greatest possible being does not automatically lead to one actually existing.

Kant does not attempt to undermine St Anselm's argument directly by virtue of his definition, but instead challenges Descartes' position. This, in turn, affects the position St Anselm takes on the nature of God. Kant shows Descartes defining God's existence through a consideration of his perfections as invalid reasoning. Kant explains that existence, which was considered a perfection possessed by God, is not a determining predicate – as existence cannot add anything to the idea of something. Only those qualities that add to the nature of God, such as omnipotence, omniscience and omnipresence, can be called predicates. Existence adds nothing new to our understanding of the nature of God and so cannot be called a predicate. This therefore undermines Descartes' position and strengthens the persuasiveness of Kant's objection.

T2: Challenges to religious belief – the problem of evil and suffering

This section covers AO1 content and skills

Specification content

The types of evil: moral (caused by free-will agents) and natural (caused by nature)

A: The problem of evil and suffering

The types of evil

Evil is often considered to be anything that causes suffering. This suffering can occur in many different forms, and can be the result of a moral action or an event that occurs in nature. Consequently, the nature of evil presents several philosophical issues. Consider the images below:

- What sort of evil do they represent?
- What is the suffering that these types of evil cause?
- How do they differ?

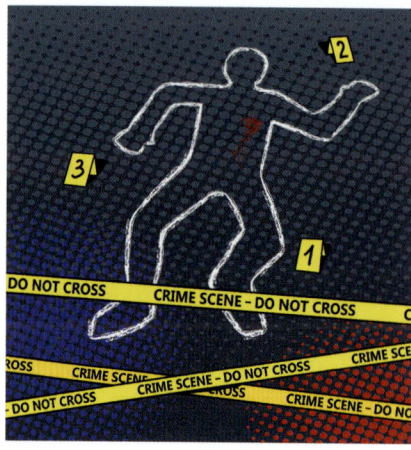

Examples of moral and natural evil

From your consideration of the images, you will have noticed how, broadly speaking, evil can be categorised into two main types: **moral evil** and **natural evil**.

Key terms

evil: anything that causes pain or suffering

moral evil: evil caused as a result of the actions of a free-will agent

natural evil: evil caused by the means of a force outside the control of free-will agents – usually referred to as 'nature'

Moral evil

Moral evil is any suffering that is brought about through the actions of a free-will agent. A free-will agent is someone who is able to make moral choices or, to put it another way, can choose to do 'good' or 'evil'. Should the agent choose evil, then their actions can cause others to suffer.

One of the main religious philosophical issues that is raised by this type of evil is that, if evil is caused by an individual that could have chosen to do good instead, does that mean that God should not be held accountable for evil's existence in the world?

Some examples of moral evil include murder, theft, violence, rape, slavery, child abuse, animal cruelty, terrorism, adultery, dishonesty, any form of negative discrimination and genocide.

Natural evil

Natural evil is any suffering that is brought about as a consequence of events outside the control of free-will agents. That means those that occur as part of nature: that is, the normal, physical workings of the world or universe.

One of the main religious philosophical issues that is raised by this type of evil is that, if evil is caused by nature, does that mean that God, as the creator of nature, should be held accountable for evil's existence in the world?

Some examples of natural evil include the suffering that results from earthquakes, tsunamis, flooding, drought, tornadoes, hurricanes, extremes in temperature (hot and cold), disease, crop failure, forest fires, pollution and global warming.

Occasionally, free-will agents can set in motion a series of events in nature that result in suffering that was not intended: for example, human activity that contributes to global warming that, in turn, results in extreme weather events. It is therefore debatable whether or not this suffering constitutes moral evil.

The logical problem of evil

Classical (Epicurus) – the problem of suffering

The problem of evil is an ancient philosophical and theological one. If a belief system suggests that the universe was created deliberately, out of nothing, by a God that is all-powerful, all-knowing and all-loving, then how is it possible that things within that universe can go wrong? Not only that, but why is it that the created beings suffer – often to appalling extremes – when they are deliberately made by this God?

It is these issues that caused the Ancient Greek philosopher Epicurus, writing in the third century BCE, to put forward what has become known as the *classical logical problem of evil*.

Any response would seem to throw up some kind of philosophical contradiction to the characteristics of this God (commonly referred to as the *God of classical theism*). This is why it remains a constant challenge to those who would believe in such a God, despite numerous attempts by religious believers, theologians and philosophers to resolve the issue.

> **Specification content**
> The logical problem of evil: classical (Epicurus) – the problem of suffering

> **" Key quote "**
>
> Either God wants to abolish evil, and cannot; or he can, but does not want to. If he wants to, but cannot, he is impotent. If he can, but does not want to, he is wicked. If God can abolish evil, and God really wants to do it, why is there evil in the world?
>
> (Epicurus, as summarised by David Hume in *Dialogues Concerning Natural Religion*, Part 10)

Specification content

J.L. Mackie's modern development – the nature of the problem of evil (inconsistent triad)

 Key terms

omnipotent: all-powerful
omnibenevolent: all-loving

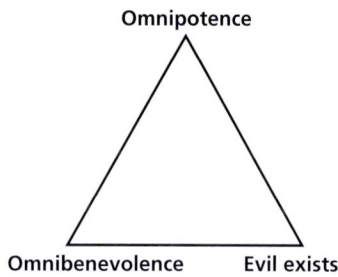

Inconsistent triad

J.L. Mackie's modern development

The nature of the problem of evil (inconsistent triad)

The Australian philosopher John L. Mackie formulated the problem of evil into an 'inconsistent triad':

1. God is **omnipotent**
2. God is **omnibenevolent**
3. Evil exists

Mackie points out that it is logically inconsistent for these three statements to exist simultaneously: that is, they cannot all be true at the same time.

The problem of omnipotence

If God were omnipotent, he would have the power to remove evil, as his omnipotence means that he is capable of any feat. The characteristic of omnipotence includes the notion that God could have created a universe where there was no evil. For Mackie, omnipotence involves a clear definition of what he calls *unqualified omnipotence*: that is, omnipotence without any restrictions due to the constraints of the world.

The problem of omnibenevolence

If he were omnibenevolent, then he, in his loving kindness towards his creation, would want to remove evil so that creation did not suffer. The idea that any omnibenevolent being would deliberately tolerate evil, and the horrendous suffering that it causes, completely contradicts the very concept of omnibenevolence.

However, the existence of evil is so tangible in its effects and its scope that any denial of its existence would be nonsensical. Therefore, it is not possible for the three statements above to co-exist.

Possible solutions

1 God is not omnipotent

An alternative solution to the problem is to try to resolve the inconsistent triad by removing one of the three points. Any such solution would read like this: If we remove the characteristic of omnipotence from God, then we can understand why evil exists because, while God loves creation and wants to prevent evil, he does not have the power to do so.

This solution echoes the philosophical stance taken by process theologians such as Whitehead, who claims that God is part of the universe and is responsible for starting off the evolutionary process that led to humanity and, as such, is responsible for what happens to his creation. However, such a God, as part of the universe, does not have sufficient power to remove evil. Process theologians regard this God as 'the fellow sufferer who understands' – being as much part of the universe as humanity.

However attractive this solution appears, ultimately it does not satisfy those religious believers who believe that their God is responsible for creating the universe *ex nihilo* ('out of nothing') – and is therefore greater than all that exists within the universe.

2 God is not omnibenevolent

So some philosophers suggest that we should remove the characteristic of omnibenevolence. In this case, evil exists and God is omnipotent. Having the power to remove evil does not mean that God wants to. If he is not 'all-loving', then why should he care if his creation suffers? Such a God may be considered malicious, and may even enjoy seeing his creation suffer.

However, such a God is so far from the imagination of all classical theistic religions as to be unrecognisable. The problem therefore remains.

3 Evil does not exist

Finally, then, we can remove from the list that 'evil exists'. In doing so, God retains his characteristics of omnipotence and omnibenevolence, and there is no contradiction for believers in terms of God's characteristics. The assertion is that evil does not exist. After all, it may be our perception that is at fault. If we were able to see the universe from a God's-eye view, then we might see that the suffering that creation faces is not the evil that we think it is, but rather it has a purpose that we do not understand because we do not have God's perspective.

Imagine the situation of a toddler playing in the kitchen while the parent is using the oven. The oven piques the toddler's curiosity and they wander over to it. Standing against the oven, they reach up to try and pull the pan off the top of the oven to see what's inside it. At this point, the parent, alarmed at what is about to happen, may swipe the toddler's hand away from the oven. In doing so, the toddler suffers from having their hand grabbed. They cannot understand why the parent has just grabbed their hand and are upset by the incident. They may even consider the parent to be cruel and unfair. However, what the toddler is unaware of is that the pan on top of the oven is full of boiling water and, had they succeeded in pulling it off the oven top, they would have been severely injured and suffered far greater pain. The toddler does not have the parent's perspective and creation, like the toddler, does not share the perspective of God (as the parent).

Attractive as this idea may at first appear, it has been largely rejected for the simple reason that the effects of evil are 'felt too widely, and its presence attested too vividly' for it to be dismissible, as Hume points out.

The inconsistent triad: summary

Mackie has brought the ancient problem, as stated by Epicurus, into the modern era. For many philosophers, however, the problem of evil is simply insurmountable. The inconsistent triad simply but devastatingly poses the question of why an all-loving, all-powerful God would allow his creation to suffer. This question seems to have no easy answer.

William Rowe

Intense human and animal suffering

In his work *The Problem of Evil and Some Varieties of Atheism* (1979), William Rowe argues that, while it seems reasonable for God to allow some limited suffering to enable humans to grow and develop, he cannot accept God allowing what he calls *intense suffering*. Animal suffering also seems pointless. Rowe uses the example of a fawn caught in a forest fire as an example of pointless animal suffering. He argues:

- An omnipotent and omniscient being would know when intense suffering was about to take place; such a being could prevent the suffering from happening.
- An all-loving being would probably prevent all evil and suffering that had no purpose and was pointless and avoidable; such evil and suffering does happen.
- Therefore, God probably does not exist.

> **Specification content**
> William Rowe (intense human and animal suffering) and Gregory S. Paul (premature deaths)

Rowe's approach is sometimes referred to as the *evidential problem of evil* (as opposed to the *logical problem of evil*, as presented by Epicurus and Mackie). It involves asking whether, and to what extent, we can use the existence of evil as evidence to argue against the existence of God.

Gregory S. Paul

Premature deaths

Gregory Paul argues that the death of so many innocent children challenges the existence of God. He estimates that, since the time that God first spoke to man, as recorded in the sacred texts of the Abrahamic religions, over 50 billion children have died naturally before reaching what he calls 'the age of mature consent'. In addition, some 300 billion human beings have died naturally but prenatally (before they have been born). Paul calls this 'the Holocaust of the children'. Using this statistical information, he argues:

- Millions of innocent children suffer and die every year, from both natural and evil causes.
- These children are too young to be able to make choices about God – they have no free will.
- No all-loving, all-powerful being would permit such suffering.
- Therefore, God does not exist.

The problem of evil stated in this way is sometimes referred to as the *statistical problem of evil*.

> **Summary**
> - The existence of evil, as something that causes suffering, seems incompatible with the idea of an all-loving and all-powerful God.
> - This problem, known as the *logical problem of evil*, was expressed by Epicurus in ancient times and by J.L. Mackie in the twentieth century.
> - Mackie formulated the idea of the inconsistent triad and suggested that a removal of any one statement from the triad could theoretically solve the problem.
> - William Rowe and Gregory Paul have respectively expressed the problem of evil in evidential and statistical forms.

> **AO1 Activity**
>
> **a** Using bullet points, outline the key ideas in both the classical and modern forms of the problem of evil.
>
> This helps with presenting a thorough and extensive knowledge and understanding of the topic area.
>
> **b** On revision cards, compile a list of examples that show occurrences of the two main types of evil. Then write an explanation of how these examples show evil and the effect on others.
>
> This helps with prioritising and selecting a core set of points to develop an answer and ensure that you are making accurate use of specialist language and vocabulary in context.

> **Specification content**
> The extent to which the classical form of the problem of evil is a problem

This section covers AO2 content and skills

Issues for analysis and evaluation

The extent to which the classical form of the problem of evil is a problem

Possible line of argument	Critical analysis and evaluation
The classical problem of evil stated	Epicurus is credited with posing, in the third century BCE, the logical problem of evil; he stated the formulation: 'Either God wants to abolish evil, and cannot; or he can, but does not want to. If he wants to, but cannot, he is impotent. If he can, but does not want to, he is wicked. If God can abolish evil, and God really wants to do it, why is there evil in the world?'
The classical problem of evil is a logical problem	Epicurus bases his assumption on an existent God who is attributed with divine power and benevolence, favourably disposed towards humanity. However, his formulation, sometimes referred to as the *Epicurean paradox*, denies that it is possible for such a God to exist alongside evil. This then is the *classical logical problem of evil*. The extent to which it is considered a problem rests, ultimately, on the point of view of the individual.
Different views of God can remove the problem of evil	Any individual who discounts the existence of God is automatically 'rewarded' by the problem of evil not being a problem at all, for evil may well exist but God does not. Alternatively, the believer may decide to attribute different characteristics to God – causing him to be a God of malevolence or limited power, or even a God who has no particular interest in the welfare of human beings; a God apathetic to innocent human suffering. This, however, is sidestepping the problem!
Evil exists because God does not care about humanity	Therefore, if an individual holds a belief in God where he or she considers God to be an almighty power but to have no particular fondness for humanity (or anything else in creation), then there is no contradiction with the existence of evil. It may also be possible to dispute Epicurus' assertion that such a God would be 'wicked', in that it may be that God simply does not care about the existence of evil. Therefore, he is not so much wicked as apathetic where evil is concerned.
Evil exists because God does not have the power to prevent it	Equally, any believer who holds faith in a God who is loving towards his creation but has no other particular attributes must be willing to concede that, despite a willingness to remove evil, he is unable to do so. This is the position that process theologians hold, who consider God as the 'fellow sufferer who understands'. In such a case, while evil still exists as an emotional and physical problem, it is no longer a logical one.
The problem of evil remains	However, for the classical theist, who holds to God's attributes of omnipotence and omnibenevolence, there is no escaping the logical problem of evil as Epicurus presented it. Such a God – able to do anything and wanting to prevent our suffering – would surely not want us, as his creation, to suffer, would he?

> **AO2 Activity**
>
> a Evaluate three lines of argument from the critical analysis and evaluation of the extent to which the classical form of the problem of evil is a problem. What are their strengths and weaknesses? Which line of argument is strongest?
>
> b Using the strongest line of argument, try to identify three key questions that might be asked – they could be critical, challenge, hypothetical or direct questions.

Specification content
The degree to which modern problem-of-evil arguments are effective in proving God's non-existence

Exam practice

Sample question
Evaluate the degree to which modern problem-of-evil arguments are effective in proving God's non-existence.

Sample answer

This is a good introduction that provides a helpful overview of the key areas for focus in the evaluation to come.

Ask almost any atheist why they do not accept the existence of God as a believable proposition and, almost invariably, they will respond with reference to the amount of evil and suffering in the world. It seems entirely inconsistent that a God who is all-loving and all-powerful and has created the universe could have put together his creation in such a way as to allow the existence of evil and suffering – often to quite appalling extremes. This undermines any counter-claim regarding his supposed goodness and power.

This paragraph presents relevant evidence, via a line of reasoning, which shows the grounds on which the problem of evil is based.

Mackie's inconsistent triad – which shows the incompatibility of God's omnipotence and omnibenevolence with the existence of evil – is an effective 'argument' for undermining the existence of God. Or so it seems. However, it must be noted that the inconsistency of the three statements is based on the assumption that God does indeed possess the stated characteristics, and this may not actually be the case.

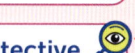

This paragraph develops the argument further, coherently making the link between this and the previous information. It also links to the overarching 'problem of evil' and refers to the inconsistent triad.

If God does indeed have both omnipotence and omnibenevolence, then it seems virtually impossible to concede that evil exists, from a logical point of view. However, the overwhelming evidence of suffering within and among the entirety of creation – not just humanity – seems to make such a conclusion entirely nonsensical. Accepting this position would seem, therefore, to lead to the inescapable alternative conclusion, that a God with the characteristics of omnipotence and omnibenevolence cannot exist.

This paragraph makes a counterpoint to provide an alternative line of reasoning. It also considers the shortcomings of the point in terms of its coherence with the overall argument.

However, if we accept, in line with Mackie's reasoning, that God is able to exist without one of those key attributes, then the modern problem of evil – much like the classical problem – no longer seems to be relevant. In other words, a God who is all-powerful, but willing to let evil exist because he either doesn't care or consciously wants his creation to suffer, would still exist, but would be significantly different from the God that the vast majority of theistic religions worship in the world today.

Perhaps, however, he is a God who is omnibenevolent and actively wants to stop the suffering that creation experiences, but is unable to do so. The laws of the universe, perhaps, may bind this being and, due to limitations of his power, he is incapable of preventing evil. He may well still exist, but would such a being be worthy of worship?

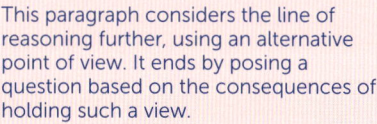

This paragraph considers the line of reasoning further, using an alternative point of view. It ends by posing a question based on the consequences of holding such a view.

Evidential arguments, such as those William Rowe proposed, which bring a whole range of suffering as evidence against the existence of God, also mount a serious challenge to God's existence. How can an omnipotent and omnibenevolent God allow such horrors to occur, and yet stand idly by while they continue to do so? Equally, the statistical problem of evil that Gregory Paul presented also shows a God who seems not to care about the destruction of literally billions of children since the time of the Abrahamic religions. The only sensible conclusion to draw from this is that God simply does not exist.

Therefore, it would seem that modern problem-of-evil arguments – such as those that Mackie, Rowe and Paul outlined – do pose a significant challenge to believers in the God of classical theism, and effectively seem to suggest his non-existence.

This paragraph accurately presents an alternative set of evidences from modern problem-of-evil arguments, and it draws a conclusion based on these.

Evaluation

This is an effective and balanced response. It considers both sides of the argument and raises questions, before putting forward a conclusion. The candidate makes accurate use both of terminology and of the views of different philosophers.

The response restates the conclusion from the previous paragraph and collates it with the evidence considered previously in the evaluation to form an overall and final conclusion.

Over to you

Below is a weak answer that a student has written in response to a question requiring evaluation of the extent to which religious solutions to the problem of evil are convincing.

Using the band level descriptors, place this answer in a relevant band. (It is obviously a weak answer and so would not be in bands 3–5.) To do this, it will be useful to consider what is missing from the answer and what is inaccurate. The accompanying analysis will assist you.

When analysing the answer's weaknesses, in a group, think of five ways you would improve the answer to make it stronger. You might have more than five suggestions, but try to negotiate as a group and prioritise the five most important things lacking from the answer.

Answer

Religious solutions such as Irenaeus' and Anselm's[1] theodicy are convincing arguments to prove God's existence in the problem of evil. It is our choice as humans to disobey our God[2] who made a world free from flaw. And this is why he designed Heaven and Hell, for the good and the bad to go to[3]. Also, evil is not a substance and therefore it cannot be claimed that God created it.[4]

In my opinion, I think that religious solutions are unconvincing. I feel that there are far too many errors in the argument for the problem of evil.[5] The main critique is that it seems impossible to say that he or any other God can be all-knowing, loving and powerful, if evil still exists in the universe.[6]

Analysis of answer

1. Incorrect philosopher's name.
2. Use of 'our God' is confessional language and not appropriate in an academic response.
3. Phrasing here is very simplistic.
4. Why? This statement needs explaining in more detail.
5. Limited in scope and expression, and no evidence or explanation given to justify the point of view.
6. There is no reasoned conclusion.

This section covers AO1 content and skills

Key person

Augustine of Hippo (AD354–430): born in North Africa, he produced a vast amount of writing, chiefly in defence of Christianity against a number of heresies popular at the time, although he also wrote very influentially on Christian belief and doctrine; his best-known works are *City of God*, *Confessions* and *Enchiridion*.

B: Religious responses to the problem of evil: Augustinian-type theodicy

The 'theodicy' of **Augustine of Hippo**, in its original form, cannot be found as a single work, but rather is a theme that runs throughout much of his writing. Some commentators have observed that Augustine was obsessed with the problem of evil and wrestled with it throughout his life – even before his conversion to Christianity. Therefore, we must remember that any presentation of his theodicy in a book such as this has to simplify Augustine's thoughts.

Adam and Eve being tempted in Eden

Key aspects of Augustine's theodicy

Evil as a consequence of sin

According to Augustine's theodicy, God's creation was originally free from evil. Evil did not exist before the sin of angels and humans. It first came into existence when angels, followed by humans, misused their will and turned from God, their creator.

According to accounts in the Bible, it is a fact of the created universe that God called all things into existence *ex nihilo* ('out of nothing') and, through corruption and decay, all things will eventually lapse back into nothingness.

Humans and angels are both part of the created order. Therefore, through this corruption and decay, they will change. This means that they have the capability of turning away from God. It is precisely this turning – which involves an act of free will – that brings about evil. However, why humans and angels would be willing to do this remains a mystery beyond human understanding, according to Augustine.

As the gift of free will necessarily includes the concept of moral responsibility, it is humans who are ultimately responsible for sin and, consequently, evil – not God. This is because humans voluntarily choose sin.

Specification content

Augustinian-type theodicy: evil as a consequence of sin; evil as a privation; the fall of human beings and creation; the Cross overcomes evil; soul-deciding

Evil as a privation

It is important to realise, however, that evil is not in any way a 'substance' or part of the created order. The significance of this is that evil, therefore, is not something God creates. If it is a substance, then God must have created it, since he creates all things. God, being an omnibenevolent creator, cannot have created evil as a substance.

Instead, evil indicates an absence, or **privation**, of part of God's created order. For example, when humans or angels 'turn away' from God, it is this 'turning away' that is a privation of God's original created order and purpose. (That is, it is an absence of following God's intended purpose for them.) The 'turning away' is therefore considered to be 'evil'.

Augustine referred to darkness as a metaphor for evil, but he referenced darkness in the sense of the absence of light. Evil has no real being of its own.

> ### Key term
> **privation:** the absence or loss of something that is normally present (e.g. *a privation of health* means that a person is ill and not healthy)

The fall of human beings and creation

As all human beings are ultimately descended from Adam (in Augustine's words, 'seminally present'), then all human beings share Adam's guilt and sin. As all share his guilt and sin, all deserve to face the same punishment. All human beings suffer through 'moral evil', as that is humankind's fault through actions it performs on the basis of free will. Another belief is that natural evil is caused by the actions of fallen angels who, like humans, chose to turn away from their creator.

The suffering that human beings face as part of the natural world (i.e. natural evil) is a direct result of the 'absence of good' caused in creation by the 'turning away' from God. Therefore, this suffering brings corruption into the created order.

The cross overcomes evil and the soul-deciding theodicy

It is this point ('to bring good out of evil') that many Christians refer to as the 'happy mistake' (*felix culpa*). This is the Christian belief that God would

For Christians, the *felix culpa* led to atonement through Jesus

T2 Challenges to religious belief – the problem of evil and suffering

Key terms

the fall: the events of Genesis, Chapter 3, where Adam and Eve face God's punishment for disobeying his divine command not to eat of the fruit from the tree of knowledge of Good and Evil

redemption: the act of saving something or someone; in the Christian context, it refers to Jesus saving humanity from evil and sin

never have needed to send Jesus into the world to save it from its sin, were it not for the events of **the fall** (the original sin of Adam and Eve and the consequences that followed their turning away from God).

Those who freely chose to accept Jesus as their saviour would be redeemed. In Christianity, this refers to being 'saved' from your sins by accepting Jesus as God's son and Christians' saviour. They would also be reunited with God in Heaven after this life. This is why the theodicy is sometimes regarded as a 'soul-deciding' theodicy.

Augustine's theodicy asserts that this chance for humanity to seek **redemption**, through Christ, not only demonstrates that God is merciful, but also underlines his justice.

> **Specification content**
>
> Challenges to Augustinian-type theodicies: validity of accounts in Genesis, Chapters 2 and 3; scientific error – biological impossibility of human descent from a single pair (therefore invalidating the inheritance of Adam's sin); moral contradictions of omnibenevolent God and existence of Hell; contradiction of perfect order becoming chaotic – geological and biological evidence suggests the contrary.

Challenges to Augustinian-type theodicies

Validity of accounts in Genesis, Chapters 2 and 3

Augustine's theodicy relies heavily on the accounts of the creation and the fall, as depicted in the biblical book of Genesis, Chapters 1–3. For the **literalist** Christian believer, this means that the accounts are to be taken as historically true, being rooted in the revelation of divine scripture. Humankind's place in the created order, and the suffering that it faces, is therefore clearly accounted for in these Genesis accounts.

However, as soon as any other view of scripture is taken, Augustine's theodicy becomes problematic.

If the view of scripture is taken as non-literal metaphorical and mythological, then any claim of historical truth relating to the accounts of creation and fall become suspect. It is from this viewpoint that the most devastating attacks upon the theodicy arise.

Key term

literalist: interpreting the text of the Bible in a literal sense – that is, every word should be taken at face value; interpretation is not required

Scientific error – biological impossibility of human descent from a single pair

The idea that all human beings deserve to be punished because they are descended from Adam fails because it is a biological impossibility. With our advancements in scientific understanding of genetics and the human mind and body, the idea that one person's 'sin' can be transferred to all of humanity is not possible; neither is the idea that all humanity originated with one pair of human beings in the first place. If the Genesis account is not scientifically valid, then Augustine's theory is not consistent or relevant to our experience of evil.

Moral contradictions of an omnibenevolent God and the existence of Hell

Key term

free will: the theological and philosophical concept that states that humans have the ability to choose freely between good and evil

If God gave humans **free will**, why did he punish them for using it? If a perfect world had been created, then how is it possible that humanity had the knowledge of good and evil necessary for free will? This implies that evil already existed; therefore, this can only be the responsibility of God. Hell is part of the created order. This suggests that, not only did God know that angels would rebel and human beings would fall, but he had also prepared a place of punishment for them. Why would an omnibenevolent (all-loving) God do this? The existence of Hell is not consistent with an all-loving God.

Contradiction of perfect order becoming chaotic

The perfect world becoming imperfect contradicts all scientific **geological** records and biological evidence. Geological evidence shows clearly that the initial physical state of the world was one of huge upheaval of the physical landscape, with volcanic activity commonplace across the surface of the Earth before it eventually began to cool. Geology sees the nature of the world even today as chaotic and unpredictable. Earthquakes are an example of this. Geologists would certainly deny a movement from initial perfection.

Evolutionary theory, according to biology, is the development of human beings because of a process of natural selection, mutation and evolution from earlier life-forms over millions of years, and is well evidenced with archaeological and genetic records. This reduces the plausibility of the creation account as a historical fact.

In addition, if human beings began by being perfect, then, even though they are free to sin, they don't have to do so. If they do, then they were not flawless to start with, and so God must share the responsibility of their fall. It is hard to clear God from responsibility for evil since he chose to create a being he foresaw would do evil.

> ### Key terms
> **geological:** the science relating to how the Earth was formed
> **evolutionary theory:** scientific theory, originally proposed in the nineteenth century, that posits that life developed from simpler to more complex life-forms via a process of natural selection and genetic mutation

Summary
- Augustine of Hippo suggested that the existence of evil is a direct result of the events of the fall, when Adam and Eve misused their free will to disobey God.
- Augustine believed that evil is best defined as an absence of God's originally perfect created order.
- Augustine believed that the sacrifice of Christ on the cross provides Christians with the opportunity for atonement and reconciliation with God.
- There have been many challenges to Augustine's theodicy based on issues relating to the historical validity and moral inconsistencies of the biblical account, as well as the contrary scientific evidence.

AO1 Activity

a Explain how Augustine uses the accounts in Genesis, Chapters 1–3 to support his theodicy.

This helps with presenting a thorough and extensive knowledge and understanding of the topic area.

b Create an information poster that summarises the key points of an Augustinian-type theodicy.

This helps with prioritising and selecting a core set of points to develop an answer and ensure that you are making accurate use of specialist language and vocabulary in context.

> **This section covers AO2 content and skills**

> **Specification content**
> Whether Augustinian-type theodicies are relevant in the twenty-first century

Issues for analysis and evaluation

Whether Augustinian-type theodicies are relevant in the twenty-first century

Possible line of argument	Critical analysis and evaluation
Evil was the result of the misuse of free will	The Augustinian-type theodicies find their origin in the works of Augustine. Based largely on the account of the fall in the Book of Genesis and the Christian understanding of the atonement through the resurrection of Jesus, the theodicy demonstrates how evil was not part of God's plan for creation, but rather was the unintended consequence of allowing free-will agents to exercise their moral choice.
How reliable are the accounts that Augustine bases his ideas on?	The questions can then be asked: how historically accurate are these accounts? Did they actually occur? If not, then why should we believe anything that is based on them? In a twenty-first-century world of scientific enquiry and healthy scepticism, such ideas seem easy to dismiss and are therefore barely relevant.
How far does free will explain the existence of evil?	The ability to have free will meant that a genuine choice between good and evil needed to be available. This meant that moral evil could theoretically thrive, if these free-will agents deliberately chose to turn away from good. Equally, the disobedience shown to God demanded a just punishment – which is where natural evil came from. This was a disruption of the perfect world God created, due to the evil choices of the free-will agents. Such a viewpoint demands an assumption that a divine being existed who 'programmed' his creation to act in a particular way. This idea seems difficult to comprehend in an age when evolutionary theory holds sway.
The account that Augustine bases his ideas on is neither credible nor relevant in the twenty-first century	The Augustinian account also presumes belief in the existence of angels. Indeed, it is the fallen angel in the form of the serpent that is the catalyst for the events of the fall. However, this is a strange notion for the twenty-first century, when there is no empirical evidence for such creatures, and certainly not in a way in which they are capable of taking the form of an animal and speaking directly with human beings. The whole account seems too fanciful for the twenty-first-century mind to take seriously.
The view that evil is a privation does not reflect reality	The view of evil as a privation depends on accepting the concept of a perfect world, where all things existed in a state of goodness and perfection and in which only by disrupting this were absences of goodness found and therefore 'evil' existed. However, in the twenty-first century, how believable is this? Evil is a very real presence in the world – as are its effects. Suggesting that evil is the 'lack of a thing' seems to belong purely to the realm of metaphysical speculation, rather than cold, harsh reality.
Christian philosophy is not relevant to those outside the religion	The salvation of human beings by acceptance of the sacrifice of Jesus is a comfort to those of the Christian faith, where a reconciled existence with God after death offers hope of a future when pain and suffering will be nothing more than a distant memory. However, for those outside of this faith tradition, no such comfort is offered and, as less than half the planet's population are promised this salvation, what relevance does it have to the majority of people in the twenty-first century?
Augustinian-type theodicies are not relevant in the twenty-first century	In conclusion, despite the appeal that they may have to believers in the Christian faith traditions, Augustinian-type theodicies lack the scientific and historical credibility to be truly relevant in the twenty-first century.

AO2 Activity

a Select three lines of argument from the critical analysis and evaluation of whether Augustinian-type theodicies are relevant in the twenty-first century. Find three references from scholars, schools of thought or religious and philosophical texts that would support those arguments.

b Using the strongest line of argument, try to identify three key quotations that might be used – they could be from scholars, religious texts or schools of thought.

Exam practice

Sample question
Evaluate the extent to which Augustine's theodicy succeeds as a defence of the God of classical theism.

Sample answer
The problem of evil is a longstanding challenge to believers in the God of classical theism. Throughout history, there have been attempts to support this belief and to attack the problem of evil. One such example can be found in the theodicies (attempts to justify God in the face of the existence of evil) associated with the works of Augustine of Hippo.

Augustine's starting point is that God is not responsible for the creation of evil. Augustine refers to evil as a lack of goodness or a 'privation of good'. One way of trying to understand what he means here is by considering the example of blindness. Blindness is the lack or privation of sight, and so this helps to explain the concept of evil being a lack or privation of good. Creating a 'lack of something' contradicts God's act of creation. If we take this point as valid, then Augustine's theodicy is already a partially successful defence of the God of classical theism.

In further defence of the God of classical theism, Augustine points out that it is the free will of humans and angels that caused suffering. It was the deliberate turning away from divine commands, as explained in the biblical account of the fall, that resulted in the destruction of the perfect order. It was not God's will for this to happen, but rather the deliberate action of free-will agents. It should be recognised that evil is a direct result of the consequences of the fall.

The Genesis account demonstrates the need for evil and suffering to exist because of actions by free-will agents. It is necessary for a just God to punish wrongdoing. The introduction of natural evil (caused by the actions of fallen angels, who wreak havoc, and human rebellion, which affected all of creation and subsequently distorted it) is therefore a deserved punishment. Again, if we accept this view, then Augustine's theodicy provides a successful defence of the God of classical theism, at least in part.

Specification content
The extent to which Augustine's theodicy succeeds as a defence of the God of Classical Theism

News reporter
This is a brief but clear introduction that provides a background for why theodicies were developed.

News reporter
The response provides an overview commentary on Augustine's understanding of evil as an 'absence' of good. It presents the information accurately, which is relevant to the question set.

News reporter
This paragraph develops the argument further, this time focusing on the concept of free will and its misuse.

Detective

Judge

The candidate summarises the argument and provides evidence for Augustine's justification of evil – a punishment from God.

T2 Challenges to religious belief – the problem of evil and suffering

This paragraph makes a counterpoint, this time attacking the flaw in Augustine's reasoning from the basis of biological science. This undermines the coherence of Augustine's point of view.

However, not all Augustine's viewpoints are as easy to accept. The assertion that all humans are 'seminally present' in Adam and therefore, according to the inheritance of guilt doctrine, all descendants of Adam (that is, all human beings) are deserving of punishment as they have inherited his sin, is a particularly difficult viewpoint to accept. This is because genetic and biological records show that it is biologically impossible (as well as genetically undesirable) for all humans to have descended from a single male. In this case, Augustine's theodicy is not a successful defence of the God of classical theism.

The candidate develops the counterpoint and raises a question that undermines the theodicy.

Equally, the proposition that God demonstrates mercy through making provision for a way of redemption through Christ, leading to the fall being referred to as the *felix culpa* ('happy mistake'), is only of relevance to Christian believers. What about theists from other faith traditions? This part of Augustine's theodicy simply does not work.

The response considers the evidence presented so far and draws a relevant conclusion.

The moral and logical issues with the various contradictions within the Augustinian theodicy further undermine its validity as a defence of the God of classical theism in the face of the existence of evil. Therefore, in conclusion, following the points made above, Augustine's theodicy fails as a successful defence of the God of classical theism.

Evaluation

This is an effective and balanced response. It considers both sides of the argument and raises questions, before putting forward a conclusion. The candidate makes accurate use both of terminology and of the views of different schools of thought.

Over to you

Below is a weak answer that a student has written in response to a question requiring an evaluation of whether Augustine's theodicy solves the problem of evil. (It is obviously a below-average answer and so would be about band 2.)

In a group, analyse the answer's weaknesses and decide on five points that you would use to improve the answer. It will be useful, initially, to consider what is missing from the answer and what is inaccurate. This time, there is no accompanying analysis to assist you.

Write out your additions, each one in a clear paragraph. Remember, it is how you use the points that is the most important factor. Apply the principles of evaluation by making sure that you:
- identify issues clearly
- present accurate views of others, making sure that you comment on the views presented
- reach an overall personal judgement.

You may add more of your own suggestions but try to negotiate as a group and prioritise the most important things to add.

Question

'Augustinian type theodicies solve the problem of evil.' Evaluate this view.

(Q4b, Component 2: Philosophy of Religion, WJEC, Summer 2017)

Answer

You could argue that Augustine was a very intelligent person and therefore was able to use this to help him put together an argument to prove that God existed, no matter what challenges were presented to him in terms of the problem of evil. Augustine knew that human beings were sinful creatures and, because of this, we were far more likely to make bad moral choices rather than good ones. This is because we had free will. It is not God's fault that we made these choices – he gave us freedom to choose and we chose the wrong thing. In this case, it is clear that the theodicy is successful.

However, Augustine's arguments are limited because of the time when he lived. We know a lot more about science and how the world works than he did, and we can see that many of his ideas make no scientific sense.

In conclusion, Augustine's theodicy does not solve the problem of evil.

This section covers AO1 content and skills

Specification content
Irenaean-type theodicy: vale of soul-making; human beings created imperfect; epistemic distance; second-order goods; eschatological justification

 Key person

Irenaeus of Lyons (second to third centuries BCE): early Christian bishop who is chiefly remembered for his writings against the heresy of Gnosticism – a major threat to Christian orthodoxy in the first few centuries of the Church's history; he also influentially stated that human beings had been made imperfect and needed to grow towards perfection, which he believed could be done only by making the proper response to God through Christ

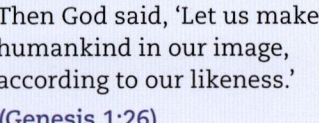

Then God said, 'Let us make humankind in our image, according to our likeness.'
(Genesis 1:26)

 Key terms

soul-making: a process where the soul is developing towards spiritual perfection by gaining the wisdom always to make the correct moral choices when faced with the ambiguities of life as a human being

epistemic distance: a distance measured in terms of knowledge rather than space or time

C: Religious responses to the problem of evil: Irenaean-type theodicy

Irenaeus of Lyons maintained that the presence of evil in the created order was a deliberate action of an omnibenevolent God who wanted his creations to develop the qualities that would make them spiritually perfect. This was unlike Augustine, who believed that free-will agents who deliberately turned away from God were responsible for the existence of evil.

Key aspects of the Irenaean theodicy and its development

Irenaeus' ideas are a result of his interpretation of Genesis 1:26 ('Let us make man in our image, after our likeness'). However, like Augustine, his theodicy was never presented as a complete work, but rather arose from his ideas about the place of humankind in the universe and the relationship that people have with God.

Human beings were created imperfectly

Irenaeus regards this life as a place where human beings, who were deliberately created imperfectly, develop their potential. They grow from the 'image' (possessing the potential qualities of God's spiritual perfection) to the 'likeness' (actually fully becoming those qualities) of God, through the trials and tribulations that they face and the decisions that they make. For every moral decision faced where a good choice is freely made, the individual develops more fully towards spiritual maturity. Irenaeus thought it was important for humans to be faced with genuine choices by being immersed in an environment where both 'good' and 'evil' were equally present and would allow for genuine choices to be made, and for genuine consequences to follow. Only then could these 'imperfect' creations have the opportunity to develop into God-like perfection.

Vale of soul-making and epistemic distance

John Hick developed Irenaeus' theodicy in his book *Evil and the God of Love* (1966). Hick describes Irenaeus' theodicy as a **soul-making** theodicy (a reference to John Keats' idea that the world was a proving ground for human beings who earned their salvation, not simply by belief in a saviour figure, but rather by working through the trials and tribulations of everyday existence). Hick also makes the point that to be truly free, human beings had to be created at an **epistemic distance** from God.

 Key person

John Hick (1922–2012): one of the most influential religious philosophers of the twentieth and early twenty-first centuries; his most famous works include *Faith and Knowledge* (1957), *Evil and the God of Love* (1966), *Philosophy of Religion* (various editions; most recent fourth edition, published 1990) and *The New Frontier of Religion and Science: Religious Experience, Neuroscience and the Transcendent* (2006)

An epistemic distance (a distance in knowledge – in this case, the knowledge of God's existence) is where humans were placed in a situation where the existence and non-existence of God were equally likely. This allowed true human freedom to exist in how they responded to God. God could not create humans who were spiritually perfect or who were immediately aware of his existence for the simple reason that, in the first instance, goodness developed through free choice is more valuable than goodness that is 'ready-made'. In the second instance, this would restrict choices, as humanity would be constantly aware of being 'watched' and would therefore make all decisions in the light of this knowledge. Hick also accepted the idea that God's mercy would allow for all human beings to complete the process of developing spiritual perfection – if not in this life, then in the next.

Second-order goods

Certain moral qualities were intrinsic to human beings, but Irenaeus' theodicy shows how second-order goods, such as courage, forgiveness and compassion, can develop only as a response to the suffering of ourselves and others. This was the essence of moving from 'image' to 'likeness'.

Evil is a necessary part of life that enables humans to develop. Without it, decisions in life would have no real value. For instance, a person would never really appreciate being in good health unless he or she had experienced being ill.

Second-order goods could never be developed if there were not the challenges in life that tested such virtues. Suffering not only enables humans to become stronger, but also allows them to appreciate goodness more. For Irenaeus, the ability for human beings to choose freely to do good was therefore a key part of achieving God's purpose for his creation.

Virtues, as second-order goods, are developed through the challenges that life brings

Eschatological justification

Irenaeus uses an analogy of God as a craftsman, working with human beings as his material. Irenaeus suggests that humans should allow God to mould them into perfection by acting in faith towards God, and by allowing the experiences of life, both good and bad, to make us into a perfectly crafted item. He also makes the point that those who resist God will be punished in the next life.

Unlike Augustine, Irenaeus' theodicy allows for God's mercy to continue into the next life, where individuals who have rejected God in this life will have the opportunity to earn his forgiveness and develop into spiritual perfection in the next. This eschatological justification for evil allowed God to remain both just and good in the face of the temporary suffering experienced by creation.

Challenges to Irenaean-type theodicies

The modern reworkings of this theodicy, with its sympathies towards scientific appreciations of the development of life on Earth, have given it a lease of life and plausibility that the Augustinian theodicy has not been able to enjoy to the same extent.

Developing into spiritual maturity has a resonance with faiths outside the Christian framework – and possibly echoes Hick's own views on religious pluralism. However, despite many of its attractions, the Irenaean theodicy has also attracted fierce criticism.

> **Specification content**
>
> Challenges to Irenaean-type theodicies: concept of universal salvation unjust; evil and suffering should not be used as a tool by an omnibenevolent God; immensity of suffering and unequal distribution of evil and suffering

If everyone ends up in Heaven anyway, what's the point of being good

The concept of universal salvation is unjust

If all humans will eventually achieve perfection, no matter what they have done in the past, how does this encourage good moral behaviour in the here and now? The concept of universal salvation seems to undermine the efforts of human beings to develop their own spiritual maturity. If God will eventually bring everyone to this state, does that suggest free will is limited? That is, do human beings have the free will to refuse this development to spiritual perfection?

Evil and suffering should not be used as a tool by an omnibenevolent God

Suffering should never be an instrument of a loving God. Hurting someone is more akin to abuse than it is to love. The concept of 'soul-making' is contrary to the central Christian belief of needing atonement through Christ. It suggests that humans alone have the ability to develop into spiritual perfection by simply making free-will choices of good over evil as they go through life. This is in direct contrast to many Christian thinkers, who say that it is only with God's grace that human beings can choose the good.

Immensity and unequal distribution of evil and suffering

The immense suffering some people endure does not make up for any possible reward of spiritual perfection. Suffering is not evenly spread; we can see this by looking at the experiences of humans across the world today. This implies inconsistency with God's mechanism of perfection. The intensity of the suffering many feel makes this a 'soul-breaking' rather than a 'soul-making' theodicy.

Summary

- Irenaeus of Lyons said evil was a deliberate part of God's plan to allow humanity to develop into a state of moral and spiritual maturity.
- John Hick developed this theodicy in the twentieth century, stating that humans had been created at a distance of knowledge from God to make their souls' spiritually perfect.
- Irenaeus stated that any evil or suffering endured would be made up for in the next, when all would eventually be reconciled to God.
- The challenges to Irenaeus' theodicy centre on issues with suffering being used as a tool by an all-loving God; an unequal distribution of suffering experienced by some; and the unjustness of universal salvation.

AO1 Activity

a   Explain how Irenaeus uses the biblical verse Genesis 1:26 to develop his theodicy.

This helps with presenting a thorough and extensive knowledge and understanding of the topic area and with making accurate reference to sacred texts.

b   Create two mind maps: one for Irenaeus and one for John Hick. Detail their ideas on their mind map so that you are clear who said what with regards to the theodicy.

> **Specification content**
> Whether Irenaean-type theodicies are credible in the twenty-first century

This section covers AO2 content and skills

Issues for analysis and evaluation

Whether Irenaean-type theodicies are credible in the twenty-first century

Possible line of argument	Critical analysis and evaluation
Humans hold a unique place in God's creation	Irenaean-type theodicies reflect on the relationship that human beings had with God and the place that they occupied in the created order. Humans were viewed as the only created being that had been made *Imago Dei* (in the image of God) and, as such, possess the potential to develop the sort of characteristics of God himself and become 'like God'. This idea was based on the verse in Genesis 1:26 'Let us make humankind in our image, after our likeness.'
Modern scientific ideas can be seen to support the theodicy	As far as the twenty-first century is concerned, this idea fits in with the scientific understanding that life on Earth develops qualities that help it survive more effectively within the natural environment (natural selection and the theory of evolution). In this sense, the Irenaean-type theodicies appear to have some credibility in the twenty-first century.
The credibility of the argument is undermined by its antiquity and key philosophy	However, others may state that basing a theodicy on a document that is nearly 3000 years old makes any claim for credibility suspect at least. The idea that the existence of evil and suffering can be explained away as some kind of 'spiritual workout' may even sound obscene to some – particularly those whose suffering is so acute that seeing any positives come from it is virtually impossible.
Evidence of the immensity of suffering undermines Irenaeus' theodicy	In fact, the very immensity of suffering that has occurred throughout human history, such as those genocides faced by Bosnian Serbs, victims of Stalin and the peoples of Rwanda and European Jewry (and those are events just from the last 80 years of recorded human history), completely undermine the idea that suffering is there to help individuals become spiritually mature. Such an idea becomes abhorrent if that is the price that needs to be paid. What sort of god would exact such a terrible cost from his creation?
The concept of development is considered credible and provides hope for religious believers	Where the theodicies may have credibility in the twenty-first century is in the promise of hope given to all. The suggestion that this process of developing from image to likeness will one day be realised by all human beings, no matter how long it takes for each individual, gives something for everyone to aspire to, in the sense that suffering and pain will be removed forever and all will be able to partake in spiritual perfection in an eternity with God; such is the hope for those who follow liberation theology – that one day suffering will be overcome, and God will restore us to him in the original relationship envisioned in Eden.
The concept of universal salvation makes good moral behaviours pointless	There are many objections to this view. Critics would claim that the idea of a universal salvation appears abhorrent. Does this mean that some of the most wicked, evil and cruel humans ever to have lived will be given precisely the same eventual reward as those humans who dedicated their lives to good works, selfless acts and the improvement of others? Do we really mean that Gandhi and Stalin will be treated the same? How does this demonstrate God's justice? Why should anyone even bother to try in this life now, if eventually we will all end up in Heaven? The idea seems preposterous and seriously undermines any credibility this theodicy may have in the twenty-first century.
The evidence against the theodicy significantly undermines its credibility	In conclusion, despite the initial attractiveness of human development and a universal hope of eternal reward, the contradictions contained in Irenaean-type theodicies are too severe for this theodicy to maintain any credibility in the twenty-first century.

> **AO2 Activity**
>
> a Evaluate three lines of argument from the critical analysis and evaluation of whether Irenaean-type theodicies are credible in the twenty-first century. What are their strengths and weaknesses? Which line of argument is strongest?
>
> b Using the strongest line of argument, try to identify three key questions that might be asked – they could be critical questions, challenges, hypothetical or direct questions.

> **Specification content**
>
> The extent to which Irenaeus' theodicy succeeds as a defence of the God of classical theism

Exam practice

Sample question

Evaluate the extent to which Irenaeus' theodicy succeeds as a defence of the God of classical theism.

Sample answer

The problem of evil is a longstanding challenge to believers in the God of classical theism. Throughout history, there have been attempts to support this belief and to attack the problem of evil. One such example can be found in the theodicies (attempts to justify God in the face of the existence of evil) associated with the works of Irenaeus of Lyons.

This start is a brief but clear introduction that provides a background for why theodicies were developed.

Irenaeus bases his main ideas on Genesis 1:26, which states: 'Let us make humankind in our image, after our likeness.' The basic thread that runs throughout Irenaeus' works (the theodicy was never written as a composite – it is a theme that runs throughout many of his writings) is that human beings were made in God's image. In other words, humans had the potential to be like God (fully actualise God's qualities within ourselves), but would develop into God's likeness only through undergoing the trials of suffering that life presents and responding to these appropriately (freely choosing to do good rather than evil).

The response summarises the key details of Irenaeus' approach to his theodicy and provides accurate and relevant commentary on key ideas and sacred texts.

Irenaeus faces the problem of evil head on and admits that evil exists. Not only does it exist, but it is also part of God's plan for humanity. God, in Irenaeus' view, has deliberately created evil so that we can develop our spiritual qualities and become better people. In this sense, the Irenaean theodicy is a successful defence of the God of classical theism because he admits the 'third corner' of the inconsistent triad, but overcomes it by stating that there is a very clear reason for the existence of evil – to help human beings achieve spiritual and moral perfection.

This paragraph develops the argument further and coherently makes the link between this and the previous information. It also links to the overarching 'problem of evil' and makes reference to the inconsistent triad.

Irenaeus speaks of God being like a craftsman, and evil being one of his tools that allows him to mould humans into perfection when they act in faith towards him: that is, when they freely choose to do good in the face of evil and suffering. The theodicy is also successful if we consider John Hick's development of Irenaeus' theodicy when he makes the point that God's mercy extends beyond this life and that, by virtue of his divine mercy, all human beings will eventually develop into spiritually perfect beings and be united with him in Heaven. This would, at first glance, seem another successful defence of the God of classical theism in the face of the existence of evil, in that the promise is that, one day, not only will evil be overcome, but also all individuals will achieve the end that God has set out for them, and all of creation will be one in harmony together.

This paragraph further supports the line of reasoning with refence to a relevant example from Irenaeus, which shows the consistency in the argument.

Unfortunately for supporters of the Irenaean theodicy, there are too many issues that are unresolved. The extent of suffering is not evenly spread. Not all humans experience the same amount of suffering in their lives, and some manage to become moral and spiritually good people even without undergoing trials of suffering and evil. In fact, some of those who undergo suffering have so much to deal with that they do not develop but actually regress – some into cycles of violence and cruelty themselves; others in taking their own lives because they cannot stand to suffer another moment.

Tennis player

The argument makes a counterpoint to show the 'flaws' in the Irenaean theodicy, providing relevant evidence and examples.

The theodicy takes neither of these into account, and both pose a serious challenge to its effectiveness as a defence of the God of classical theism. Furthermore, the concept of universal salvation seems to undermine entirely any reason for choosing to do the right thing in the here and now – what's the point if all humanity will eventually end up with God anyway? Therefore, in conclusion, following the points made above, the Irenaean theodicy fails as a successful defence of the God of classical theism.

Philosopher

Judge

The argument makes a counterpoint to show the 'flaws' in the Irenaean theodicy, providing relevant evidence and examples.

Evaluation

This is an effective and balanced response. It considers both sides of the argument and raises questions before putting forwards a conclusion. The candidate makes accurate use both of terminology and of the views of different schools of thought.

Over to you

Below is a list of several key points that a student has written in response to a question requiring an evaluation of whether the Irenaean theodicy is still credible in the twenty-first century. It is obviously a very full list.

In a group, consider what you think are the most important points to use when planning an answer to the question. This exercise, in essence, is like writing your own set of possible answers that might be listed in a typical mark scheme as indicative content. You need to decide on two things:
- which points to select
- the order to put them in an answer.

Question

'Irenaean type theodicies are still credible in the 21st century.'
Evaluate this view.

(Q3b, Component 2: Philosophy of Religion, WJEC, Summer 2019)

Indicative content

- Humans are the only created being made *Imago Dei* (in the image of God) and, as such, possess the potential to develop the sort of characteristics of God himself and become 'like God'.
- This idea is based on the verse in Genesis 1:26: 'Let us make humankind in our image, after our likeness.'
- As far as the twenty-first century is concerned, this idea fits in with the scientific understanding that life on Earth develops qualities that help it survive more effectively within the natural environment (as per natural selection and the theory of evolution).

T2 Challenges to religious belief – the problem of evil and suffering

- Basing a theodicy on a document that is nearly three thousand years old makes any claim for credibility suspect at least.
- The idea that we can explain away the existence of evil and suffering as some kind of 'spiritual workout' may even sound obscene to some – particularly those whose suffering is so acute that seeing any positives come from it is virtually impossible.
- The immensity of suffering that has occurred throughout human history from genocides completely undermines the idea that suffering is there to help individuals become spiritually mature – what sort of God would exact such a terrible cost from his creation?
- The idea of a universal salvation appears abhorrent.
- Despite the initial attractiveness of human development and a universal hope of eternal reward, the contradictions contained in Irenaean-type theodicies are too severe for this theodicy to maintain any credibility in the twenty-first century.

Challenges to religious belief – religious belief as a product of the human mind

D: Religious belief as a product of the human mind: Sigmund Freud

This section covers AO1 content and skills

Introduction

One way of resolving conflicts between religion and the physical sciences is to argue that science addresses the physical world, while religion addresses the inner world. However, the focus of **psychology** is the inner world, and it presents itself as a science. Psychology looks at human personality and experiences, and attempts to discover laws about human behaviour, as well as finding reasons why individuals hold certain beliefs. Thus, psychology states that human behaviour, experiences and beliefs can be explained without referring to the idea of a god.

Specification content

Religion as an illusion and/or a neurosis with reference to collective neurosis; primal horde; Oedipus complex; wish fulfilment and reaction against helplessness.

Sigmund Freud and human personality

One of the most influential psychologists in the twentieth century was Sigmund Freud. Born in 1856 of Jewish parents, Freud studied medicine. He was the founder of **psychoanalysis** and, by 1902, was Associate Professor of Neuropathology at the University of Vienna – a post he held until 1938. During his life, he developed his ideas about the **psyche** (personality).

He believed the psyche was divided into three parts:

- **Id**: The primitive and impulsive part of our psyche that responds to our instincts.
- **Superego**: The moral part of personality, which includes the conscience and the ideal-ego.
- **Ego**: The decision-making part of personality; the ego is the conscious self that is created by the dynamic tensions and interactions between the id and the superego, and it reconciles their conflicting demands with the requirements of external reality.

The ego experiences moral conflicts that Freud thought were reflected in dreams and neurotic symptoms.

Key terms

psychology: the study of the mind and behaviour

psychoanalysis: a method of studying the mind and treating mental and emotional disorders based on revealing and investigating the role of the unconscious mind

psyche: the mental or psychological structure of a person

id: the part of the psyche that resides in the unconscious and relates to basic needs and desires

superego: part of the unconscious mind

ego: the part of the psyche that resides largely in the conscious and is reality-orientated; it mediates between the desires of the id and the superego

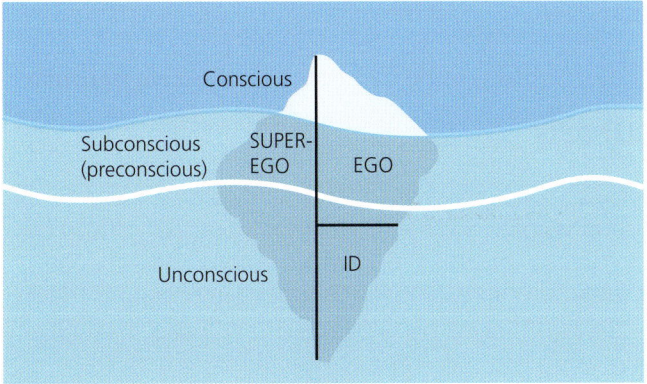

Freud's model of the psyche (personality)

Key term

obsessional neurosis: sometimes called *compulsive neurosis*; uncontrollable obsessions that can create certain daily rituals

" Key quote "

One might venture to regard obsessional neurosis as a pathological formation of a religion, and to describe that neurosis as an individual religiosity and religion as a universal obsessional neurosis.

(Freud, 'Obsessive Actions and Religious Practices')

Key terms

instinctual impulse: an instinct that is in the unconscious but active in the psyche

collective neurosis: a neurotic illness that afflicts all people

Specification content

Religion as a neurosis: the primal horde

A link between obsessional neurosis and religious ritual?

Freud sought to understand religion and spirituality. In 1907, he presented a paper to the Vienna Psychoanalytical Society entitled 'Obsessive Actions and Religious Practices'. He noted that people who suffered from an **obsessional neurosis** that involved compulsive repeated actions demonstrated similar patterns of behaviour to religious people who feel uneasy if they neglect repeated actions such as saying the rosary. In both cases, the people take great care to make sure that they carry out the details of the actions accurately.

Freud also noticed that there was at least one significant difference. He thought that people with obsessional neurosis did not understand the meaning of their actions, while

Obsessional washing of hands and the religious ritual of washing

religious people understood the meaning of their practices. Freud argued that, by means of psychoanalysis, he had found that the obsessional neurosis did have meaning. It was caused by unconscious motives derived from past events in the intimate life of the patient, and these repressed instinctual impulses (such as the sexual urge) led to a sense of guilt. Freud interpreted the repeated actions he observed as an unconscious protective measure against the temptation to give way to these instinctual impulses.

Religion as collective neurosis

In the same way, he saw that religious rituals were similarly motivated. The **instinctual impulses** of the religious person included such impulses as self-seeking, which gave rise to a sense of guilt following continual temptation. Just as in the obsessional neurosis there is displacement from the actual important thing onto another object (for e.g. from a husband onto a chair), so in religion there was a similar displacement (e.g. from doing something God disapproves of, onto the religious ritual of prayer or confession). The religious practices gradually become the essential thing; hence Freud's description of 'religion as a universal obsessional neurosis'. The neurotic compulsions and religious rituals are found universally, so he called this a **collective neurosis**.

Religion as a neurosis

The primal horde

Freud's conclusion was that religion itself was a form of neurosis, caused by traumas deep within the psyche. In 1913, Freud wrote *Totem and Taboo*, in which he sought to explain the origins of these traumas. He based his theory on Charles Darwin's suggestion that human beings had originally lived in small 'hordes' or groups.

Freud then speculated that:

- Over many generations, the horde had been dominated by single dominant males who had seized the women for themselves and had driven off or killed all rivals, including their sons.
- At some time, a band of prehistoric brothers whom the **alpha-male** group had expelled returned to kill their father, whom they both feared and respected.
- This enabled them to become dominant over the horde and gain women themselves.
- However, after the event, the young males felt guilty, as they had both loved and feared the father.
- Following their father's death, they had become rivals among themselves for possession of the women.
- Burdened with guilt and faced with imminent collapse of their social order, the brothers formed a tribe and a **totem** took the place of the father, so uniting the tribe.

> **Key terms**
>
> **alpha-male:** the dominant male in a community or group
>
> **totem:** something (e.g. an animal or plant) that is the symbol for a family or tribe
>
> **totemism:** a system of belief where human beings are said to have some kinship or mystical relationship with a spirit-being (e.g. an animal or plant)

Totemism

Freud had an interest in social anthropology, and in his book he examines the system of **totemism** among Aboriginal Australian people. He noticed that every clan had a totem (usually an animal), and people were not allowed to marry those with the same totem as themselves. Freud understood this as a way of preventing incest. The concept of the totem influenced the tribes to certain norms of behaviour, and to go against them would be taboo. According to Freud:

> The totem members were forbidden to eat the flesh of the totem animal, or were allowed to do so only under specific conditions. A significant counter phenomenon, not irreconcilable with this, is the fact that on certain occasions the eating of the totem flesh constituted a sort of ceremony ...
> (Freud, *Totem and Taboo*)

Aboriginal Australian totem

Totem as substitute

Freud saw a correlation between totemism and Darwin's primal horde theory. His psychoanalysis of the totem ceremony revealed that the totem animal was, in reality, a substitute for the father who was both loved and feared. Over time, the reputation of the slaughtered father grew to divine proportions: that is, the totem became worshipped and became a god. There was a yearly commemoration by ritual killing and eating of the totem animal. Eating and drinking are symbols of fellowship and mutual obligation. Freud argued that this insight through psychoanalysis explains the inherited sense of guilt that we all have.

> **Key term**
>
> **atonement:** making up for wrongdoing; the reconciliation of human beings with God through life, suffering and the sacrificial death of Christ

> **Specification content**
>
> Religion as a neurosis: the Oedipus complex

> **Key term**
>
> **Oedipus complex:** the theory that young boys are sexually attracted to their mothers but resent their fathers; the feelings are repressed as they fear the father – *Oedipus* refers to a character in a Greek legend that unwittingly killed his father and married his own mother

It results from a shared and inherited memory of having killed the father or having entertained such thoughts.

For Freud, this explained the Christian ritual of Holy Communion, as Christ now replaced the father as the centre of religious devotion through his offering of **atonement**. The earlier totemic meal is now replaced by Holy Communion, and identified with the son rather than a totem.

The Oedipus complex

Many people find Freud's explanation of the primal horde unconvincing as an account of the origin of the connection between the father complex and belief in God. The main reason is that the evidence base is questioned. However, his theory of the **Oedipus complex** has received more positive reactions as an account of the origins of this father complex and belief in God.

Sexual frustration and psychological consequences

Freud thought that guilt plays a fundamental role in the psyche, and that guilt operates unconsciously. He believed that the sexual drive (libido) is the most basic instinct and most capable of causing major psychological problems. Freud saw the libido as not just the desire to have sex, but also the representation of the body's desire for satisfaction, which originates in the id.

In his account of the primal horde, Freud argued that the power of the sons' bitterness towards the father stemmed from the father preventing their sexual desires from being fulfilled. Freud believed that this sexual frustration, conflict with the father and feelings of guilt are hidden deep in the unconscious, but can be identified in a child's psychosexual development between the ages of three and six. He referred to this stage as the *Oedipus complex*. It is the stage when a child begins to become sexual and to recognise him – or herself as a sexual being. A child develops a distinct sexual identity and begins to recognise the physical and social differences between men and women. This changes the dynamic between child and parent.

The Blind Oedipus Commending His Children to the Gods, Bénigne Gagneraux (1784)

Oedipus Rex

The term *Oedipus complex* was named after the character in Sophocles' Greek tragedy *Oedipus Rex*. In the play, Oedipus unwittingly kills his father and commits incest with his mother. When he realises this, he gouges out his own eyes in despair. Freud felt that the play's popularity through the ages derives from the underlying Oedipus complex in adults – an unconscious anxiety that most adults have experienced. He illustrated this unconscious anxiety using testimony from his patients.

The complex's origins in early childhood

It was Freud's opinion that boys aged three to six have a sort of love affair with their mothers. Thus, at this stage in his childhood, the son sees his father as a rival for his mother's love, attentions and affection and would like to replace him, but also fears the repercussions that might occur.

As a result, a child of this age can experience unconscious anxiety, even a castration complex, fearing the loss of his genitals. Freud suggested three reasons to explain this fear:

- With weaning, the boy has already been deprived of his mother's breast, which he thought was part of him.
- When his parents had discovered him exploring his penis and appeared upset by this, he had felt the threat of losing his penis.
- He would have discovered that some humans in fact do not have a penis and interprets this as the result of a punishment, not realising they are women.
- If the Oedipus complex goes unresolved and is repressed, then neurotic behaviour will result.

Oedipus complex and neurotic behaviour

Hence Freud linked the Oedipus complex with expressions of neurotic behaviour. He had already previously argued that the beliefs and practices of religion were merely expressions of neurotic behaviour.

As we have seen, both the primal horde theory and the Oedipus complex theory share the features of a desire to eliminate the father and a wish to possess the mother. Freud believed that both are possible explanations for the guilt and anguish that is often repressed and hidden, and which ultimately gives release to neurotic symptoms that are expressed through the belief and practices of religion.

Wish fulfilment

In *The Future of an Illusion* (1927), Freud outlined his idea of religion as an 'illusion' based on wish fulfilment of the yearnings and longings of the ideal-ego aspect of the superego. Freud's ideas were heavily influenced by the philosopher Ludwig Feuerbach, who saw God as a 'projection' of the human mind based on human longings and desires.

Freud proposed that the origin of religion lies in our deepest wishes, such as the desire for justice and the desire to escape death. Religion is seen to have emerged from such desires. Religious beliefs about life and judgement after death, such as Paradise and Hell, are two examples of this.

> **Specification content**
>
> Religion as an illusion: wish fulfilment

Freud argued that the individuals who invented the religious doctrines did so because the doctrines fulfilled their wishes. Equally, the people who embrace religious views do so out of wish fulfilment. Such wishes as a desire for justice and a desire to escape death seem common across all cultures. Therefore, it is clear why such desires are met by the claim that an eternal, omnipotent, benevolent God will resurrect the dead, punish the unjust and reward the worthy with the promise of Heaven.

A reaction against helplessness

Freud connected religious ideas to a person's obvious helplessness in the face of the forces of nature. We feel defenceless against natural forces that confront us (for e.g. droughts, floods and storms), and so need to invent a source of security. Religion creates this security with the belief that the natural forces are no longer impersonal. For example, the forces of nature might be turned into gods or goddesses we can worship.

> **Specification content**
>
> Religion as an illusion: a reaction against helplessness

By means of religious devotion, we are also no longer powerless because we believe we can control these forces of nature: for example, in the past, when it was believed that sacrifices and prayers could prevent a volcano from erupting.

Equally, we struggle with the internal forces of nature. For example:
- Religious teaching seeks to limit war and violence and introduces ideas of protecting the weak and loving one's enemies.
- The sexual drive can be controlled through strict religious laws governing sexual behaviour and relationships.

Freud concluded that, just as the father protects the child, so religious belief provides a father figure to protect the adult. Freud therefore viewed religion as a childish delusion.

Supportive evidence

Redirection of guilt complexes

Freud became convinced that the workings of the mind could be rationally explained through the scientific method of observation and analysis. His reasoning was based on his continued psychoanalysis of patients with neurosis, or who had physical symptoms with no obvious physical cause.

From his many case studies, Freud saw clear evidence of the Oedipus complex and concluded that repressed sexual feelings were at the root of these illnesses.

Case studies

Daniel Schreber

Daniel Schreber was a highly respected judge who, in his middle age, developed a religious neurosis where a mystical God occupied and penetrated his body, gradually transforming him into a woman. Although Freud did not actually meet with the judge, he studied the case and interpreted it as evidence that religious belief has its roots in the Oedipus complex, thereby showing that religion is inherently linked to neurosis.

Freud argued that, in his infancy, Schreber's libido was directed towards his father rather than his mother. These homosexual desires were repressed, but later re-emerged as a religious neurosis. Freud interpreted Schreber's belief that God was turning him into a woman as Schreber transferring desire for his father onto an acceptable object of desire: that is, God. For Freud, the case study was indicative of the general neuroses he associated with religion, where God forms a replacement for people's relationship with their father.

Little Hans

Hans had a phobia of being bitten by a horse and so tried to avoid horses. Freud interpreted this as Hans's fear of castration. Hans also showed great anxiety when he once saw a horse collapse in the street. Again, Freud saw these fears as symbols reflecting an inward conflict of the sexual drive. Hence, Freud interpreted this as an unconscious reminder to Hans of his death wish against his father, which made him feel guilty and afraid. Freud claimed that successfully treating Hans was a direct and immediate proof of his theories.

The Wolf Man

Sergei Pankejeff was a patient of Freud's but, to protect his identity, Freud referred to him as 'Wolf Man'. He had depression and went to Freud for therapy. Freud focused on a dream that Pankejeff had as a young child. The dream featured him lying in bed when the window suddenly opened and he saw six or seven white wolves. He screamed and woke up in terror of being eaten by the wolves.

> **Specification content**
>
> Supporting evidence: redirection of guilt complexes

Freud interpreted this as a repressed trauma of Pankejeff having witnessed his parents having sex. Again, Freud claimed that he was successful in treating the depression, having identified the repressed trauma.

Neurotic behaviours as redirection of guilt complexes

There has been further support in recent times for Freud's belief that repressed guilt directly causes neurotic behaviours:

- Recent research at the University of Michigan in the USA, focusing on brain activity, suggests that unconscious conflicts cause or contribute to the anxiety symptoms the patient is experiencing.
- Modern **psychotherapy**, through the Freudian interpretation of dreams, has shown a clear link from obsessions, phobias and anxieties to repressed memories and guilt.
- Therapy using hypnosis has also been successful in delving into the unconscious mind. When repressed memories have been identified, the resultant anxiety or obsessional behaviour has often ceased.
- Modern psychology recognises memory repression that can lead to denial (e.g. alcoholism) and displacement theories.
- Research on brain activity has indicated that unconscious conflicts contribute to anxiety symptoms.

Instinctive desires deriving from evolutionary basis

Freud accepted Darwinian biology as his foundation. He made it clear that the study of evolution was an essential part of the training to be a psychoanalyst, and that Darwinian theory was essential to psychoanalysis.

The theory Freud developed was based on the Darwinian idea that all behaviour is the result of a few basic animal drives produced by natural selection to aid survival. The survival genes that were passed on included those for a high sexual drive. This is why the sex drive became central in Freud's theory of human behaviour.

Challenges to Freud's interpretation

Lack of anthropological evidence for primal horde

The whole theory of the horde was based on mere speculation by Darwin. It is now thought that there was a much greater variety in the way people were grouped. It is unlikely that they were exclusively in hordes. Other issues include:

- Freud admitted that the 'primal horde' had never been observed.
- It is claimed that Darwin's words have been taken out of context and exaggerated.
- The primal horde is a concept that Darwin would not recognise – Freud's theory has misrepresented Darwin's writings.
- There is a lack of evidence that all societies had totem objects that they worshipped. Even among those that did have totem objects, not all of them had totem meals. This lack of evidence casts serious doubt on whether the primal crime actually took place.
- Even if the primal crime of the son killing the father actually happened, there appears to be no evidence for the idea that guilt can be transmitted in the way that Freud suggested. The major argument against such a theory is a recent understanding of DNA and genetics. DNA is not involved in an organism's characteristics, and an organism's characteristics do not control the composition of the DNA.

Key term

psychotherapy: treatment of mental or emotional illness by talking about problems rather than by using medicine or drugs

Specification content

Supporting evidence: instinctive desires deriving from evolutionary basis (Charles Darwin)

Key quote

Long ago he [humankind] formed an ideal conception of omnipotence and omniscience which he embodied in his gods. Whatever seemed unattainable to his desires – or forbidden to him – he attributed to these gods. One may say, therefore, that these gods were the ideals of his culture.

(Freud, *Civilization and Its Discontents*)

Specification content

Challenges including lack of anthropological evidence for primal horde; no firm psychological evidence for universal Oedipus complex; evidence basis too narrow

Malinowski with indigenous people of the Trobriand Islands

No firm psychological evidence for universal Oedipus complex

While Freud argued that the Oedipus complex accounted for people modelling God on their father, this view has been criticised for focusing only on male deities.

In some cultures, the mother is dominant and the father's role in bringing up the child is very limited. In other cultures, there is no male god figure or even no god figure at all. This seems to undermine the idea of the Oedipus complex as being universal.

Anthropologists have shown that beliefs, motives and emotional responses to situations vary remarkably from one culture to the next. For instance, Bronislaw Malinowski, a Polish anthropologist, studied the Trobriand people when he became stranded on the Trobriand Islands off the eastern coast of New Guinea. In his research he found no evidence of the Oedipus complex, even though the Trobriand people had a religion.

In Trobriand culture, children were disciplined by their paternal uncles, so the roles of sexual rival (the father) and disciplinarian (the uncle) were separated. This suggests that sex has nothing to do with religion.

A more likely explanation is that the complex does not cause religions. Rather, religions, with their strict rules on sexual behaviour and relationships, cause the Oedipus complex, which then leads to neurosis.

Freud seems to have based his theory of the Oedipus complex on five main case studies and then generalised, assuming that the Oedipus complex detected in those cases was at work everywhere.

Evidence basis too narrow

Freud constructed a theory to explain those religions he was familiar with. This is why he focused on Judaism and Christianity, arguing that the importance of the father figure developed into the male God. However, he failed to consider religions that are based upon female deities, such as the Egyptian Isis cult. Equally, he did not consider religions such as Buddhism, which do not have a god.

Freud regarded himself as a scientist and saw psychoanalysis as a new science. However, according to Karl Popper, every genuine scientific theory must be testable and therefore falsifiable, at least in principle. Freud's theory, however, cannot be falsified and so is not scientific.

A key critic of Freud's work is Adolf Grunbaum (*The Foundations of Psychoanalysis: A Philosophical Critique*, 1984). He claims that Freud's theories evade any kind of empirical test. Grunbaum challenges the view that only the psychoanalytic method can yield correct insight into the causes of neuroses, and that correct insight was necessary for a cure of those neuroses. He pointed

Freud did not consider religions that include female deities, such as the goddess Lakshmi in Hinduism

out that successful treatment had occurred without either of those two conditions being fulfilled.

There is also a feminist critique of Freud, that would argue his overall approach might be questioned on the grounds of it being considered 'Euro-centric, patriarchal and sexist'.

More recent criticism has been levelled against Freud in relation to the occurrence of sexual abuse. He reported many instances of traumas in his patients, claiming they had been seduced in very early childhood by older male relatives. Freud doubted the truth of these allegations, and replaced them with the certainty that they were descriptions about childhood fantasies.

Summary

- Sigmund Freud, following his studies of the human psyche, concluded that religious belief was a collective neurosis.
- He based his conclusions on his theories of the origins of totemism in the primal horde and the development of the Oedipus complex in early childhood.
- Freud saw religion as providing humanity with a sense of wish fulfilment and a support in the face of helplessness against natural events beyond their control.
- Despite some limited support for Freud's theories through his own case studies and modern psychology's demonstration of the link between guilt and neurotic behaviours, Freud's theories have mostly been dismissed as unscientific and lacking in an objective evidence base.

AO1 Activity

a   Examine the supporting evidence for Freud's beliefs.

This helps with presenting a thorough and extensive knowledge and understanding of the topic area.

b   On revision cards, summarise the key features of Freud's belief that religion is a collective neurosis. Include reference to the link between neurosis and ritual, the primal horde theory, the totem as substitute and the Oedipus complex.

This helps with prioritising and selecting a core set of points to develop an answer and with making accurate use of specialist language and vocabulary in context.

This section covers AO2 content and skills

Specification content
How far religious belief can be considered a neurosis

Issues for analysis and evaluation

How far religious belief can be considered a neurosis

Possible line of argument	Critical analysis and evaluation
Freud saw parallels between neurotic behaviours and ritual activity in religion	It is true that Freud's work in treating patients with neuroses drew his attention to their obsessions as having parallels with religion. In particular, the ritualistic nature of religious activity mirrored aspects of a compulsive obsessive neurosis. Therefore, it was not unreasonable to think that the same cause lay behind both – namely, repressed memories.
Unconscious racial memories are the foundations for religious belief	In addition, Freud argued that there were two universal sources of religious ideas. One was the unconscious racial memories of the slaughter of the primal father. This involved a supposedly subconscious memory of events in human history or prehistory. The strength of this proposal is that Darwinian evolutionary theory clearly supported the primal horde theory and totemism. In support of his argument, Freud considered the Holy Communion as a clear development of a totemic meal, and there are clear parallels.
Early childhood traumas contribute to the adoption of certain religious beliefs and practices	The second source was the early childhood experiences of our own parents, which he connected to a sexual trauma that he called the *Oedipus complex*. The neurosis that results is generated by the sexual component of the traumatic experience. It is this element and the associated memories that a person seeks to repress. The Oedipus complex, though a normal part of every boy's childhood, contains impulses that the person sees as shameful, including hatred of the father and desire for the mother. (This is reversed in girls and known as the Electra complex.)
	This is a little more difficult to support directly as it tends to rely upon our interpretation of religious stories, but it can certainly be seen in aspects of Hinduism, such as myths surrounding Ganesh and Ganapati. Both sources suggest that there is an underlying neurosis to certain aspects of religious belief and practice.
Evidence from Freud's case studies supports his views	Furthermore, Freud's case studies, such as Little Hans, reaffirmed Freud's view that religion was an outward expression of inner psychological conflict. The conflict is an imbalance in the personality that is reflected in certain neurotic behaviour akin to religious activity. The characteristic of a neurosis is a reawakening of repressed trauma that is accompanied by compulsive obsessional impulses. This can clearly be seen in the ritualistic and liturgical aspects of many religions.
Religious belief is a neurosis	It could be suggested, then, that this all fits exactly with Freud's understanding of the origin of religion. Therefore, religion is a neurotic illness that affects all people. Freud's position that it is a mental illness and therefore harmful is directly related to his understanding of neuroses.

AO2 Activity

a   Evaluate three possible conclusions that could be drawn from the critical analysis and evaluation of how far religious belief can be considered a neurosis. What are their strengths and weaknesses? Which line of argument is strongest?

b   Using the strongest conclusion, select three lines of argument that you would use to support this conclusion. Try to explain why you have selected these.

Exam practice

Sample question
Evaluate the adequacy of Freud's explanation of religious belief.

Sample answer

Freud's explanations are a challenge to religious belief as they see religion as a neurosis – a mental illness that is harmful. He sees religious belief as intellectually lacking, since it cannot be rationally justified, and it also devalues lives such that it makes people incapable of changing society for the better. However, is Freud right in his explanations of religious belief? Do his explanations stand up to scrutiny?

There do seem to be parallels between certain types of neurosis and religious ritual. People often display obsessional behaviour. The checking of things such as front doors, water taps and gas stove knobs can result in checking multiple times, sometimes hundreds of times and for hours on end, resulting in the person being late for work and other appointments. The checking can also cause damage to the objects that are constantly being checked. The need to clean and wash can also be a compulsion. It often involves repetitive hand washing until the person 'feels' they are clean. It is true that religion can also be seen to have aspects of obsessional behaviour. For example, Muslims are required to wash five times per day before prayer. This washing is known as *Wudu* and is a form of ritual ablution. They must wash parts of the body in a specific order and in a specific way. If they make a mistake, then they must begin the whole process again.

Freud's clinical work involving interpretation of dreams and psychoanalysis of patients was often successful in treating their obsession. This may be seen as validating his theories concerning the cause of the obsession as repressed trauma and guilt, therefore supporting the view that religion, with its religious ritual, stems from the same source: repressed memories and guilt. The repressed traumas Freud identified for religion included the subconscious memory from prehistory of the primal horde and the totemic meals that expressed sexual guilt.

Specification content
The adequacy of Freud's explanation of religious belief

This is a good introduction that provides a helpful overview of the key areas for focus in the evaluation to come, adding questions as a focal point.

This paragraph presents significant evidence, via a line of reasoning, showing the reasons why Freud considered there to be a link between neurotic behaviours and religious ritual.

This paragraph presents further evidence to support the line of reasoning.

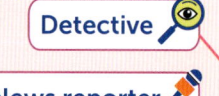

The paragraph presents further evidence to support the line of reasoning, along with a commentary.

This paragraph further develops the argument based on the concept of the need for a father figure, and then links this, via a question, to the religious belief in a father-figure god.

The response then abruptly undermines the previous line of reasoning by providing a single counterpoint, that Freud did not have any reliable evidence to support his theories.

In addition, Freud's theory of the Oedipus complex identified another form of repression involving a son's sexual attraction to his mother but resenting the father. Support for these views could be found in Darwin's theory of the primal horde; Robertson Smith's work on the totemic system; and the Oedipus complex supported by the work of Kline. There is evidence that the eating of the totem flesh constituted a sort of ceremony. It is not difficult to see in this evidence aspects of the Christian ritual of Holy Communion. The earlier totemic meal is now replaced by Holy Communion and identified with the son rather than a totem.

There can be no doubt that the 'father figure' features in religion, and the ideal father in authority is exactly the idea of God who is able to answer human longings and desires. We can see that religious doctrines reflect our wish fulfilment. Across all cultures, there is a desire for justice and escape from death. Therefore, it is clear why such desires appear in religions. Our sense of helplessness against the forces of nature drives us to invent some form of security. The sexual drive also needs controlling, so religions contain strict laws governing sexual behaviour and relationships. Is this why religious believers turn to an eternal, omnipotent, benevolent god who will answer their needs?

However, many aspects of the evidence have been challenged, including Freud's fundamental approach. It is claimed that all Freud had were theories; there was no clear verifiable evidence or statistical data. Using this line of argument, many have questioned and rejected the validity of Freud's work, both within modern psychology and beyond it.

Evaluation

This is a well-written response that mostly focuses on the theories Freud presented to support his views. These are then all undermined by a brief but condemnatory final paragraph, which brings into question the whole basis of Freud's work. The candidate's response is thorough. It gives sustained and clear views, supported by extensive, detailed reasoning and evidence.

Over to you

Below is an extract from an evaluation of whether Freud was wrong in stating that religion is a neurosis. As you read through the evaluation, try to do the following:
- Pick out the different lines of argument that the text presents and identify any evidence it gives in support.
- For each line of argument, try to evaluate whether or not you think it is strong or weak.
- Think of any questions you might wish to raise in response to the arguments.

This activity helps you to start thinking critically about what you read; it also helps you to evaluate the effectiveness of different arguments. From this, you will develop your own observations, opinions and points of view that will help with any conclusions that you make in your answers to AO2 questions.

Question

'Freud is wrong in stating that religion is a neurosis.' Evaluate this view.

(Q6, Component 2: Philosophy of Religion, WJEC, Summer 2022)

Evaluation

There do seem to be parallels between certain types of neurosis and religious ritual. People often display obsessional behaviour. This behaviour, for example, can centre on checking or contamination. The checking of things such as front doors, water taps and gas stove knobs can result in checking multiple times, sometimes hundreds of times and for hours on end, resulting in the person being late for work and other appointments. The checking can also cause damage to the objects that are constantly being checked. The need to clean and wash can also be a compulsion. It often involves repetitive hand washing until the person 'feels' they are clean. It is true that religion can also be seen to have aspects of obsessional behaviour. For example, Muslims are required to wash five times per day before prayer. This washing is known as Wudu and is a form of ritual ablution. Parts of the body must be washed in a specific order and in a specific way. If a mistake is made, then the whole process must be begun again.

Freud's clinical work involving interpretation of dreams and psychoanalysis of patients was often successful in treating the obsession. This may be seen as validating his theories concerning the cause of the obsession as repressed trauma and guilt, therefore supporting the view that religion, with its religious ritual, stems from the same source: repressed memories and guilt. In other words, religion is a neurosis.

This section covers AO1 content and skills

E: Religious belief as a product of the human mind: Carl Jung

Introduction

Carl Gustav Jung was born in 1875 in Switzerland. Like Freud, he worked with psychiatric patients after gaining his doctorate. Initially, Jung shared a similar understanding of the way the mind works, but he soon came to realise that Freud's view of the subconscious was too narrow. So, he set out to demonstrate a wholly distinctive understanding of the mind; an understanding that would see religion in a much more positive light. Unlike Freud, who saw religion as a neurosis, Jung saw it as something necessary for personal growth.

Religion necessary for personal growth

Collective unconscious

Freud (front left) and Jung (front right) at Clark University, Massachusetts, USA, in 1909

Jung and the psyche

For Jung, the psyche consists of:

- the ego – this represents the conscious mind, as it comprises the thoughts, memories and emotions that a person is aware of; it is also responsible for feelings of identity

- the **personal unconscious** – this consists of lost or repressed memories, some of which take the form of complexes; it includes things we have forgotten because they have become irrelevant or seemed unimportant at the time

- the **collective unconscious** – this idea sets Jung apart from Freud.

> **Specification content**
> Religion necessary for personal growth with reference to collective unconscious; individuation; archetypes; the God within

> **Key terms**
> **personal unconscious:** memories that have been forgotten or repressed
> **collective unconscious:** elements of unconsciousness that are shared with all other people

Just as evolution and heredity are seen as providing a blueprint for the body, so Jung saw evolution and heredity providing a blueprint for the psyche. According to Jung, the collective unconscious consists of **primordial** images and themes, derived from early human history. These include both human and pre-human experiences. Jung claimed that these images or themes could not be traced to the individual's own past experiences.

Jung called these images and themes **archetypes** and stated that, based on his research, they have universal meanings across cultures, and may show up in dreams, literature, art or religion.

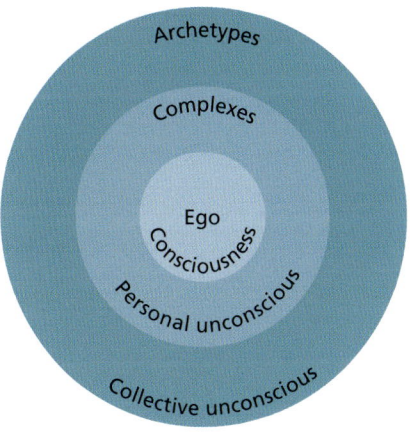

The psyche according to Jung

> ### ◉ Key terms
> **primordial:** existing from the beginning
> **archetypes:** literally meaning 'original pattern', these refer to symbolic forms that all people share in their collective unconscious; the archetypes give rise to images in the conscious mind and account for the recurring themes – these mould and influence human behaviour

Archetypes

The word *archetype* comes from the Greek meaning 'original pattern'. Archetypes are unlearned. They function to organise how we experience certain things, often evoking deep emotions. In many ways, human archetypes are similar to animal instincts in that they activate within us an automatic behaviour, such as emotions and thought patterns. Jung noted that the symbols and images from different cultures are often very similar because they have emerged from archetypes that the whole human race shares.

The archetypes are mysterious and not directly accessible to conscious thought. A person only becomes individually conscious of them when they are projected outwards, usually in the form of myths and symbols. Religious stories, symbolism and rituals, as well as art, literature and dreams, are all ways to identify the archetypes.

> ### Specification content
> Religion necessary for personal growth: archetypes

While Jung recognised that there was no actual limit to the number of archetypes potentially available to human experience, he identified four of particular significance:

- the persona
- the shadow
- the anima and animus
- the self.

The persona

This is the mask we wear to make a particular impression on others, and it may conceal our own true nature. The persona represents all the different social masks we wear among different groups and in different situations.

For example, a father may consider a trait such as disciplining as typical of a father and so adopt that trait, rather than a trait that reflects his own actual personality. Because the persona is an idealised image and not a true reflection of our personal consciousness, it can lead to inner conflicts and a repression of our own individuality.

T2 Challenges to religious belief – religious belief as a product of the human mind

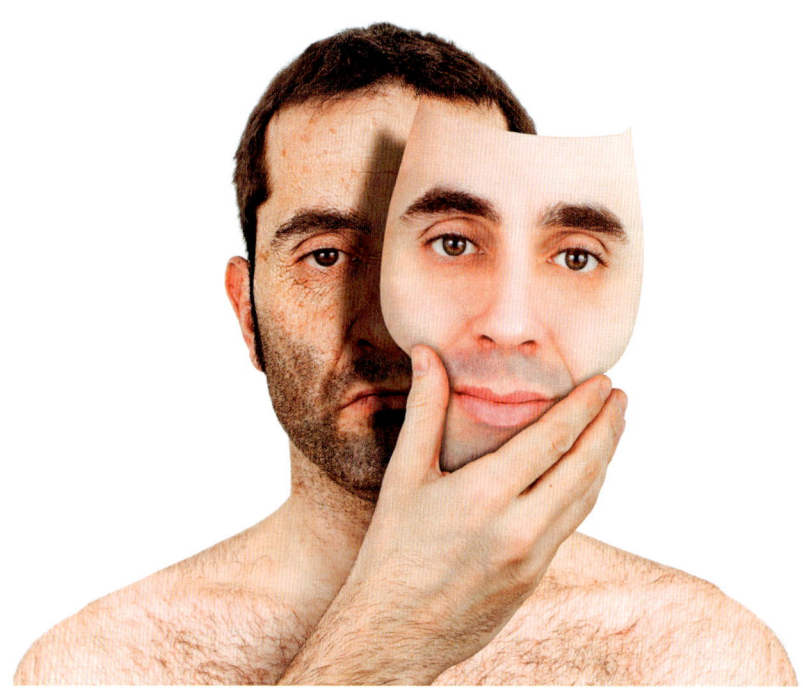

The persona archetype – the mask we wear

The shadow

The shadow refers to the suppressed, unconscious portion of the personality. It designates that side of an individual that he or she prefers not to reveal. Often it is symbolised as original sin, the devil or a snake. It is considered to be the source not only of our creative, but also of our destructive, energies.

The shadow archetype – the suppressed unconscious

The shadow is in contrast with the persona, the public self. This darker side of our personality can be a source of shame and anxiety – so we tend to deny it. The shadow, if unrecognised, is projected on others who are thought to embody those repressed tendencies that are actually resident in that person's own psyche. The most widely known shadow image is the villain archetype.

The anima and animus

These are inner attitudes that take on the characteristics of the opposite sex. Each sex manifests attitudes and behaviour of the other by virtue of centuries of living together. As people develop a gender identity, they repress the aspects of their personality that might be considered to reflect the opposite sex. For instance, a male may repress empathy in social situations because it is considered in society as a feminine trait.

The anima is the archetypal image of woman present in the unconscious of every man. It is responsible for moods and is a complication in all emotional relationships. The most widely known anima image is the mother archetype, which is represented in stories by characters such as Eve in Judaism, the Virgin Mary in Christianity and Shakti in Hinduism. The anima is often shown as a cave or a ship.

The comparable archetype in the female psyche is the animus: the woman's image of man. In the woman's unconscious, it is responsible for unreasoned opinion. It is often represented by an eagle or a bull and by phallic symbols such as towers. Both anima and animus need to be in balance.

The anima and animus archetypes – taking on characteristics of the opposite sex

The self

The most important archetype is the self, which is the midpoint of the personality – balancing (midway between) the conscious and the unconscious. The self represents the harmony and balance between the various opposing qualities that make up the psyche. The self provides a sense of unity in experience. Jung considered that the aim of every individual was to achieve a state of 'self-hood'. Because it is almost impossible for any person to embody their own self fully, this archetype is often given

The self archetype – the balance between the conscious and the unconscious

T2 Challenges to religious belief – religious belief as a product of the human mind

Key term

mandala: a geometric design symbolic of the universe, often used in Buddhism as an aid to meditation; they are usually circular in form, with one identifiable centre point

Specification content

Religion necessary for personal growth: individuation

Key term

individuation: the process of attaining wholeness and balance

expression in geometrical or abstract form, such as a **mandala**. Very well-known figures who express the self are Christ and Buddha. The self archetype comes closest to what many religions refer to as the 'soul'.

Individuation

Jung argued that, as we acquire the qualities of an archetype from the collective unconscious, we repress the attributes of our true self because they do not conform to the archetype. However, those repressed traits that are our true self must be integrated into our consciousness if we are to realise our true self. This process by which a person moves towards the achievement of the self is called **individuation**.

The integration results in the wholeness and balance of an individual's personality. The self archetype works collectively with all other aspects of a person's psyche to integrate them and become whole. It is a form of 'self-development' or 'self-realisation' – a discovery of the true self.

Therefore, individuation aims to remove from the self the false wrappings of the persona and the suggestive power of primordial images. In doing so, it will balance the contradictory nature of the archetypes and unite opposites.

An example would be the need to unite good and evil so that we see ourselves as capable of both. The lotus symbol in Asian religions reflects this uniting of opposites, where the roots of the lotus are in the dirty mud below and its flower is in the clean air above. In a similar way, Jung argued that we must get in touch with the shadow and anima/animus if we want to get in touch with the self.

The lotus flower – a symbol of individuation

The way that the archetypes are brought into our consciousness from the collective unconscious is by means of the symbols of the archetypes. These archetypal symbols mediate the process of individuation as they express and bring about the union of opposites. Jung saw these symbols as the images, dogmas and rites that form the religious traditions.

The God within

Individuation is the journey towards becoming a full individual. It is the quest to find the 'God within' and the symbol of 'the self'. In its widest sense, it is a religious quest because it is through religious images that the personality achieves its goal of integration. The religious images are simply images of the deeper self. Jung considered that the self archetype creates the same symbolism that has always expressed deity. For Jung, the self is the 'God within us'.

The following points are worth noting when it comes to Jung's concepts of God:

- It is impossible to distinguish between a symbol of the self and a God image.
- God is a deep 'inner' reality rather than an external object or person.
- God is an expression of the collective unconscious.
- A 'religious experience' with God is really an encounter with the 'self', and the experience is called 'spiritual' or 'numinous'. (Rudolf Otto, the German theologian, described a 'numinous' experience as mysterious and awe-inspiring, where the person feels in communion with a 'wholly other'.)

As we have seen, Jung's understanding of the idea of God is very different from Freud's. For Freud, God is a creation by the individual human mind and its neurotic desires. He sees it more as a mental illness, and he thought that religion would eventually die out and be replaced by science. In contrast, Jung sees religion as helpful for balancing mental health, and as a key to the process of integration and individuation.

> **Specification content**
> Religion necessary for personal growth: the God within

Supportive evidence

Recognition of religion as a source of comfort

It is generally agreed that Jung's theories were experience driven. He constructed his concepts from evidence he derived from his personal experience and clinical observations. He concluded that the archetypes occur universally in all cultures and historical periods. Myths and religions contain similar themes that were also found in the dreams of his patients. Jung believed that the archetypes provided a way of interpreting dreams, as well as myths and features of traditional religions.

Indeed, Jung viewed religion as a positive factor of psychological value. Although he saw religion as error, nevertheless it is a positive error in that it provides humankind with assurance and strength. He viewed the idea of God and religious phenomena as symbols that express and draw human beings towards psychic wholeness.

> **Specification content**
> Supportive evidence including recognition of religion as a source of comfort

Loss of religion and the rise of psychoneurosis

Jung became aware that the horrors of the First World War posed a spiritual problem for the modern person as the religious, social and political certainties had been torn down. As a result, people had become disconnected from humanity and spirituality. Uncertainty and disillusionment followed, and civilisation became dominated by materialism, science and technology. The religious symbols that projected the archetypes were often absent, and Jung maintained that this led to psychoneurosis. This was because neurosis and depression result from a disharmony between consciousness and unconsciousness. Healing and wholeness must come from restoring harmony within oneself and between oneself and the external world.

In 1932, he reported that:

> Among all my patients ... over thirty-five – there has not been one whose problem in the last resort was not that of finding a religious outlook on life ... every one of them fell ill because he had lost what the living religions of every age have given to their followers, and none of them has been really healed who did not regain his religious outlook.
> (Jung, 'Psychotherapists or the Clergy')

The task of the psychologist

He saw the psychologist's task as one of regaining the inner vision for each of his patients, and he argued that this was achievable by establishing a connection between the psyche and the sacred images.

There was a need to pay attention to messages from the unconscious and the spiritual realms through dream analysis; word associations; and interpretation of symbols, metaphors and creative activities. For Jung, understanding the symbolic meaning of the unconscious archetypes was a major step towards attaining meaningful living.

Recognition of religion as promotion of personal and social mindsets arising from religious belief

Jung saw support for his theories in his observation that human beings have collective ideas and common ethics that could be found in all religions. Indeed, he saw religious belief as aiding individuation and leading to wholeness of the individual.

Jung appreciated that there was a significant difference between Western and Asian minds. The Western mind, he saw as extroverted and in search of an outer reality. In contrast, he saw the Asian mind as introverted and in search of the source of all existence, the psyche itself. Therefore, he saw particular value in the Asian techniques of meditation.

Buddhist meditation and the self archetype

In Buddhist meditation, for example, removing ignorance is vital: this involves removing hindrances such as sensuous desires, ill-will and restlessness. The meditation seeks to uncover misconceptions about who and what we are. For example, the *Brahma Viharas* (Buddhist Virtues) are meditative states, thoughts and actions to be cultivated in Buddhist meditation. These four Buddhist Virtues are loving kindness, compassion, altruistic joy and composure. This meditative practice is similar to the God archetype that involves the development of positive, wholesome images for reflection. Therefore, the idea of the self archetype organising and harmonising the 'fuller picture' of reality is similar to the idea of meditation leading to enlightenment (*nibbana* or *nirvana*).

Failure of organised religion

Jung felt that the way inward for people in the West was more difficult. There was nothing in the West really comparable to the Asian meditation tradition except psychotherapy. This involved such techniques as dream analysis, and the aim was to guide the patient to a personal confrontation with the collective unconscious and its archetypes. For Jung, symbols worked only if they were dynamic. He believed that many symbols in organised religion had become just objects and had therefore lost their meaning and their power to actualise the God archetype. Jung concluded that organised religion was a failure.

> **Specification content**
>
> Supportive evidence including recognition of religion as promotion of personal and social mindsets arising from religious belief

Religious behaviours and positive mental health

Surveys on mental health, happiness and social benefits show a positive rating for those who are religious. This suggests that religion aids wholeness and helps to integrate conscious and unconscious contents into a coherent psychic totality.

Surveys suggest that social cohesion and social support are found among church members. Religious behaviour is a source of social integration for those often rejected by wider society. Religion is also seen as a source of comfort, as it offers meaning to life and freedom from fear of death.

Challenges to Jung's interpretation

Lack of empirical evidence for Jungian concepts

Jung's central claims concerning archetypes do have some support in that they appear in myths and religions of some cultures and also in people's dreams. However, there are criticisms of his approach. These include:

- It has not been possible to devise any method of research that could fully verify Jung's claims.
- Jung's claim of a collective unconscious that contains the archetypes cannot be demonstrated by **empirical evidence**.
- Similar effects do not necessarily mean similar causes. Therefore, there may be other theories to account for the fact of parallel imagery.
- The psychologist Gordon Allport pointed out that a far better explanation is that the images result from a conformity to culture.
- Hall and Lindzey accused Jung of relying on clinical and armchair techniques of research, rather than on experimentation and quantification.
- Jung is making an unprovable assumption when he states that human beings have an *a priori* disposition to construct God-images: that is, that God-images and therefore religious beliefs are innate.
- Jung avoided making predictions based on his theories, and that freed him from ever being proved wrong.

Reductionist views regarding religious belief

While in many ways Jung is positive about the essential role that religion plays in psychological health, his own understanding and interpretation of religion and religious belief does not always take into account the fullness of religious beliefs and experiences. He has therefore been regarded by some as taking a reductionist view of religion.

Some of these critiques include:

- Many would argue that an experience that stems from the mind and, as such, is in no way external to the subject cannot be termed religious. Christ, for example, is more than just a symbol for something else. He is a historical person whom many regard as the Son of God.
- What is important to Jung is not the historical Jesus and whether he was an actual person, but the psychic experience that the title 'Christ' causes. For Jung, Jesus is the exemplification of an archetype. For Christians, such an understanding of Jesus and Christianity would be unacceptable.
- Equally controversial was Jung's book *Answer to Job* (1951), in which he argues that both good and evil are aspects of God.

> **Specification content**
> Challenges including lack of empirical evidence for Jungian concepts and reductionist views regarding religious belief arising from acceptance of Jung's ideas

> **Key term**
>
> **empirical evidence:** knowledge received by means of the senses, particularly by observation and experimentation

T2 Challenges to religious belief – religious belief as a product of the human mind

> **Key term**
>
> **Theravada Buddhism:** a school of Buddhism that draws its scriptural inspiration from the Pali canon

- It seems that Jung did not believe in the existence of God in the traditional sense of an external being. He does not dismiss the possibility, but thinks that we can never know whether God exists.
- Jung believes that no argument from experience can prove the existence of anything that lies beyond the boundaries of human experience. However, he argues that human beings possess the property of formulating God-images, and so infers that our collective unconscious contains the archetypal God-form.
- Jung seems to ignore the existence of atheists and non-theistic faiths, such as **Theravada Buddhism**.
- The term *religion* becomes so broad in scope in Jungian use that it seems an applicable term to use for any system of ideas. This makes it virtually impossible for anyone to be referred to as a non-believer.

Summary

- Jung developed ideas about the psyche, seeing Freud's view as too narrow. His key idea was that of the collective unconscious.
- Jung believed that to be psychologically healthy we need to achieve a state known as *individuation*, something attainable only after accessing the archetypes of the collective unconscious – which we do through myths, symbols and dreams.
- It was because of this that Jung argued that religion is helpful in the quest for positive mental health and a key part of the process of psychological integration and individuation.
- While it is generally agreed that Jung used a more balanced evidence base for his theories about religious belief, he is still regarded as reductionist in his views on religion. There is also criticism of his theory of the archetypes and the collective unconscious due to a lack of empirical evidence.

AO1 Activity

a   Examine the supporting evidence for Jung's beliefs.

This helps with presenting a thorough and extensive knowledge and understanding of the topic area.

b   On revision cards, summarise the key features of Jung's belief that religion is necessary for personal growth. Include reference to the collective unconscious, the archetypes, the God within and individuation.

This helps with prioritising and selecting a core set of points to develop an answer and with making accurate use of specialist language and vocabulary in context.

> **Specification content**
> The extent to which Jung was more positive than Freud about the idea of God

This section covers AO2 content and skills

Issues for analysis and evaluation

The extent to which Jung was more positive than Freud about the idea of God

Possible line of argument	Critical analysis and evaluation
Reasons Freud's views on the idea of God are often considered negative	Freud is usually portrayed as being negative about the idea of God, while Jung is seen as more positive. Freud likened religion to mental illness. It was just another form of neurosis (in particular, a sexual neurosis), where both the religious worshipper and the obsessional neurotic spend hours carrying out certain rituals. If the rituals are omitted or not performed in the correct way, then the person becomes anxious and apprehensive. Therefore, just as the obsessional neurotic needs therapy and treatment to rid him – or herself of this neurosis, so also the religious worshipper needs therapy to be free from neurosis. Seen in this light, religion is harmful and limiting.
Freud's view of religion was that it was harmful to psychological health	Although Freud considers different causes of the neurosis (primal horde theory, totemism, Oedipus complex, father figure), they all share the same theme – the neurosis is the result of repression. Religion is not something that heals and makes whole, but rather something that needs healing and curing. Religion is infantile and can lead to people not taking action to better society. They turn to pray to an omnipotent, benevolent father figure rather than act themselves. Freud sees the idea of God as a creation of the individual human mind and its neurotic desires. He believed the neurosis of religion stems from the conflict between the conscious and unconscious mind, with the individual repressing impulses and past associations.
Reasons Jung's views on the idea of God are more positive than Freud's	In contrast, Jung appears to present a much more positive view of religion. He rejects the idea of religion as a sexual neurosis. Instead, by unlocking the deepest level of the unconscious, it leads to the focus on the primordial and archetypal images of humanity: namely, the collective unconscious. It is from the collective unconscious that we acquire the qualities of an archetype that, in turn, mould and influence our behaviour. For Jung, God is an expression of the collective unconscious.
God is a psychic reality and accessing the God archetype is beneficial for psychological health	Hence, religion is positive. It is about the evolving process in the development of the psychic personality – integrating the conscious and unconscious aspects of the psyche. Freud saw religion as a mixture of guilt-ridden repressions and obsessions expressed through ritual. Jung, however, saw religion as a natural and legitimate dimension of psychic activity. Religious images are simply images of the deeper self and, through these religious images, the personality achieves its goal of integration. Therefore, for Jung, God is a reality from the deepest part of the human collective unconscious.
For psychological health, the unconscious and the conscious mind need to be integrated	Religion is therefore both positive and beneficial since it is necessary for human psychic development. A lack of religious feelings or belief implies a failure by the person to integrate the unconscious and the conscious mind. Whereas Freud saw symbols as a way an individual sought to avoid reality, Jung saw symbols as the way to gain knowledge of realities that in themselves are unknowable. Symbols transformed rather than led to neurosis.
Conclusion: Jung was more positive than Freud about the idea of God	Overall, the weight of evidence from the work of both Jung and Freud would suggest that Jung was more positive than Freud about the idea of God.

> **AO2 Activity**
>
> a Analyse three possible conclusions that could be drawn from the critical analysis and evaluation of the extent to which Jung was more positive than Freud about the idea of God. What are their strengths and weaknesses? Which conclusion is strongest?
>
> b Using the strongest conclusion, select three lines of argument that you would use to support this conclusion. Try to explain why you have selected these.

> **Specification content**
>
> The effectiveness of empirical approaches as critiques of Jungian views on religion

Exam practice

Sample question

Evaluate the effectiveness of empirical approaches as critiques of Jungian views on religion.

Sample answer

Empirical evidence includes the record of someone's direct observations or experiences, and these can be analysed both quantitatively and qualitatively. Jung's methodology involved the inclusion of descriptions of certain observable psychic 'facts' such as dreams and visions. They are 'facts' in that they provide knowledge of our own psychic world. Jung maintained that using subjective personal experiences was valid as an empirical method, since the psyche's imaging of reality is the only reality for the individual who creates it.

This is a good introduction that provides a helpful overview of the key areas for focus in the evaluation to come.

In *Psychology and Religion* (1938), Jung claimed that 'although I have often been called a philosopher, I am an empiricist and adhere as such to the phenomenological standpoint'. For Jung, facts denote psychic phenomena since they provide knowledge of our own psychic world. Indeed, Jung argued that only psychic existence is immediately verifiable and so, when empiricists investigate the world, they discover facts that by necessity are psychic.

This paragraph explores a line of reasoning that draws on relevant evidence to show how Jung considered himself to be an empiricist.

The problem appears to be that, while we can criticise empirical approaches for being selective, unrepresentative, not entirely proof and subject to interpretation, we can also similarly criticise Jung's view of religion because there is no empirical proof in the sense of physical proof. However, we should always remember that, just as any physical experiment has an element of observation and interpretation, so too Jung's methodology is based on the same two principles of observation and interpretation.

This paragraph considers an issue with the consistency of the initial line of reasoning.

It could be argued that Jung's research into ancient myths and legends provided empirical evidence. The images he referred to clearly exerted a hold on the human mind. Further support came from his observation that human beings have collective ideas and common ethics found in all religions. The constant recurrence of symbols from mythology in personal therapy supports the idea of an innate collective cultural residue.

This paragraph presents a reflection on Jung's use of empirical evidence, with relevant evidence and examples.

Alternatively, we could argue that a basic test of a scientific statement is whether it is falsifiable. Since Jung's evidence is derived from inner psychological states, the 'observation' of this is not really the same as observing the boiling point of water. Jung is concerned with the state of mind that the subject is experiencing; he is not concerned with whether the subjective experience has any grounding in a reality that is separate from the subject. Whatever is derived from the experience is subjective. This means that truth in these circumstances is not about whether the experience corresponds to reality, but about whether the subjective experience is a genuine experience.

Jung argued that the truth of a psychic experience does not depend on whether it corresponds to reality, but solely on whether the subject 'feels' it to be true. He rarely, if ever, made predictions, and so this freed him from being proved wrong. His own dreams, thoughts and introspection, in addition to those of his patients, shaped his theories. Many would claim that these observations are not an adequate scientific basis for a major theory on human personality.

A line of argument might be to challenge the value of empirical evidence on the grounds that we should be sceptical about our senses. As Hilary Putnam noted, we could all be a brain in a vat, stimulated electrically in such a way as to give us the delusive experience of living the life we are familiar with. Indeed, we could also doubt our reasoning abilities. Such an approach to empirical evidence would mean that any critique of Jung's use of empirical approaches would be of no importance in weighing up Jung's view of religion.

Some would argue that these criticisms are sufficient to reject Jung's views about religion. Should we consider his methodology flawed? Are his conclusions invalid? Perhaps … however, they appear to be no more invalid than those of religious believers. Others are more reluctant to dismiss Jung's explanations. They draw attention to Jung's study of comparative mythology, which supports his theories. Indeed, many see his theories as a bridge between the scientific and the religious that is both respectful and non-judgemental by avoiding issues of empirical verification. Overall, we could coherently argue that, even if the evidence is not verifiable, Jung's theories still give an explanation for religious beliefs that is consistent with the evidence.

Evaluation

This is a good response. It considers both sides of the argument and raises questions before putting forward a conclusion. The candidate makes accurate use both of terminology and of the views of different schools of thought.

Over to you

Below are brief summaries of two different points of view concerning the extent to which Jung's explanation of religion as a product of the human mind is convincing.

Use these two views and lines of argument as the basis of an evaluation. To achieve a fully developed argument, rewrite the two views in a fully evaluative style, adding further reasons and evidence linked to the arguments they raise.

When you have completed the task, refer to the band descriptors for A2 (WJEC) or A Level (Eduqas) and, in particular, look at the demands described in the higher band descriptors, which you should be aspiring towards. Ask yourself:

- Is my answer a confident, critical analysis and perceptive evaluation of the issue?
- Does my answer convey a confident and perceptive analysis of the nature of any possible connections with other elements of my course?
- When used, is specialist language and vocabulary both thorough and accurate?

Question

'Jung's argument that religious belief is a product of the human mind is convincing.' Evaluate this view.

(Q3, Component 2: Philosophy of Religion, WJEC, Summer 2023)

Point of view 1

Jung shows, through his study of world religions, the similarity between the different religions, particularly in their images and symbols. It seems reasonable to assume that those similarities are not just coincidental, but originate from similar sources. Jung concludes that these symbols are symbols of archetypes that are in the collective unconscious. His psychoanalysis of patients is evidence that our repressed traits are brought into our consciousness by the archetypal symbols. They need to be integrated into our consciousness so we can realise our true self. This is a religious quest, since religious images are simply images of the deeper self. A religious experience is an encounter with the self. This understanding of religion is closer to Asian than to Western religions. It explains religion for the twenty-first century.

Point of view 2

Jung's explanation of religion as a product of the human mind is, firstly, without evidence and, secondly, not about religion. He claims to be scientific, but he offers theories that cannot be verified. His whole evidence rests on subjective personal experiences, but he seems unconcerned whether the content of these experiences accurately relates to reality. Equally, it describes religion, but that is not what is meant traditionally by religion. Jung talks about Christ, but not in the way Christians understand Christ. It fails on a third area: that Jung fails to explain atheism. Jung's explanation does not convince us.

F: Issues relating to rejection of religion: atheism

Rejection of belief in deities

Atheism in the ancient world

It is generally accepted that Diagoras of Melos was the first atheist. He lived in the fifth century BCE and was a Greek poet and **sophist**. Only anecdotes remain about his views concerning the worship of national gods, but his views seemed sufficiently offensive at the time to force him to flee Athens in fear for his life.

Possibly an even earlier example of atheism can be found in the Asian religions of Jainism, Buddhism and Taoism, since they do not include a deity as such and can be dated as far back as the sixth century BCE.

However, many would argue that this is a simplistic view of those religions that stems from their rejection of the idea of a creator god. The word *atheistic* appears in ancient Greek and has the meaning of 'godless' or 'disrespecting the local gods', even though they may have believed in other gods.

A good example is Socrates (470–399BCE), who was accused of corrupting Athenian youth by encouraging them not to believe in the city's gods. Socrates regarded Homer's gods as corrupt, vain and self-serving. He described them as like human beings on a bigger scale, complete with vices and virtues.

The Greek word *atheoi* can be found in the New Testament in Ephesians 2:12. Here, it means 'without God'. In other words, the people had no real knowledge of God, rather than refusing to believe in God.

Papyrus 46 showing the word *atheoi* from Ephesians 2:12

Justyn Martyr, the Christian apologist, pointed out in the second century that Christians such as himself 'were even called "atheists" – which we are in relation to what you consider gods, but are most certainly not in relation to the Most True God'.

> **This section covers AO1 content and skills**

> **Specification content**
> Rejection of belief in deities

> ⊙ **Key term**
>
> **sophists:** Greek teachers and writers particularly skilled in rhetoric and reasoning

T2 Challenges to religious belief – religious belief as a product of the human mind

Key terms

Renaissance: period of European history between the fourteenth and seventeenth centuries that was a time of great revival of art, literature and learning

Reformation: the religious movement in Europe in the sixteenth century that led to the creation and rise of Protestantism

Age of Enlightenment: an intellectual and philosophical movement in Europe in the eighteenth century

Atheism: AD 1500–1900

It was the great European movements of the **Renaissance** and the **Reformation** that coined the term *atheist*. The term was used exclusively as an insult, according to the author Karen Armstrong, as nobody wanted to be regarded as an atheist since it implied the person lacked moral restraint.

Two further movements in the eighteenth century made an impact on challenging belief in God. The first was the **Age of Enlightenment**, which encouraged individuals to think for themselves and appealed to both human reason and the scientific method as the means of finding truth. Secondly, the French Revolution of 1789 mobilised intellectuals who saw the Church as an outmoded institution that propped up the monarchy.

By the 1770s, atheism was ceasing to be a dangerous accusation; so much so that it was evolving into a position that some felt they could openly claim. The word *atheism* had now taken on the meaning of a denial of the existence of God or, at the very least, the claim that one should live one's life with disregard towards a god.

The last person who was jailed for being an atheist in Britain was George Holyoake in 1842. He was sentenced to six months' imprisonment. In 1880, Charles Bradlaugh was elected as the Liberal MP for Northampton. His refusal to take a parliamentary Oath of Allegiance on the Bible, rather than just to affirm his Oath of Allegiance without religious basis, resulted in him not being allowed to take his seat. He was re-elected several times over five years, but did not take his seat until 1886. When he eventually took his seat, he became Britain's first openly atheist Member of Parliament.

Atheism in the twentieth and twenty-first centuries

During the twentieth century, atheists in Western societies became more active, and even state atheism emerged in eastern Europe and Asia, particularly in the Soviet Union and in Communist China.

Through increased travel and communication, people became aware of other religions. As a result, it seemed that there were contradictions between the religions. They appeared to say different and incompatible things about the nature of ultimate reality, divine activity and the destiny of the human race. It was argued that which religion you follow depends on where you are born and has little to do with truth.

The 1960s saw a movement from within the Christian Church that many viewed as closer to atheism than theism. This theological movement claimed it was no longer tenable to hold the traditional view of God being 'out there'. God is just a very powerful symbol, but has no 'real' objective or empirical existence.

The Anglican bishop John Robinson popularised these views in Britain. His book *Honest to God* (1963) describes God as 'the ground of our being', instead of the traditional view that God is an objective personal force. Traditional theistic thinking placed God outside and above the world. However, Robinson placed God deep in the human person. So he argued that everyone needs to look inside themselves to find God.

In the 1980s, Don Cupitt, who was both an Anglican priest and Dean of Emmanuel College, Cambridge, presented a TV series entitled *Sea of Faith*. The title was taken from the poem 'Dover Beach' by Matthew Arnold, in which the poet expresses regret that belief in a supernatural world is slowly slipping away. In his TV series, Cupitt charted the transition from some form of traditional belief in God to a rejection of the supernatural world. God existed as an idea in the minds of believers rather than as an external, objective being. This new understanding of religious faith gave rise to the 'Sea of Faith' Movement.

A feature of the twenty-first century has been the high-profile promotion of a more militant form of atheism termed **New Atheism**, which was associated with people like Christopher Hitchens and Richard Dawkins. It sees religion as a threat to the survival of the human race. It sees the concept of God as a totalitarian belief that destroys individual freedom.

> **Key term**
>
> **New Atheism:** also known as *antitheism*; the belief that religion is a threat to the survival of the human race

The atheist bus campaign, 2008–9

T2 Challenges to religious belief – religious belief as a product of the human mind

The differences between agnosticism and atheism

> **Specification content**
> The differences between agnosticism and atheism

As we have seen above, the definition of *atheism* has changed through the centuries. Alister McGrath defines atheism as 'the religion of the autonomous and rational human being, who believes that reason is able to uncover and express the deepest truths of the universe'.

There are various shades of atheism. Antony Flew, in his book *The Presumption of Atheism* (1972), first introduced the terms *weak* and *strong* atheism. He argued that atheism should be the default position.

Different perspectives of atheism

Term	Explanation	What this atheist would say
Negative (weak) atheism	This is where the atheist does not make the positive claim that God does not exist. It is the theist who makes the assertion, and therefore it is the theist who bears the burden of proof. The atheist merely says that she does not believe any deities exist, but does not assert as true that no deities exist.	'I don't believe that God exists, but tell me why do you believe in God?'
Positive (strong) atheism	In this case, both the atheist and the theist have to give reasons to defend their belief. A positive atheist asserts that she knows that God or gods do not exist. In a similar way, the theist asserts that God exists.	'I know God does not exist, and here are my reasons, so why do you believe in God?'
Protest atheism	This is a revolt against God on moral grounds. In Dostoyevsky's novel *The Brothers Karamazov*, the atheist Ivan recounts a story about a young boy who was torn apart by hunting dogs in front of the boy's mother. Ivan comments that even if God did exist (which he did not believe anyway), he would want nothing to do with him.	'Even if God did exist, I could not morally accept God.'
New Atheism (antitheism)	This is the belief that religion is a threat to the survival of the human race. This view of atheism is a hostile reaction to theism and is expounded by Richard Dawkins in his book *The God Delusion*.	'I don't believe God exists and neither must you.'

Thomas Huxley (1825–95)

In contrast, agnosticism is commonly used to indicate a suspension of the decision to accept or reject belief in God. The term *agnostic* was first used by the English biologist Thomas Huxley in a speech at a meeting of the Metaphysical Society in 1869. The word is derived from the Greek, meaning 'without knowledge'.

Therefore, agnosticism embraces the idea that the existence of God or any other ultimate reality is, in principle, unknowable. Our knowledge is limited and we cannot know ultimate reasons for things. It is not that the evidence is lacking; it is that the evidence is never possible.

Many people are convinced that agnosticism is some sort of 'middle way' or 'third way' between atheism and theism. But agnosticism is not about belief in God; it is about knowledge. It is not a creed, but a methodology. Huxley argued that people should not pretend that conclusions that are not demonstrated or demonstrable are certain.

Just as with atheism, there are various shades of agnosticism. In recent years, the meaning of *agnosticism* has shifted again. The philosopher Nicholas Everitt, in *The Non-existence of God* (2004), uses it to apply to someone who thinks God's existence and his non-existence are equally probable.

Different perspectives of agnosticism

Term	Explanation	What this agnostic would say
Strong agnosticism	Strong agnosticism is the assertion that it is impossible to know whether or not God exists. It is unknowable because our knowledge is limited, and we cannot know ultimate reasons for things. It is not that the evidence is lacking; it is that the evidence is never possible.	'I don't know whether or not God exists and neither do you.'
Weak agnosticism	This is the belief that the existence of God is currently unknown, but it is not necessarily unknowable. God may exist or may not exist, but judgement has to be withheld until evidence becomes available. This is the common usage of agnosticism, where it indicates the suspension of a decision.	'I don't know whether or not God exists, but maybe you do.'

The rise of New Atheism (antitheism)

On 11 September 2001, there was a series of four co-ordinated terrorist attacks by Islamic terrorists on the United States. In the aftermath, there began a powerful attack on religion, as religion was seen as the main cause of the catastrophe. It triggered a movement that saw not just religious extremists, but religion in general, as dangerous and deluded.

The first person to express this view was Sam Harris, who published his views in his bestselling book *The End of Faith* (2004). By 2006, two other voices had joined the debate, publishing popular books of their own. Richard Dawkins wrote *The God Delusion* and Daniel Dennett wrote *Breaking the Spell*. In that same year, the term *New Atheism* came into being. Its originator was Gary Wolf, who wrote an article about the three authors for the British magazine *Wired*. A year later, Christopher Hitchens wrote a bestseller called *God Is Not Great*, expressing similar views, and the phrase 'the Four Horsemen (of the Non-Apocalypse)' soon began to be used to refer to the four writers.

Atheists in the past have argued that those who believe in God are wrong, but have shown little or no hostility towards religious belief or practice. However, New Atheism is antitheism. It displays an intense anger towards religion and sees it as harmful.

> **Specification content**
>
> The rise of New Atheism (antitheism); its main criticisms of religion; non-thinking; infantile world-view; impedes scientific progress

New Atheism's main criticisms

Religion is non-thinking

One of the core defining characteristics of New Atheism is its emphasis on rationality and its vehemently held view that faith and religion are irrational.

Dawkins argues that religion involves faith, and faith by nature is opposed to evidence. He considers that all faith is blind trust and intellectually irresponsible. According to Dawkins:

> Faith is the great cop-out, the great excuse to evade the need to think and evaluate evidence ... Faith is not allowed to justify itself by argument. (Dawkins speaking in 1992)

In *The God Delusion*, Dawkins argues that religious people are non-thinking. He claims that religious people know, without evidence, that the faith of their birth is the one true faith; all others being aberrations or downright false. Faith is infantile, so Dawkins points out that Christian and Muslim children are brought up to believe unquestioningly. Belief in God is something forced upon children by adults, so it should be rejected. Dawkins likens faith in God to believing in Santa Claus and the Tooth Fairy. When you grow up, you grow out of it. His analogy contends that both represent belief in non-existent entities.

For New Atheists, the accusation about non-thinking goes far beyond just sloppy thinking or irrationality. Religion is dangerous and leads to fanaticism. Even mild and moderate religion helps to provide the climate of faith where extremism naturally flourishes. In *The God Delusion*, Dawkins asks why nineteen well-educated middle-class men traded their lives in this world for the privilege of killing thousands. His conclusion was that they believed they would go straight to Paradise for doing so. It is religion itself that is to blame, not religious extremism. In contrast, though atheists have also done terrible things, they did not do them because of atheism but for other reasons.

The key voices of New Atheism – known as the Four Horsemen. From top left to right and then bottom left to right: Sam Harris, Richard Dawkins, Daniel Dennett, Christopher Hitchens

"Key quotes"

Many of us saw religion as harmless nonsense. Beliefs might lack all supporting evidence but, we thought, if people needed a crutch for consolation, where's the harm? September 11 changes all that.

(Dawkins, 'Has the world changed?', *The Guardian*)

I'm not even an atheist so much as I am an antitheist; I not only maintain that all religions are versions of the same untruth, but I hold that the influence of churches, and the effect of religious belief, is positively harmful.

(Hitchens, *Letters to a Young Contrarian*)

Religion has an infantile world-view

New Atheism sees the religious view of reality as deficient and impoverished compared with its own world-view. New Atheists claim that the kinds of views of the universe that religious people have traditionally embraced are very limited in comparison to the way the universe actually is.

Some of the criticisms that are specific to religion having this limited view include:

- Dawkins sees the universe presented by organised religion as 'a poky little medieval universe, and extremely limited', whereas science offers a bold and brilliant vision, seeing the universe as grand, beautiful and awe-inspiring.

- New Atheism claims that deep space, the billions of years of life's evolution and the microscopic workings of biology and heredity contain more beauty and wonder than do 'myths' and 'pseudoscience'.
- Natural selection is regarded as sufficient to explain the apparent functionality and non-random complexity of the biological world.
- New Atheism rejects the idea of the supernatural. New Atheists claim that such beliefs fail to do justice to the sublime grandeur of the real world. These beliefs represent a narrowing down from reality; an impoverishment of what the real world has to offer.
- God is not required as an explanation for the existence of the universe. God's existence cannot explain the world because he must be at least as complex, and therefore as improbable, as the world itself; and such an improbable entity would also require explanation.
- Indeed, in *The God Delusion*, Dawkins launches into a long list of the supposed faults of Yahweh, including 'jealous and proud of it; a petty, unjust, unforgiving control-freak; a vindictive, bloodthirsty ethnic cleanser; a misogynistic, homophobic, racist, infanticidal, genocidal, filicidal, pestilential, megalomaniacal, sadomasochistic, capriciously malevolent bully'.

Religion impedes scientific progress

New Atheism affirms a materialist world-outlook. Since matter is law-governed, it can be subject to scientific investigation. Hence, scientific theories are based only on evidence, while religion, New Atheists claim, runs away from evidence.

Viewpoints relating to this include:

- Atheism is rational and scientific, while religion is irrational and superstitious. Just as non-thinking and blind faith lead to fanaticism and violence, so blind faith and religious fundamentalism subvert science.
- New Atheists see blind faith in the truth of the holy book as unquestionable for religious believers. Therefore, if the book is true and evidence seems to contradict it, then the evidence, rather than the book, needs to be thrown out. Dawkins argues that when a science book is wrong, someone eventually discovers the mistake and it is corrected in subsequent books. However, that does not happen with holy books.
- Religion impedes scientific progress because it teaches us not to change our minds. It saps the intellect. Dawkins sees fundamentalist religion as hell-bent on ruining the scientific education of thousands of young minds, and religion in general as furthering the idea that unquestioning faith is a virtue.

Religious responses to the challenge of New Atheism

The views expounded by New Atheism have been widely challenged. The fundamental criticism of New Atheism is that it simply attacks easy and lazy caricatures or degenerate forms of religion, ignoring the mainstream reality. It also fails to forward a positive and compelling approach of its own. Its aggressively negative stance led Paul Kurtz to describe it as 'atheist fundamentalism'.

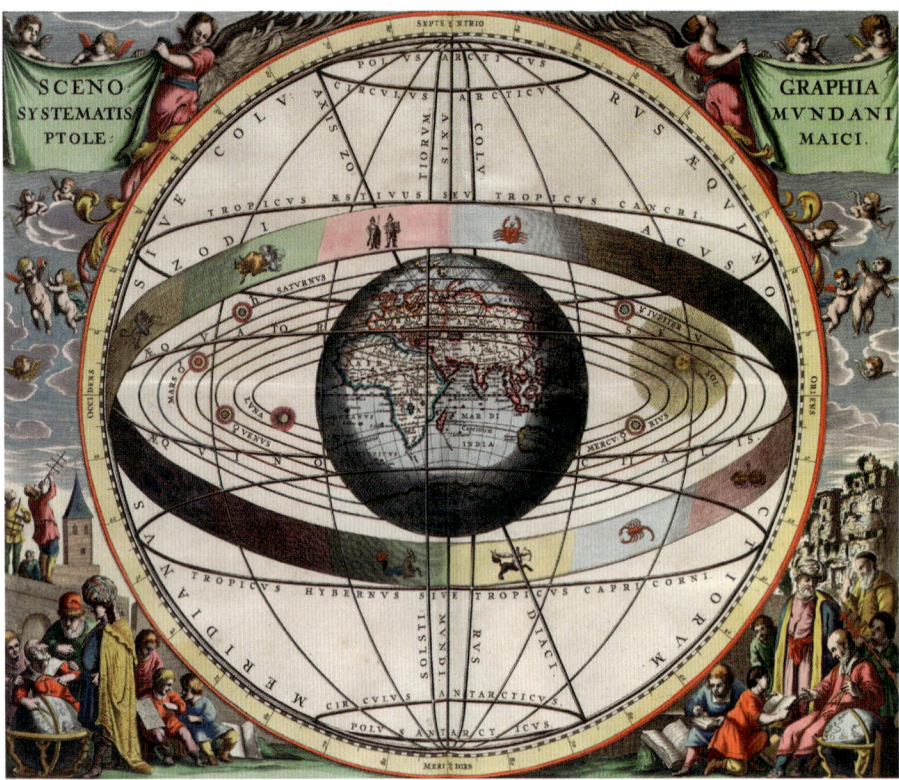

An ancient diagram of the universe

One of the most prolific writers who has addressed the challenges posed by New Atheism is Alister McGrath, a former atheist and now a Christian who, before he retired, was Andreas Idreos Professor of Science and Religion at Oxford University, as well as Professor of Divinity. McGrath comments that New Atheism defines itself by what it is against rather than by what it is for.

Incompatibility of science and religion

As we have seen, New Atheism takes a strongly positivist view of science, arguing that it explains (or has the potential to explain) everything, including matters traditionally regarded as lying within the religious realm. It denies the idea of multiple explanations of the same things, arguing that only the scientific explanation can be valid. Therefore, science and religion are depicted as offering competing explanations.

However, John Polkinghorne sees no competition. He argues that different levels of explanation need weaving together to provide a rich and comprehensive whole. For example, a scientific description of the world may describe the Big Bang and the evolution of living creatures. The religious may speak of God bringing the world into existence and directing it towards its intended outcome. Some see it as a process involving divine action. For others, it is God creating and working through natural forces.

These two accounts supplement rather than contradict each other. The natural world can be interpreted, without any loss of intellectual integrity, in a number of different ways. Indeed, two areas of thought that lie beyond the scope of the natural sciences are the notions of value and meaning – since they are non-empirical.

> **Specification content**
>
> Religious responses to the challenge of New Atheism: rejection by religious groups of New Atheist claims regarding incompatibility of science and religion; increase in fundamental religious activity relating to morality and community; increase in religious apologists in media

Alister McGrath argues that evidence and belief in religion is akin to evidence and belief in the natural sciences. Both involve showing that there are good reasons for thinking something is right, without having total confirmation. Dawkins wrongly defines religious faith as believing in something that has no supporting evidence. He fails to make the distinction between the 'total absence of supporting evidence' and the 'absence of totally supporting evidence'.

Increase in fundamentalist religious activity

Morality and community

Religious beliefs involve a world-view that is embedded in a person's thinking and behaviour. Therefore, religion cannot be a purely private matter for religious believers. The public and private dimensions of life can never be truly kept separate. The attack on religion from New Atheism has led to some religious groups being more outspoken in their opposition to atheistic trends within society. They see traditional social norms being undermined.

In particular, there has been an upsurge in both Islamic and Christian fundamentalism. The word *fundamentalism* has the meaning of unwavering attachment to a set of irreducible beliefs. As society is viewed as moving away from these fundamental beliefs, so these religious groups become more active in opposing the changes by seeking to influence law and public policy.

For instance, the Christian Right in the USA is an informal coalition of evangelical Protestants and Roman Catholics who seek to apply their understandings of the teachings of Christianity to politics and to public policy. They try to influence and motivate the electorate on particular social issues. The key social issues have been homosexuality, same-sex marriage, gender identity, abortion and embryonic stem-cell research.

In the UK, organisations such as The Christian Institute promote a conservative Christian viewpoint founded on a belief in biblical inerrancy. The Institute campaigns on social and moral issues and seeks to influence Parliament; on occasions, taking legal action.

The term *Islamic fundamentalism* has negative connotations as it is a term associated with groups such as ISIS, designated a terrorist organisation by the United Nations. However, like Christian fundamentalism, it can also apply to law-abiding groups who follow Islam and seek to influence society through social and political action.

Increase in religious apologists in the media

The rise of New Atheism has led to much public discussion about Christianity. As a result, it has given a platform for Christian apologists to reaffirm and represent the reasonableness of the Christian faith. It has allowed for a much fuller and more authentic public articulation of the nature and characteristics of Christianity. The Church seems to have been prompted to recover (revive) an apologetic tradition. The agenda of New Atheism has defined the areas that Christian apologists have had to focus on, such as an appeal to the natural sciences in support of faith.

Alister McGrath commented that argument does not create conviction, but the lack of it destroys belief. What seems to be proved may not be embraced; but what no one shows the ability to defend is quickly abandoned.

New Atheism has had a high profile in the media, particularly through the regular television, radio and internet appearances of Richard Dawkins. The large number of public and university debates featuring one or more of the 'Four Horsemen' has given a platform to various religious apologists, such as William Lane Craig debating with Christopher Hitchens. In particular, social media have opened the debate to a wider audience.

> ### Summary
> - The concept of atheism has a long tradition, traceable back to the time of the Ancient Greek philosophers. However, the meaning of the term has changed over time.
> - There are several key definitions of *atheism*, and implications associated with these definitions, in contemporary society.
> - The concept of New Atheism arose in response to the attacks of 11 September 2001 and triggered a series of high-profile publications and debates about the role of religion in society.
> - The result of New Atheism's public attacks on religion produced a response from religious apologists, and saw an increase in fundamental religious activity.

AO1 Activity

a Explain the key challenges to religious belief from New Atheism.

This helps with presenting a thorough and extensive knowledge and understanding of the topic area.

b On revision cards, record quotations from those who support and those who challenge New Atheism.

This helps with selecting relevant material to support an answer and provide an extensive range of views of scholars/schools of thought that are used accurately and effectively.

> **Specification content**
> The success of atheistic arguments against religious belief

> **This section covers AO2 content and skills**

Issues for analysis and evaluation

The success of atheistic arguments against religious belief

Possible line of argument	Critical analysis and evaluation
New Atheist ideas demonstrate that religion is irrational	New Atheism presents atheism as the only option for the thinking person. Richard Dawkins argues that religion is 'the root of all evil' because it goes against all scientific principles and promotes ignorance. It promotes 'non-thinking', and belief is not based on evidence. Rather, it is blind faith, and he sees religion as irrational. Religion should be abandoned since humanity has progressed and advanced in scientific knowledge.
Scientific explanations have replaced religious ones	New Atheism claims that advances in science have now eliminated God from any explanation required of the universe. Science answers our questions about the origin of life and the world without the need for a religious explanation.
Religion and science should not necessarily be viewed as conflicting with one another	The perceived failure of the arguments for God that Dawkins discusses raises doubts about God's existence. He sees religious faith as a delusion – a fixed false belief. However, such a view appears nonsense since there are many scientists who would claim to hold a religious faith and see no conflict between science and religion. Religion deals with ethics and spirituality, and science with empirical questions.
The negative behaviours of some religious believers do not in themselves disprove the existence of God	New Atheism's depiction of religion has been accused of being a caricature. It is claimed it misrepresents religion and religious teaching, choosing to focus only on those who are extreme and resort to violence. No matter how badly religious persons behave, it does not disprove God or religious teachings. It merely shows that some believers live inconsistently with such teachings. In fact, it could be argued that such actions demonstrate the truth of most religions that people have a sinful nature.
New Atheism is selective in the evidence it uses to attack religious belief	New Atheism also fails to be realistic about the darker side of atheism (e.g. Lenin and his attempts through violence to eradicate religious belief). It is estimated that atheist and secular regimes in the twentieth century alone have killed well over 100 million people – more than a hundred times the total deaths caused by Christians from the Crusades until the present. New Atheists also ignore the teaching of non-violence and forgiveness in world faiths.
It could be argued that New Atheism is successful due to its influence in contemporary culture	Perhaps we should measure the success of atheistic arguments, not by the persuasiveness of the academic/intellectual arguments, but by their influence in the public arena and everyday thinking. Certainly, New Atheism has enjoyed a high profile, and many feel it has diminished the relevance of religious authority in contemporary society.
Other atheists have challenged New Atheist arguments against religion	However, it is interesting that New Atheism has also come under attack from other atheists. For example, C.J. Werleman in *The New Atheist Threat: The Dangerous Rise of Secular Extremists* describes the New Atheists' uncritical devotion to science, their childish understanding of religion, their extreme Islamophobia and their intolerance of cultural diversity. It seems clear that atheism has not gone unchallenged in its arguments against religious beliefs.

> **AO2 Activity**
>
> a Evaluate three lines of argument from the critical analysis and evaluation of the success of atheistic arguments against religious belief. What are their strengths and weaknesses? Which line of argument is strongest?
>
> b Using the strongest line of argument, try to identify three key questions that might be asked – they could be critical, challenges, hypothetical or direct questions.

Specification content

The effectiveness of empirical approaches as critiques of Jungian views on religion

Exam practice

Sample question
Evaluate the extent to which religious responses to New Atheism have been successful.

Sample answer

This is a good introduction that provides a helpful overview of the key areas for focus in the evaluation to come.

New Atheism's attack on religious beliefs has not gone unchallenged. New Atheism argues that science has disproved God and religious believers are in denial about the advances of science to explain the universe. However, it is interesting that some of the voices challenging New Atheism have come from scientists themselves. Indeed, many scientists hold a religious belief and see no contradiction between science and religion. Professor Lennox, a Christian, has held many public debates with Dawkins, yet neither has been persuaded to change his view.

This paragraph presents a New Atheism argument and a response and then provides commentary on these.

New Atheism attacks faith, claiming it is a belief that is held in the total absence of evidence, while science is based on evidence and so compels us to accept the truth. Alister McGrath challenges this view of both faith and science. He accuses the New Atheists of failing to make the distinction between 'the total absence of supporting evidence' and 'the absence of totally supporting evidence'. Faith is acting on what you have good reason to believe is true. The evidence in science does not lead automatically to one conclusion. For example, scientists disagree about whether there is a single universe or a series of universes.

This paragraph examines the coherence of part of the argument.

However, it might be claimed that the truth of the scientific disagreement can be resolved in the future, while the religious claims cannot. In response, the religious person might argue that, if there is a God, then there is a possible eschatological verification or God may even make himself known on Earth or through religious experience.

The candidate explores an alternative line of reasoning, drawing on the work of contemporary religious thinkers and linking their thinking to recent scientific theory as a means of supporting their views.

Religious arguments for the existence of God point out that they are not proofs, nor were they ever claimed to be. They are *a posteriori* (reasoning based on observation) demonstrations of the coherence of faith. Nevertheless, religious believers such as the Christian William Lane Craig and Richard Swinburne defended the traditional arguments for God, showing them to be justifiable rather than proven. Alister McGrath also notes that the cosmology of the twenty-first century is much more sympathetic to Christian belief than a century ago.

Another major attack on religion from New Atheism has been the charge that religion is the root of all evil, especially regarding violence. The religious response has been to challenge the use of the word *religion* and to challenge the claim that religion causes violence. *Religion* is a false universal in that *religion* as such does not exist, but rather individual religions exist. The individual religions also have teachings about peace, non-violence and forgiveness as major aspects of their beliefs: for example, *ahimsa* in Asian faiths and forgiveness in Christianity and Islam. New Atheists focus just on a small group of extremists and label all with the same charge. For New Atheists, faith means the rejection of evidence-based thinking.

This paragraph takes a forensic view of the evidence, looking at the use of the word *religion* as well as examining the breadth of religious teachings that New Atheists have ignored.

The philosophy of religion has enjoyed a part revival in attempting to address some of the arguments the New Atheists have put forward. As well as a new defence of the traditional arguments for God by people such as Craig and Swinburne, philosophers have debated the issue of objective morality. Atheism seeks to remove any religious claims to moral authority and looks to science to guide us. But given that atheism views ethical standards as mere private notions of morality, they cannot appeal to any form of objective morality. Morality becomes more a case of individual personal taste. Therefore, religion has responded to atheism's attacks on morality and evil.

This paragraph presents a new line of reasoning, focusing on the perception of morality, making point and counterpoint.

If anything, the attacks by atheism seem to have led to a strengthening of religious belief, rather than a decline. Religious believers have been forced to address the charges, and it has provided an unexpected public platform and welcome interest in the whole area of religious beliefs. Faiths have had opportunities to express their beliefs and to justify them. You have to wonder whether it would have been more effective for atheism to say nothing, rather than engage in high-profile debate?

It does seem that the religious responses have been successful, since New Atheism has failed to deal the knockout blow to religion that it had sought. Instead, possibly because of its caricatures or possibly because of religious responses, New Atheism seems in decline. Many have come to see it as a form of intolerant fundamentalism that focused more on ridiculing opposition than engaging in intellectual debate.

The response now considers the evidence presented so far and draws the conclusion, following a pertinent question, that New Atheism may have inadvertently scored an 'own goal' in its efforts to discredit and weaken religious belief.

Evaluation

This is an effective and balanced response. It considers both sides of the argument and raises questions before putting forward a conclusion. The candidate makes accurate use both of terminology and of the views of different scholars/schools of thought.

Over to you

On the next page is part of an evaluation of whether or not religious responses to New Atheism are successful.

Respond to this argument by thinking of three key questions you could ask the writer that would challenge their view and further defend their argument.

Question

'Religious responses to New Atheism have been unsuccessful.' Evaluate this view.

(Q4, Component 2: Philosophy of Religion, WJEC, Summer 2018)

Evaluation

If anything, the attacks by atheism seem to have led to a strengthening of religious belief, rather than a decline. Religious believers have been forced to address the charges, and it has provided an unexpected public platform and welcome interest in the whole area of religious beliefs. Faiths have had opportunities to express their beliefs and to justify them. One wonders if it would have been more effective for atheism to say nothing, rather than engage in high-profile debate. Many books have appeared defending the rationality of religious belief. However, it is also true that traditional religion, if measured by attendance at worship, is declining, at least in the West, although there has been growing interest in Asian faiths.

It does seem that the religious responses have been successful, since New Atheism has failed to create the knockout blow to religion that it had sought. Instead, possibly because of its caricatures or possibly because of religious responses, New Atheism seems in decline. Many have come to see it as a form of intolerant fundamentalism that focused more on ridiculing opposition than engaging in intellectual debate.

Religious experience (1)

A: The nature of religious experience

Visions

We can define a **vision** as something someone sees, while awake or asleep, but not by ordinary sight. It is a supernatural or prophetic sight, and usually conveys a revelation or message of some form.

There are different types of vision. Like other types of religious experiences, various scholars have classified and grouped them differently. In the main, in terms of their nature, they have either **sensory** or **dream-based** qualities, and they can often contain an **intellectual** aspect.

Sensory visions

A vision has a sensory characteristic if it involves the recipient's senses. In other words, it is where external objects, sounds or figures appear before the recipient.

Sensory visions can be summarised in three ways:

1. Group visions are seen by more than one person. An example is the Angels of Mons where, during the First World War, a vision of St George and a phantom bowman halted the Kaiser's troops. Others claimed that angels had thrown a protective curtain around the British troops, saving them from disaster.

2. Sensory visions can also be individual; seen by only one person. An example is St Bernadette who claimed to have been instructed by an apparition of the Virgin Mary to dig a hole so that a healing spring would appear. The place was Lourdes.

3. A slight variation is that a sensory vision can be **corporeal** in nature: that is, have an object that is external and appears to be physical in nature, but is visible only to certain people. An example is appearances of angels.

Visions can also contain fantastic creatures or figures, such as Ezekiel's vision of four living creatures (Ezekiel 1:6–14). Each of the four had the face of a human being, and on the right side each had the face of a lion, and on the left the face of an ox; each also had the face of an eagle (Ezekiel 1:10).

Intellectual visions

A vision can have an intellectual quality if the vision brings the recipient(s) a message of inspiration, insight or instruction; it can also contain warnings!

The actual content of intellectual visions can be very varied. For example, there could be an image or event that provides a message, such as Peter's vision of a large sheet descending (Acts 10:9–16). The sheet contained all kinds of four-legged animals and reptiles and birds. A voice told Peter to kill and eat. When he refused, the voice told him that he should not call anything impure that God has made clean. Peter then realised that he could eat with a Gentile.

A vision could deliver a very specific message: for example, the final judgement and images of the end of the world in the Book of Revelation (Revelation 20:12–15). This describes the dead being judged according to what they had done. Anyone whose name was not found written in the book of life was thrown into the lake of fire (Revelation 20:15).

> **This section covers AO1 content and skills**

> **Specification content**
> The nature of religious experience with particular reference to visions – sensory; intellectual; dreams

> **Key terms**
> **vision:** the ability to 'see' something beyond normal experiences (e.g. the vision of an angel); such visions usually convey information or insight concerning a specific religious tradition
> **sensory:** a vision where external objects, sounds or figures convey knowledge and understanding to the recipient
> **dream-based:** in terms of visions, the unconscious state where knowledge or understanding is gained through a series of images or a dream-narrative, which would not normally be available to the individual in the conscious state
> **intellectual:** in terms of visions, what brings the recipient(s) knowledge and understanding
> **corporeal:** of a material nature, physical

T3 Religious experience (1)

Dream-based visions

Some dreams can involve visions where, in the unconscious state, individuals experience a series of images or a dream-narrative that would not normally be available to them in the conscious state.

Individual visions are often imaginative or dream-based internal visions, where the image is produced in the person's imagination and has no existence external to that person. An example is John's visions of strange creatures in the Book of Revelation. This also brought a message to understand. Therefore, in addition to having the specific quality of being dream-based, it can also be intellectual. Another example of a dream-based religious experience is when the wise men were warned in a dream not to return to Herod (Matthew 2:12).

A dream vision could contain religious figures. St Teresa of Avila's most famous vision was of an angel holding a long spear, with something like a fire at the end of the spear. This seemed to pierce her heart several times, and when it was withdrawn, it left her 'completely afire with a great love for God'.

These classifications of visions are interchangeable, and a particular vision may have more than one quality. The very nature of visions as religious experiences is wide ranging, and therefore we can classify them in more than one way.

Conversion

The word **conversion** means a 'change in direction' or 'turning around'. It is a process of change that alters a person's view of the world and their personal place in it.

Individual/communal conversion

An example of an individual conversion can be found in the account of a British singer-songwriter who, under the name of Cat Stevens, first rose to international fame in the 1960s. In the 1970s, following battles with mental health, substance addiction and recovery from a serious illness, Stevens felt his life had lost direction. In 1977, he was involved in a near-drowning incident and prayed that, if divine intervention would save his life, he would spend the rest of it dedicating himself to the service of God. Although Stevens was raised in a Christian context, it was following the reading of the Qur'an that he found himself drawn to the message of Islam. He converted soon after and changed his name to Yusuf Islam and, since then, has been a significant popular voice in promoting Islam through his music and humanitarian work.

Conversions are usually a personal experience, but not always. There are many examples of communal conversions. The classic example of communal conversion is in Acts of the Apostles, Chapter 2. The disciples were gathered in a room and received the Holy Spirit:

> When the day of Pentecost came, they were all together in one place. Suddenly a sound like the blowing of a violent wind came from Heaven and filled the whole house where they were sitting. They saw what seemed to be tongues of fire that separated and came to rest on each of them. All of them were filled with the Holy Spirit and began to speak in other tongues as the Spirit enabled them. (Acts 2:1–4)

Although this is a dramatic communal religious experience, it is what happened next that is also relevant here as a conversion experience. The Book of Acts goes on to describe how, being 'filled with the Holy Spirit', the disciples then went out into the streets of Jerusalem and began preaching, speaking in tongues, healing people and, because of their actions, converting people.

> **Specification content**
> The nature of religious experience with particular reference to conversion – individual/communal; sudden/gradual

>  **Key term**
> **conversion:** in a religious context, the change of state from one form of life to another

Paul's conversion on the way to Damascus. The Book of Acts describes several conversion experiences

Sudden/gradual conversion

The psychologist and philosopher William James looked at conversion from a psychological perspective. He noted that a conversion can be either gradual or sudden.

A gradual conversion is one that may take many years to happen, before the individual finds him- or herself fully accepting a belief system (or even rejecting a belief system).

Gradual conversions tend to be less dramatic than sudden conversions. There is some evidence suggesting that the length of time it takes for an individual to convert is related to the length of time that the conversion lasts for. That is, a gradual conversion is more likely to last, while a sudden conversion may not.

However, even sudden conversions may have had prior subconscious development. In other words, the individual may have considered ideas relating to the system he or she converted to for many years prior to the actual conversion event. One example of this can be found in the account of John Wesley. While already considering himself to be a Christian, he had a deep conversion experience when he felt his 'heart strangely warmed to faith'.

Nature of conversion experiences

A conversion can be from no religion to a faith. For example, Augustine, who became Bishop of Hippo in AD395 and was a key thinker in the development of the Christian Church, writes of his conversion, 'As I came to the end of the sentence, it was as though the light of confidence flooded into my heart and all the darkness of doubt was dispelled.'

Conversion can also be from one faith to another faith. For example, Sundar Singh, who was raised a devout Sikh, was dissatisfied with Sikhism and sought ultimate meaning in Hinduism and Christianity. Disenchanted with both, he decided to kill himself unless God revealed himself. Then he had a vision of Jesus and became an active Christian for the rest of his life.

T3 Religious experience (1)

A conversion is often volitional or self-surrendering. This means that the conversion might involve giving up personal will, either freely (*volitional*) or with resistance and an internal battle (*self-surrendering*).

A conversion can be passive or active, which means either the experience comes upon the individual somewhat unexpectedly without being deliberately sought, or someone might specifically seek a spiritual experience by going to an evangelistic meeting.

Sometimes a conversion can be a matter of intellectual persuasion. This involves conflict between two systems of thought, where the new one is seen as 'true'. It can also be one of moral transformation; this is where someone adopts a new moral approach to their life and decision making (for example, giving up eating animal products).

Mysticism

Overview

A departure from a logical, rational view of religion is the experience cited by religious believers of **mysticism**. The term has become somewhat loosely translated in recent times to refer to a range of experiences, often incorrectly linked to a vague kind of 'new-age' approach to religious practices and experiences. While there may well be veins of mystical experiences to be found within such areas, the history of mysticism is older by far.

Mystical experiences are described in the most ancient religious traditions that we know of. From ancient texts such as the Bhagavad Gita in Hinduism to accounts of medieval mystics such as Julian of Norwich and Meister Eckhart, mysticism has a rich and diverse history.

> **Specification content**
> The nature of religious experience with particular reference to mysticism – transcendent; ecstatic and unitive

> **Key term**
> **mysticism:** a religious experience where union with God or the absolute reality is sought or experienced

Mystical experiences occur in many different religious traditions

Nature of mystical experience

What then is the *nature* of mystical experience? To this question there are numerous responses, but certain themes run throughout all of them. Ed Miller regards it as 'the pursuit of a transcendent, unitive experience with the absolute reality' (*Questions that Matter*, 1995) and summarises the nature of mystical experience as:

- **transcendent**: not localisable in space or time
- **ineffable**: not expressible in language
- **noetic**: conveying illumination and/or truth
- **ecstatic**: filling the soul with bliss and/or peace
- **unitive**: uniting the soul with reality.

> **Key terms**
> **transcendent:** everything that lies beyond the everyday realm of the physical senses
> **ineffable:** something that a person cannot speak of as no words can describe the experience
> **noetic:** knowledge gained through mystical experience that would otherwise not be available to the recipient through ordinary means
> **ecstatic:** an overwhelming feeling of bliss or peace
> **unitive:** the feeling of complete oneness with the divine

Miller is not alone in using these particular terms to define mystical experiences. Commentators such as William James (who makes use of several of the categories above) and Walter Stace define mystical experiences in different ways, but admit to a series of common features that all such experiences are said to have.

Religious mystics often speak of a mystical ascent, which is in some ways similar to the Platonic view of reality, where there is, effectively, a ladder or staircase. These steps begin in the earthly, mundane world but, with regular practice and divine assistance, individuals can transcend their own reality and ascend this ladder, to gain unity with the ultimate reality. It is often described metaphorically as a journey from darkness to light.

Transcendent mystical experience

Transcendent mysticism is associated with the mystical experiences that take the practitioner 'beyond' the realm of the normal everyday experience. Transcendental realities are often described in language that refers to 'other worldly' or 'different dimensions', both of which are vague descriptions of a feeling of moving beyond this physical realm to the realm of the 'other' – the realm of the spirit.

Such experiences include other types of mystical experience, such as ecstasy and unitive experience, as the believer feels that he or she has become one with the transcendent reality, while effectively disengaging for a while from the temporal and physical world of the empirical senses.

Example of transcendent mystical experience: Sufism

Most religious traditions have aspects of transcendental mysticism within them. One of the most notable of these is Sufism, the mystical group within Islam that focuses on divine union with Allah through meditation, dance and other mystic practices. Rumi, a thirteenth-century Persian poet and arguably the most famous Islamic mystic, was associated with this tradition.

Rumi believed that all individuals have a yearning within them that is due to the feeling of separation that all beings instinctively feel. He recognised that, while Allah was both high in the heavens and closer to man than his own jugular vein, humankind was still separated from Allah. Only by spiritual purification through love could union with God (*tawhid*) be truly achieved. Rumi believed that the human spirit was designed for the singular underlying purpose of drawing into a deeper relationship with God.

He developed the practice known as *Sema*, a sacred dance where Sufis constantly turn on the left foot. The turning, according to Rumi, is a metaphor for 'a blessed state of every fibre of an individual's being turning on the axis of the merciful and compassionate creator and sustainer of all things'. This turning is meant to generate a spiritual ascent to Allah.

'The Song of the Reed Flute'

The message of yearning to be united with Allah forms the central message of Rumi's poem 'The Song of the Reed Flute'. Here, Rumi invites the listener to understand the secret of human existence by 'hearkening to the message hidden in the plaintive tones of the reed flute'. If, reasons Rumi, the most basic purpose of the human spirit is to put a person in a relationship with the divine, then all other relationships within the created order, especially those with other human beings, are mystical gateways into a closer relationship with the creator.

This highly significant part of Rumi's mystical experience was played out in his own relationship with his mentor, Shams. He noted how, through this close relationship, he felt that he became closer in his relationship with Allah. Rumi believed poetry, music and dance were all direct doorways to the divine and, due to these convictions, he founded the Mevlevi order of Sufis, famous for their Whirling Dervishes.

Whirling Dervishes practising Sema

Ecstatic mystical experience

The ecstatic mystical experience is well documented and discussed in the work of a wide range of mystics, philosophers and scholars from various traditions.

Teresa of Avila regards ecstasy as the suspension of the exterior senses: 'One perceives that the natural heat of the body is perceptibly lessened; the coldness increases, though accompanied with exceeding joy and sweetness' (Teresa, *Autobiography*).

Others in the Christian tradition describe it as the closest a mortal being can get to the feeling of what it must be like for departed souls to be in the presence of God. Followers of Eastern religious traditions also describe feelings of mystical ecstasy – often centred around intense meditative practices such as those in the later stages of Vipissana meditation in Buddhism and Yogic practices in Hinduism.

Broadly speaking, ecstasy can be described as having two effective states:
- an interior sensation, where the mind becomes utterly focused on a subject (usually religious in nature)
- the physical suspension of the normal activity of the senses, such that individuals appear to be in a trance-like state in which they are not easily disturbed. However, upon wakening, most are able to describe, in some measure, the intensity of their experiences, albeit in highly symbolic language.

Unitive mystical experience

The concept of union involves removing the separation between the individual and God. Thus, the unitive type of mystical experience tends to cover a range of similar types of experiences, rather than describing a single identifiable experience.

Many Christian mystics have claimed such experiences, including St Bernard of Clairvaux, the French Cistercian abbot, who described the experience as a 'mutuality of love'. The medieval German mystic (and student of Meister Eckhart) Henry Suso stated that the experience was like a man who:

> ... is entirely lost in God, has passed into him, and has become one spirit with him in all respects, like a drop of water which is poured into a large portion of wine. Just as this is lost to itself, and draws to itself and into itself the taste and colour of the wine, so it likewise happens to those who are in complete possession of blessedness. (Suso, *The Little Book of Truth*)

Prayer within the mystical tradition

Teresa of Avila

Born on 15 March 1515 in Spain, her family inspired the young Teresa to take her religious life seriously and, in 1535, she joined an order of Carmelite nuns. After a severe illness left Teresa partially paralysed for three years, she became somewhat disillusioned with her religious practices, especially **prayer**. However, a vision of the 'sorely wounded Christ' was to re-energise Teresa's spiritual journey and inspire her to write her great works on prayer.

Teresa's approach to mystical experience was through her four stages of prayer. She believed that true union with God could be achieved only by intense concentration and disciplining oneself through a life of prayer that would, by a series of stages, allow a person to reach that union:

> To say something, then, of the early experiences of those who are determined to pursue this blessing and to succeed in this enterprise ... it is in these early stages that their labour is hardest, for it is they themselves who labour and the Lord Who gives the increase. In the other degrees of prayer the chief thing is fruition, although, whether at the beginning, in the middle or at the end of the road, all have their crosses, different as these may be. For those who follow Christ must take the way which He took, unless they want to be lost. (Teresa, *Autobiography*)

The garden metaphor

Teresa firmly believed that it was not possible for an individual to achieve that union by him- or herself; only through God's grace could a person move through the various stages:

> The beginner must think of himself as of one setting out to make a garden in which the Lord is to take His delight, yet in soil most unfruitful and full of weeds. His Majesty uproots the weeds and will set good plants in their stead. Let us suppose that this is already done – that a soul has resolved to practise prayer and has already begun to do so. We have now, by God's help, like good gardeners, to make these plants grow, and to water them carefully, so that they may not perish, but may produce flowers which shall send forth great fragrance to give refreshment to this Lord of ours, so that He may often come into the garden to take His pleasure and have His delight among these virtues. (Teresa, *Autobiography*)

Teresa is often associated with teaching on the various stages of prayer. She compares these stages to the ways in which a garden can be watered:

1. *Drawing water from a well.* This involves great physical labour and is not very efficient.

> **Specification content**
> The nature of religious experience with particular reference to prayer – types and stages of prayer according to Teresa of Avila

> **Key term**
> **prayer:** in simple terms, communication with the divine

Teresa of Avila

2. *Waterwheel and buckets.* Less constant physical labour is needed here, but it still requires a machine to be built and placed. It is more effective than using the well.
3. *A stream.* This waters the ground much better, for it 'saturates it more thoroughly and there is less need to water it often'. The gardener has less work to do here.
4. *Heavy rain.* This is the most efficient method as it requires no intervention from the gardener, and it waters the entire area of the garden.

The waterwheel as a metaphor for prayer

The interior castle

While her definitions of prayer from her autobiography are highly significant, many observers believe that the real insight into mystical experience is found in Teresa's final work: *The Interior Castle*.

Moving on from her analogy of a watered garden, Teresa now considers the soul to be like a castle that contains seven suites or mansions. The first three mansions refer to the type of prayer that Teresa speaks about in detail in earlier works, such as her *Autobiography*. These prayers, while allowing the individual to come closer to God, do not give the same level of union that can eventually be gained. This union is to be found within the fourth to the seventh mansions, where Teresa represents the various degrees of mystical prayer.

The fourth mansion: the Prayer of Quiet

The first of these, found in the fourth mansion, is the Prayer of Consolations from God, better known as the Prayer of Quiet. Teresa describes this as a state where the human will is completely captivated by God's love. This has the individual operating on the mystical level and, as such, experiencing peace and spiritual delight. Sometimes the experience is so intense that the individual can faint or appear semi-comatose – St Teresa refers to this state as a 'sleep of the faculties' (*faculties* is an alternative term for the senses).

The fifth mansion: the Prayer of Simple Union

Within the fifth mansion, Teresa describes the next stage as the Prayer of Simple Union: 'God implants himself in the interior of the soul in such a way that, when it returns to itself, it cannot possibly doubt that God has been in it and it has been in God.' Teresa is stating that, at this stage of prayer, the individual is convinced that he or she has been with God and that he has been with them.

The sixth mansion: Spiritual Marriage

The sixth mansion contains the longest of Teresa's mystical descriptions. It is occasionally disputed as to precisely what she was describing, but it is commonly known as the stage of Spiritual Marriage. The main experiences associated with this stage can include rapture, feelings of painful longing, spiritual ecstasy and visions. The overriding characteristic is the sense of wanting to be able to spend every possible moment alone with the divine 'spouse', and the complete rejection of all things that can get in the way of such moments.

The seventh mansion: Mystical Marriage

The seventh and final mansion is, for Theresa, the highest possible state of prayer that is achievable on Earth. The soul is regarded as having reached a state of transforming union or, as it is more commonly known, the stage of Mystical Marriage. It is the stage where the individual feels complete unity with the divine, to the extent of intuitively feeling an intimate and perceptive awareness, knowledge and understanding of the person of the divine.

> **Summary**
>
> ★ Religious experiences can occur in a variety of forms, including visions, conversion, mysticism and prayer, and there are examples of these in the majority of known religious traditions.
>
> ★ Visions can be sensory, intellectual or dream-based, whereas conversions can occur both individually and communally.
>
> ★ Mysticism and mystical experiences can be defined in various ways, and the work of William James and Ed Miller has helped to clarify some of these.
>
> ★ Prayer within the mystical tradition is explained through the work of St Teresa of Avila, who describes various stages and states of prayer in both her garden and mansion metaphors.

> **AO1 Activity**
>
> **a** Explain Teresa's examples in her studies on prayer.
>
> This helps with presenting a thorough and extensive knowledge and understanding of the topic area.
>
> **b** On revision cards, summarise the key features of visions, conversion and mysticism. Use relevant examples to support each of these.
>
> This helps with prioritising and selecting a core set of points to develop an answer and with making accurate use of specialist language and vocabulary in context.

> This section covers AO2 content and skills

> **Specification content**
> The impact of religious experiences upon religious belief and practice

Issues for analysis and evaluation

The impact of religious experiences upon religious belief and practice

Possible line of argument	Critical analysis and evaluation
Religious experiences may not be physical but can still have impact	Some may argue that religious experiences are not the same as sense experiences. God is not material. God does not have a definite location. How would you recognise it was God that you were experiencing? However, just as people are known to each other by a kind of awareness and understanding of the mind rather than through our physical body, so in the same way people claim to experience God, who is non-physical, and this has great impact upon both religious belief and practice.
The act of conversion is a demonstrable way of proving the impact of religious experiences	A way of assessing the impact of religious experiences upon religious belief and practice is with the experience of conversion. A conversion essentially initiates two things: firstly, the belief in God's existence or the truth of another religion; and, secondly, a change of behaviour in the new convert. For example, Augustine, who became Bishop of Hippo in AD395 and was a key thinker in the development of the Christian Church, converted from atheism to believer and had a major impact on the belief and practice of others. In the same way, Sundar Singh, who was raised a devout Sikh, had a vision of Jesus and became an active Christian for the rest of his life.
Richard Swinburne's principles support the idea that religious experiences have impact	Swinburne has proposed the principles of credulity and testimony. These state that it is reasonable to believe that the world is probably as we experience it to be. He argues that other people's testimony of religious experiences provide good reason to believe that God exists. Many people, on the basis of apparent direct experiences of God, take it that God exists. This also has impact upon others, who may base their belief in God upon the acceptance of another's religious experience.
The work of William James, although subjective, supports the idea that religious experiences have impact	William James was particularly interested in the effects of religious experience on people's lives and believed that the validity of the experience rests upon the effects it produces. He saw that the effects of these experiences were powerful and positive. They changed the lives of communities and individuals so much that he saw this as powerful evidence for both a belief in God and the validity of such belief. However, some argue that James is too subjective as he focuses more on the truth of the experience for the individual.
There is a variety of impacts from religious experiences	Overall, religious experience inevitably impacts on belief and practice, but there is a range of impacts from just an individual to worldwide communities, in the case of religious founders.
The impact of religious experiences is limited	In conclusion, it is probably best to admit that, while religious experience does inevitably have a powerful impact upon religious belief and practice, its impact is limited to those who believe and cannot extend to providing sound and firm philosophical proof that the object of that religious experience is objectively real.

> **AO2 Activity**
>
> a Evaluate three lines of argument from the critical analysis and evaluation of the impact of religious experiences upon religious belief and practice. What are their strengths and weaknesses? Which line of argument is strongest?
>
> b Using the strongest line of argument, try to identify three key questions that might be asked – they could be critical, challenge, hypothetical or direct questions.

Exam practice

Sample question
Evaluate whether different types of religious experience can be accepted as equally valid in communicating religious teachings and beliefs.

Sample answer

The main issue here is whether or not all religious experiences have the same value for communicating or evidencing religious belief and specific teachings. There are so many different types, all of which have varying impact. In addition, as regards the religious teachings, it could be argued that the messages, visions, information and beliefs apparently transmitted in religious experiences are so diverse and contradictory that it is impossible for the majority of religious experiences to be real and accurate, and therefore a valid tool for communicating religious truths.

For example, in Zen Buddhism, religious experiences do not lead to Buddhists' claims of a creator god, but meditation makes you fully in touch with the true nature of reality. Opposed to this is the claim of some Christians that they meet with God or Jesus in their religious experiences. It appears, then, that religious experiences could suggest that God, or the impersonal spiritual experience, is relative to, and dependent upon, cultural beliefs that we understand and interpret.

However, accounts of different experiences do not mean they are all in error. Maybe only one religion is correct, so the other religious experiences are false, but those of that one religion are true. This is more an internal debate between religions. Some may say that their religious experience allows them to have a pluralistic outlook, for example, Hick and Gandhi. Others may have a more exclusivist approach and claim that their religious experience is the single truth.

Aside from this problem, there is another issue. This is the key problem of ineffability. Many religious experiences are beyond verbal description. There are no words that can describe the experience, so it is not possible for others to understand. The experience is subjective and private; it is not open to anyone else. The experience is personal; it is not possible to understand fully unless we have the experience. If all this is true, then how can ineffable religious experiences be as valid in communicating or evidencing religious belief and specific teachings as other forms of religious experience?

Equally, we should consider the primary purpose of a religious experience. Is it for the individual alone? Is it meant only to deepen faith, or is it there to be used as an exemplar for teaching others and sharing the experience? What if others misunderstand the experience? Does it demean its original value for the recipient? Certain types of religious experience may be considered 'superior' to others within a faith tradition, for the alleged value they may have in communicating or consolidating a particular belief or faith tradition, thereby potentially making those who do not experience this feel inferior or unworthy.

Despite this, it may be safe to conclude that religious experiences are a valid way of communicating or evidencing religious belief and specific teachings for religious believers. However, the real question of whether or not they all have an equal impact for this purpose is quite clearly dependent upon the type of religious experience it is.

Specification content
Whether different types of religious experience can be accepted as equally valid in communicating religious teachings and beliefs

News reporter
This is a good introduction that provides a helpful overview of the key areas for focus in the evaluation to come.

Detective
This paragraph presents relevant evidence showing the difficulty in coming to an agreed view on the issue.

Explorer
This paragraph presents an alternative line of reasoning, referring to relevant examples to support this.

Detective

Critical thinker
The candidate explores another line of reasoning, drawing on relevant evidence to show the complexity of providing a single definitive response.

Philosopher
This paragraph poses a series of questions to explore the issue further.

Judge
The response then considers the evidence presented so far and draws a conclusion, while recognising that the issue is dependent on a variety of factors and therefore can have a variety of outcomes.

Evaluation

This is an effective and balanced response. It considers both sides of the argument and raises questions before putting forward a conclusion. The candidate makes accurate use of both evidence and examples.

Over to you

Below is a list of indicative content that could be used in response to a question requiring an evaluation of whether visions are the most effective way of communicating religious teachings and beliefs. The problem is that it is not a very full list and needs completing!

As a group, consider what is missing from the list. You need to add at least six points (three in support and three against) that you would use to improve the list, and/or give more detail to each point that is already in the list. Remember, it is how you use the points that is the most important factor.

Apply the principles of evaluation by making sure that you:
- identify issues clearly
- present accurate views of others, making sure that you comment on the views presented
- reach an overall personal judgement.

Then, as a group, agree on your final list and write out your new list of indicative content, remembering the principles of explaining with evidence and/or examples. Put this list in order of how you would present the information in an essay. You will then have your own plan for an ideal answer.

You may add more of your own suggestions, but try to negotiate as a group and prioritise the most important things to add.

Question

'Visions are the most effective way of communicating religious teachings and beliefs.' Evaluate this view.

(Q3b, Component 2: Philosophy of Religion, WJEC, Summer 2022)

List of indicative content

In support:
- Visions are more effective than having the information second-hand.
- They begin and/or deepen commitment to religious belief and practice in a unique way.
- Your added content …

Against:
- Religious upbringing has a greater impact.
- Sacred writings are more important than religious experiences from belief and practice.
- Your added content …

B: Mystical experience

William James' four characteristics of mystical experience

William James' *Varieties of Religious Experience* (1902) is regarded as one of the most significant and influential studies of religion in the twentieth century. Among other subjects, James (1842–1910) details a classification of mysticism within Lectures 16 and 17 of the work. These are notable observations of mystical experience, and no serious study of the subject would omit reflecting on James' contributions.

Explanations of the classifications follow in James' own words (all quotations come from James' *The Varieties of Religious Experience*):

Ineffability

> Ineffability – The handiest of the marks by which I classify a state of mind as mystical is negative. The subject of it immediately says that it defies expression, that no adequate report of its contents can be given in words. It follows from this that its quality must be directly experienced; it cannot be imparted or transferred to others. In this peculiarity mystical states are more like states of feeling than like states of intellect. No one can make clear to another who has never had a certain feeling, in what the quality or worth of it consists. One must have musical ears to know the value of a symphony; one must have been in love one's self to understand a lover's state of mind. Lacking the heart or ear, we cannot interpret the musician or the lover justly, and are even likely to consider him weak-minded or absurd. The mystic finds that most of us accord to his experiences an equally incompetent treatment.

James notes that the main characteristic of a mystical experience is often ineffability. That is to say, the experience defies description – it cannot be put into words. Mystics such as Teresa of Avila, Eckhart, Rumi and others also mention this characteristic. It underlines how profound, how deep, how meaningful the experience is for the person or persons undergoing it. The very value of the experience, according to James, is that it has to be lived through – to be directly experienced – to fully appreciate it, as words are not adequate. This means that no description can ever pass on to another person what the experience was like. For James, the value of the mystical experience was being in the experience, and there can be no substitute for this.

Of course, the very nature of this ineffability also presents a challenge, in terms of being able to prove its authenticity to someone else. James recognises this, but states that, just because it cannot be 'proved', this does not reduce its value. For James, it has more to do with the deficiency of empiricists (those who look for knowledge based on directly observable physical evidence) than with any deficiency of the mystic, that the experience cannot be described.

Noetic quality

> Noetic quality – Although so similar to states of feeling, mystical states seem to those who experience them to be also states of knowledge. They are states of insight into depths of truth unplumbed by the discursive intellect. They are illuminations,

> This section covers AO1 content and skills

> **Specification content**
> William James' four characteristics of mystical experience: ineffable, noetic, transient and passive

> **" Key quote "**
>
> One may say truly, I think, that personal religious experience has its root and centre in mystical states of consciousness.
>
> (William James, *The Varieties of Religious Experience*)

Ineffability – where you don't have the words to describe the experience

Mystical experiences that have a noetic quality mean the recipient gains knowledge

revelations, full of significance and importance, all inarticulate though they remain; and as a rule they carry with them a curious sense of authority for after-time.

The gaining of a special kind of knowledge, or insight, is another hallmark of the work of mystics down the ages, and this is what James refers to when he considers the *noesis* (the gaining of knowledge) of the mystics' experiences. This means that the outcome of the mystical experience for the recipients is that they are now in possession of knowledge that previously they were not and, for many religious believers, this knowledge cannot be obtained through any other medium than mystical religious experience.

Transiency

Transiency – Mystical states cannot be sustained for long. Except in rare instances, half an hour, or at most an hour or two, seems to be the limit beyond which they fade into the light of common day. Often, when faded, their quality can but imperfectly be reproduced in memory; but when they recur it is recognised; and from one recurrence to another it is susceptible of continuous development in what is felt as inner richness and importance.

In the third characteristic, James discusses the mystical experience in terms of its length and disproportionate effects. He states that it is quite common for mystical experiences to be brief, in terms of the time that they take to occur. However, he notes that, while the experience may be brief (**transient**), the effect of it often lasts far longer than the experience itself – often due to the intensity of the mystical encounter. For the recipient, the consequences of a brief mystical experience may well be lifelong.

> ### ● Key term
>
> **transient:** an experience that is short-lived yet has far-reaching and/or long-lasting consequences

Passivity

Passivity – Although the oncoming of mystical states may be facilitated by preliminary voluntary operations, as by fixing the attention, or going through certain bodily performances, or in other ways which manuals of mysticism prescribe; yet when the characteristic sort of consciousness once has set in, the mystic feels as if his own will were in abeyance, and indeed sometimes as if he were grasped and held by a superior power. This latter peculiarity connects mystical states with certain definite phenomena of secondary or alternative personality, such as prophetic speech, automatic writing, or the mediumistic trance. When these latter conditions are well pronounced, however, there may be no recollection whatever of the phenomenon and it may have no significance for the subject's usual inner life, to which, as it were, it makes a mere interruption. Mystical states, strictly so called, are never merely interruptive. Some memory of their content always remains, and a profound sense of their importance. They modify the inner life of the subject between the times of their recurrence.

The fourth and final classification notes the important feature that the experience tends to be 'done to' recipients (that is, they are **passive** recipients) and that, even when the recipient goes searching for the experience, the actual moment itself is governed by a being or force external to the will of the mystic. James provides several examples of mystics behaving in a certain way or completing certain actions that appear to be beyond what they could normally do – as if something else is 'controlling' them in either their speech or their actions. James also notes that these events can significantly change individuals and their lives, even though they may not be able to recall exactly what it was that they were doing while undergoing the mystical experience.

Rudolf Otto

The human predisposition for religious experience

Otto's approach, in his *The Idea of the Holy* (1917), was to look at the aspects of religious experience that were beyond the scope of rational and empirical reasoning. He was interested in how religious experiences affected people. Human beings seemed to have a predisposition for religious experience. He focused on how these religious experiences made people feel, rather than on the actual events themselves.

Otto drew on the history of religion, as he was familiar with it. Combining it with his interest in **anthropology** and **naturalism**, he produced an investigation into the subjective field of religious and mystical experiences.

Concept of the numinous

For Otto, the word *holy* had several wide-ranging connotations, not all of which he found helpful when trying to describe feelings in a religious or mystical experience. Therefore, to describe the feelings that people had as a result of their experience with a supernatural or divine power, he coined the term *numinous*.

This word comes from the Latin word *numen*, which refers to a supernatural divine power. This sets it apart from the ethical and moral meanings that the word *holy* may also have. Thus, individuals who experience the numinous feel the presence of a supernatural or divine power as part of their religious or mystical experience.

Otto considered that the numinous was a state of mind that was unique, and unrelated to any other. He stated that this meant it was therefore not possible to adequately define it. Otto believed that it was only by experiencing the numinous that an individual could properly come to a realisation of what it meant. It could not be taught, it could only be '...evoked, awakened in the mind; as everything that comes "of the spirit" must be awakened.' (*The Idea of the Holy*, Otto, 1923, OUP)

Mysterium tremendum et fascinans

Otto recognised that, as these numinous experiences were different from everyday experiences, they could not be described in everyday, rational ways. Instead, he said that they were non-rational events. Otto is not stating that experiences of the numinous were irrational; rather, they were non-rational in the sense of not being definable in rational terms.

For Otto, these numinous experiences were 'the deepest and most fundamental element' that religious believers could undergo. To sum this up, he called these experiences *mysterium tremendum et fascinans*.

Mystical experiences are usually characterised by their passive quality

Key terms

passive: in the context of mysticism, where the mystical experience is 'done to' the recipient – it is not instigated by the individual or group, but is instead due to some kind of external force or influence

anthropology: the study of human beings, their culture and social development

naturalism: something that arises from real life or the world of nature

Specification content

Rudolf Otto – the concept of the numinous; *mysterium tremendum*; the human predisposition for religious experience

A numinous experience?

T3 Religious experience (1)

Otto described it thus:

> The feeling of it may at times come sweeping like a gentle tide, pervading the mind with a tranquil mood of deepest worship. It may pass over into a more set and lasting attitude of the soul, continuing, as it were, thrillingly vibrant and resonant, until at last it dies away and the soul resumes its 'profane', non-religious mood of everyday experience. It may burst in sudden eruption up from the depths of the soul with spasms and convulsions, or lead to the strangest excitements, to intoxicated frenzy, to transport, and to ecstasy. It has its wild and demonic forms and can sink to an almost grisly horror and shuddering. It has its crude barbaric antecedents and early manifestations, and again it may be developed into something beautiful and pure and glorious. It may become the hushed, trembling, and speechless humidity of the creature in the presence of - whom or what? In the presence of that which is a Mystery inexpressible and above all creatures. (*The Idea of the Holy*, Otto, 1923, OUP)

The *mysterium tremendum* was therefore a 'profound and deeply felt' religious experience. This showed that the numinous was an expression of religious awe and wonder through encounter with the divine.

Otto described how participants in numinous experiences may experience any of the following states of emotion: *awefulness* (a sort of profound unease), *overpoweringness* (inspires a feeling of humility), *energy* or *urgency* (compelling), *wholly other* (totally outside normal experience) and *fascination* (causes the subject of the experience to be caught up in it).

Summary

- William James wrote one of the most influential academic texts on mystical religious experiences.
- He categorised them as having four key characteristics: ineffability, noetic quality, transiency and passivity.
- Rudolf Otto looked at the aspects of mystical religious experience that were beyond the scope of rational and empirical reasoning.
- He coined the terms *numinous* and *mysterium tremendum* to help provide a way of describing these mystical religious experiences.

AO1 Activity

a Outline William James' four characteristics of mysticism. Then, in pairs, take turns testing each other on the four definitions.

This helps with presenting an extensive and relevant response that answers the specific demands of the question set. In an examination situation, it can be easy to mix up ideas, terms and definitions – so regular memory testing with a partner can help avoid this.

b Taking an example from the world religion in your course of study, record how a religious experience in that tradition might be considered 'numinous'.

Use this example in any answer that addresses Otto's concept of the numinous.

This helps with prioritising and selecting a core set of points to develop an answer and with making use of accurate and relevant knowledge and understanding of religion and belief.

> **Specification content**
> The adequacy of James' four characteristics in defining mystical experience

> **This section covers AO2 content and skills**

Issues for analysis and evaluation

The adequacy of James' four characteristics in defining mystical experience

Possible line of argument	Critical analysis and evaluation
Are the features that James identifies adequate for defining mystical experience?	William James' characteristics of mystical experience have been the standard for classification of the features of a mystical experience now for many years. Many scholars have used, debated, accepted, challenged or developed them. The issue really is: are the features James identified adequate in the light of the work of other scholars?
The adequacy of each characteristic	James identified four features of mystical experiences. ● The first feature is *ineffability*. This means that no adequate account of the experience can be given in words. It defies expression. Phrases such as 'the dissolution of the personal ego' are empty to those who have not experienced such things. ● A second feature is their *noetic* quality: that is, apparent insight into the depths of truths unobtainable by the intellect alone. Mystical experiences have a force of certainty and reality. ● Mystical experiences are also *transient*, which means that the states cannot be maintained for long periods of time. Though the states are remembered, they are imperfectly recalled. They usually leave the recipient with a profound sense of the importance of the experience. ● Finally, mystical experiences have the feature of *passivity*, whereby there is a sense of feeling that the individual is taken over by a superior power.
Otto's work highlights the adequacy of James' characteristics	These all appear to be perfectly sound, but whether or not they are adequate depends upon whether any other scholarly observations have added, superseded or challenged them. If we compare Otto's numinous classification of religious experience, we can see that really it adds nothing new to James' characteristics of mystical experience. Otto identified a number of elements, such as *awefulness* (a sort of profound unease), *overpoweringness* (inspiring a feeling of humility), *energy* or *urgency* (compelling), *wholly other* (totally outside normal experience) and *fascination* (causing the subject of the experience to be caught up in it). Most of these are really elaborations upon, or alternative definitions for, James' four features.
The work of Happold also shows the adequacy of James' characteristics	In a way, we can say the same of the philosopher F.C. Happold, who identified another three characteristics of mystical experience: consciousness of the oneness of everything; a sense of timelessness; and the idea that the ego is not the real 'I' but that there is something that lies behind the usual experience of self. These appear to have similarities with both numinous and James' four characteristics.
There are different perspectives on mystical experience that James' characteristics do not address	However, if we look at the work of the Italian medieval theologian and philosopher St Bonaventure, we can see a different perspective on mystical experience that really focuses on the process of mysticism rather than on analysing its common features. Bonaventure identified three stages of a mystical experience: the purgative stage, when the mystic is purified and prepared for the experience through meditation; the illuminative stage, when the mystic is affected both cognitively (intellectually) and emotionally; and the unitive stage, when the mystic gains a continuing union with God.

Possible line of argument	Critical analysis and evaluation
James' characteristics are adequate but not definitive	In conclusion, it appears that James' four characteristics of mystical experience are adequate as they have stood the test of time. Nonetheless, this does not mean that they are definitive and, as we have seen, there are other more elaborate articulations of mystical experience.

AO2 Activity

a Analyse three possible conclusions that could be drawn from the critical analysis and evaluation of the adequacy of James' four characteristics in defining mystical experience. What are their strengths and weaknesses? Which conclusion is strongest?

b Using the strongest conclusion, select three lines of argument that you would use to support this conclusion. Try to explain why you have selected these.

Specification content
The adequacy of Otto's definition of *numinous*

Exam practice

Sample question
Evaluate the adequacy of Otto's definition of *numinous*.

Sample answer

News reporter
This is a good introduction that provides an overview of the issue for the evaluation to come.

Rudolph Otto, in his book *The Idea of the Holy*, tried to identify and describe what made a religious experience uniquely religious, as opposed to just an ordinary experience. The main issue here is not just Otto's definition, but really the basis of that definition and the implications that it brings. Rudolph Otto said of the numinous experience, 'there is no religion in which it does not live as the innermost core and without it no religion would be worthy of the name'. In other words, the claim of the numinous is that it is the one essential and valid religious experience, as opposed to just an experience.

Detective
This paragraph presents further evidence, relevant to the topic, highlighting the individual and personal as key to appreciating fully the impact of a 'numinous' experience.

Central to this investigation, however, was the underlying assumption and conviction that a personal encounter with God is for every religious believer. Again, Otto was convinced that everyone could have a personal encounter with the spiritual or the divine, and that it does not necessarily have to involve overt dramatic sensory or dream experiences. Otto's numinous was a very individual and personal experience.

Detective
This paragraph further develops the argument and makes use of relevant terminology to explain the point accurately.

Despite this, Otto also held that its dramatic nature lay in what the religious experience invoked within the individual; namely, that the *mysterium tremendum* also prompted the *fascinans* – that is, an intense fascination with the experience itself. This then provided a platform for a religious believer to interpret the world around them.

Critical thinker
This paragraph challenges the argument presented so far, and shows the technical aspect of the word *numinous* lacking any specific detail about either the experience or the divine.

The problems with this account of the numinous is that it has very little to say about the nature of God or the specific details of a specific religious belief. It provides no instruction or clear explanation other than a sense of awareness of the 'other'. Indeed, Otto himself held that God cannot be known through the senses or through the process of rational thought; God was 'wholly other'. Other objections include that it is too vague as regards how any theological ideas could follow from the experience due to the *fascinans*, as Otto held. In this sense, it appears limiting, especially as there are well-documented types of experience that are entirely different from the numinous.

Another criticism suggests that Otto reduces the concept of religious experience to a simple 'feeling', when there is clearly much more to religious experiences than that. But the most powerful critique of Otto's numinous really involves what he set out to demonstrate – that every individual can experience the divine. The real question is, however, due to such a general and diluted description of the religious experience as the numinous, how do we know that God is the object of this experience?

In conclusion, it would seem that Otto's numinous is adequate in describing what some, if not all, religious experiences may 'feel like', but beyond that it has clear limitations, as the criticisms above attest. It really tells us nothing more. However, it may be possible to use the definition of numinous in conjunction with other terms describing religious experiences as a basis for study. This may be as far as its adequacy extends.

The candidate further examines the coherence of the argument and poses a pertinent question as a result of this examination.

The response now considers the evidence presented so far and draws the conclusion that, while the term has its uses, it also has its limitations, both of which affect how far it can be considered 'adequate'.

Evaluation

This is an effective and balanced evaluation. It considers both sides of the argument and is clearly a response that successfully identifies and thoroughly addresses the issues the question raises.

Over to you

Below are some conclusions that could be drawn in response to a question that asks you to evaluate whether William James' four characteristics adequately define mystical experience.

Consider each of the conclusions and collect evidence and examples to support each argument from the AO1 and AO2 material you have studied in relation to James' four characteristics of mystical experience. Select the conclusion that you think is most convincing and explain why it is so. Now contrast this with the weakest conclusion in the list, justifying your argument with clear reasoning and evidence.

Question

'James' four characteristics adequately define mystical experience.' Evaluate this view.

(Q3b, Component 2: Philosophy of Religion, WJEC, Summer 2022)

Conclusions

1. James' four characteristics are adequate for defining mystical experience.
2. James' four characteristics in defining mystical experience are just one of many different ways of studying mystical experience.
3. James' four characteristics are more than adequate in defining mystical experience because they are the standard set in the study of mystical experiences.
4. James' four characteristics in defining mystical experience have been better developed and expressed by others.
5. James' four characteristics in defining mystical experience are adequate but not definitive.

> **This section covers AO1 content and skills**

> **Specification content**
>
> Challenges to the objectivity and authenticity of religious experience: with reference to Caroline Franks Davis (description-related, subject-related and object-related challenges). Claims of religious experience rejected on grounds of misunderstanding; claims delusional – possibly related to substance misuse; fantastical claims contrary to everyday experiences.

C: Challenges to the objectivity and authenticity of religious experience

Caroline Franks Davis

Caroline Franks Davis, in her 1989 work *The Evidential Force of Religious Experience*, lists three distinct challenges to claims of religious (mystical) experiences being real.

Description-related challenges

When people describe any event as an experience of 'God' or the 'divine', they are making a claim that they cannot prove. This is because there is no agreed-upon empirical (or other) proof for the existence of such things. The only conclusion that can be drawn is that it is not valid to base such claims on agreed foundations, such as empirical knowledge.

Furthermore, the claim is inconsistent or contradictory with normal everyday experience and, for this reason, should be rejected. It is not a claim that is in any sense valid. It is instead merely a misunderstanding of the experience on the part of the recipient, and must therefore be rejected as having any basis in fact.

Subject-related challenges

In these challenges, it is the recipients (subjects) of the religious experience that are put under suspicion. It may be claimed that they are unreliable as a source; they may be considered to be mentally ill or to have delusions brought about, perhaps, by some sort of substance misuse.

Their claims are considered unreliable because of who they are. It is believed that they are not in a position to understand properly what they have experienced for the reasons given above. Due to this, any claims that they make about a religious experience must not be taken seriously, but must be dismissed.

Object-related challenges

The final type of challenge focuses on the alleged object of the experience. What this means is that the experience being claimed is put under suspicion because it is considered to be a work of fantasy – something that goes against everyday experiences. The likelihood of people having experienced something such as they claim is so unlikely as to be entirely untrue.

The suggestion of God (the object) having been experienced is no more likely to be true than a claim of having seen a 3-metre-tall green alien or a flying antelope. As we are unlikely to believe anyone who claimed experience of the latter two examples, why should we believe the claim of someone who is said to have experienced God?

> **" Key quote "**
>
> With arguments against the plausibility of religious doctrines and reductionist accounts of religious experiences now widely accepted, and with many people leading atheistic lives … religious individuals can no longer assume that experiences judged to be 'genuine' by fellow believers are immune from further attack. They are challenged on all sides, by philosophers, psychologists, sociologists, anthropologists, members of other religious traditions and even by members of their own tradition with widely differing views.
>
> (Caroline Franks Davis, *The Evidential Force of Religious Experience*)

Religious experiences lack objectivity and authenticity

The very nature of mystical experiences (whatever their type and whoever undergoes them) seems to belong to a bygone era. Reading accounts of mystical experiences in ancient religious texts seems perfectly natural, as does considering the experiences of the famous mystics from the traditions of the various world religions.

However, when faced with such claims in an age seemingly dominated by empiricism, science, rationality and evidential proofs, doubt and disbelief tend to come into play. We question the objectivity and authenticity of such experiences and, particularly for those outside religious traditions, we dismiss the realm of the mystical experience as having no believable basis in reality.

As we have seen, in trying to establish the reliability of any mystical experience, the criteria for establishing truth must first be agreed upon. However, due to the very nature of mystical experiences, most philosophers agree that such criteria are virtually impossible to verify. This is because mystical experiences, by their very nature, are subjective and not objective.

If something is objective and verifiable, it relates to external facts that can be agreed upon by observers. It is possible to prove by one or more of the five senses; it can be described; and multiple observers will come to the same conclusion about the same thing – for example, the colour of the car is red.

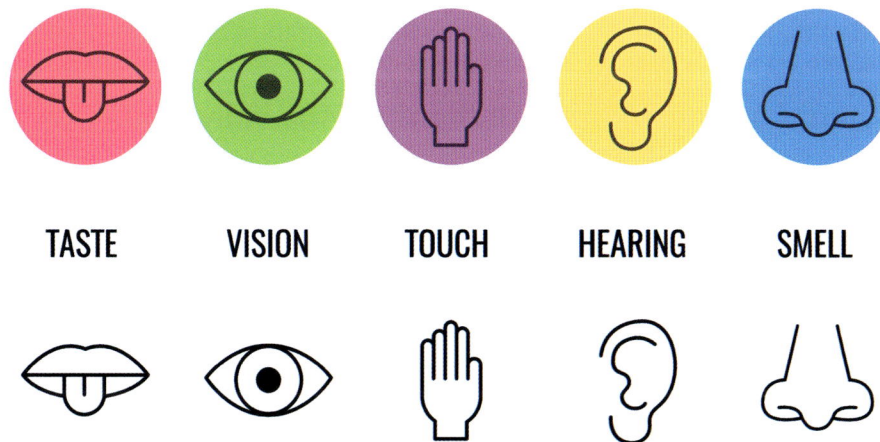

In the modern world, being able to prove experiences through the five senses is considered important

If something is subjective, then it tends to be based upon opinion, personal judgement, belief or assumption, and is more difficult to verify. It is likely to be interpreted in different ways by multiple observers, and these views may change according to time and context – for example, this is the best car in the world to drive.

David Hume, in *An Enquiry Concerning Human Understanding* (1748), stated that it was not impossible for miracles to occur; it was merely impossible ever to prove that one had, in fact, occurred. Transferring this naturalistic view to religious experiences, a similar problem is faced. Due to their highly individualistic nature (for the most part), religious experiences are not open to rational enquiry and, therefore, are treated with suspicion at best and derision at worst.

> **Specification content**
>
> Challenges: individual experiences valid even if non-verifiable; claims could be genuine – integrity of individual; one-off experiences can still be valid even if never repeated

Responses to these challenges

Individual experiences are valid, even if they're non-verifiable

Due to the very fact that communicating religious experiences depends entirely on the perception of the experience by the recipient – or, in some cases, the witnesses to the recipient – it is considered a subjective experience. As scientific empiricism tends to reject subjective accounts out of hand, this presents a serious challenge to the 'truth' of any mystical experience. However, equally, the experience remains valid for the individual, or group of individuals, even if, by its very subjectivity, it is non-verifiable.

Basil Mitchell underlined this point when he spoke at the Symposium on Theology and Falsification in 1971. He demonstrated in his parable of the partisan and the stranger that it is the trust, or faith, that an individual has that is significant when it comes to the validity of belief in something. This extends to a belief in the truth of a religious experience. Even if evidence is presented that might undermine the claim of the individual's religious experience, as long as the individual has faith in their belief, it remains valid..

We may not be able to prove or disprove something, but that does not mean that such a thing does not actually happen. Indeed, there may well be a belief that such things do actually happen, despite the lack of evidence either for or against them – and such ideas and beliefs are held to be meaningful. Richard Swinburne gives the example of the 'toys in the cupboard' coming to life – even though there could be no evidence to support (or deny) this assertion, the idea is still meaningful to those who hear it.

Claims could be genuine: integrity of the individual

With regard to the integrity of the individual, one of the best-known defences is that from Richard Swinburne. He proposed the *principle of credulity*, which states that what someone claims to perceive is probably the case unless there are special reasons for thinking the experience is false. The special reasons that might cast doubt on the validity of the event are:

- if the person is unreliable (e.g. in a highly emotional or irrational state)
- if similar perceptions are shown to be false (e.g. induced by taking drugs such as LSD)
- if there is strong evidence that the object of the experience was not present or did not exist (e.g. a mirage)
- if the experience can be accounted for in other ways as a reality and not just in someone's imagination.

In the absence of these special considerations, Swinburne argues, people's testimony about their religious experience provides good reason to believe that their experience is valid. This is Swinburne's *principle of testimony*.

In this way, religious experiences are validated according to Swinburne. The integrity of the individual is maintained, and people's religious claims could well be genuine.

One-off experiences can still be valid even if they're never repeated

A challenge to many religious experiences is that they are one-off events and, as such, are not open to the same scrutiny that can be applied to regularly repeated events. The suggestion is that their very uniqueness casts doubt on their authenticity. If there were no witnesses to the one-off event, then why should others accept it as valid?

However, this is to look at the validity of events through the reductionist lens of an empiricist, and is not necessarily a valid view itself. A one-off experience can still be valid – a repetition of the event is not required for it to retain its validity. It may be more difficult to provide irrefutable proof, but that should not undermine the validity of an event.

Religious experiences give hope to many people – should their validity be questioned?

Summary

- Religious experiences seem to belong to an age gone by, and many have questioned their place as objective and authentic experiences in a world that values empirical proof above all else.
- Caroline Franks Davis proposed three key challenges to claims of religious (mystical) experiences being real: description-related; subject-related; and object-related.
- Hume's essay on miracles is the classic work covering the significance of empirically based challenges.
- There has been a response to these challenges from philosophers including Basil Mitchell and Richard Swinburne; the relevance of faith and the individual's integrity are at the heart of their defence.

AO1 Activity

a Explain each of Franks Davis' challenges to the authenticity of religious experience.

This helps with presenting a thorough and extensive knowledge and understanding of the topic area.

b On revision cards, summarise the replies to these challenges offered by philosophers such as Mitchell and Swinburne.

This helps with prioritising and selecting a core set of points to develop an answer and with demonstrating extensive depth and breadth in your answer. It also helps with making excellent use of evidence and examples.

> This section covers AO2 content and skills

> **Specification content**
> The extent to which the challenges to religious experience are valid

Issues for analysis and evaluation

The extent to which the challenges to religious experience are valid

Possible line of argument	Critical analysis and evaluation
Religious experiences are not the same as sense experiences	The first challenge to religious experiences is that they are not really the same as sense experiences, even if they have sensory elements to them. However, we could argue that, just as we are known to each other by a kind of direct apprehension rather than through our physical body, so in the same way we may be able to experience God who is non-physical, and so the challenge has its obvious limitations.
Is direct experience of God impossible?	Another challenge is that a direct experience of God is impossible, as the empiricist philosopher David Hume suggested. This claim of a direct experience of God does not really make sense for many people. The response of religious believers, however, could be that it may be possible for God to enter time and space, and it is also a reasonable argument to believe that God would seek to interact with creation.
Are religious experiences only valid if they can be verified?	The Logical Positivists argued that a religious experience cannot be verified. The nature of religious experiences is such that they have their own level of 'reality' or 'fantasy' that is quite separate from meaningful logical analysis. Pitted against this is the fact that some religious experiences appear to be shared by many people and so cannot be fabricated or 'fantasy'. Indeed, there may be criteria external to the experience that would add weight to its validity: for example, if the experience makes a noticeable difference to the religious life of the person. Swinburne adds to this that the onus is on the sceptic to show the experience is delusive.
Religious experiences appear to be too varied and contradictory to be valid	Although some experiences may be experienced by more than one person, there is still the issue of a lack of overall uniformity of religious experiences. They are very different and sometimes contradictory. Which one is valid, and which one is true? However, God may reveal himself in terms of cultural beliefs that we understand and interpret, and there being accounts of different experiences does not mean they are all in error. Maybe only one religion is correct, so the other religious experiences are false, but those of that one religion are true?
Science can explain away religious experiences	Science has provided challenges to religious experiences: for example, in the field of physiology and neurology and by Persinger's experiments. Such challenges conclude that religious experiences have clear materialistic explanations. However, it could be argued that the neurological changes associated with religious experiences may mean such activity does in fact perceive a spiritual reality, rather than the explanation being that it is solely the brain that is causing those experiences.
Are psychological challenges valid?	Finally, there are psychological explanations that Freud suggested, such as collective neurosis, the primal horde and the Oedipus complex, and the arguments of Jung that provide a positive but materialistic account of religious experiences. However, such theories, especially on the part of Jung, were never intended to debate issues of authenticity or validity regarding the truth claims of religious experiences. Instead, they simply provide a suitable explanation for the process by which human beings encounter such experiences.
The validity of the challenges to religious experience is not certain	In conclusion, key questions remain despite the challenges and their counterarguments. For example, if there is a God, why doesn't he reveal himself to everyone, especially if he wants us to believe in him? Although challenges are clearly valid, the solutions are far from confirmed.

> **AO2 Activity**
>
> a Select three lines of argument from the critical analysis and evaluation of the extent to which the challenges to religious experience are valid. Find three references from scholars, schools of thought or religious and philosophical texts that would support those arguments.
>
> b Using the strongest line of argument, try to identify three key quotations that could be used – they could be from scholars, religious texts or schools of thought.

Exam practice

Sample question

Evaluate the persuasiveness of Franks Davis' different challenges to the authenticity of religious experiences.

Sample answer

Franks Davis put forward three distinct challenges to the authenticity of religious experiences. To assess their persuasiveness, we need to consider each challenge in turn. The first challenge is the description-related challenge, which argues that a description of any event that claims itself to be an experience of 'God' or the 'divine' is a claim for which there is no proof. This invalidates the description because the claim is inconsistent or contradictory with normal everyday experience. A religious experience, therefore, is merely a misunderstanding of the experience on the part of the recipient.

While this challenge seems reasonable, there is a major flaw in the reasoning. Aside from the issue of 'proof', which has its own problems in philosophy, the real problem with this challenge is with the limited understanding of 'experience'. This is a very materialist-based assumption similar to Hume's empiricism. Experience may not just be a matter of normal everyday experience. Indeed, what makes religious experience different is that it could be argued to be an experience of the 'abnormality' of a possible spiritual realm that filters into the normal.

The second challenge is to do with subject-related challenges. This challenge suspects that the recipient (subject) of the religious experience is unreliable as a source, and that they may have a mental illness or delusions brought about by some sort of substance misuse. Impaired perceptions and understanding mean that the recipient's claims must be dismissed.

Again, this challenge seems quite logical. However, aside from the objections raised to scientific and psychological explanations, the work of Richard Swinburne uses principles of credulity and testimony as a strong defence of those who claim to have had a religious experience.

Swinburne proposed the principle of credulity, stating that it is reasonable to believe that the world is probably as we experience it to be unless there are special reasons for thinking the experience is false. He argues that religious experiences

> **Specification content**
>
> The persuasiveness of Franks Davis' different challenges

News reporter ✏️

This is a clear introduction that provides an overview of the first challenge with appropriate commentary.

Critical thinker

This paragraph further examines the challenge and raises technical points regarding the terms *proof* and *experience*.

News reporter ✏️

This paragraph presents an overview of the second challenge with relevance and accuracy.

Tennis player 🎾

Detective

This part presents a detailed counterpoint, showing thorough, sustained and clear views supported by extensive, detailed reasoning and evidence.

can therefore be verified. Then Swinburne uses the principle of credulity as part of his argument to derive his principle of testimony, which argues that other people's testimony of religious experiences provides good reason to believe that God exists, because what someone seems to perceive is probably the case (principle of credulity). This is because many people, based on apparent (perceptual rather than inferred) direct experiences of God, take it that God exists and, in the absence of special considerations, it is reasonable to believe that the experiences of others are probably as they report them (principle of testimony).

Although Swinburne uses this as part of his overall argument for the existence of God, the points he makes do challenge the persuasiveness of Franks Davis' subject-related challenges.

This paragraph presents and evaluates the third challenge appropriately.

Finally, the object-related challenges centre on the chances of having experienced something such as the recipient claims being so unlikely as to be entirely untrue. However, it could be argued that the nature of the experience is very different from the hypothetical experience of a flying antelope, and some would also suggest that it merely points to the possibility for something else 'existing' in a way different from how we normally perceive: that is, in a spiritual sense.

This is a brief conclusion that takes into account the previous lines of reasoning as the basis for a final assessment of the issue.

In conclusion, although the challenges Franks Davis put forward do appear persuasive, it is clear that if these challenges are themselves challenged, their persuasiveness can also be questioned.

Evaluation

This is an effective and balanced response. It considers both sides of the argument before putting forward a conclusion. The candidate makes accurate use both of terminology and of the views of different schools of thought.

Over to you

Your task is to write a response, under timed conditions, to a question requiring an evaluation of the extent to which the challenges to religious experience are valid.

You need to focus for this and apply the skills that you have developed so far. A suggested approach is given below.

Question

'Challenges to religious experience are not valid.' Evaluate this view.

(Q3b, Component 2: Philosophy of Religion, WJEC, Summer 2023)

Suggested approach

1. Begin with a list of indicative content. Perhaps discuss this as a group. It does not need to be in any order. Remember, this is evaluation, so you need different lines of argument. The easiest way is to use 'Support' and 'Against' headings.
2. Develop the list using examples.
3. Now consider the order in which you would like to explain the information.
4. Then write out your plan, under timed conditions, remembering to apply the principles of evaluation by making sure that you:
    - identify issues clearly
    - present accurate views of others, making sure that you comment on the views presented
    - reach an overall personal judgement.
5. Use the band descriptors to mark your own answer, carefully considering the descriptors.
6. Ask someone else to read your answer and see whether they can help you improve it in any way. You could do the same for them.

Use this technique as revision for each of the topic areas that you have studied.

T3 Religious experience (1)

Religious experience (2)

This section covers AO1 content and skills

Specification content
The influence of religious experience on religious practice

D: The influence of religious experience on religious practice and faith

Religious experience and religious practice

Alister Hardy

In 1969, the English marine biologist Alister Hardy set up the Religious Experience Research Unit in Oxford, with the objective of examining the extent and nature of the religious experiences of people in Britain. Hardy had just retired from his Chair at Oxford as a scientist but had a lifelong interest in religion.

In compiling a database of religious experiences, what soon became obvious to Hardy and the other researchers was the sheer breadth and variety of such experiences. Among those accounts were reported the more traditional religious experiences, which were centred on followers of various religions.

Hardy recognised that there was a wide range of religious experiences

According to Hardy, a religious experience 'often induces in the person concerned ... a conviction that the material everyday world is not the whole of reality and that there is another part to life' (Hardy, *The Spiritual Nature of Man*).

> **Key quote**
>
> We only have to glance at religious history to see the enormous vitality and significance of experience in the formation and development of religious traditions. Consider the visions of the Prophet Muhammad, the conversion of Paul, the enlightenment of the Buddha. These were seminal events in human history. And it is obvious that the emotions and experiences of men and women are the food on which the other dimensions of religion feed: ritual without feeling is cold, doctrines without awe or compassion are dry, and myths which do not move hearers are feeble.
>
> (Ninian Smart, *The World's Religions*)

Religious practice and religious faith

This theme focuses on the influence of religious experience on religious practice and faith. Religious practice includes **ritual**, religious ceremonies and festivals, but also daily life, involving religious duties and reflections.

Ritual, as well as being a religious experience in itself, can also be a trigger for further religious experience. In addition, prayer and fasting are often preparation for certain ritual actions, ceremonies or festivals and are also personal or communal religious experiences.

Often, festivals are celebrations of a past event that is grounded in a significant religious experience. For example, during Ramadan, Muslims celebrate the time when the verses of the Qur'an were revealed to the prophet Muhammad. All these forms of religious practice and faith have been influenced by religious experience and can also lead to religious experience.

Faith is a key feature of many religions. Most thinkers define religious faith in terms of some mixture of an action of the will, trust and belief in a body of truths expressed in statements or propositions.

It seems that a religious experience can move people into faith, and faith can lead people into a religious experience. In addition, there are many types of religious experiences. These include quiet reflection and contemplation of the divine: for example, private prayer or meditation. They also include more obvious public expressions of faith: for example, through the experience associated with charismatic worship – 'speaking in tongues'.

Value of religious experience for the religious community

Affirmation of the belief system

Religious experiences can affirm (that is, verify) a belief system by their very occurrence. In many religions, there is often a central figure who is linked to the founding of that religion. In many cases, these figures experience a particularly significant event that marks the start of their ministry. Their authority is often associated with their religious experience, which is seen as a confirmation and affirmation of their message.

Buddhism

In Buddhism, the significant religious experience that marked the affirmation of Siddhartha Gautama was that, as he sat under the Bodhi Tree in meditation, after several weeks, he achieved **Enlightenment**. It was from this moment on that he became known as the *Buddha* ('Awakened One' or 'Enlightened One').

Christianity

In Christianity, the **revelation** through the appearance of angels to Mary and Joseph affirms the doctrine of the **incarnation** and virgin birth. The experience at Jesus' baptism by John the Baptist – where the heavens are described as opening and the voice of God is heard declaring Jesus as his son – is an affirmation of Jesus' status for Christians.

Specification content

The influence of religious experience on faith

 Key term

ritual: a set of actions that have a deeper, religious or spiritual significance

Specification content

The influence of religious experience on religious practice and faith: value for religious community: affirmation of belief system

 Key terms

Enlightenment: in Buddhism, the experience of awakening to insight into the true nature of things

revelation: a supernatural disclosure to human beings

incarnation: the Christian belief in the embodiment of God the Son in human flesh as Jesus Christ

Paul is also seen as an influential figure of the Church. Over half the books in the New Testament have traditionally been attributed to him. These contain the core of Christian theology. Paul changed from being someone on a mission to arrest Christians, to someone preaching and suffering for proclaiming Jesus of Nazareth as the Jewish Messiah and Son of God. What triggered the change was a number of religious experiences, including a conversion experience when the resurrected Jesus allegedly appeared to Paul on the road to Damascus; Ananias receiving a vision about Paul; and Paul being filled with the Holy Spirit.

Judaism

Exodus 3 tells how Moses saw a burning bush that was not consumed. God spoke to him from the bush and commissioned Moses as a prophet and liberator of the people of Israel.

Sikhism

Likewise, Guru Nanak received a revelation, which is at the start of every chapter and sub-chapter in the Sri Guru Granth Sahib (the sacred scripture of the Sikhs). Guru Nanak tells how he took a dip in the river and disappeared into the waters. He was missing for two days and nights. On the third day, he reappeared out of the water with a verse on his lips that is now referred to as the Mool Mantra.

The Mool Mantra (Mool Mantar in Punjabi)

Summary

In all these accounts, a particular individual is confirmed as the person for a specific religious task by means of some type of religious experience. Through those individuals, revelation is given. It is the religious experiences that convince followers that the person has been specially chosen, and so affirms their authority and status as a trustworthy receiver of revelation.

Promotion of the faith value system

> **Specification content**
>
> Value for religious community: promotion of faith value system

As well as religious experiences being seen as the guarantor of received revelation about doctrine and beliefs, religious experience can also be the source of ethical standards.

Buddhism

The Buddha's enlightenment experience is an example of meditation to be emulated by others. The Buddha placed great emphasis on searching for oneself just as he did, and the practices of meditation are examples of this.

Christianity

Christianity sees Jesus and Paul as revealing and clarifying ethical standards and behaviour. The Gospels record that Jesus summarised Jewish Law in the words 'Love the Lord your God with all your heart, with all your soul, with all your mind and with all your strength and love your neighbour as yourself.' Jesus is seen by Christians as the Son of God, whose authority was confirmed by his miracles, death and resurrection.

Judaism

Likewise, Moses is honoured among Jewish people as the 'lawgiver of Israel'. He received the Ten Commandments inscribed on two stone tablets, along with the laws of the covenant, which included both customary law and ritual ordinances. These provide explicit moral guidance, and so govern the behaviour of believers.

Strengthening the cohesion of a religious community

A religious community celebrating a past religious experience or expressing worship together, for example, can be occasions when a religious community is strengthened by religious experience. The very act of coming together as a religious community to participate in worship or to commemorate an event of significance has essential value for the religious community and is the lifeblood of religious living.

Such community gatherings provide an opportunity for further religious experiences and spiritual benefits, such as:

- strengthening the community spiritually through collective worship
- creating a greater sense of unity through fellowship
- establishing a common identity
- highlighting a common purpose through specific events – for example, festivals and rites of passage
- reaffirming faith – for example, creeds, reading religious texts and hymns
- expressing and sharing one's spirituality with others – for example, testimonies and personal experiences.

Value of celebrating a past religious experience for strengthening cohesion

This type of celebration usually occurs by means of festivals or pilgrimage. For many Buddhists, Wesak celebrates the Buddha's enlightenment. Homes are decorated and there are special temple services.

In Islam, the festival of Ramadan celebrates the time when the Qur'an was first revealed to Muhammad. Fasting during the month of Ramadan is obligatory for Muslims. Ramadan is seen as a time to spend with friends and family. The fast will often be broken by different Muslim families coming together to share in an evening meal.

Eid ul Adha is another Muslim festival. It remembers Abraham's willingness to sacrifice his son when Allah ordered him to. Eid usually starts with Muslims going to the mosque for prayers. It is also a time when they visit family and friends, as well as offering presents. At both these Islamic festivals, the religious community comes together – sharing in the same rituals and beliefs.

In Judaism, the festival of Pesach commemorates the events of the Passover, when the enslaved Israelites were spared from the plague of the death of all the firstborn and escaped from Egypt. Everyone takes part in retelling the story over the Seder meal with family and friends. This sharing expresses their common identity as members of the religious community.

Moses Smashing the Tablets of the Law, Rembrandt (1659)

> **Specification content**
> Value for religious community: strengthening cohesion of religious community

Value of present-day worship and rituals for strengthening cohesion

The experience of present-day religious followers as they gather for worship each week can be seen as a religious experience that strengthens cohesion for a religious community. The following provide examples of this:

- Shared worship can lead to a special kind of communal experience.
- The reading and preaching of the sacred text can be a trigger for religious experience. Most religions consider their scriptures as the revealed word of God. Through these texts and others, God speaks to the individual.
- Jesus said that where two or three are gathered together for prayer, there he is also. This suggests that there is something special about the gathering together of religious believers. The Friday prayer at the mosque and the Sabbath gathering at the synagogue are specific occasions that strengthen the cohesion of particular religious communities.
- Ritual also reinforces the communal experience. It gives a feeling of group solidarity and unity and a sense of belonging to something that is greater than the individuals who comprise it. Rituals such as the Eucharist (Mass or Holy Communion) in Christianity are special times when, for a community worshipping together, there is an experience and mystery that Hardy described as 'another dimension to life'.
- Christian **charismatic worship** has an emphasis on and expectation of the Holy Spirit at work among the worshippers. This group expectation of meeting with God is a shared religious experience, and so can strengthen the cohesion of that religious community.

> **Key term**
>
> **charismatic worship:** exuberant and expressive forms of worship, often involving ecstatic religious experiences (e.g. speaking in 'tongues' and healing miracles)

> **Specification content**
>
> Value for individual: faith restoring

Value of religious experience for the individual

Faith restoring

Both one's own religious experience and the testimony and accounts of the religious experience of others can be of value to the individual.

If one's own faith is struggling and doubt setting in, then having a religious experience – a meeting with God – can clearly remove doubts and renew faith. Such an experience might come from:

- a time of prayer or meditation
- the reading of a sacred text
- being with others of the religious community
- participating in a religious ritual such as the Eucharist.

It can be any occasion when people open themselves up to seeking or listening to God.

A time of prayer may help believers restore or renew their faith

The faith-restoring experience may also come through others:
- A testimony of one person's religious experience may lead to another's own renewal of faith, after hearing how God has influenced that person's life.
- The religious experience gained from going on a pilgrimage can rekindle dwindling faith and commitment. For example, in Islam the Hajj is one of the five pillars and all Muslims are expected to undertake this pilgrimage at least once in their life.

Strengthening faith in the face of opposition

Individuals may be strengthened in their faith in the face of opposition as they hear of other believers' experiences of facing opposition themselves. This may include some account of an act of God when they were rescued from a situation, or an account of when a believer was given strength to face and overcome an opposing point of view.

It may even be accounts of martyrs that inspire faith in the face of opposition. There are often stories in the sacred texts of followers who faced persecution. The story of the origin of the **Khalsa** in Sikhism, where five Sikhs were willing to die for their faith, can be a source of inspiration and a trigger for religious experience.

The founding of the Khalsa

The following account is taken from SikhiWiki:

> After [the Guru's] inspirational discourse, he flashed his unsheathed sword and said that every great deed was preceded by equally great sacrifice. He asked, with a naked sword in his hand, 'I need one head. Is there anyone among you, who is ready to die for his faith?'
>
> When people heard his call, they were taken aback. Some of the wavering followers left the congregation, while other began to look at one another in amazement.
>
> After a few minutes, a brave Sikh from Lahore named Daya Ram stood up and offered his head to the Guru. The Guru took him to a tent pitched close by, and after some time, came out with a blood-dripping sword. The Sikhs thought Daya Ram had been slain.
>
> The Guru repeated his demand calling for another Sikh who was prepared to die at his command. At this second call, even more people were shocked and some were frightened. A few more of the wavering followers discreetly began to filter out of the congregation.
>
> However, to the shock of many, another person stood up. The second Sikh who offered himself was Dharam Das. This amazing episode did not end there. Soon three more, Mohkam Chand, Sahib Chand and Himmat Rai, offered their heads to the Guru. Each Sikh was taken into the tent and some thought that they could now hear a 'thud' sound – as if the sword was falling on the neck of the Sikh.

> **Specification content**
> Value for individual: strengthening faith in face of opposition

> **Key term**
> **Khalsa:** literally meaning 'pure'; the name for those who have undergone the Amrit ceremony in Sikhism

> **Key term**
>
> **Amrit:** literally meaning 'immortality'; the name of the holy water that the Khalsa drink in the baptism ceremony in Sikhism

Guru Gobind Singh founded the Khalsa in Sikhism

> **Specification content**
>
> Value for individual: renewal of commitment to religious ideals and doctrines

Now the five Sikhs were missing with the Guru in the tent. It was a nerve-racking time for the sangat (congregation). There was pin-drop silence as all focused intensely on the tent opening. After what seemed an eternity, the tent opening moved and the Guru came out of the tent. No naked sword this time!

Soon the five Sikhs were presented alive to the congregation wearing brand new decorated robes. They constituted the *Panj Pyare*: the Five Beloved Ones, who were baptised as the *Khalsa* or the Pure Ones with the administration of **Amrit**.

The Guru declared: 'From now on, the Khalsa shall be baptised with Amrit created with water stirred with a double-edged sword – Khanda, while the words of Gurbani are uttered.'

Prayer and meditation in the face of opposition

Prayer and meditation in the face of opposition can lead to a religious experience in which the person gains strength and faith to confront the situation. The sense of God being with the believer because of a religious experience he or she has had enables the person to stand firm and continue despite threats of persecution.

In the early Christian Church, there is the account of a religious experience at Pentecost when the Holy Spirit was claimed to have come upon the disciples. The result of this was that they proclaimed about Jesus and, when facing persecution, they said that they couldn't stop. They had to obey God rather than human beings.

Renewal of commitment to religious ideals and doctrines

Most religions have occasions when followers of the faith have an opportunity to renew their commitment to their faith and ideals. Often, this takes the form of a public commitment, where the person confirms their faith. The decision to make such a commitment can be a religious experience.

Initiation into a faith can also be a time of renewal of commitment, when individuals renew the commitment that their parents made at birth on their behalf or when they renew the commitment previous generations made as full members of that religious community. Most religions have some kind of initiation ceremony.

In Sikhism, the Amrit ceremony is the initiation rite. During the ceremony:

- Hymns are recited from the Sikh scripture.
- Prayers are said and the principles of Sikhism are affirmed.
- Candidates then drink some of the Amrit from the same bowl, and have it sprinkled on their eyes and hair.
- Each person recites the Mool Mantra.

Undergoing the Amrit ceremony means the person has joined the Khalsa.

The original Sikh Amrit ceremony

The following account is taken from SikhiWiki:

> Upon administering Amrit to the Five Beloved Ones (*Panj Pyare*), the Guru asked them to baptise him in the same manner, thus emphasising equality between the Guru and his disciples.

> Guru Gobind Singh named the new ceremony, *Khande di Pahul*, namely the baptism of the double-edged sword, which is also known as *Amrit-Sanchar*.
>
> He stirred water in an iron bowl with the sword, reciting five major compositions, *Japji*, *Jaap*, *Savaiyye*, *Benti Chaupai* and *Anand Sahib*, while the five Sikhs stood facing him.
>
> The Guru's wife, Mata Sahib Kaur, put some sugar-puffs into the water. The nectar thus obtained was called *Khanday-da-Amrit* or simply just *Amrit*.
>
> This implied that the new Khalsa brotherhood would not only be full of courage and heroism, but also filled with humility.

Public declarations of faith

In Christianity, adult baptism and confirmation are similar religious services, where Christians make a public commitment to their faith. They often give a testimony of their journey of faith at this time.

Festivals and seasons

Festivals can also be occasions when religious believers are moved to renew their commitments to a religious way of life.

In Judaism, **Rosh Hashanah** marks the beginning of the ten-day period of atonement leading to **Yom Kippur**, when Jewish people are commanded to search their souls and make amends for sins they have committed. Yom Kippur is the holiest day of the Jewish year, and many Jewish people spend the entire day in prayers at the synagogue.

The time of **Lent** provides Christians with a similar opportunity to reflect and renew their commitment to Christianity. Lent is a period of six weeks when many Christians observe a period of fasting, repentance, self-denial and spiritual discipline. The goal, as in other religions, is to develop a closer relationship with God.

Fasting

A common feature of religions is the act of fasting, which is intended to help teach self-discipline. It is seen as a time to take our eyes off the things of this world and instead focus on God. This is the focus of Ramadan for Muslims, who see this month of prayer and fasting as an annual time for spiritual renewal.

Significant religious places

Holy places can also be triggers for a religious experience that leads to renewal and recommitment to religious beliefs. Usually, they are places where either something happened or people feel something sacred. It may be that worship has taken place there for a great length of time: for example, Jerusalem and the Western wall or the Sikh Golden Temple at Amritsar. Often, holy places become places of pilgrimage, such as Makkah. These types of locations are believed to be places where there is a sacred meeting between the spiritual and the physical.

> **Key terms**
>
> **Rosh Hashanah:** the Jewish New Year
> **Yom Kippur:** in Judaism, the day of Atonement and the holiest day of the year
> **Lent:** in Christianity, a season of 40 days of prayer and fasting before Easter

Ramadan is an important time for spiritual renewal for Muslims

> **Summary**
> ★ In the second half of the twentieth century, Alistair Hardy set up the Religious Experience Research Unit as a way of scientifically collecting information about religious experiences and the impact they had on people.
> ★ There are a wide range of religious experiences, and all of these have some influence on either religious practice or religious faith in the way that they affect both religious individuals and religious communities.
> ★ Their value for religious communities is that they affirm belief systems, promote the faith's value system (laws, ethics and so on) and can bring the religious community closer together, both physically and spiritually.
> ★ Their value for religious individuals is that they can restore and strengthen faith – particularly when faced with opposition to that faith – and can also provide opportunities for individuals to renew their commitment to the beliefs, values and teachings of their particular religious tradition.

AO1 Activity

a   Explain the value of religious experiences for an individual.

This helps with developing a response that demonstrates extensive depth and/or breadth, with excellent use of evidence and examples.

b   On one side of a revision card, write a religious belief or practice from the world religion that you are studying. On the reverse side, explain how that belief or practice is underpinned by a religious experience. For example, in Judaism the celebration of Pesach is based on the experience of the Hebrew people's flight from Egypt and freedom from captivity.

This helps with prioritising and selecting a core set of points to develop an answer and with making accurate use of specialist language and vocabulary in context.

> **Specification content**
> The impact of religious experiences upon religious belief and practice

> This section covers AO2 content and skills

Issues for analysis and evaluation

The impact of religious experiences upon religious belief and practice

Possible line of argument	Critical analysis and evaluation
Religious experiences are intrinsic to religious belief and practice	It can be difficult to separate religious experience from religious belief and practice, if we understand religious experiences to refer to those experiences that are recognisably religious (e.g. religious assembly, reading of sacred writings). In support of this, an individual's prayer to God is clearly a religious experience for that person. The practice of prayer is therefore a religious experience. William James described prayer as 'the very soul and essence of religion', and so its impact upon religious belief and practice is significant.
The act of religious practice can be considered a religious experience and therefore has impact	Just as prayer is a religious experience, a baptism or participation in a rite of passage is equally a religious experience. Indeed, it could be argued that the Roman Catholic understanding of the meaning of *Eucharist* (that is, *transubstantiation*) brings with it the religious experience of the transformation of the bread and wine into the body and blood of Christ. Therefore, the very act of a religious practice may itself be considered a religious experience and so have significant impact.
Intention is key to the impact of religious experiences upon religious belief and practice	However, others might question this view. Just participating in a religious practice does not guarantee that the person participating is the receiver of a religious experience. The participation could be almost mechanical, particularly if it is an act that is often repeated. For instance, saying the Mool Mantra or the Lord's Prayer could be acts where the actual words are repeated by rote, almost unconsciously. Indeed, if we take this line of argument, then the impact of such experiences is significantly less than those who have true intent or, as Muslims would express it, *niyyah* or *niyat*, which is the only thing that validates a religious act.
Religious experiences are often the reason for religious practices	Religious experiences influence belief and practice since they are often the reason for a religious practice, such as a religious pilgrimage or a religious festival. For example, during Ramadan, Muslims celebrate the time when verses of the Qur'an were revealed to the prophet Muhammad. *Wesak* ('Buddha Day') is when Buddhists celebrate the life of the Buddha and his teachings, and revelations about the nature of death, karma and rebirth, suffering and desire.
Religious experiences, through belief and practice, provide cohesion to the religious community	Clearly these beliefs and practices are important to religious believers. They are reminders to them of why and what they believe – the affirmation of their faith. They demonstrate what is important to them and are a witness to others outside the faith. They serve to unite the religious community and give it a distinctive identity. They strengthen the religious community. The reason for assembling at a place of worship is also usually linked to some religious experience of the past. Hence, it seems that religious experiences do have a significant impact upon religious belief and practice.
Conversion experiences clearly impact the lives of religious believers	Conversion experiences are clearly examples of religious experience impacting on the religious beliefs of the individual. They change the beliefs and practices of the person who has had the experience. Examples include John Wesley, St Paul and Yusuf Islam (formerly known as Cat Stevens). The conversion might be from one denomination to another within the same religion: for example, from Baptist to Catholic or Sunni to Shi'a. Alternatively, the conversion might be from one religion to another, or from no religion to a religion. Joining a religion often involves some initiation ceremony marking membership. Usually, members of the religion witness or participate in the ceremony, and this can have an impact on them in terms of renewing their own religious commitment.

Possible line of argument	Critical analysis and evaluation
Religious experiences clearly impact on religious belief and practice	William James emphasised the fruits of the religious experience as evidence that religious experiences impact positively on a person's life. Perhaps this is a sufficient lens with which to view the impact of religious experiences on religious belief and practice? We can therefore conclude that, while it may vary in its character and extent, the impact of religious experience on religious belief and practice is irrefutable.

> **Specification content**
> Whether religious communities are entirely dependent on religious experiences

> **AO2 Activity**
> a Evaluate three lines of argument from the critical analysis and evaluation of the impact of religious experiences upon religious belief and practice. What are their strengths and weaknesses? Which line of argument is strongest?
> b Using the strongest line of argument, try to identify three key questions that might be asked – they could be critical, challenge, hypothetical or direct questions.

Exam practice

Sample question
Evaluate whether religious communities are entirely dependent on religious experiences.

Sample answer

This is a comprehensive introduction, with a wide range of examples, that sets up the contention that religious communities are dependent on religious experiences.

Religious faiths have various beliefs and practices that derive from past religious experiences. Certainly, the foundation of the faith usually has some sort of religious experience to show the authority of the central figure of the faith. In Judaism, we have Abraham's covenant experience; Christianity is based on the resurrection of Jesus; the Buddha's whole enlightenment experience is the very basis of Buddhist teaching and practice. Not only is the revelation of the Qur'an to Muhammad through Angel Jibril a religious encounter, the Qur'an itself is seen as the final miracle to humanity from Allah. The Vedas in Hinduism are the product of the insights of the seers of ancient Hinduism, and in Sikhism, Guru Nanak's religious experience in the river where he disappeared for three days is the turning point in his ministry. All are clear examples of the primary, albeit indirect, level of dependency of religious communities on the religious experience of their founders.

This paragraph presents relevant evidence, via a line of reasoning, showing a clear link between religious experiences and religious communities.

In a similar way, particular events in the religious faith are often associated with a religious experience. These are remembered and celebrated through festivals and pilgrimages. For instance, the festival of Pesach remembers the events of the Passover, when the enslaved Israelites were spared from the plague of the death of all the firstborn and escaped from Egypt. This establishes a common identity and reaffirms faith. Family and friends meet together for the Seder meal, when they retell the story and everyone takes part. This coming together to remember the past religious experience and share in the same rituals and beliefs creates a great sense of unity.

However, in the twenty-first century, many of these religious experiences have been challenged and doubted as historical happenings. Rather, they are interpreted as symbolic or mythological. The extent to which this interpretation challenges the importance of such religious experiences to religious communities is difficult to gauge. If the events never happened and there was no religious experience, can the account still be vital to the religious community? Some may argue, for instance, that the account of the resurrection of Jesus, if interpreted as symbolic, can still inspire and be meaningful to the religious community.

The candidate considers an alternative view that challenges the historicity of the events and poses the question of whether they are still vital to the religious community.

It remains true to say that beliefs and practices are derived from past experiences. Believers still interpret them as events that promote a faith value system and guide a religious community, even if they do not interpret their historicity in a literal sense. If there were no religious experiences from the past, then there would be no religious communities.

This paragraph provides a simple counterpoint to the suggestion that events need to be literal to be valid.

Another line of argument involves making some distinction between the different religious experiences. For example, prayer and worship form the basic practice of religious believers worldwide and therefore are an essential part of what it means to be religious. However, the experiencing of visions and mystical events may not be open to all religious believers and therefore does not constitute an essential element of what it means to be religious.

This paragraph considers an alternative line of argument, differentiating between different types of experiences and their relative significance to the issue.

Religious communities are not entirely dependent on religious experience since religious belief can be the result of rational enquiry. A reasoned faith does not demand a religious experience. However, some religious believers argue that being religious is about knowing God, and they often express it in terms of the need for both head and heart knowledge. It is the heart knowledge that demands a religious experience. In other words, believers may argue that individuals need a personal experience of God rather than second-hand accounts. Taking this view, religious experience may be essential for the individual as much as for a religious community.

This is an exploration of another line of reasoning, giving an alternative consideration.

Recent debate about the origin of religious experiences has cast some doubt on their whole nature. Physiological factors, such as drugs and research into stimulation of the temporal lobes, have suggested natural explanations for religious experiences. In a similar way, psychological factors, such as certain personality traits and the work of Jung, have raised doubts about the validity of religious experiences.

The candidate raises the technical issue relating to the authenticity of religious experiences.

In response, philosophers such as Richard Swinburne have defended their validity through his argument based on the principle of credulity and the principle of testimony, which argue that religious experiences can be rationally seen to be genuine, given rigorous testing according to certain criteria. Therefore, the issue may not be so much about whether religious communities are dependent on religious experiences, but more about whether they ever should be dependent, given possible doubts about the validity of any religious experience.

The candidate makes a counterpoint followed by a question that, looking at the issue from a different viewpoint, also forms the conclusion to the argument.

Evaluation

This is a well-considered and balanced response. The candidate gives sustained and clear views, supported by extensive, detailed reasoning. There is accurate use of specialist language and vocabulary in context throughout.

Over to you

Below is an evaluation of whether religious experiences can influence religious beliefs and practices. It has no quotations at all to support the argument it presents. Beneath the evaluation are two quotations that could be used to improve the outline.

Your task is to rewrite the outline, making use of the quotations. Such phrases as 'according to …', 'the scholar … argues' or 'it has been suggested by …' may help.

When you have completed the task, try to find another quotation that you could use and extend your evaluation further.

Evaluation

In most religions, there is often a pivotal figure who is linked to the founding of that religion. Usually these figures experience a particularly significant event that marks the start of their ministry. Their authority derives from their religious experience as it is seen as confirmation and affirmation of their message. As a result, their revelation is trusted and forms the basis of the faith. It is embraced by the individual believer and influences their religious beliefs and practices.

However, historical critical methods, such as that involved in biblical criticism, have questioned the reliability of ancient sacred texts. It seems likely that the accounts of religious experiences should be interpreted more as symbolic or mythological than as historical and literal, and should therefore not influence religious beliefs and practices.

David Hume asserted that religious experiences such as miracles cannot be used as influencing a belief system, since many religions have such accounts and they therefore contradict each other. If a religious experience is appealed to, to confirm a belief, then what about all those other religious experiences in other faiths that confirm their beliefs?

Influencing belief and practice through religious experiences assumes that there are already reasons for believing in God and the supernatural. Therefore, religious experiences may not entirely influence religious beliefs and practices.

Quotation 1

'The mystic does not give us any information about the external world, he merely gives us indirect information about the condition of his own mind.' (Ayer)

Quotation 2

'When one person suffers from a delusion it is called insanity. When many people suffer from a delusion it is called Religion.' (Pirsig)

E: Different definitions of miracles

This section covers AO1 content and skills

Introduction

The word *miracle* comes from the Latin word for 'wonder'. The main characteristic of a miracle is that it is in some way unusual or extraordinary, so that it provokes wonder.

An early definition of a miracle was given by St Augustine (354–430 CE), who held that a miracle is not contrary to (i.e. against the laws of) nature because the hidden potentials in nature that make miracles possible have been placed there by God. Hence, a miracle is contrary only to our knowledge of nature.

A number of other different philosophical definitions of a miracle have been offered. Four of the main ones are discussed below.

Specification content
Miracles, the definitions of

Specification content
St Thomas Aquinas (miracles different from the usual order)

St Thomas Aquinas

St Thomas Aquinas developed St Augustine's understanding. Aquinas defined a miracle as 'that which has a divine cause, not that whose cause a human person fails to understand'. A key feature of Aquinas' thought is that he believed that everything that exists has a nature; everything has things that it is able to do or is meant to fulfil (that is, its *telos*).

He also believed that there was an order to all things. He said of miracles, 'Those things must properly be called miraculous which are done by divine power apart from the order generally followed in things.'

A miracle for Aquinas is therefore an event beyond the natural power of any created being. It has a 'divine cause' and, as stated above, is not a normal part of the nature or order of things. God alone can perform miracles, since he is un-created.

Aquinas distinguished between three kinds of miracle:

- events where God does something that nature could never do – for example, the Sun going back on its course across the sky
- events where God does something that nature can do, but not in that order – for example, life following death, as in the case of Jesus' resurrection in Christianity
- events where God does something that the working of nature usually does, but without the operation of the principles of nature – for example, someone being instantly cured of an illness that usually takes much longer to cure.

God is active in all three events.

Thomas Aquinas (1225–74)

Key quote

A miracle is … that which has a divine cause, not that whose cause a human person fails to understand.

(Aquinas, *Summa Contra Gentiles*)

David Hume

By the seventeenth century, any talk concerning the behaviour of things being given a nature by God had been replaced by the terms the **laws of nature** or *natural laws*. Therefore, by David Hume's time, it was thought that natural laws were universal and governed all events. In Section X of Hume's book *An Enquiry Concerning Human Understanding*, he defines a miracle as 'a violation of natural law'.

Hume develops this by offering a fuller definition: 'a transgression of a law of nature by a particular volition of the Deity, or by the interposition of some invisible agent'. For Hume, a miracle not only had to be an event that broke the laws of nature, but also had to express divine cause.

An example of this would be raising a person from the dead. It breaks our regular experience of the laws of nature and demands an intervention by

Specification content
David Hume (transgression of a law of nature)

Key term

laws of nature: the scientifically agreed physical laws by which the universe usually operates

T3 Religious experience (2)

Jesus walking on water

David Hume (1711–76)

God or some supernatural agent. It is a miracle, regardless of whether or not anyone recognises it.

Other examples might include healing a man with a withered arm; instantly turning water into wine; or walking on water, with no support under the water and without the feet sinking into the water.

Hume's understanding of a law of nature has been understood by philosophers in two different ways. The first is often referred to as the 'hard' interpretation. This assumes that laws of nature are unalterably uniform. If miracles are a 'violation' of what cannot be altered, then miracles are impossible.

A similar 'hard' interpretation argues that what appears to be a violation of a law of nature is a misstated law of nature. The laws postulated need to be adjusted to take in the new circumstance, so that a new law of nature is now derived that now has no exceptions. Once again, the view is that there can be no violation of a law of nature.

An alternative understanding of a violation of a law of nature is referred to as the 'soft' view. This sees natural laws not as fixed laws that are unalterable in any circumstance, but rather natural laws that can have exceptions. Therefore, natural laws are seen as regular normal patterns of events but can be altered, for example, by the intervention of God. This then makes the issue for belief in miracles not about a logical impossibility but about whether the evidence for the altered law is credible and convincing..

R.F. Holland

Ray Holland (1923–2013) presents a completely different approach to defining a miracle. He argues that a miracle need involve neither breaking the laws of nature, nor an intervention by God. For Holland, a miracle can be spoken about only against a religious background where the miracle is taken as a sign. Hence, a miracle can be defined as 'a remarkable and beneficial coincidence that is interpreted in a religious way'. Holland refers to this as a **contingency miracle**.

The illustration that Holland uses is of a child caught between rail tracks in his toy car, with a train fast approaching out of sight of the boy. The mother can see both the boy on the tracks and the train approaching. She realises that the boy will be hit by the train as there is too little distance for it to stop, once the driver sees the boy. However, the train suddenly starts to slow down and eventually stops about a metre away from the boy. The mother still says it is a miracle, even when she is later told that the reason for the train stopping is that the driver had suffered a heart condition and passed out, causing the automatic braking system to come into play and so stop the train.

In Holland's illustration, the mother thanks God. A non-religious person would describe the event as extraordinarily lucky. However, even though it doesn't break the laws of nature, the religious person sees it as a miracle. It is not about a real action undertaken by a supernatural being.

> **Key quote**
>
> Nothing is esteemed a miracle, if it ever happens in the common course of nature.
>
> (Hume, *An Enquiry Concerning Human Understanding*)

Specification content
R.F. Holland (contingency miracle)

Key term
contingency miracle: a remarkable and beneficial coincidence that is interpreted in a religious fashion

It is therefore the interpretation of an ordinary event that makes it a miracle. Only if a person interprets the event as a miracle can the event be called a miracle. Otherwise, it is just a 'remarkable and beneficial coincidence'.

Richard Swinburne

Richard Swinburne (born 1934) endorses Hume's definition and accepts that a miracle is an objective event in which God intervenes. However, he also makes a significant change and an addition:

1. He borrows a phrase from Ninian Smart, to overcome what he regards as a misleading phrase that Hume used. Instead of Hume's phrase 'a violation of a law of nature', Swinburne uses the phrase 'an occurrence of a non-repeatable counter-instance to a law of nature'.

By this, he means:

- In most circumstances, laws of nature (L) occur.
- In the case of a miracle, an event (E) occurs that (somehow) replaces a law of nature. Swinburne calls 'E' a counter-instance to a law of nature.
- In addition, Swinburne regards 'E' as being a non-repeatable event.
- Because 'E' is a non-repeatable event, it would make no sense to replace the usual 'L' with a modified version that includes 'E' – the non-repeatable nature of 'E' means that it will not occur again and a modified 'L' would therefore make no sense.
- Therefore, if we leave 'L' as it is, we have good reason to believe it would give correct predictions in all other conceivable circumstances.

Consider the following example:

- An electric kettle is a device that boils water. It does this by sending a large electric current to the heating element, which heats up the water around it, eventually causing it to boil.
- We may consider this the 'law of nature' (L) for how an electric kettle works.
- Therefore L = every time we switch on the filled kettle, it will eventually boil the water.

However:

- Imagine if one day we fill the kettle up, switch it on and, instead of the water boiling (L), for some unaccountable reason, it freezes. We could therefore consider this a 'counter-instance to a law of nature' (E).
- We would not expect this occurrence to repeat itself – because if we modified our understanding of an electric kettle to a device that sometimes boils water and sometimes freezes it, then it would not be fit for purpose!
- Therefore, the event of the kettle freezing water is considered a non-repeatable counter-instance to a law of nature (E).
- As it is non-repeatable, we can assume that we don't need to get our kettle repaired because it is reasonable to believe that in the future it will just boil the water as it is supposed to (L).

Holland's example of a miracle

> **Specification content**
>
> Richard Swinburne (religious significance)

T3 Religious experience (2)

A working electric kettle should produce boiling water, not ice!

(The example above would not be considered a miracle, though, as it does not fulfil Swinburne's second condition – see below. The only way it could be considered as such is if the kettle's owner for some reason was in desperate need of ice and perhaps even prayed for some!)

2. Miracles hold some deeper religious significance than just breaking laws of nature. To be a miracle, an event must contribute significantly towards a holy divine purpose for the world. Miracles are also seen as signs from God. The word *sign* is used in John's Gospel to refer to Jesus' miracles in a way that always seem to point to something beyond the actual event. The miracles are not seen as an end in themselves.

> **Key quote**
>
> If a god intervened in the natural order to make a feather land here rather than there for no deep ultimate purpose, or to upset a child's box of toys just for spite, these events would not naturally be described as miracles.
>
> (Swinburne, *The Concept of Miracle*)

Why religious believers accept that miracles occur

A religious believer accepts that God exists. God's existence may be independently supported by traditional theistic arguments, such as the design argument. If there is also strong historical evidence that a miracle has occurred, then it seems reasonable to believe that it has, as long as there seems a suitable motive for God acting in this particular way.

Swinburne argues that natural theology establishes the probability that God would produce a revelation, which would need to be confirmed as authentic. Miracles could be the vehicle for this as long as the miracle could be judged as actual on the basis of historical investigation.

The nature of God as loving and compassionate may be another reason why religious believers accept that miracles occur. God in his love might be expected to intervene through compassion. The various world religions understand God to be loving and caring for his people. Therefore, God may be expected to intervene on occasions through miracles to show that love and care.

Specification content

Considerations of why religious believers accept that miracles occur: evidence from sacred writings

Swinburne also suggests that additional evidence for believing a miracle occurs could include the miracle happening in answer to a prayer, and if the prayer was addressed to a named person: for example, Jesus or Allah. If the world is God's creation, it becomes much more likely that he would wish to intervene and respond to requests to do so, in the form of a miracle.

Evidence from sacred writings

The sacred writings of many religions record supernatural events to demonstrate the significance of those who are accepted as God's messengers on Earth.

Judaism

In Judaism, for example, there are accounts of Moses parting the Red Sea to let the Hebrew people escape from the pursuing Egyptians. Furthermore, the feeding of the Hebrew people with manna from heaven and the miraculous defeat of Amalek also show the importance of Moses as a spiritual leader, validated by God working miracles through him.

Other accounts of miracles in Jewish scriptures are similarly used to confirm the significance of certain individuals and their being in receipt of God's favour, such as the miracles associated with Elijah, Ezekiel and Daniel.

Christianity

In Christianity, there are accounts of the miracles of Jesus, and Jesus' resurrection, as well as the miracles performed by the Apostles Peter and Paul.

Some historians, such as Carl Becker, argue that miracles cannot be the object of historical investigation since miracles claim to involve a supernatural being. However, this has been challenged. Consider the resurrection of Jesus, which Christians claim was performed by God. The event can be examined by historians since it is associated with other historical information not written by Christian authors, such as contemporary records by historians such as Tacitus and Josephus, for example:

- the crucifixion, death and entombment of Jesus
- Jesus' tomb discovered to be empty some days after his death
- the claim by Jesus' followers that they saw Jesus alive several days after his death and entombment.

It is true that the historian cannot identify the supernatural agent who is said to perform the miracle. However, it may be possible to detect through historical investigation various aspects of the supernatural agency of an alleged miracle. This is particularly true for religious believers, who see the world as a place where God is active in human events.

Buddhism

Buddhism is non-theistic, so it rejects the idea of a miracle as a 'sign of God'. There are examples in early Buddhist texts of people who developed supernatural powers from mystical practices, but the Buddha did not encourage this.

Islam

Although Islam accepts the supernatural, Muhammad refused to do wondrous signs to strengthen his authority. The performance of miracles for some Muslims is a sign that a person's intention is still directed towards worldly approval, and not exclusively towards God. Although, for many Muslims, the only miracle is the production of the Qur'an, there are some Muslims who nevertheless believe in miraculous stories associated with Muhammad.

Summary

Therefore, many religious believers claim they have reason to accept that miracles occur: their sacred writings, which are considered the word of God, contain accounts of miracles.

For Christians, the resurrection of Jesus affirms his status as the son of God

Affirmation of faith traditions

Many religious believers claim that only the 'true' religion has 'true' miracles, while other religions have either no miracles or 'false' miracles.

Miracles function like a divine signature, confirming the authority and truth claims of a particular faith tradition. The Judaeo-Christian tradition supports this view, for example:

> This salvation, which was first announced by the Lord, was confirmed to us by those who heard him. God also testified to it by signs, wonders and various miracles ... (Hebrews 2:3–4)

If God had an interest in communicating with people and if God desired that they were able to recognise some message as being from him, then it might be expected for miracles to occur. For instance, there is an account in some traditions of Islam that the people of Makkah asked Muhammad to show them a miracle. So Muhammad split the Moon into two by a gesture of his index finger. The halves of the Moon appeared one behind the mountain and the other in front of it. The miracle confirmed the authority of Muhammad to the people.

Many Christians would argue that the resurrection of Jesus confirms that Jesus is the Son of God and that Christianity is the one true religion. In both examples, for the religious believer, the miracle affirms the faith tradition.

Miracles can also be an essential element of the actual revelation. For example, according to the Christian tradition, Jesus entered the world by means of the virgin birth. Jesus died, overcame death by his resurrection and was victorious over evil. Christians see Jesus as the revelation itself, rather than as the one who *receives* the revelation.

Some religious believers may take the evidence of miracles in other religions to support the claim that those religions also make valid or true claims. They would argue that there is no reason why God should not work miracles within any religion, as each contains a valid response to the reality of God.

Personal experience

Miracles can generate and support faith in individuals, especially if they experience them personally. Good examples are the healing miracles that are claimed to have taken place at the Roman Catholic shrine at Lourdes. Since 1858, there have been 69 verified miracles or cures in Lourdes.

> **Specification content**
> Considerations of why religious believers accept that miracles occur: affirmation of faith traditions

> **Specification content**
> Considerations of why religious believers accept that miracles occur: personal experience

The most recent case occurred in 2008, but was not officially confirmed until 2018, after extensive investigation by a medical committee. The person healed was Sister Bernadette Moria, who lived with severe neurological conditions that modern medical science had been unable to alleviate. The medical committee concluded that her sudden healing at Lourdes was scientifically unexplainable.

The reason that religious believers go to Lourdes is that they believe in a personal God, and they have faith that God answers prayers. Therefore, they pray for God's intervention. The prayer for a miracle usually relates to a prayer for healing.

For religious believers, miracles are not just events in the past that happened to individuals to confirm their authority, but they are events that can happen in the present. They believe that God is active within his creation and works within the world to answer prayer.

Lourdes

Testimonies of personal healing are a feature of charismatic Christianity. Believers have a world-view where miracles, signs and wonders are expected to be present in their lives.

Therefore, one reason why religious believers accept that miracles occur is that they claim they have personal experience of them or that they know others who have.

Summary

- ★ The definition of miracles given by Aquinas recognises that miracles universally involve the action of God, whereas Hume's definition centres around the concept of (scientific) natural laws and the alleged intervention of a supernatural agent.
- ★ Holland's definition focuses on the way that certain events are interpreted as miraculous due to the witness's perspective. He regards miracles as beneficial coincidences.
- ★ Swinburne believes that for an event to be a miracle it needs to hold a deeper religious significance and be a one-off event, where the laws of nature could be temporarily altered to allow the miracle to occur.
- ★ Religious believers tend to accept the existence of miracles based on personal experience or due to evidence of such events in the sacred writings of their religion. They regard them as events that confirm the authority or truth of their religious tradition.

AO1 Activity

a Examine Hume's definition of *miracle* and his understanding of what constitutes a law of nature.

This helps with ensuring that you are making accurate use of specialist language and vocabulary in context.

b On revision cards, record the key reasons that religious believers accept that miracles exist.

This helps with presenting a thorough and extensive knowledge and understanding of the topic area.

> **This section covers AO2 content and skills**

> **Specification content**
> The adequacy of different definitions of miracles

Issues for analysis and evaluation

The adequacy of different definitions of miracles

Possible line of argument	Critical analysis and evaluation
There is debate over the criteria for what constitutes a miracle	The criteria for an event to be called a miracle has long been debated. What in the past may have caused wonder, may in the twenty-first century no longer be a cause for wonder. But does that necessarily stop it being a miracle? Certainly, Holland did not think so. His definition was not about a real action undertaken by a supernatural being. It was the interpretation of an ordinary event that made it a miracle.
Can we consider Holland's definition adequate?	In one sense, we could consider Holland's definition to be adequate since it is consistent with many people's world-view of a non-supernatural universe, and the meaning of the word *miracle* has been changed to fit in with that world-view. However, other people may not see it as adequate since it appears to call any unexpected beneficial event a miracle without any reference to a supernatural agent causing the event.
We can consider Holland's view adequate	One line of argument is that even Holland's definition is consistent with the idea of supernatural intervention. It is not a breaking of a law of nature so much as the supernatural agent working with the laws of nature and in the timing of the events. The result is a beneficial outcome. On this view, Holland's definition may be regarded as adequate.
How adequate is Aquinas' definition?	Thomas Aquinas gave an early definition of *miracle*. He linked the act of a miracle with divine cause, since miracles were events that were not a normal part of the nature of things. Although Aquinas' definition clearly involves a supernatural agent, many may judge his definition inadequate. This is because of his understanding that everything that exists has a nature given by God; our modern-day understanding is of the laws of nature as scientific and empirical events, independent of any supernatural cause.
How adequate is Hume's definition?	Hume provided one of the most popular definitions of *miracle*. He referred to 'a transgression of a law of nature by a particular volition of the Deity, or by the interposition of some invisible agent'. His definition has the idea of divine action and objectivity. However, much discussion has arisen over the idea of 'violating a law of nature'. To some, this description seems to imply that God is going against his own laws.
Views of the laws of nature are significant in the debate	Others, such as Alistair McKinnon, maintain that defining miracles as a violation of a law of nature is a contradiction in terms. Laws of nature exert no opposition or resistance to anything. They are simply highly generalised shorthand descriptions of how things do in fact happen. He suggests that it would be more accurate to replace the phrase 'natural law' with 'the actual course of events'. This means that his understanding of natural laws includes whatever happens. Therefore, Hume's definition is inadequate.
We can consider Swinburne's view adequate	Swinburne's definition attempts to overcome the problems of Hume's by rephrasing 'violations of a law of nature' as 'an occurrence of a non-repeatable counter-instance to a law of nature'. Swinburne also emphasises the purpose of miracles as 'signs'. Richard Purtill, in a chapter in *In Defence of Miracles*, identifies five parts to the definition of a miracle.

Possible line of argument	Critical analysis and evaluation
	- First, the exception to the natural order is temporary.
- Second, it is an exception to the ordinary course of nature.
- Third, unless you have the idea of a way things ordinarily happen, the idea of a miracle cannot be clear.
- Fourth, a miracle must be caused by the power of God.
- Finally, it must address the purpose of miracles – they must be a sign of God acting.

Taking this view, it seems that Swinburne's definition is the most comprehensive. |

AO2 Activity

a Analyse three possible conclusions that could be drawn from the critical analysis and evaluation of the adequacy of different definitions of miracles. What are their strengths and weaknesses? Which conclusion is strongest?

b Using the strongest conclusion, select three lines of argument that you would use to support this conclusion. Try to explain why you have selected these.

Exam practice

Sample question
Evaluate how far different definitions of miracles can be considered as contradictory.

Sample answer
The four definitions that are specified for study are those by Aquinas, Hume, Holland and Swinburne. One of the most obvious contradictions between these different definitions is that, while Hume and Swinburne see God as interventionist and breaking laws of nature, Holland sees natural courses of events and amazing coincidences. However, this may not in fact be a contradiction. They could be describing different types of miracles. Holland's definition refers to 'contingency' miracles. It is when several events, all with natural causes, come together that an event becomes unusual.

News reporter

This is a good introduction that provides a helpful overview of the key areas for focus in the evaluation to come.

If the context is of a believer who has an expectation of divine agency acting, possibly because of praying, then the event might well be described as a miracle. Norman Geisler refers to such events as a 'class two miracle'. The 'violation miracle' is what Hume and Swinburne described, where it appears that a law of nature has been violated. Both types of miracles involve divine agency, but working at different levels. So, is that really a contradiction? Aquinas' definition also supports divine agency but, because of scientific understanding at the time, he does not couch it in terms of breaking a law of nature. However, he does make clear that miracles are events that are different from the usual order. For Aquinas, a miracle is an event beyond the natural power of any created being. It has a 'divine cause' and so is not a normal part of the nature of things.

Detective

This paragraph presents significant evidence, via a line of reasoning, showing the grounds for considering the definitions as potentially contradictory.

Critical thinker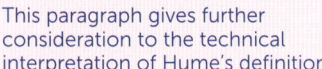

The candidate presents a line of reasoning that looks at the factors of subjectivity and objectivity as a technical aspect of the debate, examining how the different viewpoints contribute towards a coherent understanding of the issue.

Another line of argument focuses on the apparent contradiction between the relative subjectivity and objectivity of the miracle. The *contingency miracle* is subjective and becomes a miracle when someone interprets events in this way – usually from within the circle of believers. In contrast, the *violation miracle* is objective in that everyone – both sceptics and believers – identify the breaking of the law of nature. However, some may disagree. Those who reject the supernatural (*naturalism*) would argue that no law of nature has been broken. Rather, it is that we had an incomplete law and there exists a law of nature that incorporates the particular circumstance that occurred.

Critical thinker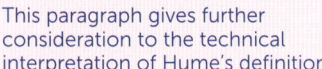

This paragraph gives further consideration to the technical interpretation of Hume's definition.

Another line of argument considers whether the definitions contradict in terms of the extent they allow for the possibility of miracles to happen. We can see some contradiction, depending on whether we adopt the 'hard' or 'soft' interpretation of Hume's definition. The 'hard' view understands the definition to rule out any possibility of miracles: that is, miracles cannot happen, by definition. The 'soft' interpretation of Hume's definition allows for the possibility that miracles *could* occur, rather than that they *have* occurred.

Detective

The candidate presents evidence to clarify the issue further around apparent contradiction.

Another possible area of contradiction involves the issue of the purpose of miracles. Hume does not consider this in his definition. Therefore, he does not link or associate miracles with some 'sign' from God or some beneficial intervention. In contrast, both Holland and Swinburne make clear that these are key elements of their definitions. We could argue that there is no contradiction between any of the definitions. They are merely focusing on different aspects and acknowledging two different types of events that can be called miracles (contingency and violation).

Philosopher

Judge

The response considers the evidence presented so far and draws the conclusion, following two pertinent questions, that it is ultimately the significance of the miracle to the religious believer, not the definition, that matters.

Indeed, this line of argument could accept that every definition of miracle is in itself correct, but just not the fullest definition we could offer. Such an argument would say that each definition is useful to a religious believer in the way they use it to strengthen their faith. Overall, perhaps the most important response to this issue would be 'does it really matter?' Surely, different or contradictory does not mean that this destroys the meaning, purpose or integrity of the miracle? After all, whether or not a miracle violates a law of nature or works within nature, the significance of either definition is what really matters for the religious believer.

Evaluation

This is an effective and balanced response. It considers both sides of the argument and raises questions before putting forward a conclusion. The candidate makes accurate use both of terminology and of the views of different philosophers.

Over to you

Below is an evaluation of whether definitions are suitable for identifying miracles. It has no references at all to support the arguments it presents. Beneath the evaluation are three references to the works of scholars that could be used to improve the evaluation.

Your task is to rewrite the evaluation, making use of the references. Such phrases as 'in his book … (scholar) argues that …', '… makes an interesting argument in support of this, suggesting that …' or 'the work of (scholar) has made a major contribution to the debate by pointing out …' may help.

In published work, references are often presented as footnotes, but for an answer in an A Level essay under examination conditions this is not expected. An awareness of which book or article your evidence comes from is also useful, although not always necessary.

When you have completed the task, try to write another reference that you could use and extend your evaluation further.

Evaluation

Before you can decide whether a miracle has happened, you must know how you would identify a miracle. Theists usually appeal to the definitions that involve a violation of a law of nature. However, it is not clear how you would know a law of nature had been broken. How is it possible to distinguish between an unusual event in nature, a law of nature that is not complete and a miracle? Equally, to appeal to a divine agency as the cause assumes that a divine being exists. Some would argue that it is a circular argument that appeals to miracles to prove the existence of God.

In response, some theists argue that events like the resurrection of Jesus are so unusual that a divine cause is the only explanation. However, no historical event can be justifiably identified as an act of God.

Theists may respond by arguing that there are other reasons for believing that there is a God. Others may argue that both the theist and the naturalist argue from a faith position. Neither side is able to falsify the other. Once the naturalists agree that they hold a faith position, then in all fairness they must allow other alternative world-views the same opportunity.

Reference 1

The problem of 'miracles' … must be solved in the realm of historical investigation, not in the realm of philosophical speculation. (Montgomery)

Reference 2

The odds for getting a perfect bridge hand are 1 in 1,635,013,559,600. But it happened – naturally! The argument from the odds to God amounts to saying that adding more zeros to the end of a probability ratio can transform an unusual event into a miracle. (Geisler)

Reference 3

If a miracle is merely a portent [that] is not contrary to nature, but contrary to our knowledge of nature, it has no real apologetic value. (Flew)

> This section covers AO1 content and skills

F: Contrasting views on the possibility of miracles: David Hume and Richard Swinburne

David Hume

Essay and scepticism of miracles

Although Hume's essay on miracles, which makes up Chapter 10 of his book *An Enquiry Concerning Human Understanding* (1777), is scarcely 20 pages long, it is regarded as a major contribution to the debate about miracles. He wrote it to convince readers that appealing to miracles could not demonstrate the truth of Christianity or religion in general.

The essay is in two parts:

- Part 1 attempts to show on philosophical grounds that the evidence against the occurrence of a supposed miracle strongly outweighs the evidence in favour of the occurrence.
- Part 2 attempts to show that although, in theory, the evidence in favour could outweigh the evidence against, in practice this never happens.

Hume was an **empiricist**, and therefore believed that all questions of truth had to be based on experience. This approach required the assessment of evidence. He felt that this was particularly important for any historical enquiry, since 'a wise person proportions their belief to the evidence'.

For example, if someone claims that an event has happened, then an investigator will weigh the evidence in favour of the event happening against the evidence that it did not happen. Part of that evidence will include the testimony of witnesses and the investigator's experience of what usually happens.

Hume's challenge relating to testimony-based belief

Given that a wise person 'proportions' their belief to the evidence, Hume examined the evidence for miracles. He concluded:

- Statement A: Where the experience (that is, what has happened) has been constant (i.e. it happened the way it has always previously happened), then this constitutes full proof.
- Statement B: Where it has been variable (i.e. it doesn't always happen in the same way), then it is a case of weighing the proportionate probability of the experience having happened against not having happened.

Where the belief is about miracles, a difficulty arises. This is because a miracle (according to Hume) is a violation of the laws of nature – something that is contrary to both Statements A and B.

In such a case, even the most impressive testimony would merely equal the improbability of the miracle, at best. Hume concludes that only testimony so strong that its falsehood would itself be more miraculous than the alleged miracle would convince him that a miracle had taken place – something that is highly unlikely, if not impossible.

Hume does not seem to deny the possibility of miracles as such, but examines the balance of probability. What is more likely: that a miracle occurred or that a witness is either lying or mistaken?

Miracles are, by definition, exceptional events, while people lying or being mistaken is common. Therefore, the probability seems against the miracle occurring; it is, on balance, more likely that a lie has been told or a mistake has been made.

Specification content

David Hume – his scepticism of miracles including challenges relating to testimony-based belief

---

Key term

empiricist: a person who believes that all knowledge is based on sense experience

---

" Key quote "

There is not to be found in all history, any miracle attested by a sufficient number of men, of such unquestioned good sense, education and learning …

(Hume, *An Enquiry Concerning Human Understanding*)

Hume's challenges relating to credibility of witnesses and susceptibility of belief

In Part 2 of his essay, Hume attempts to demonstrate that the quality of the testimony required to establish that a miracle has occurred needs to be of such high quality that it can never pass this test. For this reason, miracles can never be proved. He highlighted four reasons against the possibility of miracles, three of which concern the credibility of witnesses and susceptibility of belief. Those three reasons are:

1. No miracle has a sufficient number of witnesses. What is required is a quantity of educated, trustworthy witnesses to a public event in 'a celebrated part of the world'. They would have to be 'of such unquestioned good sense as to secure us against all delusions in themselves'. In particular, the witnesses would need to have a lot to lose if they were found to be lying. Hume claims that, in all history, such witnesses to a miracle have never been found.

2. People are prone to look for marvels and wonders. The passion and surprise arising from miracles, being an agreeable emotion, gives a tendency towards belief in those events. Hume contends that a religious believer may know the miracle is false, but 'perseveres in it, with the best intentions in the world, for the sake of promoting so holy a cause'. That is, he or she had a vested interest and was biased. Hume believes that these aspects can easily account for delusions about miracles.

3. The sources of miracle stories are ignorant people. This seems to refer partly to uneducated Galilean peasants, a possible reference to the New Testament gospels. Hume noted that there were no equivalents in his day that compared to the miracles recorded in the Bible. Therefore, he focused on the testimony of those in the distant past. The miracle stories acquired authority without critical or rational inquiry. If they had originated in 'a city renowned for arts and knowledge', rather than in some remote country, Hume maintains they would not have been believed.

> **Specification content**
> Challenges relating to the credibility of witnesses; susceptibility of belief

Hume's challenges relating to the contradictory nature of faith claims

Hume's fourth and final reason against miracles concerns his argument about religious traditions counteracting each other. Different religious traditions making competing claims of miracles make the claims unreliable.

For example, if an Islamic miracle supports Islam and so discredits Christianity as a true religion, then, equally, any claim of a Christian miracle will likewise discredit Islam. Therefore, evidence for one is evidence against the other, and vice versa.

Every supposed miracle is used to establish that particular tradition and therefore is an indirect attempt to destroy the creditability of other religions. Miracles are therefore self-cancelling as witnesses to the truth of a religious system.

> **Specification content**
> Challenges relating to the contradictory nature of faith claims

Richard Swinburne

Natural laws and miracles

Whereas Hume seems to reject the possibility of rational belief in miracles, Swinburne argues that there can be evidence that a law of nature has been contradicted, and so accepts that rational belief in miracles is possible. His main writings on miracles can be found in his book *The Concept of Miracle* (1970).

> **Specification content**
> Richard Swinburne – his defence of miracles, including definitions of natural laws

As discussed earlier, Swinburne accepted the basis of Hume's definition of a miracle but, instead of a miracle violating the laws of nature, Swinburne used the phrase 'a non-repeatable counter-instance to a law of nature'. He avoids the word *violation*.

Identifying a non-repeatable counter-instance to a law of nature

According to Swinburne, a non-repeatable counter-instance to a law of nature would have to fulfil three observations:

1. If we have good reason to believe that an event E has occurred contrary to predictions of L (what we assume is a law of nature), and we have good reason to believe that events similar to E would not occur again in similar circumstances, then there is every reason to think that L is indeed a law of nature.

2. It would have to be the case that if we tried to modify the law of nature to try to predict event E, then the modified law of nature will give false predictions in other circumstances.

3. If we leave the law of nature unmodified, we have good reason to believe that the unmodified law will give correct predictions in all other conceivable circumstances.

Can a non-repeatable counter-instance be believed to have happened?

Swinburne then addresses the question of what would be a good reason for believing that an event E, if it occurred, was a non-repeatable counter-instance to what we had assumed was the law of nature L, and not a repeatable counter-instance.

This is crucial because, if the event E is in fact a repeatable counter-instance, then all we would need to do would be to modify L to form a true law of nature that could also predict these repeatable counter-instances.

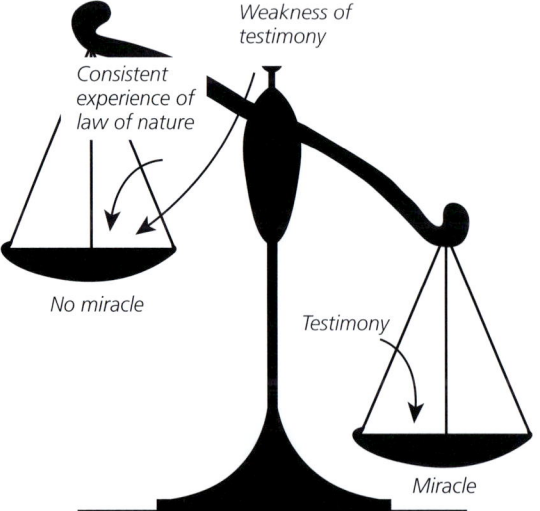

The issues involved in weighing up miracles

The philosopher Antony Flew commented that the reason Hume rejects historical evidence of witnesses and favours the law of nature not being violated is that the historical evidence is often appealing to a singular past event that is no longer possible to examine directly. In contrast, the supposed law of nature can be tested at any time by any person.

However, Swinburne points out that both historical and scientific evidence give only limited support to any claim. Also, both can be tested at any time by any person. The historical evidence is not just written or verbal testimony. It is also about the character, mind and competence of the original witnesses, as well as physical traces of the event or even present effects resulting from the event.

He concludes that 'the wise man in these circumstances will surely say that he has good reason to believe that E occurred, but also that L is a true law of nature and so that E was a violation of it'. As Swinburne comments, 'Whether there is such evidence is, of course, another matter.'

A non-repeatable counter-instance identified as a miracle

For a non-repeatable counter-instance to a law of nature to be a miracle, it has to be caused by a god or have some religious significance. (This was Swinburne's second condition in his definition of miracles.) To conclude that it was brought about by a rational agent would be to give a different kind of explanation.

If there is other evidence for the existence of God, then if event E is the sort of thing that is consistent with God's character and is otherwise unexplained, then Swinburne argues that it is reasonable to believe that God caused the event. In particular, he reasons that, if events occur that normally occur by the intentions of human beings but they occur without human beings, then it would be justifiable to claim a non-material being caused it: that is, a god.

Challenge to Hume on the contradictory nature of faith claims

Hume states that miracles in different religious traditions are contradictory and self-cancelling. If miracles are appealed to as evidence for the truth of religion, then miracles in another religious tradition would destroy the evidence of that religion, and vice versa.

However, Swinburne points out that Hume's argument is valid only if the two miracles are in conflict and incompatible. Swinburne claims that most alleged miracles do not give rise to conflict: for example, there is no conflict or contradiction between the resurrection of Jesus in Christianity and Muhammad splitting the Moon in Islam.

Swinburne gives a fictional example of two such miracles that would illustrate a conflicting claim:

1. A devout Roman Catholic priest might be praying for a miracle to demonstrate the truth of the doctrine of **transubstantiation**, when the **tabernacle** containing the **Sacrament** levitates.
2. A dedicated Protestant minister might pray for a miracle to show that the doctrine of transubstantiation is idolatrous. Then lightning strikes out of a cloudless sky and destroys the tabernacle.

These are conflicting miracles concerning doctrine, and Swinburne makes the point that religious miracles are not of this type.

A miracle in the context of Hinduism and one in the context of Islam will not usually show that specific details of their respective religions are true. Most, if they occurred, would show only the power of God or gods and their concern for the needs of people.

Challenge to Hume on the credibility of witnesses

Swinburne accepts that Hume's three arguments against miracles involving the credibility of witnesses are valid. However, he makes the point that the

Specification content
Richard Swinburne's defence of miracles — contradictions of Hume's arguments regarding contradictory nature of faith claims

Key terms
transubstantiation: the Roman Catholic doctrine that, in the Eucharist, the whole substance of the bread and wine changes into the substance of the body and blood of Christ
tabernacle: in Roman Catholicism, a box-like vessel for the exclusive reservation of the consecrated Eucharist
Sacrament: one of the Christian rites considered to have been instituted by Christ to confer or symbolise grace

Specification content
Richard Swinburne's defence of miracles — contradictions of Hume's arguments regarding credibility of witnesses

standards of evidence that Hume sets are very high, questioning what exactly constitutes a sufficient number of witnesses.

One of the purported miracles in Hume's essay concerns the Tomb of Abbé Paris. In this case, Hume considers the credibility of the witnesses in terms of their number, integrity and education as irrelevant, though they are of an exceptional quality. Hume regards the miraculous nature of the event sufficient to reject it.

The second of Hume's points against miracles concerns the love of gossip and the bias that some people have, such that they spread a miracle story even when they know it isn't true. Again, Swinburne does not deny that this happens, but comments that there are other people who are scrupulously honest and only historical investigation will show which group the witnesses to any alleged miracle are in. In contrast, Hume seems to assume all believers are either deceivers or deceived.

Hume's third point against miracles centres on their origin in what he takes to be ignorant and barbarous nations. Swinburne comments that Hume seems to identify an ignorant nation as one that believes miracles happen. To make such a connection would seem unjustified.

Swinburne lists three principles for weighing conflicting evidence, besides the most basic principle of accepting as many pieces of evidence as possible:

1. Evidence of different kinds ought to be given different weights. For instance, our own memory ought to count for more than the testimony of another witness, unless circumstances suggest otherwise: for example, 'I am sleep deprived'.
2. Different pieces of evidence ought to be given different weights in accordance with any empirical evidence that may be available about their different reliability. For instance, we can weigh the different conflicting testimonies by looking at how reliable previous testimonies by these witnesses have been.
3. Multiple similar testimonies from different witnesses ought to be given more weight against a lesser number of contrary testimonies, unless there is strong evidence of falsehood. For example, if five people all claim the same thing, then it is more persuasive than one person saying something contrary, unless we can explain why the five people all said the same: for instance, they had plotted together to give false testimony.

Swinburne argues that these principles for assessing conflicting evidence are relevant to weighing up the evidence for miracles.

AO1 Activity

a. Examine Hume's arguments against miracles.

This helps with presenting a thorough and extensive knowledge and understanding of the topic area.

b. Write a conversation between Hume and Swinburne about miracles. Each scholar should say one thing in turn, and then go back to the first philosopher for the second point, and so on. Think of questions each one would ask the other.

This helps with consolidating who said what and the objections they may have towards other definitions.

It also helps with presenting thorough, accurate and relevant knowledge and understanding of the topic area.

Summary

- Hume's essay on miracles sets out a definition for them, along with his philosophical arguments to demonstrate the unlikelihood of them occurring.
- Hume's essay also sets out to undermine the evidence base of those who claim miracles occur.
- Swinburne responds to Hume by examining the relationship between the concept of laws of nature and events claimed as miraculous, and finds that there need not be a contradiction between them.
- Swinburne suggests that Hume's philosophical arguments against miracles are unsound and that Hume's attack on the evidence base for miracles is unjustified.

> **Specification content**
> The effectiveness of the challenges to belief in miracles

This section covers AO2 content and skills

Issues for analysis and evaluation

The effectiveness of the challenges to belief in miracles

Possible line of argument	Critical analysis and evaluation
Are miracles just natural events that have been misunderstood?	If miracles are understood in the sense of 'contingency miracles', then many would argue that there is no problem in believing in such events happening. They are just natural events that are amazing coincidences. The theist would see God working through natural events, while the naturalist would not interpret the events as involving any divine agency.
Claiming a supernatural cause for an event makes no sense when there are laws of nature	The main challenges to belief in miracles have come from the more traditional understanding of miracles involving the breaking of a law of nature for a purpose by a divine being. One line of argument is to challenge the view that a divine agency is the necessary cause of the event. To claim that it must be ascribed to supernatural agents is to say something that no one could possibly have the right to affirm on the evidence of the event alone. Therefore, we should not use the term *miracle* in such instances.
Is it possible to break a law of nature?	Another challenge is the problem of being able to identify whether a law of nature has been broken. It could be that the law was just incomplete and there is a law that includes the circumstance that occurred. Swinburne attempted to address this problem by rephrasing what we mean by the breaking of a law of nature. He defines a miraculous event as the occurrence of a non-repeatable counter-instance to a law of nature. If the law is left unmodified, then we have reason to think it would give good predictions in all other conceivable circumstances. In this sense, it might be judged valid to claim that a law of nature has been broken in this one instance.
Belief in miracles, based on the testimony of believers, is unreasonable	Hume argued that it is unreasonable to believe in miracles. He considered that it will always be more reasonable to believe that the law of nature has not been broken than to believe testimony that the law of nature has been broken. Testimony to miracles has inherent weaknesses and so is likely to be unreliable and weaker than our everyday experiences of the regularity of nature.
We can accuse Hume's approach of being inconsistent	Hume himself gave an example in his essay 'On Miracles' that a large number of credible people had witnessed publicly – yet he dismissed the account as unreliable on the grounds that it was impossible. This suggests Hume decided it was unreasonable to believe in miracles regardless of the evidence.
The problem of evil raises a significant issue regarding miracles	The problem of evil remains a major problem for many people. If God is able to intervene, then why doesn't he address the real problems of the world more directly by means of miracles? This is part of the problem of evil and suffering. God has the means (power) and the motivation (love, goodness) to eliminate evil and suffering. Yet there is evil and suffering. God seems indifferent to the continued existence of suffering in the world.
Do we need to revise our understanding of what a law of nature is?	Perhaps we can solve the issue by looking at our understanding of the laws of nature. If laws of nature are generalisations formulated retrospectively to cover what has happened, then there cannot be miracles, for whenever any event happens that is outside of the established natural laws, it would simply mean that we must widen the law to cover this new case. Taking this understanding, supposed laws of nature are not broken but are better described as incomplete laws that we need to adapt to include the new happening. However, this still leaves us with the concept of a miracle that works within the laws of nature.

AO2 Activity

a Select three lines of argument from the critical analysis and evaluation of the effectiveness of the challenges to belief in miracles. Find three references from scholars, schools of thought or religious and philosophical texts that would support those arguments.

b Using the strongest line of argument, try to identify three key quotations that might be used — they could be from scholars, religious texts or schools of thought.

This is a good introduction that signposts the key points of the response, followed by a consideration of the first point.

This paragraph presents evidence showing Swinburne's response to Hume and the reasons for the response to be considered as valid.

This paragraph provides further evidence, before an evaluation that provokes a question about the validity of Hume's view.

The candidate further examines the inconsistency of Hume's attack on miracles, and questions the coherence of his argument.

This paragraph makes a further point, with commentary, regarding Hume's view.

Specification content
The extent to which Swinburne's responses to Hume can be accepted as valid

Exam practice

Sample question
Evaluate the extent to which Swinburne's responses to Hume can be accepted as valid.

Sample answer

Swinburne's responses to Hume cover three main areas. The first concerns Hume's actual definition of miracles. Swinburne interprets the definition as the 'soft' meaning rather than the 'hard' meaning. Swinburne's rephrasing of 'a violation of a law of nature' seems helpful. It makes clear that identification of the breaking of a law of nature requires that the exception to the natural order is temporary and it is an exception to the ordinary course of nature. Many scholars feel that Swinburne's addition to the definition that includes 'purpose' is important. This fits in with the idea of religious 'signs' rather than a God who just 'shows off'.

The second area in which Swinburne responded to Hume concerned claims that miracles in different religious traditions were contradictory and therefore self-cancelling. The reasoning is that if miracles are appealed to as evidence for the truth of a religion, then miracles in another religious tradition would destroy the evidence of that religion. However, it is not clear that miracles do actually give rise to conflict. They tend to show the power of God or gods, and their concern for the needs of people. For them to be contradictory would require a miracle to authenticate two opposing doctrines. Swinburne claims this has not occurred.

Swinburne's third area responding to Hume concerns the credibility of witnesses. Hume cites a number of reasons, including the absence of a sufficient number of quality witnesses. We could argue that Hume's argument is reasonable since the witnesses must be trustworthy and reliable. However, a weakness in the argument is that it is not clear how many witnesses are required to qualify for 'sufficient'. Is belief ultimately based on the number of witnesses? Maybe the nature of the event and the extent to which it is consistent with the nature of God and his purposes are more significant than how many witnesses there are to the event.

Hume seems to write as if all believers are either deceivers or deceived. In his chapter on miracles in his book An Enquiry Concerning Human Understanding, he cites some miracles that occurred in France that supposedly took place in his own lifetime. Hume acknowledges that the events were witnessed by people of unquestioned integrity. However, Hume refuses to credit such testimony on the grounds of 'the absolute impossibility or miraculous nature of the events which they relate'. This implies that Hume rejected miracles regardless of the evidence. However, as an empiricist he surely should go by the evidence. It raises the wider question as to the extent that weight of evidence can persuade us to change our minds.

Another aspect of testimony that Hume raises against miracles concerns the love of gossip and bias of people who tend to spread stories of miracles – especially if the account is used to establish a religion – even though they know the miracles to be false. Hume also claims that the origins of miracles were from ignorant and barbarous nations, resulting in the miracle stories acquiring authority without critical or rational inquiry.

WJEC/Eduqas Religious Studies for A Level Philosophy of Religion

Certainly, Swinburne seems correct in drawing attention to the different weighting that should be given to various witnesses. For instance, multiple similar testimonies from different witnesses ought to be given more weight than a lesser number of contrary testimonies, unless there is strong evidence of falsehood: for example, they had plotted together to give false testimony. However, we do know that accounts can undergo change as they are passed on. It has also been argued that miracles cannot be open to historical research, since a miracle is ascribed to an agent that is non-empirical and supernatural and so cannot be detected by historical methods.

Critical thinker

This paragraph evaluates Swinburne's response and considers the coherence of the argument.

Another line of argument is to follow Swinburne's positive reasons for believing in miracles. He argues that we should expect miracles because God needs to communicate with his creatures and to authenticate his message. He further argues that, if the event happens in response to prayer and is consistent with the nature of God, then it is acceptable historical evidence. Some may conclude that Swinburne raises valid responses to Hume's arguments. However, it may well be that the believer and the naturalist, with their different world-views, will remain unconvinced of the other's position.

Judge

The response considers the evidence presented so far and draws the conclusion that the persuasiveness of each form of argument may be an entirely subjective matter, based on preference.

Evaluation

This is an effective and balanced response. It considers both sides of the argument and raises questions before putting forward a conclusion. The candidate makes accurate use both of terminology and of the views of different philosophers.

Over to you

Below is an evaluation of whether Hume displayed a contradictory approach to miracles. As it stands, it is a weak argument because it has no quotations or references as support it.

This time, find your own quotations (about three) and use your own references (about three) to strengthen the evaluation. Remember, sometimes a quotation can follow from a reference, but you can also use them as separate points.

The result will be a fairly lengthy answer. You could check it against the band descriptors for A2 (WJEC) or A Level (Eduqas) and, in particular, look at the demands described in the higher band descriptors, which you should be aspiring towards. Ask yourself:

- Is my answer a confident, critical analysis and perceptive evaluation of the issue?
- Have I used the views of scholars/schools of thought extensively, appropriately and in context?
- When used, is specialist language and vocabulary both thorough and accurate?

Evaluation

Scholars disagree as to the extent that Hume's essays contain contradictory ideas. One area that appears contradictory is whether Hume thought that miracles were impossible. Both in his definition and in his assessment of particular miracles, he seems ambiguous. Certainly, if we take a 'hard' interpretation of his definition, it seems that laws of nature cannot be violated regardless of alleged evidence to the contrary. However, if we take the 'soft' interpretation, then it appears it is more an issue of the strength of the evidence as to whether a miracle occurred.

It is not clear whether Hume contradicts his supposed empiricist position when he assesses miracles. An empiricist should be led by the evidence, yet his approach seems to contain some *a priori* arguments.

T4 Religious language (1)

> **This section covers AO1 content and skills**

> **Specification content**
> Limitations of language for traditional conceptions of God such as infinite and timeless

A: Inherent problems of religious language

Limitations of language for traditional conceptions of God: infinite and timeless

Our communication depends on language. This may sound like an obvious statement to make, but the implications are significant and it is important that we set these out from the beginning. Whether we are speaking to someone, listening to someone, writing something or reading something, we make many assumptions about the nature of communication that we take for granted.

One such assumption is that we can be understood.

If this is not true, then our communication is ineffective. Our speaking and writing is nothing more than random sounds and shapes, as our intended audience cannot interpret what we are trying to say. Equally, if we do not possess the tools that allow us to decode what we hear and what we read, then communication is again rendered ineffective.

Experience-based language

All our language is based on experience. Communication is about, among other things, sharing ideas, experiences and realities with each other. For these to be meaningful, we must be able to relate in some way to what we are being told. In other words, we need to have some shared experience base upon which to build our understanding of the language that we also share. Language that communicates common experiences (e.g. my house is made of red bricks, my car is black and so on) presents no difficulty for interpretation, which is rooted in a shared experience.

For example, to discuss what it means for water to be wet, it is necessary for us to have experienced water and to understand what the concept *wet* refers to. Once we have an agreed common understanding of these things, then such statements become both understandable and meaningful.

How would you describe the 'wetness' of water if you had never experienced it?

Perhaps, importantly, even if we did not have access to either of these things, we could understand what the meaning was in principle, as we would understand how we could gain the experience necessary to understand them.

We exist in space, a space that can be measured in three dimensions – that of height and width and depth. We quantify the world around us by reference to this finite (measurable) space. It has edges, corners, limits, boundaries. It is observable and can be experienced empirically. It makes sense to us – our disciplines of physical science and engineering depend on us having a definable sense of what finite space is. To discuss something as being 'infinite' is to talk about something that can't be observed, can't be measured, and therefore can't be experienced in a quantifiable, measurable way. How then can the concept of infinite make sense to us?

Equally we have a concept of time – it is how we measure our days, our existence. It is how we refer to our histories and it is a framework by which we discuss our futures. We live in time; we experience time. Time is therefore meaningful to us. To suggest that something is 'timeless' is therefore to suggest something that is beyond our experience, something that is abstract and intangible. It makes no sense to our lived experience.

Issues with metaphysical language

The vast majority of everyday communication is about the physical world: that is, after all, the world we inhabit. However, there are also forms of communication that deal with aspects of our lives that are not to be found in the physical world. Language about emotions, ideas, expressions of artistic preferences, ethical discussions and language about religion all go beyond what is found in our physical realities. Such concepts are sometimes referred to as **metaphysical**.

For some, such language is often dismissed as not having the same level of meaning as language about the physical world, because there can be no objective agreement on the experiences being discussed. Indeed, some like David Hume consider such language to have no value in the empirical world.

Key term

metaphysical: something that is beyond, or not found in, the physical world

>
>
> If we take in our hand any volume; of divinity or school metaphysics, for instance; let us ask, Does it contain any abstract reasoning concerning quantity or number? No. Does it contain any experimental reasoning concerning matter of fact and existence? No. Commit it then to the flames: for it can contain nothing but sophistry and illusion.
>
> (Hume, *An Enquiry Concerning Human Understanding*)

While this is not a direct attack on the use of metaphysical language as such, it provided a foundation for others later to attack this type of language. We will see this when we look at the work of the **Logical Positivists**.

Key term

Logical Positivists: philosophers who supported the claim that language could be meaningful only if it could be verified by empirical means

How can we talk meaningfully about an infinite God?

Limitations of experience-based language

As our language is based on experience, and our experiences are generally confined to the empirical world and our interactions with it, our language is somewhat limited in its scope to discuss things beyond this. For example, we can describe any object in a three-dimensional physical space but, were someone to ask us how we might describe the same object in five-dimensional space, we would struggle. This is because our experiences are rooted in three-dimensional physical spaces. We do not exist in five dimensions.

Therefore, talk about such ideas becomes problematic – unless we are mathematicians. A mathematician might talk about five dimensions with some confidence – albeit in terms of an abstract concept. Other mathematicians might well understand this discussion, but it is unlikely that people who are not mathematicians familiar with fifth-dimensional mathematical constructs would be able to make sense of it.

The same might be said of religious language. Indeed, the language used to express the 'Ultimate' or 'God' within a religious tradition encounters the same problems. For example, God as infinite and timeless appears more like a mathematical, abstract claim than a reality that we see and experience in the world around us. God is often considered transcendent, a spirit, beyond this world of experience or, in the case of Buddhist nirvana, impossible to express.

The main problem remains, then, that religious language about God is unverifiable in relation to our common base of experiences that give language its meaning.

The challenge to sacred texts and religious pronouncements as unintelligible

> **Specification content**
> Challenge to sacred texts and religious pronouncements as unintelligible

If language is the method of communication, then religious language is the method of communicating about religion. In simple terms, religious language might be used to describe physical objects with religious connotations, such as places of worship or collections of sacred writings; or it might be describing the physical action that a religious believer undertakes during a specific

Different places of worship all use specific and different religious languages

religious ritual. In all such cases, the language is understandable and relatable because it deals with the observable and experienced empirical world.

However, once the religious language goes on to describe the divinities that are worshipped in such buildings or the teachings relating to an afterlife that may be contained within sacred writings – or even how the ritual actions being performed can purify an individual's soul – then suddenly what is being communicated may not be either understandable or relatable.

For instance, how does a non-believer know what is meant when he or she is greeted on entering a Pentecostal Church with the question, 'Have you been washed in the blood?' or told that 'God's presence is here' or even that 'Heaven and Hell are religious truths'? The same can be said for other religious traditions and their particular descriptions of beliefs and experiences.

The challenge that religious language is not a common shared base and experience

For this reason of unintelligibility, there are some philosophers who consider that religious language is inherently problematic, purely on the basis of it not communicating ideas that can be agreed upon by all as possessing an empirically knowable 'truth'. When talking about the traditional conceptions of God, there is no common or shared experience universally applicable to those with a faith commitment and those without. Our language is experience based – and our experiences are time limited: that is, they are based within the confines of time, in that they have a past, present and

> **Specification content**
> Challenge that religious language is not a common shared base and experience

future. Therefore, to talk about things beyond our experience means to move away from that which can be known. To talk about things beyond time – with concepts such as infinity or timelessness – means to talk about ideas that can only ever be expressed in abstract terms. At this point, the empirical understanding of language breaks down.

To reiterate: if I talk about the place of worship that I attend, then I can describe its physical location and features. What I am talking about can be 'known' by others via empirical and experience-based means. There is no problem with my description. Once I begin to talk about my belief of an infinite, timeless, transcendent divinity that loves me and has a specific plan and purpose for my eternal soul, then no empirical or experience-based means could establish the truth of what I have just said.

In a similar way, the experience of darshan for a Hindu performing puja in a Hindu temple, the Buddhist experience of the jhanas, the presence of the Holy Spirit during worship and sacraments for a Christian and the experience of Shekhinah during worship for a Jewish devotee are all beyond the empirical or experience-based means that could establish the truth of what, in fact, they have all proposed to have 'experienced'. This is because all such language is specific to the individual or community that describes it. It is this fact, for many philosophers, that immediately removes it from the possibility of universal **verification**.

This, in summary, is the inherent problem of religious language.

> **Key term**
>
> **verification:** proving something true by using evidence that counts towards it

> **Specification content**
>
> The differences between cognitive and non-cognitive language

The differences between cognitive and non-cognitive language

Philosophers who are considering how language is used generally divide it into two main forms. These forms are **cognitive** and **non-cognitive** language. While these terms may appear complex, their meaning is quite straightforward. Applying them to the way that we use language is particularly useful when we attempt to consider whether or not language is meaningful. The act of cognition is the act of knowing something; not by intuition, but by knowledge and understanding that is gained through experiences and the senses.

Cognitive language

Cognitive language is any form of language that makes an assertion, which is usually factual in the sense that it can be demonstrated to be true or false by objective means. These means might be through verification or **falsification**

> **Key terms**
>
> **cognitive:** language that is empirically verifiable and makes assertions about objective reality
>
> **non-cognitive:** language that is subjective, not empirically verifiable or falsifiable, but instead expresses an attitude towards something
>
> **falsification:** proving something false by using evidence that counts against it

Non-cognitive language is not always clear to another because it expresses opinions, attitudes, feelings and emotions (see Theme 4, Section B). Scientific language – in the sense of language used in science to describe the external world – is exclusively cognitive; expressed in terms of what is known or can be known.

Religious language, however, is not as straightforward. When religious language is used in a cognitive sense, it is referring to a statement that is believed to be true, such as in the statements used in the traditional theistic proofs. These statements purport to be able to determine that God exists as an external reality that can be shown to be true via empirically verifiable means: for example, in the cosmological argument when the series of causes and effects are linked to the concept of there being an initial first cause, which theistic philosophers claim to be God.

Non-cognitive language

When language is non-cognitive, it is not used to express empirically knowable facts about the external world. It is not something that can be held up to objective scrutiny. This is because non-cognitive language is language that expresses opinions, attitudes, feelings and/or emotions. It is language that relates to individuals' views of what reality may mean to them – and this may differ from the view of someone else, even though he or she may be experiencing the same reality. Both views are held to be valid – but in a non-cognitive sense. For instance, have you ever woken up in a bad mood? Has it affected the way you have viewed the people and world around you? This is because your non-cognitive view of the world has a reality that is 'true' for you – even if it is not an empirically verifiable fact of the actual external reality of the people and world around you! (If you woke up in a really good mood, the same world and people would impact on you differently again.)

Non-cognitive language is often used in religious communication, according to several religious philosophers. This is because it is language that is making claims about believers' attitude towards the world around them, based on their religiously held beliefs.

Summary

★ We make many assumptions about the nature of communication that are not always justified and therefore can lead to misunderstandings in what we are trying to communicate.

★ All the language we have is based on our lived experience; therefore, to understand anything, we need to have a shared experience of what that 'thing' is. This causes issues when we communicate about anything metaphysical as it is impossible to know for certain (empirically speaking) what it is we are communicating about.

★ This is the basis of the main challenges to the meaningfulness of religious language. It is an inherent problem that religious language has, as it communicates ideas about metaphysical concepts such as the divine and the afterlife as well as ethics.

★ Philosophers make a distinction when talking about language as to whether it is cognitive (objective) or non-cognitive (subjective).

AO1 Activity

a Examine the inherent problems of religious language.

This helps with presenting a thorough and extensive knowledge and understanding of the topic area.

b Using revision cards, on one side write a key word or phrase that identifies a problem and on the reverse write an explanation of the problem.

This helps with prioritising and selecting a core set of points to develop an answer and with making accurate use of specialist language and vocabulary in context.

> This section covers AO2 content and skills

> **Specification content**
> The solutions presented by religious philosophers for the inherent problems of using religious language

Issues for analysis and evaluation

The solutions presented by religious philosophers for the inherent problems of using religious language

Possible line of argument	Critical analysis and evaluation
There are both challenges and defences to the meaningfulness of religious language	While the challenges to the meaningfulness of religious language have been considerable, there have also been a number of responses that attempt to stave off these challenges.
Aquinas argues that analogy is a meaningful way to talk about God	Aquinas considers that meaningful talk about religion, and specifically God, is limited by our experience as human beings. Therefore, we have to find ways within our limited experience to express ideas and truths about the divine. For Aquinas, this is by way of analogy, and his two forms of analogical language – that of *attribution* and that of *proportion* – provide meaningful insights into a reality that human beings could only ever hope to glimpse part of.
There is disagreement regarding the validity of Aquinas' views	Of course, the challenge to Aquinas' assertions is that analogy does not give us a full understanding of what it is that is being discussed, nor an objectively agreed idea about what we mean when discussing such ideas. However, Aquinas would say that to try and qualify religious language in such a way is to miss the point of the function of religious language.
Responses to falsification provide effective solutions to the problems of religious language	Philosophers such as Antony Flew raise other issues. He considers that, unless religious believers would allow something to count against (falsify) their beliefs, then those beliefs are meaningless. However, philosophers such as Richard Swinburne say that concepts exist that we can easily imagine but cannot find evidence against, but the concept still has meaning for us (e.g. toys in a cupboard that dance across the floor when nobody is watching).
Meaningfulness comes from deeply held beliefs	Religious language expresses an attitude towards life, as much as it expresses ideas about external reality. R.M. Hare demonstrated through his idea of the *blik* that a deeply held belief is meaningful to the individual, even when the language about that belief cannot be shown to be empirically verifiable. The way individuals live their life, and how they view the world around them, is deeply meaningful to them because of their religious beliefs, irrespective of what others may be able to understand.
Those who consider religious language to be inherently problematic are too reductionist in their views	While those who have a reductionist view of the function of language, such as Logical Positivists, may challenge religious language in terms of its meaningfulness, it retains meaning for those who hold religious beliefs. There is a continued debate over whether religious language should have to be shown to be meaningful via empirical means to overcome its perceived 'inherent problems'.

AO2 Activity

a Evaluate three lines of argument from the critical analysis and evaluation of the solutions presented by religious philosophers for the inherent problems of using religious language. What are their strengths and weaknesses? Which line of argument is strongest?

b Using the strongest line of argument, try to identify three key questions that might be asked – they could be critical, challenge, hypothetical or direct questions.

Exam practice

Sample question

Evaluate the exclusive context of religious belief for an understanding of religious language.

Sample answer

To claim a belief that 'God loves me'; that 'Allah is The One, The Indivisible'; that 'Vishnu is the Preserver' is to use language that, without context, may appear confusing at best, meaningless at worst. Each of these phrases reflects not just a particular religious tradition, but also a deeply held set of beliefs about the character of the divine being that is referenced. Such beliefs are often viewed as not being discoverable outside of those religious traditions, as there is no objectively agreed reality in reference to each of them, that is universally accepted both inside and outside of religious belief.

We can therefore ask whether this language can have any meaning at all outside of religious belief. Is religious language ultimately an entirely exclusive form of communication, inaccessible to those outside of the tradition?

In his theory of language games, Ludwig Wittgenstein considers that the way to understand language is by considering how it is used ('ask not for its meaning but for its use'). Wittgenstein considers that each area of human activity can often be recognised by its specialised use of language. He refers to these as 'language games', and suggests that, unless you understand the 'rules of the game', you will not be able to access the meaning of the language. In the same way that you would not play the game of cricket using the rules of backgammon, you would not expect to be able to play the game of 'religious language' using the game of 'secular language'.

Considering D.Z. Phillips' development of Wittgenstein's ideas, the theory of language games is an anti-realist view of the 'truth'. In other words, as long as the community that uses language and associated beliefs understands and agrees on them, then they have the same value as any other similar sets of languages and beliefs in alternative communities. This reinforces the idea that only those who hold the religious beliefs can understand religious language.

> **Specification content**
> The exclusive context of religious belief for an understanding of religious language

This is a good introduction that provides a helpful overview of the key areas for focus in the evaluation to come. It also raises relevant questions.

This paragraph presents evidence, focusing on the contribution of Wittgenstein and providing accurate and relevant examples to support the line of reasoning.

This paragraph develops the previous point, with additional commentary and relevant evidence supporting the argument.

This paragraph provides a counterpoint regarding the way language is understood. The answer gives a good understanding of how this newly introduced concept applies to the debate.

This paragraph explores an alternative line of reasoning, drawing on relevant evidence to show how religious language can be understood in the same way as moral claims.

This section presents a different line of reasoning that argues, with significant supporting evidence and examples, that religious language has a specific purpose and it should not matter whether those outside religion do not understand it.

The response considers the evidence presented so far and asks a series of questions that, by the conclusion that they lead to, effectively undermine the assumption that there is an exclusivity of religious language.

A response from other philosophers, such as Swinburne, suggests that this is a misunderstanding of how language functions, and that religious language and its meaning are equally valid in the 'realist' theory of truth. By this they mean that, when religious believers state their beliefs, the beliefs are not just some community-agreed beliefs that do not extend beyond that community, but are instead beliefs that correspond to an objective reality beyond the community. (This is why others, such as the Logical Positivists, believe that they can legitimately challenge the meaningfulness of religious language, as they dispute this belief.)

To dispute the claim further that religious language is exclusive to the context of religious belief, philosophers such as R.B. Braithwaite claim that religious language is meaningful to those outside of religion, in a similar way that moral claims are meaningful. His view is that religious statements are expressions of a particular attitude or intention of how life is to be lived and, as such, are very similar to the way moral language is used: that is, to express an opinion or attitude about the relative ethical value of a belief or action, and to live life accordingly. For Braithwaite, religious language is meaningful, whatever the context, as it is a non-cognitive form of language. It is not a form of language that has any empirical significance, but it is understandable as an attitude towards life.

Religious language is used to transmit religious beliefs – this is a clearly understandable idea. It is used, most commonly, by people who name themselves as religious – again, an understandable idea. However, we should also remember that, in the vast majority of cases, these people also operate in other spheres of life – beyond that of just their religion. They therefore engage in other forms of life and language. Is it sensible to suggest that their use of language when discussing religion is intelligible only to those who share their beliefs?

When the Roman Catholic priest speaks of transubstantiation, that the blessed sacrament is the body and blood of the saviour Christ, it is clearly important that Roman Catholic believers understand what he is saying. The communication between these two parties is intimately linked to the beliefs of the religion, and it is not important that anyone outside the tradition actually understands the meaningfulness of these faith claims.

Equally, the Islamic believer who discusses the concept of the Ummah with another Muslim understands what is meant and how the practices of zakah and salah help to reinforce this belief as an essential part of what it means to be Muslim. Again, it is not important whether anyone outside the tradition understands these things – they are serving a specific purpose: to provide the believers with a context where they can make sense of their faith and understand the contributions of their various actions towards it.

In neither of these cases is it being argued that the religious language cannot be understood by those outside the religion; rather it is argued that it is not important for the practice of the religion whether or not they can. If this is so, then how does a religious person 'share their faith' with a non-religious person? Where does this leave the evangelist? How can the theist have a meaningful debate with an atheist? If the view is (seriously) held that religious language is truly exclusive to the context of religious belief, then it would appear that religion is doomed to an insular existence without possibility of conversion, interaction or debate beyond the confines of the seminary, yeshiva or madrassa. The very fact that there is religious debate and discussion between members of different faiths, as well as between those of faith and those of no faith, would suggest that this view of exclusivity is quite simply untrue.

Evaluation

This is an effective and well-balanced response. It considers different views of the argument and raises questions before putting forward a conclusion. The candidate makes accurate use of both terminology and the views of different schools of thought.

Over to you

Below is a one-sided view concerning a possible solution to the inherent problems of religious language. It is around 150 words long.

Presenting one side of an argument or one line of reasoning is not really evaluating it. Add a counter argument or alternative line of reasoning to the paragraph to make the evaluation more balanced. Write about 150 words for your counter argument or alternative line of reasoning.

Then, think of another line of argument or reasoning that might support either argument, or even a completely different argument, and add it to your answer.

Finally, ask yourself: will my work, when developed, contain thorough, sustained and clear views that I have supported with extensive, detailed reasoning and/or evidence?

One-sided view

We should not consider religious language as a statement that can be empirically verified in the way that a scientific statement about the nature of reality can be. To do so is to misunderstand what type of language religious language is. Religious language is not cognitive language; it is not language that expresses empirically verifiable, objectively knowable, facts about the world. That is not its purpose or its function. Instead, we should consider religious language as non-cognitive, in that it is something that expresses an attitude towards something else. For example, a religious believer who states that 'I believe that the world was created by a divine being', is in fact stating their belief that it is a sacred place, and that a being exists with the power to create it. As non-cognitive language, it is not subject to the same criticisms as cognitive language.

> **This section covers AO1 content and skills**

> **Specification content**
>
> Logical Positivism – verification by Alfred J. Ayer (A.J. Ayer) – religious ethical language as meaningless; there can be no way in which we could verify the truth or falsehood of the propositions (e.g. God is good, murder is wrong); falsification – nothing can counter the belief (Antony Flew).

>  **Key terms**
>
> **tenets:** key beliefs or principles
> **tautological:** a self-explanatory statement in which something is repeated in different words (e.g. 'The summit was at the top of the mountain'.)

B: Religious language as cognitive, but meaningless

Logical Positivism

Logical Positivism was a philosophical movement that grew out of the work of a group of philosophers known as the Vienna Circle. This highly influential group of philosophers met in the 1920s and 1930s, and considered their task to be a philosophically driven systematic reduction of all knowledge to basic scientific and logical formulations.

In other words, in considering language as the means by which all human knowledge is transmitted, they applied the same criteria as they used in mathematics and scientific investigation, and thus moved to a position that acknowledged two things:

1. Anything outside of basic logical and scientific **tenets** is meaningless, since it is unverifiable.
2. What remains are **tautological** (self-explanatory) statements and statements that could be verified by observations from first-person sense experience (this can also be regarded as empirical experience).

The Vienna Circle disbanded when the Nazi Party came to power in Germany in the 1930s. Many of its members subsequently emigrated to the USA and were able to continue working and developing the ideas associated with the Vienna Circle in the academic institutions there. However, one of its key founding members, Moritz Schlick, remained and was killed by a Nazi sympathiser in Vienna in 1936. The ideas that the Vienna Circle promoted, such as the principles of both verification and falsification, remained popular until the mid-twentieth century.

Verification

To verify something is to show something to be true – to authenticate it – by some form of testimony or evidence. The Logical Positivists viewed scientific knowledge as the paradigm of knowledge (experiments and observations), since it had proved successful and resulted in agreed knowledge. Therefore, according to Logical Positivism, the only two forms of knowledge were logical reasoning and statements that were open to empirical evidence. These were:

- tautological statements
- mathematical statements
- synthetic statements (a statement that could be verified by some form of sense experience or experiment – for example, 'my car has four wheels')
- analytic statements (where the truth of the statement is determined within the statement itself – for example, 'all spinsters are unmarried females').

Statements that lay outside of such logical reasoning and empirical evidence were considered meaningless.

For Schlick and the Logical Positivists, this became known as the *verification principle*: the meaning of a statement is its method of verification. That is, we know the meaning of a statement if we know the logical or empirical conditions that would show that the statement is either true or false.

A.J. Ayer

The spread of the Logical Positivist movement in Britain is credited to A.J. Ayer. In 1936, he wrote the influential *Language, Truth and Logic*. In this book, he set out the criteria for how language could be considered meaningful: a synthetic statement is meaningful if and only if it has some relation to observation. Ayer also attacked metaphysics, regarding it as essentially meaningless – being nothing more than a misunderstanding of how reality should be described. He regarded metaphysicians as 'devoted to the production of nonsense'.

In rejecting metaphysical statements (such as 'God is good' and 'murder is wrong'), Ayer (and Logical Positivists in general) rejected as meaningless any statement that did not fit their criteria of meaning. These statements were rejected as there was no way of being able to determine their 'truth'. What sense experience or logical reasoning could be used to demonstrate the truth of what was being asserted? (This meant a rejection of not only religious language but also language that was related to ethics, and statements relating to any form of abstract thought – which would include statements relating to an appreciation of art, music or literature.)

The verification principle was an attempt to establish a criterion of meaning for how we use language about the world

Verification in practice and in principle

Ayer, however, recognised that the principle of verification, as set out by the Logical Positivists, had a clear limitation. It could not take into account those statements that were made about things that were accepted as meaningful even though they were not considered to be immediately verifiable in practice. For example, there is no observation possible now that could verify the truth of historical statements such as 'Lord Nelson won the Battle of Trafalgar'. However, clearly most people would argue that this is meaningful (and indeed true).

Similarly, scientific statements such as 'water always boils at 100 degrees Celsius' (meaningful but actually false) are not verifiable by observation. We cannot experience firsthand (and therefore verify) events of the past, and it is not possible to observe (and therefore verify) that all water boils at 100 degrees Celsius.

It was for these reasons that Ayer made a distinction between verifiability 'in practice' and verifiability 'in principle'.

> In the first place, it is necessary to draw a distinction between practical verifiability, and verifiability in principle. Plainly we all understand, in many cases believe, propositions which we have not in fact taken steps to verify ... But there remain a number of significant propositions, concerning matters of fact, which we could not verify even if we chose; simply because we lack the practical means of placing ourselves in the situation where the relevant observations could be made.

> A simple and familiar example of such a proposition is the proposition that there are mountains on the farther side of the moon! No rocket has yet been invented which would enable me to go and look at the farther side of the moon, so that I am unable to decide the matter by actual observation. But I do know what observations would decide it for me, if, as is theoretically conceivable, I were once in a position to make them. And therefore I say that the proposition is verifiable in principle, if not in practice, and is accordingly significant.
> (Ayer, *Language Truth and Logic*)

Therefore:

- The criterion of 'in practice' refers to those statements whose truth or falsehood could be determined by some observation or experiment that could be carried out in the present day.
- The criterion of 'in principle' allows verifiability (and so the statement is meaningful), but only in theory.

For instance, historical events could have been verified had you have been present at the time they happened. Likewise, with 'water always boils at 100 degrees Celsius', since we know what it would take to verify it – namely to observe every drop of water. In other words, we establish meaningfulness of a statement by relating it to some set of observation sentences. The observations do not actually have to be made. All that is required is that we could in principle make those observations, that is, I know under what circumstances it would be verifiable.

However, this still did not allow for religious statements such as 'I saw God last night' as we do not even know in principle what sense experience would count in its favour.

Strong and weak verification

Ayer then introduced another distinction between what he called 'strong verification' and 'weak verification':

> A further distinction which we must make is the distinction between the 'strong' and the 'weak' sense of the term 'verifiable'. A proposition is said to be verifiable, in the strong sense of the term, if, and only if, its truth could be conclusively established in experience. But it is verifiable, in the weak sense, if it is possible for experience to render it probable.
> (Ayer, *Language, Truth and Logic*)

He was aware, for instance, that universal claims are not conclusively verifiable. It is in the very nature of these statements that their truth cannot be established with certainty by any finite series of observations. In such cases, the verification is said to be 'weak'. Sense experiences merely count towards establishing the truth value of a statement. However, it is still meaningful since it is linked to sense experience.

In contrast, if the verification is conclusive, then Ayer said that it was 'strong' verification. He made this distinction so it would include statements that people regarded as meaningful. In essence, Ayer moved away from focusing on what can be derived from observation claims to focusing on what observation claims might be relevant in order to verify a statement. However, once again religious statements were still not included. For instance, Ayer would have argued that the statement 'God performs miracles' is meaningless since it cannot be verified even in the 'weak' sense.

Falsification

Falsification is the idea that, for something to be meaningful, there has to be evidence that could count against the statement: that is, empirically to refute it. If this is possible, then what has been stated clearly has an empirically meaningful basis, otherwise there would not be the possibility to find evidence that counts against it. This idea was championed in the early part of the twentieth century by Karl Popper.

Karl Popper and falsification

Popper's assertion was that, if a principle is robustly scientific, then it should be inherently disprovable (that is, you would know 'how' to disprove it; you would know what it would take to find things that count against it). Thus, scientific theories (e.g. gravity) can be tested to see whether any evidence can be found against them (e.g. an object would float away from the Earth if gravity were disproven). In this sense, they are falsifiable and, therefore, meaningful. Karl Popper argued that science did not move from observation to theory, but rather from theory to observation. Theories are considered true until some evidence shows them false. So, for science, the criterion is falsifiability rather than verifiability.

Falsification and the meaningfulness of language

Some philosophers, therefore, saw that this criterion could apply to language in general rather than just to science. If it was known what would have to be the case for a statement to be considered false, then the statement was meaningful. Alternatively, if no observation could ever count against a statement, then the statement was considered meaningless. If the statement asserts nothing (since it is consistent with every possible observation), then it cannot mean anything.

So what about religious statements such as 'God exists'? According to the criterion of falsification, there seems no way to disprove it (since God has no empirical attributes).

Flew and falsification

Antony Flew developed this and, with reference to John Wisdom's parable of the invisible gardener, set out his view that religious statements could not be falsified and were therefore meaningless. Flew writes:

> Let us begin with a parable. It is a parable developed from a tale told by John Wisdom in his haunting and revelatory article 'Gods'. Once upon a time two explorers came upon a clearing in the jungle. In the clearing were growing many flowers and many weeds. One explorer says, 'Some gardener must tend this plot.' The other disagrees, 'There is no gardener.' So they pitch their tents and set a watch. No gardener is ever seen. 'But perhaps he is an invisible gardener.' So they set up a barbed-wire fence. They electrify it. They patrol with bloodhounds. (For they remember how H.G. Wells' *The Invisible Man* could be both smelled and touched though he could not be seen.) But no shrieks ever suggest that some intruder has received a shock. No movements of the wire ever betray an invisible climber. The bloodhounds never give cry. Yet still the Believer is not convinced.
> (Flew, 'Theology and Falsification')

> ### Key quote
>
> 'But there is a gardener, invisible, intangible, insensible to electric shocks, a gardener who has no scent and makes no sound, a gardener who comes secretly to look after the garden which he loves.' At last the Sceptic despairs, 'But what remains of our original assertion? Just how does what you call an invisible, intangible, eternally elusive gardener differ from an imaginary gardener or even from no gardener at all?'
>
> (Flew, 'Theology and Falsification')

 Key term

God of classical theism: God as defined in religions such as Christianity, Islam and Judaism – a God who is held to possess certain attributes such as omnipotence, omniscience and omnibenevolence

Specification content

Criticisms of verification: the verification principle cannot itself be verified; neither can historical events; universal scientific statements; the concept of eschatological verification goes against this

Flew continues with the believer's claim, see the Key quote in the margin.

The parable of the gardener demonstrated the problems in falsifying religious language and truths

Flew specifically chooses to challenge God's existence with evidence of the existence of evil and suffering in the world. He asks why religious believers would not allow such evidence to count against their beliefs in a supposed all-loving, all-powerful God; the characteristics associated with the traditionally held **God of classical theism**.

Flew states that believers do not allow such evidence to count against their theistic beliefs and, as a consequence, these beliefs are not falsifiable (and therefore not meaningful), having 'died a death of a thousand qualifications', in that the believers would always justify such evidence with an 'Oh yes, but ...' response.

Challenges to falsification
Criticisms of verification

While, on the face of it, the standpoint of verification as a means of testing the meaningfulness of language seems both sensible and even laudable, it is not without its problems – the most obvious coming from the original verification principle itself.

'The meaning of a statement is its method of verification' is neither logically obvious nor supported by empirical evidence – thus, the statement itself is not verifiable. A self-defeating principle is not a suitable bedrock upon which to build a criterion for establishing the meaningfulness of language.

As Ayer recognises, the fact that the initial criteria for the verification principle did not take into account historical statements or even universal scientific statements (all bodies expand when heated, the Sun always rises in the east and so on) as meaningful further undermines its usefulness. This is why Ayer needed to amend the principle so that a 'weak' form could be established that would allow for such statements to be meaningful.

Hick and the Celestial City parable: a criticism of verification

Religious philosopher John Hick makes a further observation. He argues that, in fact, the Christian concept of God is verifiable in principle.

Hick writes:

> Two men are travelling together along a road. One of them believes that it leads to a Celestial City, the other that it leads nowhere; but since this is the only road there is, both must travel it. Neither has been this way before, and therefore neither is able to say what they will find around each next corner. During their journey they meet both with moments of refreshment and delight, and with moments of hardship and danger. All the time one of them thinks of his journey as a pilgrimage to the Celestial City and interprets the pleasant parts as encouragements and the obstacles as trials of his purpose and lessons in endurance, prepared by the king of that city and designed to make of him a worthy citizen of the place when at last he arrives there. The other, however, believes none of this and sees their journey as an unavoidable and aimless ramble. Since he has no choice in the matter, he enjoys the good and endures the bad. But for him there is no Celestial City to be reached, no all-encompassing purpose ordaining their journey; only the road itself and the luck of the road in good weather and in bad … Their opposed interpretations of the road constituted genuinely rival assertions, though assertions whose assertion-status has the peculiar characteristic of being guaranteed retrospectively by a future crux. (Hick, 'Theology and Verification')

Using his parable of the journey to the Celestial City, Hick demonstrates that, while the knowledge that the Christian God exists may not be immediately verifiable in practice, there is the possibility that it can be verified in the future: that is, after death. This concept is known as **eschatological verification** (quite literally, 'to verify in the end times').

> **Key term**
>
> **eschatological verification:** John Hick's assertion that certain religious statements may be verifiable at a future point (i.e. after death); in this sense, they are 'verifiable in principle' and should therefore be regarded as meaningful

Hick's analogy of the road to the Celestial City asserts that the problems of verifying religious language will be answered at the end of the journey

Criticisms of falsification

Richard Hare

Much like verification, the concept of falsification has been criticised as a philosophical method to establish the meaningfulness of language or concepts.

> **Specification content**
>
> Criticisms of falsification: Richard Hare – bliks (the way that a person views the world gives meaning to them even if others do not share the same view)

> **Key terms**
>
> **symposium:** a meeting, often academic or legal in nature, where a particular topic or subject is discussed
>
> **blik:** a term used by R.M. Hare to describe the point of view that someone may hold that influences the way he or she lives

R.M. Hare, in a **symposium** with Antony Flew and Basil Mitchell, suggested that the concept of meaningfulness comes from the impact that a belief has on an individual – not from the empirically verifiable or falsifiable nature of the belief. It does not matter if others do not share that belief.

As such, he proposed the idea of **bliks** – a term coined to describe a way of looking at our lives and our experiences. Hare suggested that a blik has the power radically to affect our behaviour and the relationship that we have with the world (and people) around us. In this sense, the blik is meaningful – even if it cannot be falsified. To illustrate this, Hare tells the parable of the university dons and the paranoid student who believes that all the dons are dedicated to causing him harm.

Hare writes:

> A certain lunatic is convinced that all dons want to murder him. His friends introduce him to all the mildest and most respectable dons that they can find, and after each of them has retired, they say, 'You see, he doesn't really want to murder you; he spoke to you in a most cordial manner; surely you are convinced now?' But the lunatic replies, 'Yes, but that was only his diabolical cunning; he's really plotting against me the whole time, like the rest of them; I know it I tell you.' However many kindly dons are produced, the reaction is still the same.
>
> Now we say that such a person is deluded. But what is he deluded about? About the truth or falsity of an assertion?
>
> Let us apply Flew's test to him. There is no behaviour of dons that can be enacted which he will accept as counting against his theory; and therefore his theory, on this test, asserts nothing. But it does not follow that there is no difference between what he thinks about dons and what most of us think about them – otherwise we should not call him a lunatic and ourselves sane, and dons would have no reason to feel uneasy about his presence in Oxford.
>
> Let us call that in which we differ from this lunatic, our respective *bliks*. He has an insane *blik* about dons; we have a sane one. It is important to realise that we have a sane one, not no *blik* at all; for there must be two sides to any argument – if he has a wrong *blik*, then those who are right about dons must have a right one. Flew has shown that a *blik* does not consist in an assertion or system of them; but nevertheless it is very important to have the right *blik*.
> (Hare, *Symposium on Theology and Falsification*)

> **Specification content**
>
> Basil Mitchell – partisan and the stranger (certain things can be meaningful even when they cannot be falsified)

Basil Mitchell

In the same symposium, Basil Mitchell suggested to Flew that he had fundamentally misunderstood the religious believers' perspective when Flew had stated that religious believers allow nothing to count against their beliefs. Mitchell argued that this was simply not true. He stated that religious believers are frequently faced with challenges to their belief and with evidence that seems to be contrary to their beliefs. It was a matter of faith as to how the individual dealt with those challenges, but it was not true to say that such evidence had no impact on the religious believer.

Mitchell uses another parable, that of the **partisan** and the stranger, to illustrate his point:

> In time of war in an occupied country, a member of the resistance meets one night a stranger who deeply impresses him. They spend that night together in conversation. The Stranger tells the partisan that he himself is on the side of the resistance – indeed that he is in command of it – and urges the partisan to have faith in him no matter what happens.
>
> The partisan is utterly convinced at that meeting of the Stranger's sincerity and constancy and undertakes to trust him. They never meet in conditions of intimacy again. But sometimes the Stranger is seen helping members of the resistance, and the partisan is grateful and says to his friends, 'He is on our side.' Sometimes he is seen in the uniform of the police handing over patriots to the occupying power. On these occasions his friends murmur against him; but the partisan still says, 'He is on our side.' He still believes that, in spite of appearances, the Stranger did not deceive him. Sometimes he asks the Stranger for help and receives it. He is then thankful. Sometimes he asks and does not receive it. Then he says, 'The Stranger knows best.' Sometimes his friends, in exasperation, say, 'Well, what would he have to do for you to admit that you were wrong and that he is not on our side?' But the partisan refuses to answer. He will not consent to put the Stranger to the test. And sometimes his friends complain, 'Well, if that's what you mean by his being on our side, the sooner he goes over to the other side the better.' The partisan of the parable does not allow anything to count decisively against the proposition 'the Stranger is on our side'. This is because he has committed himself to trust the Stranger. But he of course recognises that the Stranger's ambiguous behaviour *does* count against what he believes about him. It is precisely this situation which constitutes the trial of his faith.
> (Mitchell, *Symposium on Theology and Falsification*)

Mitchell's point, therefore, is that such beliefs constitute a 'trial of faith' – a test for an individual's religiously held beliefs. The evidence against the beliefs is not discounted and the believers do not lose meaningfulness in their beliefs through 'the death of a thousand qualifications'. To believe that is to misunderstand both the purpose and challenge of holding a religious faith. Consequently, Mitchell stated, religious beliefs, expressed in religious language, should be regarded as meaningful.

Richard Swinburne

Furthermore, Richard Swinburne notes that there are plenty of instances where human language is used in ways that people accept as meaningful, even without the empirical evidence to support it. Just because an idea cannot be falsified does not mean, necessarily, that the idea should be automatically discounted as meaningless. We may not be able to disprove something, but that does not mean that such a thing does not actually happen. Indeed, there may well be a belief that such things do actually happen, despite the lack of evidence either for or against it – and such ideas and beliefs are held to be meaningful.

As evidence for this, Swinburne gives the example of the 'toys in the cupboard' coming to life – even though there could be no evidence to

Key term

partisan: person who holds a particular political view, usually someone who holds an opposing point of view from the ruling political powers; Basil Mitchell probably uses 'partisan' to refer to members of the resistance movement in the Second World War

Hare used the example of a murderous university don to illustrate his idea of a blik

Specification content

Richard Swinburne – toys in the cupboard (concept meaningful even though falsifying the statement is not possible)

support (or deny) this assertion, the idea is meaningful to those who hear it.

Understanding that toys can come to life when we're not watching them may not be falsifiable but it is meaningful

Summary

★ A key challenge to the meaningfulness of religious language arose from the work of the Logical Positivists of the early twentieth century. They claimed that language could be meaningful only if it adhered to a set of empirically agreed criteria. These became known as the *verification* and *falsification* principles.

★ A.J. Ayer developed the verification principle to take into account those things that could be verified in practice (strong verification) and those that could be verified in principle (weak verification).

★ There have been criticisms of both the verification and falsification principles as not taking into account the full range of religious language and, in the case of the verification principle, contradicting its own criteria.

★ Criticisms in the form of parables from Hick, Hare, Mitchell and Swinburne all demonstrate issues with the Logical Positivists' approach to language.

AO1 Activity

a Explain both the verification and falsification principles and how they challenge the meaningfulness of religious language.

This helps with presenting a thorough and extensive knowledge and understanding of the topic area.

b Using revision cards, write key points from your notes on Logical Positivism. Record a key word or phrase on one side and an explanation of this on the reverse.

This helps with prioritising and selecting a core set of points to develop an answer and with making accurate use of specialist language and vocabulary in context.

Issues for analysis and evaluation

The persuasiveness of arguments asserting either the meaningfulness or meaninglessness of religious language

> **This section covers AO2 content and skills**

Possible line of argument	Critical analysis and evaluation
Language is meaningful if it relates to agreed criteria	We can argue that we should consider meaningful a statement, or form of language, that relates very clearly to something that can be objectively experienced. If a person claims that 'the bird has wings', then it is generally understood that the person is referring to an object, present in the world of the animal kingdom and definable and identifiable by an agreed set of criteria as a 'bird'. Furthermore, we can readily identify the physiological structure of this object by visual observation and a basic awareness of the different parts that can constitute a body, as well as how we can define them in terms of shape and function, so as to lead us to identify whether or not there is truth to the statement that this 'bird' object does indeed possess the physical characteristic of 'wings'.
Verification is key to meaningfulness	Such is the view of Logical Positivism – that any language that can be reduced to a set of observable criteria should be understood to be meaningful. Equally, tautological statements such as 'all spinsters are unmarried females' can also, by definition, be understood to be meaningful. In this sense, the established criterion for the verification principle that the Logical Positivists proposed is both meaningful and, as a means for understanding language, persuasive.
Not all statements are equally verifiable	The difficulty comes when a person makes a claim such as 'the angel has wings'. While, superficially, this appears to be the same sort of statement as the previous one, the difficulty comes when we attempt to define the word *angel*. Unlike the bird, which can clearly be categorised as belonging to the empirical world and is readily identifiable through an agreed set of criteria, the same cannot be said for the 'angel'.
Statements that cannot be verified are meaningless	While we can, as previously noted, understand what is meant by the word *wings*, how do we know that the wings of an angel are comparable to the wings of a bird? The lack of verifiable information about the angel means that such a statement is therefore meaningless. It has no corresponding reality to the empirical world and can be proven neither by sense experience nor by tautological understanding. Logical Positivism makes a powerful case about our understanding of what can be understood to be meaningful and therefore is particularly persuasive, when understood in such a way.

> **Specification content**
>
> The persuasiveness of arguments asserting either the meaningfulness or meaninglessness of religious language

Possible line of argument	Critical analysis and evaluation
Logical Positivism has misunderstood the use of religious language	However, to treat religious language in the way that Logical Positivists treat it is to understand religious language to be cognitive: that is, it is a form of language that contains information that is objectively knowable about the external, empirically experienced, world. Religious philosophers, such as R.B. Braithwaite, consider this to be a fundamental misunderstanding of both the purpose and function of religious language. They suggest that the Logical Positivists have 'missed the point', and therefore undermine the persuasiveness of their points of view.
Meaningfulness of language should be derived from the impact it has on an individual	Braithwaite, and those who agree that religious language has a non-cognitive, rather than cognitive, function, point out that, to understand religious language, we need to appreciate that it is expressing an attitude towards a form of life. It is not expressing 'facts' about the world in a scientific sense. The language is meaningful because it affects the way individuals choose to live their life and relate to the world around them, including how they view their relationship with other human beings.
Categorisation of religious language influences how its meaningfulness is viewed	Whether we accept that religious language is cognitive or non-cognitive influences whether or not we consider that the challenges to its meaningfulness are successful.

AO2 Activity

a Select three lines of argument from the critical analysis and evaluation of the persuasiveness of arguments asserting either the meaningfulness or meaninglessness of religious language. Find three references from scholars, schools of thought or religious and philosophical texts that would support those arguments.

b Using the strongest line of argument, try to identify three key quotations that might be used – they could be from scholars, religious texts or schools of thought.

Exam practice

Sample question
Evaluate how far Logical Positivism should be accepted as providing a valid criterion for meaning in the use of language.

Sample answer
The philosophical movement of Logical Positivism considered their task to be a philosophically driven systematic reduction of all knowledge to basic scientific and logical formulations. The requirement for all language to be subject to a scientific form of 'enquiry', in that it needed to be empirically verifiable, became the focus of their work.

In considering how language was used, the forms of language regarded as analytic and synthetic were identified. Analytic language – that which was self-explanatory or self-defining (true by definition) – was held to be a meaningful form of expression, and it was true *a priori* (independent of experience). Such statements as 'all spinsters are unmarried females' is an example of an analytic statement – and it is easy to see why the Logical Positivists considered this to be a valid criterion for understanding 'meaning' when language was used. Tautological and mathematical statements were equally accepted under this criterion for meaning.

The other form of language, synthetic language, was regarded as meaningful simply because the language could be understood, *a posteriori*, as it was based on empirically provable first-person observations. Language such as 'the spinster wore a red hat' was deemed to be meaningful as it could be clearly provable, in practice, via sense experience. Synthetic statements corresponded neatly with the sort of observations the scientific community was making, and were therefore readily accepted as having valid meaning due to their empirical basis.

It is clearly the case that such a criterion for establishing meaning in the use of language should be readily accepted in the arenas for which it was intended. However, what happens when that criterion is applied to areas of knowledge and human activity that lie beyond those readily found in the empirically observable external world?

For Logical Positivists, the lack of correspondence of religious belief and religious language to their criterion for meaning demonstrated that religious activity was essentially meaningless, to the scientific mindset. It was something that could not be empirically verified and therefore should not be accepted as anything other than meaningless. However, those outside the Logical Positivist movement considered the criterion of meaning they established to be flawed, and therefore not an adequate way of providing an appropriate criterion for understanding the meaning of language. Critics have argued strongly that the insistence on the strict adherence to the principle of verification is clearly problematic, as the principle itself cannot be verified.

A.J. Ayer attempted to navigate the challenge of the limitations of the verification principle by proposing an amendment to the criterion and by suggesting that, while it was entirely laudable to have a situation where something could be verified in practice (what he later referred to as the 'strong' form of the verification principle), it was equally acceptable to appreciate that this was not always possible; however, it was possible to verify something in principle. He later referred to this as the 'weak' form of the verification principle: the means and criteria that could be used to 'verify' the truth or falsity of a particular statement were known.

> **Specification content**
> How far Logical Positivism should be accepted as providing a valid criterion for meaning in the use of language

News reporter
A good introduction that provides a helpful overview of the key areas for focus in the evaluation to come.

Detective
News reporter
The response provides evidence, with commentary, of the criteria by which language can be considered meaningful according to Logical Positivism.

Detective
News reporter
This paragraph presents further relevant evidence of the criteria Logical Positivism used, again with appropriate explanatory comments.

Philosopher
The response briefly summarises the information so far and then invites the reader to consider an alternative point of view via a question.

Tennis player
Detective
The candidate provides a response to the previous question, from the standpoint of Logical Positivism, and then develops a counterargument that highlights the flaw in the principle of verification.

Detective
This paragraph presents evidence that is relevant to the question, and explains it in a highly accurate way, showing how Logical Positivism amended its approach to the verification principle.

The response then develops the previous point further, before showing clearly how this development applies to religious language, with accurate and relevant reference to a philosopher and his viewpoint. This then leads to a conclusion regarding the meaningfulness of religious language.

Ayer's moderated form of the verification principle allowed for both historical statements (e.g. the Battle of Waterloo was fought in 1815) and universal scientific statements (all metals expand when heated) to be verifiable (in principle), and therefore to be potentially regarded as meaningful. The strong form had not allowed for this. In this way, Ayer, as a Logical Positivist, put forward a criterion of meaning for the use of language that seemed far more acceptable.

In fact, using an extension of this reasoning, religious philosopher John Hick suggested that, if there was an afterlife, then the truth of God's existence would be verifiable after death. This became known as *eschatological verification* and is a form of verification that establishes that religious language is indeed meaningful.

Evaluation

This is a good response. It considers relevant information in a systematic and coherent way, before stating an appropriate conclusion. The candidate makes accurate use both of terminology and of the views of different schools of thought.

Over to you

Below is an evaluation of Logical Positivism in response to a question about religious language. The evaluation is around 150 words long.

At the end of the paragraph, there is an intermediate conclusion that we have put in italics. As a group, try to identify where you could add more intermediate conclusions to the rest of the passage.

When you have done this, you will see clearly that in AO2 it is helpful to include a brief summary of the arguments you have presented as you go through an answer, and not just leave it until the end to draw a final conclusion. In this way, you demonstrate that you are sustaining evaluation throughout an answer and not just repeating information you have learned.

Question

'Issues surrounding religious language are relevant in the 21st century.' Evaluate this view.

(Q5, Component 2: Philosophy of Religion, WJEC, Summer 2024)

Evaluation

Logical Positivism has suggested a simple method for determining the meaningfulness of any given statement. It applies scientific principles in the form of statements that we can consider to be self-explanatory (analytic) and practically verifiable via empirical methods (synthetic) as the only criterion for establishing meaning. Some consider this criterion to be too restrictive as it does not take into account as meaningful either historic statements or universal scientific statements; that was considered to undermine it as a useful method for establishing meaning. Ayer therefore modified it to include a verifiable in practice (strong) and verifiable in principle (weak) form. Religious philosophers point out that something can be considered to be meaningful by virtue of the effect it has on a person, rather than just by whether it is empirically verifiable. *They have pointed out that the Logical Positivists have misunderstood the purpose of religious language.*

C: Religious language as non-cognitive and analogical

Proportion and attribution (St Thomas Aquinas)

Long before the Vienna Circle's debates regarding the meaningfulness of religious language, philosophers in the Middle Ages were considering the use of words in the relationship between God and humans. One of the most significant of these contributors was St Thomas Aquinas (1225–74) who, in several of his writings, considers the function of language and how we can further understand the mysteries of the divine nature. God, according to the writings of Aquinas, is essentially unknowable. However, certain properties can be attributed to God and, according to Aquinas, it is the task of the believer to develop increasingly deep insights into him by reflecting on creation and the teachings of holy scripture and the Church.

Aquinas recognised that language was often used in two main ways – **univocally** and **equivocally**.

> **This section covers AO1 content and skills**
>
> **Specification content**
> Proportion and attribution (St Thomas Aquinas) and qualifier and disclosure (Ian Ramsey)
>
> ### Key terms
> **univocally:** where something has one universal and unambiguous meaning
> **equivocally:** where there is more than one meaning, usually in relation to a word or phrase

Univocal language

When language is used univocally, it is used in the sense that a certain term means the same thing whatever the context. In other words, it has exactly one and the same, identical meaning, whenever and wherever it is used. For example, when I use the noun *carpet*, I mean the same thing when I put it in different contexts: 'the bedroom carpet'; 'the carpet in the mosque'; 'the camper van's carpet'; 'the carpet for sale in the carpet shop'. In every usage, I am referring to a floor covering usually made from a thick woven fabric.

Equivocal language

When language is used equivocally, a term has completely different meanings according to context. For example, when I use the noun *set*, I could be referring to a mathematical device, a television, a place where a play is performed, a hair arrangement, a number of repetitions used in bodybuilding and so on. Here, the context changes the meaning of the word – in fact, without understanding the specific context, you would have no insight into what I mean by the word *set*.

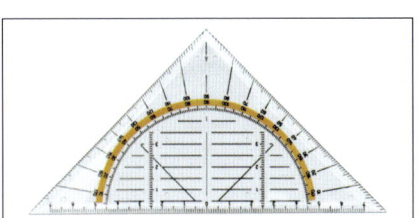

The word *set* can have a different meaning when associated with 'square', 'TV' and 'film'

T4 Religious language (1)

> **Key term**
>
> **analogy:** where something (that is known) is compared with something else (usually something unknown) to explain or clarify

William Paley used the analogy of a watchmaker to help understand religious teachings that the universe was designed

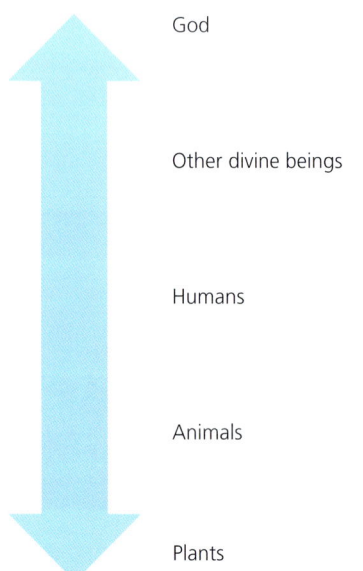

Aquinas believed that the universe exists in a hierarchy, with everything having its set place, order and purpose according to whereabouts it exists in that hierarchy

Analogy

Clearly, neither of these language uses is helpful for the believer in trying to gain a deeper insight into the nature of God. On the one hand, univocal language could not possibly describe God – God is so different from us that any use of a univocal word would be hopelessly inadequate. Equally, using equivocal language would just put us into a place where we knew the word had a different meaning but we would have no knowable terms of reference, or understandable context, to explain what it meant – in which case the word may as well be a nonsense word.

Aquinas therefore settled on the use of **analogy**.

Analogy gives a middle ground because, on the one hand, it accepts that part of what is being said is imperfectly understood (and, for Aquinas, human beings could never fully understand God as human beings are too limited and God is too great). On the other hand, the object referenced in the analogy is fully understood, and this is required for the analogy to work.

The example of Paley's watchmaker is one of the more notable uses of analogy in the history of religious philosophy. It has long been debated as to how effective it is in showing the supposed correlation between a complex mechanism designed by an intelligent human being and the complex universe designed by the intelligent divine being.

One of the key features of a successful analogy is ensuring that there is some link or relationship between the two things being compared.

For Aquinas, God was the source of all existence; the source of all creation. The account in the Judeo-Christian scripture Genesis contains a direct reference to God making humans in his image (Genesis 1:26: 'Let us make humankind in our image, in our likeness'). Thus, for Aquinas, there is a definitive link between human beings and God. It therefore follows that speaking about God could be understood with reference to our understanding of what it means to be human – from both human nature and human purpose.

> **❝ Key quote ❞**
>
> From what we have said, therefore, it remains that the names said of God and creatures are predicated neither univocally nor equivocally but analogically: that is, according to an order or reference to something one ... Thus, therefore, because we come to a knowledge of God from other things, the reality in the names said of God and other things belongs by priority in God according to His mode of being, but the meaning of the name belongs to God by posteriority. And so He is said to be named from His effects.
>
> (Aquinas, *Summa Contra Gentiles*)

The analogy of proportion

Aquinas considered that the universe is inhabited by different orders of things. These were hierarchical in the sense of status. So, for example, God would be above all creation (as well as its source). Humans are lower than God, but higher than animals. Animals are higher than plants, and so on. Therefore, each order possesses particular characteristics appropriate to its hierarchical status, even though the same adjective may be applied.

Adjectives

For instance, we could consider what it means for a human to be intelligent and for an animal – for example, a fox – to be intelligent. These occupy different positions within the created order and therefore, according to Aquinas, we should consider what we mean when we apply the word *intelligence* to each.

Clearly, there are common features in the use of the word (relating to ability, judgement, intuition and so on) but we do not understand the word *intelligence* to mean exactly the same thing when applied to both a human being and a fox. The intelligence is relative. It is also appropriate. In this sense, we can see the link but we understand there is a difference – in **proportion** to the reality that the thing being spoken about possesses.

In other words, a human being is intelligent in the appropriate way that it is for a human being to be intelligent; a fox is intelligent in the appropriate way it is for a fox to be intelligent.

To put it yet another way:
- A human being is intelligent in proportion to what it means for a human being to be intelligent.
- A fox is intelligent in proportion to what it means for a fox to be intelligent.

For Aquinas, it was therefore possible to talk analogically about God by referring to human qualities. So, to talk about God as 'good' makes sense analogically because we understand what it means for a human being to be good; therefore:
- A human being is good in proportion to what it means for a human being to be good.
- God is good in proportion to what it means for God to be good.

> **Key term**
>
> **proportion:** relating to the relative value of something according to its nature

The intelligence of foxes and human beings is proportionately different

The analogy of attribution

The second analogous way that Aquinas believed it was possible to talk about God in a meaningful sense was through the analogy of **attribution**.

An *attribute* is a characteristic or feature that something possesses. Common positive attributes to describe human beings might be such words as *good*, *loving*, *wise* and so on. However, Aquinas believed that these attributes are entirely divinely inspired. Human beings can be good only because they come from God. God's goodness is the attribute that human beings, who have come from God (as has all creation), are therefore good, in the sense that their goodness comes from God. Human beings are not good independently of God, but good because they are dependent on God.

> **Key term**
>
> **attribution:** relating to the attribute or characteristic an object possesses

Aquinas argued that food in itself is healthy only in that it is a cause of good health in humans through attribution; in itself, it is just food

To make this clearer, consider the word *healthy*. If I talk about an animal having good health, I could attribute my definition of the animal as having good health because I know that its blood is healthy, its diet is healthy, its exercise regime is healthy. None of these three things is *healthy* in itself (that is, blood is not intrinsically 'healthy'; diet is not intrinsically 'healthy'; and neither is an exercise regime), but they derive their 'healthiness' from the relationship they share with the animal. This is why some philosophers refer to this as the analogy of *reference*.

Because of this relationship, where the attribute comes from God, we can gain an insight into what it means in relation to God, as long we understand the equivalent human quality.

Qualifier and disclosure (Ian Ramsey)

In 1957, Ian Ramsey, later to become Bishop of Durham, wrote arguably his most famous work *Religious Language*. In this, he wanted to examine how we use language and how he felt it should be understood. Ramsey's own beliefs, which are clear from this and other of his theological works, were that all experience is effectively a religious experience because, for him, all experience is essentially a continual encounter between God and his creation. It was through this particular framework that Ramsey developed his distinctive teachings regarding **disclosure**.

For Ramsey (1915–72), the religious language that grows out of religious situations becomes revelatory in the sense that those religious experiences are variously referred to as *disclosures*. Here, disclosures are moments where the person is often able to grasp an understanding of the divine, although not all moments of disclosure are considered religious. Instead, these are moments where the believer not only appreciates the superficial moment itself, but also realises that there is something else going on; something that could not easily be described in normal language. What is also common among these moments of disclosure is the degree of commitment they provoke from the individual. To try and make sense of this, Ramsey developed his idea of disclosure 'models'.

Referring to key terms used for God that are common throughout the Christian Bible, such as *Father*, *Shepherd*, *King* and *Rock*, Ramsey recognised within each of these terms a particular view about a reality that the believer was committing to (i.e. a father protects, as does a shepherd; a king protects and rules; whereas a rock provides strength and stability, and is a firm foundation upon which to build). In other words, they provide a disclosure (or disclosure 'model') about God.

However, on their own they are still insufficient ways properly to refer to God. This is why Ramsey believed we need to make use of a **qualifier** – words or phrases that we add to these earlier terms to provide them with the quality and sense that they are greater than what their normal reality represents.

Thus, words and phrases such as *transcendent*, *almighty*, *everlasting* and *all-loving* add another dimension to these terms by 'qualifying' them in relation to God. The *Father* becomes the 'Almighty Father'; the *Shepherd*, the 'all-loving Shepherd'; and so on. With these qualifications, 'the penny drops, the light dawns' (Ramsey) and the believer is brought into a meaningful disclosure through religious language.

> **Key terms**
>
> **disclosure:** where something is made known that previously was hidden or unknown
>
> **qualifier:** a term used by Ramsey to mean a word or phrase used to give a deeper meaning to the model that the qualifier precedes

Challenges to analogy and qualifiers

While, in many ways, analogy is a useful way of helping to gain insights into the meaningfulness of religious language, it is not without its limitations.

Firstly, as Hume recognised in his *Dialogues Concerning Natural Religion*, an analogy is only as good as the point at which the two things being compared are similar. The issue for religious language in using analogy, which was central to the concerns raised by the Vienna Circle, can be summarised in these two questions:

- What do we mean when we use the word *God*?
- How do we 'know' what 'God' actually is (in an empirical sense)?

If we are unable, in some way, to answer these questions, then our point of comparison fails. If this fails, then so does the analogy, thereby rendering analogical language not only meaningless but, in a very real sense, useless – as far as talking about God is concerned.

Secondly, both Aquinas and Ramsey assume God's existence and, with such an assumption, their assertions regarding analogy have some weight. However, if we dismiss the assumption, then we run into a serious philosophical issue as far as analogous religious language is concerned – without the existence of God, there can be no point of comparison.

Thirdly, even if we accept Aquinas' and Ramsey's assumption in relation to the existence of God, our lack of empirical knowledge of what God actually is means that the best hope we can have of using language about God is to use it equivocally. In this sense, we know that God is different (even if we can't say precisely how) and therefore the meaning of the words is different – but this takes us back to square one in terms of trying to find a meaningful way to talk about God, as we saw in why Aquinas originally rejected equivocal language as a meaningful way to talk about God.

Finally, Ramsey's use of qualifiers serves only to underline that we do not fully understand what we mean when referring to God – we can only ever get an insight. Ramsey admitted that this was part of the 'mystery' of what it means to have faith: 'They disclose but do not explain a mystery' (Ramsey, *Models and Mystery*). That does not necessarily satisfy the non-religious believer when considering whether analogy is a suitable way to talk meaningfully about God.

> **Specification content**
> Challenges including how far analogies can give meaningful insights into religious language

How we can use Aquinas' and Ramsey's views to understand religious teachings

Regardless of the challenges to the use of analogy in talking meaningfully about God and other forms of religious language, the work of both Aquinas and Ramsey has been useful for those who have a religious belief.

Religious teachings, expressed through religious language, can often be hard to understand from the perspective of those outside a tradition. (They can also sometimes be difficult for those within!) However, considering the idea that there is a connection between a creator God and his human creation means that we can draw a suitable point of reference between the two, thereby shedding some light on what would otherwise be virtually impossible to understand.

To talk about God is to talk about something that is the source of all human activity. Understanding this means gaining insights into religious belief and practice by considering their root in the realm of human experience.

> **Specification content**
> How we can use Aquinas' and Ramsey's views to understand religious teachings

These human experiences, known and understood, form gateways into the realm of the divine. Religious teachings are therefore illuminated by association. Believers have clear points of reference to begin to try and understand the mysteries of their religious tradition. Analogies of proportion and attribution give clear ways for accessing a meaningful context to begin to come to terms with the spiritual realm – anchored as they are in the physical one.

Ramsey's models that help to disclose divine attributes, and his qualifiers that make sense of the impossibility of describing God, help religious believers understand how it is possible to talk about things that relate to God. At the same time, this helps religious believers appreciate that things of this nature are far beyond our actual understanding, and that we merely grasp at what they might mean. Far from making religious language meaningless, they assist religious believers by providing insights into something that otherwise has no point of reference.

Thus, the many different religious teachings that relate to God, the revelation of scripture, divine election, angels, salvation, life after death and so on, are well served by the work of both Aquinas and Ramsey. They provide a useful means by which to talk about them, to communicate the ideas to others and to reflect on their meanings, while retaining a sense of how they relate to our everyday experience of the empirical world.

Summary

- Aquinas showed that the usual ways of using language (*univocal* and *equivocal*) are not meaningful when talking about God, but he believed language about God could be meaningful by using analogy.
- Aquinas proposed an analogy of proportion and an analogy of attribution, both based on the connection between God and humanity established through creation.
- In the twentieth century, Ramsey developed the use of analogical language to talk meaningfully about God by introducing the idea of *disclosures* and *qualifiers*.
- Challenges to the use of analogy discuss how far we can gain an accurate insight into something that we ultimately have no way of determining empirically: that is, what do we actually mean by the word *God*? However, others have rejected these challenges and show how analogies have helped to provide insights where otherwise there would be no point of reference.

AO1 Activity

a Explain Aquinas' analogy of proportion and analogy of attribution.

This helps with presenting a thorough and extensive knowledge and understanding of the topic area.

b On revision cards, summarise the key points from your notes on the use of analogy as a non-cognitive but meaningful form of language.

This helps with prioritising and selecting a core set of points to develop an answer and with making accurate use of specialist language and vocabulary in context.

> **Specification content**
> The extent to which the challenges to Logical Positivism provide convincing arguments to non-religious believers

> **This section covers AO2 content and skills**

Issues for analysis and evaluation

The extent to which the challenges to Logical Positivism provide convincing arguments to non-religious believers

Possible line of argument	Critical analysis and evaluation
Non-religious believers supported Logical Positivism	The work of the Logical Positivists was firmly based upon the scientific principles. The use of empirical observation and a systematic application of what became known as the *verification principle*, for determining the meaningfulness of any statement, would prove to be a highly influential idea for many years. This approach was appealing to those who were not of a religious background, and it could be argued that the default position towards Logical Positivism, among non-religious believers, would be one of firm support.
Logical Positivism lost credibility as the century progressed	However, the challenges to Logical Positivism grew as the twentieth century progressed. This is because ideas such as language games became more widely accepted. It is also fair to say that many philosophers, by the mid-twentieth century, realised that the verification principle was actually self-defeating. Those from both the religious and non-religious philosophical communities accepted these criticisms.
Logical Positivism was viewed as being too reductionist	The Logical Positivists stated that only those statements that were analytic or synthetic could truly be accepted as meaningful. This was because analytic statements were self-defining – and thereby 'true' by definition – or because synthetic statements could be rendered meaningful by some sense experience or observation. This led to a conclusion that any form of metaphysical statement, being neither analytic nor synthetic, had to be considered meaningless. While this posed an issue for statements about religion, it also dismissed commonly experienced facets of human existence, such as emotions and morality, as being ultimately meaningless. This provoked a reaction from philosophers outside the Logical Positivist tradition who saw this as a reductionist approach to the 'meaningfulness' of statements beyond the analytic/synthetic scope.
Logical Positivists misunderstood religious language	The religious philosopher R. Braithwaite observed that Logical Positivism misunderstood how religious language was used. He noted that religious language was about expressing attitudes towards life that were meaningful by virtue of the impact that they had on the believer's life. To express a religious belief was also to adopt a particular attitude towards the self and those around you.
Weak verification paves the way for religious statements to be verifiable in principle	Another religious philosopher, John Hick, pointed out that Ayer's weak form of verification would actually permit some religious statements to be meaningful, as some sense experience could be identified that would count towards them – particularly historical religious claims. Hick also pointed out that, if there was an existence after death, then faith claims such as 'God exists' would theoretically be verifiable. Hick called this *eschatological verification* and, if his logic is accepted, this is a convincing argument for both religious and non-religious believers.

Other forms of Logical Positivism can be successfully challenged	Religious philosophers also challenged the Logical Positivist position of falsification. Richard Swinburne pointed out, in his 'toys in the cupboard' example, that we can consider some statements to be meaningful to us, even when we cannot disprove them. Non-religious believers can accept this point, as it depends on understanding concepts that do not depend on an acceptance of any religious belief (i.e. the idea that toys can physically move when not being watched).
The challenges to Logical Positivism can be considered convincing	Therefore, meaningfulness is as powerfully expressed through a non-cognitive understanding of language as it is through a cognitive understanding. Again, this must surely be a convincing challenge to Logical Positivism for non-religious believers.

AO2 Activity

a Analyse three possible conclusions that could be drawn from the critical analysis and evaluation of the extent to which the challenges to Logical Positivism provide convincing arguments to non-religious believers. What are their strengths and weaknesses? Which conclusion is strongest?

b Using the strongest conclusion, select three lines of argument that you would use to support this conclusion. Try to explain why you have selected these.

Specification content

Whether non-cognitive interpretations are valid responses to the challenges to the meaning of religious language

Exam practice

Sample question

Evaluate whether non-cognitive interpretations are valid responses to the challenges to the meaning of religious language.

Sample answer

The challenges to the meaningfulness of religious language have been met over the last century or so with a series of robust philosophical defences, often based on the view that religious language is a form of language that is more properly understood to have a non-cognitive rather than a cognitive function. The responses of Braithwaite demonstrated that religious statements were expressions of a particular attitude or intention of how life was to be lived and, as such, were very similar to the way in which moral language is used: that is, to express an opinion or attitude about the relative ethical value of a belief or action, and to live one's life accordingly.

News reporter

This is a good introduction that provides a helpful overview of the key areas for focus in the evaluation to come. The answer successfully identifies some of the key issues.

However, the challenges to the meaningfulness of religious language were specific, in the sense that they were levelled at the idea that religious language said nothing that could be either verified or falsified. Religious language was not self-evident (*analytic*), nor could any sense experience or experiment count towards it (*synthetic*). Both of these assumed that religious language had a function similar to other forms of language. Whether or not we accept this particular point forms the crux of how far we consider non-cognitive interpretations of language to be valid responses to the challenges to the meaning of religious language.

Tennis player
Detective

This paragraph present evidence along with a recognition that there are two potentially equally valid lines of reasoning, dependent on point of view.

The function of any form of language is to communicate. Communication is the exchange of ideas between individuals or groups. Where there is a shared understanding of what is being communicated (and this usually comes from experience), then what is being communicated can generally be regarded as meaningful. This holds true for both cognitive and non-cognitive forms of language. Therefore, if we accept this point, then we consider non-cognitive interpretations of language to be meaningful, and they are therefore suitable responses to the challenges to the meaning of religious language.

News reporter
Critical thinker

This paragraph provides a commentary relating to the issue of how language can be understood and the consequence of that for the issue in question.

However, some philosophers identified a particular difficulty with the non-cognitive approach. If we accept the idea that religious statements are expressions of a particular attitude or intention of how life is to be lived, then, by logical extension, they are not making statements about any kind of reality that could be described as 'objective'. By this, we mean not only that they are not making any 'factual' comments, but that, if religious language is purely to be understood as non-cognitive, then it is incapable of making such statements.

Critical thinker

This paragraph examines a further technical point and raises an issue with the potential validity of non-cognitive statements for religious believers.

This poses an issue for the religious believers who might state that 'God exists' or 'sacred writings are the word of God' or 'I believe in a life after death'. These are not just expressions of attitude for the religious believer. They are, in fact and in the context appropriate to the particular religion, assertions about how reality actually is. In a very real sense, the religious believer considers these to be statements about the external world – in other words, the believer is using them in a cognitive, not non-cognitive, sense. This brings us back to the original challenge from Logical Positivism: that is, that such statements are neither analytic nor synthetic – they cannot be verified.

Critical thinker
Explorer

Following on from the previous point, this paragraph looks at the issue for religious believers in more detail before drawing a conclusion that has significant consequences in relation to the question.

This seems to be conclusive but, again, appearances can be deceptive. Our line of reasoning, which took the view that religious claims are not the same as religious attitudes, does not take into account the context of making such claims in the views that Hare expressed. To make such a claim as part of someone's blik could be argued as making a cognitive claim within a non-cognitive framework – in the sense that a person is making statements about what they perceive to be reality, not just their 'attitude' towards it (although the attitude influences the statements being made). If this is held to be true, then the concept of a blik, as a non-cognitive concept, provides a context that successfully meets the challenges to the meaningfulness of religious language. They are meaningful, and they do successfully meet the specific criticisms that the likes of Logical Positivists levelled at religious language, along with any others who may consider religious language to be a meaningless form of communication.

Critical thinker
Judge

The response draws a conclusion based on an understanding of the difference between what an objective reality is and what a perceived reality is. It then measures the influence the reality has on an individual, rather than any other criteria.

Evaluation

This is an effective and balanced response. It considers both sides of the argument and raises questions before putting forward a conclusion. The candidate makes accurate use both of terminology and of the views of different schools of thought.

Over to you

Below are listed three basic conclusions drawn from an evaluation of whether non-cognitive interpretations are valid responses to the challenges to the meaning of religious language.

Develop each of these conclusions by identifying briefly its strengths (referring to some reasons underlying the conclusion), but also showing an awareness of challenges to it (these may or may not be weaknesses, depending on your view). The result should be three very competent paragraphs that could form a final conclusion of any evaluation.

When you have completed the task, refer to the band descriptors for A2 (WJEC) or A Level (Eduqas) and, in particular, look at the demands described in the higher band descriptors, which you should be aspiring towards. Ask yourself:

- Is my answer a confident, critical analysis and perceptive evaluation of the issue?
- Is my answer a response that successfully identifies and thoroughly addresses the issues the question raises?

Conclusions

1. Non-cognitive interpretations are insufficient for responding to the direct challenge of Logical Positivism.
2. The meaningfulness of religious language can be found in the way that it directly affects the way that a person lives their life.
3. Religious language expresses more than just an attitude – it makes actual claims about how the world is, and so should be treated as a cognitive form of language, not as non-cognitive.

T4 Religious language (2)

D: Religious language as non-cognitive and symbolic

> This section covers AO1 content and skills

Overview

We shall consider the ideas of two key thinkers who have contributed, firstly, to the understanding of the role of symbols as a form of non-cognitive language.

J.H. Randall who, in 1958, wrote *The Role of Knowledge in Western Religion*, attempted to bring together some of the key ideas that had presented themselves to the world of theology from philosophy, psychology and science over the preceding century. Randall recognised that religion and science were human activities that performed different functions, yet both had a vital role to play in the cultural life of human beings.

The other thinker, Paul Tillich, was described by influential twentieth-century American theologian Reinhold Niebuhr as 'a giant among us'. In 1957, Tillich wrote in his book *Dynamics of Faith* about symbols opening up levels of reality to help humans to engage with their 'ultimate concern'.

> **Specification content**
> Religious language as non-cognitive and symbolic

Symbols can be found in all religious traditions

J.H. Randall and the functions of symbols

When we think of symbols, we think of those pictures from everyday life that, to us, have different meanings according to our own experiences and cultures. These symbols are rich in meaning and therefore can be interpreted in many different ways. Sometimes the meaning of the symbols can change. These changes occur because society itself changes; our priorities change; our understanding of our own selves changes. Even those things that to us once had prime importance in our lives, because of the passage of time, fade in significance from what they once were.

Understanding the function of these symbols has long been a matter of interest for those individuals and groups who wish to find the deeper

> **Specification content**
> Religious language as non-cognitive and symbolic: functions of symbols (John Randall)

meaning of the pictures and words that point to the very heart of what it means to be human. Symbols can be found in all walks of life and in all areas of human interest and activity. Therefore, it should be no surprise that religion and particularly religious language have a rich and diverse history of symbols and symbolism.

Religion and science – a shared purpose?

In the early part of the twentieth century, American philosopher John Herman Randall undertook an academic journey to explore not only how religious language carries both meaning and knowledge, but also how this form of communication both differs from and shares similarities to other disciplines, such as the world of science. In considering the function of religious language as a vehicle for conveying knowledge, Randall concentrated specifically on the forms of communication within religion that give believers the greatest insights into their commonly held beliefs, ideas and cultural identities.

Randall's work moved beyond looking at the historical issue of the conflict between religion and science, which he saw as having been largely resolved (if still misunderstood by those outside of academia). He then looked at the relationship between religion and philosophy; particularly those ideas that came from the philosophy of Ancient Greeks.

Randall did not believe that religion and science were in direct competition with each other

He realised that the great Christian thinkers of the early Church, such as Augustine, who were influenced by Greek philosophers, saw philosophy as central in recognising the twin pillars of faith and reason.

Turning his attention to natural science – particularly the post-Enlightenment period that developed from the work of Newton – Randall realised that the worlds of natural science and **natural theology** had a common purpose. That purpose was to reveal the workings of the world and universe within which we live.

The function of religious belief

Far from seeing the development of rational thought as a threat to religion, Randall realised that the religious ideas of the Middle Ages needed to develop alongside, and along with, the discoveries brought about by science. Randall identified the central role of religious belief in understanding what it means to be religious, since religious beliefs lead onto religious practice, which is itself a religious experience:

> If the function of religious beliefs is not to generate knowledge and truth, what is their function? Very early in every great religious tradition, reflective men came to see that the ordinary ideas entertained and used in worship, prayer and ritual could not be 'literally' true. The idea of God, for example, employed by the unreflective in the actual practice of the religious arts, could not be adequate to the true nature of the divine.
> (Randall, *The Role of Knowledge in Western Religion*)

The unifying ability of ideas

Randall recognised that religious ideas have consequences: they result in unifying people, from tribes to city-states, from kingdoms to nations. They give people an identity: individual, corporate, cultural, national. In doing so, they provide a common vision of the values that hold people together – in essence, this became the core of what would be recognised as a cultural and religious identity. It provides a common way of communicating, providing a shared set of values. This translates quite literally into a common form of language; at its heart, the religious language – a language highly symbolic, representing those very things that give people their identity. For Randall, this is the role of religious experience.

It is against this background that Randall's identification of the functions of symbolic religious language can be understood.

Religion as human activity

Randall went on to observe that religion, as far as he was concerned, is not independent of humanity's secular knowledge. For Randall, religion is a human activity that demands 'careful observation and description, explanation, reflective understanding, and intelligent criticism'. Randall believed that all religious beliefs are mythology: that is, all religious beliefs are religious symbols. If such symbols are held to contain any kind of truth, Randall believed that this is not the truth of factual statements of the empirical sciences or any other realist-based rational discipline. Randall seems to have held a coherence theory of truth in relation to religious belief. That is to say, when it comes to belief in God and other such **theological propositions**, Randall can be said to accept anti-realism.

Key term

natural theology: philosophical reasoning based on information that can be rationally gained about the physical world and that leads to revelation about the divine

"Key quote"

All ideas of God, like all other religious beliefs, are without exception religious symbols. This means that they perform what is primarily a religious function. They are employed in religious experience, and serve to carry on the religious life. They are techniques, instruments, in terms of which ritual and the other religious arts are conducted.

(Randall, *The Role of Knowledge in Western Religion*)

Key term

theological propositions: beliefs or ideas put forward in the context of religious doctrines or philosophies

Insight and function

Further, Randall believed that religion gave humans a valuable insight into what it means to exist as a being within the universe. He did not believe that religion provides additional truths about the world or humanity or God, but instead that it leads to an enhanced view of the experience of existence. Randall stated:

> ... religion gives men more, and how much more only the participant can realise. In this it is like art, which likewise furnishes no supplementary truth, but it does open whole worlds to be explored, whole heavens to be enjoyed.
> (Randall, *The Role of Knowledge in Western Religion*)

According to Randall, the primary role of religious symbols is to provide a function. This function is sometimes described as a *revelation of truth*. Randall believed that to describe how this works is a complex matter. He acknowledges the work he shared with Tillich in developing this understanding of the function of religious symbols as a form of communication within the religious sphere.

Signs and symbols

Like Tillich, Randall drew a distinction between signs and symbols. The random sign was something that provoked the same human response as another thing, for which it could stand as a kind of surrogate or substitute. A sign, therefore, according to Randall, 'stands for or represents something other than itself: it is always a sign of something else'. It points to the thing that it is there for – it is not the thing itself; it does not aim to provoke a deeper or emotional response from us.

In contrast, a symbol serves an entirely different function, in Randall's view. A symbol is not representative in any sense; it doesn't stand for anything other than itself. The function of the symbol is quite unique, in that a symbol provokes a response from those who see it or use it. In Randall's words, 'it is important to realise that religious symbols are not signs; they belong rather with the nonrepresentative symbols which function in various ways in both intellectual and the practical life'.

A sign is not a symbol

> **Key term**
>
> **empirical knowledge:** knowledge that is acquired (or acquirable) through the five senses; it is knowledge that provides information about the external, physical world

Cognitive and non-cognitive symbols

Randall also draws a distinction between symbols that we use in the scientific field and symbols used in the arts and religion. The former, Randall believed, can be identified as cognitive symbols: that is, they provide factual knowledge about the empirical world. Such symbols can be found in scientific equations, hypotheses and theorems. Randall believed that they serve an entirely different function from the symbols found in the world of the arts and religion; these are exclusively non-cognitive, in that they produce an emotional response – they do not provide **empirical knowledge**.

Symbols as motivators

As a form of communication, religious symbols act as motivators; they lead those who are influenced by them to forms of action. These responses tend to be common or shared because of the nature of the symbol and the identity of the community that shares it. These symbols are also able to communicate qualitative or shared experiences; experiences that are often considered to be difficult to put into words. The power of the symbol is to evoke the feelings of those shared experiences, which give a particular power to the symbol itself.

Symbols as revelation

Religious symbols also hold a unique characteristic, according to Randall, in that, unlike the symbols found within art, religious symbols have the ability to reveal or disclose something about the world in which they function. This, for Randall, is particularly important because it is at this juncture that the religious symbol and religious knowledge share common ground. He writes:

> Religious symbols are commonly said to reveal some truth about experience. If we ask what it is that such symbols do reveal or disclose about the world, it is clear that it is not what we should call in the ordinary sense knowledge, in the sense already defined. This revelation can be styled knowledge or truth only in a sense that it is equivocal or metaphorical. It is more like direct acquaintance than descriptive knowledge: it resembles what we call insight or vision. Such symbols do not tell anything that is verifiably so; they rather make us see something about our experience and our experienced world.
> (Randall, *The Role of Knowledge in Western Religion*)

Thus, religious symbols, for Randall, serve as instruments of revelation. It is only through symbols that human beings can approach the divine. It is only through symbols and symbolic language that we can truly live a religious life in any meaningful sense.

Paul Tillich: God as that which concerns us ultimately

The functions of symbols

Working as a contemporary to Randall but publishing one year earlier, Paul Tillich, in his book *Dynamics of Faith*, also contributes to the understanding of symbolic language. The text describes the contributions of symbols to an understanding of faith. To appreciate properly Tillich's work on symbols, we must first give a brief sketch of his work on faith. Tillich saw faith as the state of being ultimately concerned.

Beyond the basic needs, such as those recognised in Maslow's hierarchy of needs (i.e. food, shelter, warmth, water and so on), Tillich also saw the need to fulfil spiritual concerns: cognitive, aesthetic, social and political. These concerns led to humanity's ultimate concern.

> **Specification content**
>
> Religious language as non-cognitive and symbolic: God as that which concerns us ultimately (Paul Tillich)

> **" Key quote "**
>
> … it is not the unconditional demand made by that which is one's ultimate concern, it is also a promise of the ultimate fulfilment which is accepted in the act of faith. The content of this promise is not necessarily defined. It can be expressed in indefinite symbols or in concrete symbols which cannot be taken literally … Faith is the state of being ultimately concerned.
>
> (Tillich, *Dynamics of Faith*)

In Tillich's words:

> Man's ultimate concern must be expressed symbolically, because symbolic language alone is able to express the ultimate. This statement demands explanation in several respects. In spite of the manifold research about the meaning and function of symbols which is going on in contemporary philosophy, every

writer who uses the term symbol must explain his understanding of it. Symbols have one characteristic in common with signs; they point beyond themselves to something else. The red sign at the streetcorner points to the order to stop the movements of cars at certain intervals. Red lights and the stopping of cars have essentially no relation to each other, but conventionally they are united as long as the convention lasts. The same is true of letters and numbers and possibly even words. They point beyond themselves to sounds and meanings ... Sometimes such signs are called symbols; but this is unfortunate because it makes the distinction between signs and symbols more difficult because it is the fact that signs do not participate in the reality of that to which they point, while symbols do. Therefore, signs can be replaced for reasons of expediency or convention, while symbols cannot. (Tillich, *Dynamics of Faith*)

Characteristics of symbols

Tillich identifies six characteristics of symbols. In brief, these are as follows:

1. Symbols point beyond themselves to something else.
2. Symbols participate in the reality of that to which they point.
3. Symbols open up levels of reality that are otherwise closed to us.
4. Symbols unlock dimensions and elements of our soul that correspond to the dimensions and elements of reality.
5. Symbols cannot be produced intentionally. They grow out of the individual or collective unconscious and cannot function without being accepted by the unconscious dimension of our being.
6. Symbols, like living beings, grow and die. They grow when the situation is ripe for them, and they die when the situation changes.

Symbols have six different characteristics, according to Tillich

Symbolic language and ultimate concern

Tillich explains the relationship between symbolic language and the ultimate concern as follows:

> We have discussed the meaning of symbols generally because, as we said, man's ultimate concern must be expressed symbolically! One may ask: why can it not be expressed directly and properly? If money, success or the nation is someone's ultimate concern, can this not be said in a direct way without symbolic language? Is it not only in those cases in which the content of the ultimate concern is called 'God' that we are in the realm of symbols? The answer is that everything which is a matter of unconditional concern is made into a god. If the nation is someone's ultimate concern, the name of the nation becomes a sacred name and the nation receives divine qualities which far surpass the reality of the being and functioning of the nation. The nation then stands for and symbolises the true ultimate, but in an idolatrous way. Success as ultimate concern is not a natural desire of actualising potentialities, but is readiness to sacrifice all other values of life for the sake of a position of power and social predominance. The anxiety about not being a success is an idolatrous form of the anxiety about divine condemnation. Success is Grace; lack of success, ultimate judgement. In this way concepts designating ordinary realities become idolatrous symbols of ultimate concern. The reason for this transformation of concepts into symbols is the character of ultimacy and the nature of faith. That which is the true ultimate transcends the realm of finite reality infinitely. Therefore, no finite reality can express it directly and properly. Religiously speaking, God transcends his own name. This is why the use of his name easily becomes an abuse or a blasphemy. Whatever we say about that which concerns us ultimately, whether or not we call it God, has a symbolic meaning. It points beyond itself while participating in that to which it points. In no other way can faith express itself adequately. The language of faith is the language of symbols. (Tillich, *Dynamics of Faith*)

For Tillich, therefore, the language of symbols is the language of power. Tillich viewed God as the fundamental symbol of ultimate concern. In this sense, the language of symbols is entirely non-cognitive in that it brings about a response at the deepest emotional level of the believer to the symbol, reality and ultimate concern that is God.

Tillich also saw the symbols of faith as closely linked to the idea of myth. Myths, like symbols, participate in human activity. According to Tillich, they give rise to human cultural and religious traditions and, like symbols, are 'present in every act of faith because the language of faith is the symbol'.

Challenges to the adequacy and insights of symbols

The function of symbols

We have seen that the work of Randall and Tillich does much to help us appreciate how symbols and symbolic language can be used to communicate deep and powerful meanings for individuals, groups and societies. The symbol is a key component of religious life, religious

> **Specification content**
> Challenges including whether a symbol is adequate or gives the right insights

experience and therefore religious language. The deep-seated emotional responses that some symbols can bring about demonstrate that symbolic language is meaningful for those who engage with it. However, even with all that said, there have been criticisms.

The limitation of symbols as non-cognitive

Firstly, and by his own admission, Randall recognised that the language of the symbol is inherently non-cognitive. As such, symbolic language does not provide information about the empirically knowable, objective world in an objective and empirical way – for to do so would make it cognitive language, which it is not. This immediately puts it at odds with the conclusions of the Vienna Circle and later Logical Positivists, in that symbolic language – not being verifiable, falsifiable, analytic, synthetic or mathematical – is rendered essentially meaningless, in a cognitive and empirical sense.

Philosophical confusion

Paul Edwards, the American professor of philosophy, criticised Tillich's work on symbols as 'philosophical confusion'. Edwards noted that Tillich himself recognises, in his *Systematic Theology*, the inability to express in literal terms anything meaningful about God. Edwards wrote:

> The concession by an author that he is using a certain word metaphorically is tantamount to admitting that, in a very important sense and a sense relevant to the questions at issue between metaphysicians and their critics, he does not mean what he says. It does not automatically tell us what he does mean or whether in fact he means anything at all. (Edwards, 'Professor Tillich's Confusions')

Edwards recognises that this undermines Tillich's attempt to say anything meaningful by virtue of symbolic language, and references back to the Logical Positivists to support this criticism of Tillich:

> Granting this, it seems to me the Logical Positivists nevertheless deserve great credit helping to call attention to certain features of many sentences (and systems) commonly called metaphysical. The metaphysicians are sometimes obscurely but never, to my knowledge, clearly aware of these features. On the contrary, they manage by various stratagems to hide these features both from themselves and others. (Edwards, 'Professor Tillich's Confusions')

How do we know whether symbols provide the right insight?

Changing meanings

Another point at which it can be shown that a symbol may not be adequate is that symbols change over time. Tillich recognises this himself, yet it did not deter him from believing that symbolic language can still provide meaningful insights into deep and powerful truths. However, if people take a symbol and change its meaning, then they are not just altering the symbol but are also altering something more fundamental: that is, the association of that symbol for a particular culture.

There are a number of examples of such symbols changing over time. One example is the *ichthus* – a symbol used by early Christians to signify a safe place for meeting and to hide their basic creed. The word arises from the Greek acronym Jesus (**I**) Christ (**Ch**), God's (**Th**) Son (**U**), Saviour (**S**). The symbol itself was originally used in pre-Christian times as a fertility symbol, with the shape being associated with the womb of the Great Mother goddess.

Another example, with a more recent historical connotation, is the swastika, which was originally a symbol from Eastern religions. It was often associated with the universal principle of harmony and peace, before being perverted into a symbol of hatred for many in the West because of its association with the Nazis in the twentieth century.

The changes of meaning are significant. Therefore, what insight can a symbol truly provide, if its meaning can change over time? Equally, how adequate is it at providing that necessary spiritual insight, if the context of the symbol can change the meaning entirely? In both cases, changes of meaning undermine the idea that symbolic language is a meaningful form of language. If the meaning changes, how can the symbol be considered to be anything other than ultimately meaningless?

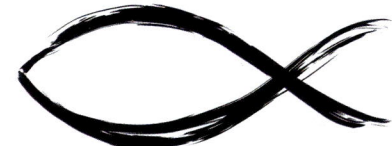

The ichthus and swastika have changed their symbolic meaning over time

How can Randall and Tillich's views be used to help understand religious teachings?

Religious teachings can vary, from clear instructions on how to behave in a religious setting, to how to act in a religious ritual or even how to make moral decisions. They can also relate to the wider mysteries of the universe, the soul and human existence. In terms of the first type of religious teachings, the views of Randall and Tillich have little to say. However, in relation to the second type, their views can help shed light on those teachings. A note of caution, however: neither Randall nor Tillich laid claim to having a theological 'Rosetta Stone': in other words, a firm declaration about such mysteries. Instead, their work was to show how symbols can help us gain insight into the world of religion.

> **Specification content**
>
> A consideration of how these two views (Randall/Tillich) can be used to help understand religious teachings

Randall's views

For example, J.H. Randall's views were that religious beliefs (and the teachings that arose from them) were not to be understood in a literal sense:

> Very early in every great religious tradition, reflective man came to see that the ordinary ideas entertained and used in worship, prayer and ritual could not be literally true. The idea of God, for example, employed by the unreflective in the actual practice of the religious arts, could not be adequate to the true nature of the Divine. God could not be 'really' the animal, or natural force, or carved image, the imaginative picture, in which the average man conceives the Divine. He could not be even the highest human image, the 'Father', or the kind of person who in the present fashion seems appropriately approached in terms of the 'I-Thou' experience ... They cannot be taken as literal accounts of the divine. They are imaginative and figurative ways of conceiving the relations of men and their ideals to the nature of things and to its religious dimension. (Randall, *The Role of Knowledge in Western Religion*)

Randall goes on to explain how these ideas should be understood symbolically instead – for, in that non-cognitive structure, they make more intellectual sense to the 'reflective man'.

Randall thought that early religious worshippers understood that they were to understand the objects they worshipped symbolically, rather than literally

As Randall develops his work, the idea that symbols are able to convey knowledge about the world becomes a central theme. This is not knowledge in the cognitive sense, but an almost intuitive knowledge, where insight is gained (even though Randall is not precisely clear about what he means by this) and truths about the world are revealed. Thus, it could be argued, by understanding symbols, we are led to a greater understanding of religious beliefs and their associated teachings.

Tillich's views

For Tillich, the key aim of his work was to show how symbols could point beyond themselves and lead believers to their ultimate concern. By participating in the reality of that to which it pointed, the symbol sheds light on the meaning of the object or idea that it represents, and provides an insight that would not have been possible through any other means. One such example of this is the reference to God, as expressed by Tillich:

> God is the basic symbol of faith, that's not the only one. All the qualities we attribute to him, power, love, justice, are taken from finite experiences and applied symbolically to that which is beyond finitude and infinity. If faith calls God 'almighty', it uses the human experience of power in order to symbolise the content of its infinite concern, but it does not describe the highest being who can do as he pleases. So it is with all the other qualities as with all the actions, past, present and future, which men attribute to God. They are symbols taken from our daily experience, and not information about what God did once upon a time or sometime in the future. Faith is not the belief in such stories, but it is the acceptance of symbols that express our ultimate concern in terms of divine actions. (Tillich, *Dynamics of Faith*)

Understanding how symbols work in the everyday world, therefore, Tillich provides guidance to how religious teachings can be understood: that is, as ideas expressed symbolically, to be interpreted by those who participate in them and who therefore accept them for what they are. In this, believers are led to their ultimate concern.

Rejection of their views – religious teachings as cognitive and objective

However, neither Randall's nor Tillich's views are universally accepted. Some find the idea that their religious beliefs and teachings are to be understood purely symbolically, or in a solely non-cognitive way, as potentially offensive, as it suggests that they have no basis in objective reality. That is, they do not relate to the world as it is experienced by human beings on a day-to-day basis. They argue that religious teachings depict reality as it really is and should therefore be understood cognitively. For such believers, the views put forward by Randall and Tillich – that this is not the actual intention of religious language – may cause them considerable concern.

Summary

- In the mid-twentieth century, in separate but contemporary works, J.H. Randall and Paul Tillich produced key texts showing how symbols and symbolic language could convey meaning.
- Randall considered the function of symbols in religion and in society and noted that their key role is to 'generate knowledge and truth'. He considered the role that symbols have in unifying peoples and providing them with an identity, acting as motivators and providing revelation.
- Tillich considered that symbols have key characteristics and listed six of these. He saw symbols as carrying a language of power and ultimately as the language in which faith best expresses itself. Tillich saw myths as the key vehicle for carrying symbols in society and across time.
- Some have challenged the concept of symbols, suggesting that unless the context is known the symbol remains meaningless. There is also concern that symbols can be misinterpreted, particularly with their tendency to change meaning over time. However, the work of Randall and Tillich is recognised as supporting religious believers in understanding, at a greater depth, the teachings of their religious traditions.

AO1 Activity

a   Outline Randall's ideas in ten bullet points. Learn these bullet points and test yourself on them or ask someone else to test you until you can accurately repeat them.

This helps with presenting a thorough and extensive knowledge and understanding of the topic area.

b   On revision cards, summarise the key features of Randalls' and Tillich's characteristics of symbols.

This helps with prioritising and selecting a core set of points to develop an answer and with ensuring your response has an excellent standard of coherence, clarity and organisation.

> **This section covers AO2 content and skills**

> **Specification content**
> Whether symbolic language can be agreed as having adequate meaning as a form of language

Issues for analysis and evaluation

Whether symbolic language can be agreed as having adequate meaning as a form of language

Possible line of argument	Critical analysis and evaluation
Symbols provide us with a means of representing the indefinable	Understanding language in a non-cognitive sense allows us to move beyond a literalistic and empirical interpretation, into one that is more associated with emotions, feelings or the expression of something that relates to some indefinable mental state or image. Symbols effectively evoke these things and provide a more than adequate meaningfulness to how we use and understand language.
Symbols convey meaning	Tillich, who worked with Randall on the function of symbols, stated that there are six key aspects, including the ideas that symbols point beyond themselves to something else, as well as participating in the reality of what they point to. Symbols, then, possess a very real, very meaningful quality that operates on a far deeper level than empirical, scientific language. For these reasons, the work of both Randall and Tillich very much supports the idea that symbols can provide adequate meanings as a form of language.
The work of prominent sociologists and psychologists supports the validity of symbols to convey meaning	It would seem, then, that symbolic language is unassailable in terms of the levels of meaning that it can bring to those who engage with it. The individual and social interactions that occur through engagement with symbolic language are clearly undeniable. The work of sociologists such as Émile Durkheim, and psychologists such as Carl Jung, recognise the significant value that symbols have within human culture as means of providing identity and meaning in an existential sense.
Symbols and their meaning are liable to change over time, impacting on their meaningfulness	However, not all would agree with the ability of symbols to provide meaning. Indeed, one of the key features of symbols that Tillich recognised was that symbols 'grow and die'. He means that there were historically chronological points for the relevance of symbols and, once those times had passed, the symbols' relevance passed too. This would suggest that, for all their significance, symbols do not provide a constant or consistent meaning that can be interpreted 'at all times and in all places'. Symbols are inextricably linked with cultural norms. As these change, so do the meanings of the symbols.
Symbols are sensitive to cultural referencing, making them unreliable as vehicles of meaningfulness	The very fact that symbols are sensitive to cultural norms means that different cultures can, quite literally, treat symbols in entirely different ways. Perhaps an obvious example is that of the swastika. Long used in the religions and societies associated with Asia, the swastika represented peace and the universality of the organising principle. Its inclusion in the art of Buddhism, Hinduism and Sikhism is well documented. Its use in Puja to provide inspiration as well as devotion is equally well known. However, in the twentieth century, the swastika took on an altogether different meaning. It became linked with a political movement that is historically regarded and associated with fear, hatred, prejudice and some of the worst documented atrocities visited by human beings upon each other. Since then, it still has associations with cultural examples of discrimination and ignorant hatred. If such a symbol can have such diverse meanings, how is it that symbols can provide any constant, reliable and, above all, adequate guide to meaning – particularly when used in symbolic language?

Possible line of argument	Critical analysis and evaluation
Symbolic language should be dismissed as meaningless	Rational thinking should dismiss symbols and symbolic language as flights of fancy that entertain at best, but distract people from the true meaning of life at worst. They promote navel-gazing activities that detract from useful contributions to society and we should therefore dismiss symbolic language as both meaningless and, ultimately, useless.
The ability of symbolic language to convey meaningfulness is a matter of perspective	To draw these arguments together, it seems that the question is not straightforward. Quite simply, if non-cognitive language is considered as a valid vehicle for language to transmit meaning, then symbolic language does indeed fulfil that role. However, if this idea is rejected, then symbolic language is ultimately meaningless and cannot provide any adequate meaning as a form of language.

AO2 Activity

a Evaluate three lines of argument from the critical analysis and evaluation of whether symbolic language can be agreed as having adequate meaning as a form of language. What are their strengths and weaknesses? Which line of argument is strongest?

b Using the strongest line of argument, try to identify three key questions that might be asked – they could be critical questions, challenges, hypothetical or direct.

Exam practice

Sample question

Evaluate how far the works of Randall and Tillich provide a suitable counter-challenge to Logical Positivism.

Sample answer

The influence of Logical Positivism at the beginning of the twentieth century was significant, as far as philosophy was concerned. For the first time, in a systematic way, the empiricism of the scientific world was being rigorously applied to the world of ideas; and the challenges to that world were, to say the least, significant. Luminaries such as Schlick and Carnap and associates with the Vienna Circle such as Ayer, Popper and Wittgenstein were contributing radical ideas that included the fierce rejection of metaphysics due to, in the definition of the empirical thought being proposed, it having nothing meaningful to say about the external world.

At its heart, Logical Positivism was proposing an adoption of a rigid criterion for meaning that was based on the ability to verify a statement. This proposition fitted comfortably with the empirical world of the physical sciences and was therefore regarded as a litmus test for meaning. Analytic and synthetic statements, along with mathematical and tautological statements, were all regarded as meaningful, yet anything that fell outside of these was regarded as ultimately meaningless.

Specification content
How far the works of Randall and Tillich provide a suitable counter-challenge to Logical Positivism

News reporter
This is a good introduction that provides a helpful overview of the background to the evaluation to come.

Detective
The response presents evidence, via a line of reasoning, showing the grounds for Logical Positivism to consider language meaningful.

Tennis player

This paragraph introduces the views of Randall and Tillich as a counterpoint to the views of Logical Positivism.

Being exposed to the ideas of Logical Positivism, both Randall and Tillich took an oppositional view in terms of what constituted meaning. They viewed language non-cognitively – not as something that can be held up to objective scrutiny. This is because non-cognitive language is language that expresses opinions, attitudes, feelings and/or emotions. It is language that relates to a person's view of what reality may mean to them – and this may differ from the view of another, even though they may be experiencing the same reality. Both views are valid – but in a non-cognitive sense.

News reporter

The candidate explains Randall's viewpoints, with commentary, as a line of reasoning in supporting the meaningfulness of religious language.

Randall was interested in the way that religious language worked. He believed that religious language carried both meaning and knowledge. He also recognised that this form of communication both differed from and shared similarities with other forms of language – including the language of the world of the physical sciences. In considering what the function of religious language was as a vehicle for conveying knowledge, Randall concentrated specifically on the forms of communication within religion that gave believers the greatest insights into their commonly held beliefs, ideas and cultural identities.

Explorer

This paragraph presents further evidence, this time from a different angle, demonstrating how Randall saw common ground in the purpose of religion and science.

Randall realised that the worlds of natural science and natural theology had a common purpose. That purpose was to reveal the workings of the world and universe where we live. Looking at religious beliefs, expressed through religious language as key to this understanding, Randall stated in his *The Role of Knowledge in Western Religion*: 'If the function of religious beliefs is not to generate knowledge and truth, what is their function?'

Tennis player

This paragraph makes another counterpoint, this time attacking the flaw in inductive reasoning: namely, that the conclusion is not definitive.

Randall recognised that religious beliefs resulted in unifying people together; they gave people an identity. They provided a common way of communicating, and a shared set of values. This translated, quite literally, into a common form of language; at its heart, the religious language – a language highly symbolic, representing those very things that give the people their identity. This was the role of religious experience. As such, Randall's view of religious language was that it was entirely meaningful – in a powerful, yet non-cognitive way, and his views appear to offer a significant counterpoint to the ideas of the Logical Positivists.

The candidate explores an alternative line of reasoning, through the work of Tillich, and provides appropriate commentary on his views and on how they relate to the issue.

Similarly, Tillich saw the meaningfulness of religious language through the way it was used. Regarding religious language as having a unique ability to communicate symbolically, he recognised that the meaning came through the function that religious language provided. He believed that symbols not only pointed beyond themselves, but were also participatory in the reality they pointed to. For instance, a Christian regarding the symbol of the crucifix is immediately drawn into the symbolism associated with incarnation, atonement and sacrifice, as expressed through the Christian tradition. Symbols therefore allow those who encounter them the opportunity to have levels of reality opened to them that may not have been accessible otherwise. Spiritually, this is invaluable. Symbolic language, for Tillich, was the language of the soul – and as such was meaningful at the deepest level possible for a human being, albeit not necessarily in the way that the Logical Positivists may have defined meaningfulness.

Judge

The response then considers the evidence presented so far and draws a conclusion while pointing out that Randall and Tillich are viewing the issue through a different lens.

In fact, both Randall and Tillich's approaches to language were, as we have seen, significantly different from the approach of the Logical Positivists. As such, it could be argued that their views offer an effective counterargument to Logical Positivism, even though they are not necessarily approaching the subject from the same philosophical starting point.

Evaluation

This is an effective and balanced response. It considers both sides of the argument and draws a suitable conclusion. The candidate makes accurate use both of terminology and of the views of different philosophers and schools of thought.

Over to you

Your task is to write a response, under timed conditions, to a question requiring an evaluation of the effectiveness of the solutions to the problem of symbolic language. This exercise is best done as a small group at first.

A suggested approach is given below.

Question

Evaluate the effectiveness of the solutions to the problems of symbolic language.

Suggested approach

1. Begin with a list of indicative arguments or lines of reasoning, as you may have done previously. This does not need to be in any particular order at first, although as you practise this you will see more order in your lists, particularly by way of links and connections between arguments.
2. Develop the list by using one or two relevant quotations. Now add some references to scholars and/or religious writings.
3. Write out your plan, under timed conditions, remembering the principles of evaluating with support from extensive, detailed reasoning and/or evidence.

When you have completed the task, refer to the band descriptors for A2 (WJEC) or A Level (Eduqas) and, in particular, look at the demands described in the higher band descriptors, which you should be aspiring towards. Ask yourself:

- Is my answer a confident, critical analysis and perceptive evaluation of the issue?
- Is my answer a response that successfully identifies and thoroughly addresses the issues the question raises?
- Does my work show an excellent standard of coherence, clarity and organisation?
- Will my work, when developed, contain thorough, sustained and clear views that I have supported with extensive, detailed reasoning and/or evidence?
- Have I used the views of scholars/schools of thought extensively, appropriately and in context?
- Does my answer convey a confident and perceptive analysis of the nature of any possible connections with other elements of my course?
- When used, is specialist language and vocabulary both thorough and accurate?

> **This section covers AO1 content and skills**

E: Religious language as non-cognitive and mythical

Myth as a unique and specialised form of language

The term *myth*

In the world today, the term *myth* is often seen as meaning the same as 'falsehood'. For many, a myth is another type of story that has fantastical elements to it, but bears no resemblance to the truths found within the empirical world – the world that we live in and experience every day. Myths, according to the view of many in contemporary society, are regarded as 'fairy stories' – something to entertain children, but that have little or no value beyond this particular sphere of life. However, to reduce a myth to these elements is fundamentally to misunderstand the purpose of this form of language. This is particularly true within the field of religious studies, where *myth* is actually a highly specialised term that refers to accounts that contain truths that are communicated in the form of picture imagery and symbolic text.

> **Specification content**
>
> Complex form of mythical language that communicates values and insights into purpose of existence. Myths help to overcome fears of the unknown; myths an effective way of transmitting religious, social and ethical values.

> **" Key quote "**
>
> A myth is a story, imagined or true, that helps us make sense of reality ... Without a myth there is no meaning or purpose to life. Myths do more than explain. They guide mental processes, conditioning how we think, even how we perceive.
>
> (D.C. Matt, *God and the Big Bang*)

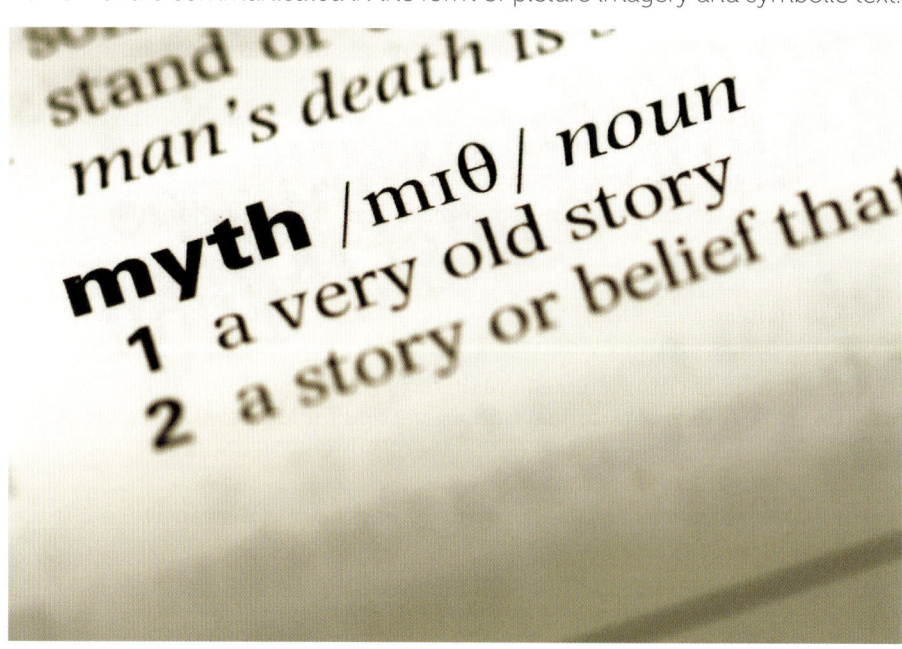

The term *myth* is often misunderstood in modern society

Interpreting myths

To **deconstruct** myths purely by empirically based methods is to miss the meaning of these accounts. Such reductionist approaches, which were particularly popular in the nineteenth and early twentieth centuries, led to the popular view today of myths being little more than fantasies, which provided simplistic views of the complexities surrounding the natural world and events such as the beginning of the universe and the formation of life on Earth.

To dismiss myths as simplistic, as previously stated, is factually inaccurate. Myths do require interpretation, but to do so requires care. Understanding the original context of the myth is important.

German biblical scholars of the twentieth century, when looking at the New Testament within the Christian tradition, spoke of the need to understand the **Sitz im Leben** of the New Testament writers. (*Sitz im Leben* means 'situation in life' – the particular social and historical context of the time.) This would

> **● Key terms**
>
> **deconstruct:** analyse a text by taking it apart to work out what it means
>
> **Sitz im Leben:** a German phrase meaning 'situation in life'; used as a theological term to refer to the context where an account is written usually influencing the writer because of the particular circumstances of the context

allow the meaning of those documents to be properly understood. They also cautioned against applying our own *Sitz im Leben* when interpreting them – because to do so would be to add perspectives that are not relevant to the time of the writers; this would lead to a misunderstanding of the original meanings of such documents. This is why a cautionary approach to interpreting myths will bring a more accurate understanding of the original context and purposes of the myths themselves.

The purpose of myths

Myths exist in all human cultures. The very fact that this is so demonstrates the value that they have for all societies. These myths provide insights into a range of elements that each society holds as significant, though not all societies and cultures have myths for all the same elements. There are commonly recurring ones, such as the creation of the universe; the roles and persons of the gods; heroic myths; how and why the world operates in the way that it does (including ethical codes); the struggle between good and evil, and so on.

Understanding mythical language is essential to help us understand myths. However, studying myths and the language they are written in is a matter of interpretation. Therefore, armed with the best knowledge that we have, we should remember that interpretations are not necessarily always definitive. The myth is a powerful form of literature; it is also, as has already been mentioned, extremely complex. As such, different times and different people may interpret the myth is different ways. As we look at various myths, later in this section, we will further explore these differences of interpretation, as appropriate.

Another issue with the myth is that many myths are remarkably similar to one another – if not in content, then in structure. An example of this is the *ex nihilo* creation myths that begin with voids, water and a divine figure or figures. The ability to appreciate that these represent images and beliefs deeply rooted in the culture from which they arise allows for each myth to be interpreted accordingly – so, while the content may have similarities, the interpretations may differ somewhat.

 Key term

ex nihilo: literally 'out of nothing'; a Latin term often associated with creation myths

Myths as complex forms of literature

Myths are a complex form of literature. Mythical language is also complex, being formed of metaphorical, symbolic and analogical terms – having meanings 'hidden' beyond the literal reading of the text. Over the last century, with the work done on mythical language in religious studies, psychology and anthropology, scholars have determined that, far from the simplistic and childish fantasies that many in contemporary society mistakenly label *myths*, they serve a far more significant purpose.

Myths talk about events surrounding the natural world and how it came to be, but not purely as simple narratives. They hold within them deep and lasting truths that are integral to the identity of the culture and society to which they belong. At their very heart, myths explore what it means to be human, what our relationship should be with the world we inhabit, how we should relate to each other and what our responsibilities are to the powers that, they claim, we owe for our very existence.

Myths and religion

Myth is an integral part of religion. Many of the aspects of religion depend on myth to provide a means of expressing those fundamental religious truths that cannot be expressed in any other form of language – for to do so would be to simplify them or devalue them.

Because myths and mythical language are highly complex and contain metaphorical, symbolic and analogical aspects within them, attempting to find literal meanings to myths inevitably leads to error. This is the case both for those who may adopt a fundamentalist and literalist approach to their reading of religious texts, and for those who may criticise religion as meaningless in the contemporary scientific world.

Meaningful discussion regarding myth needs to take into account the highly specific way myths employ language. Discussion then needs to begin to explore and understand the richness of the text as it unveils mythical truths about human existence, the universe we inhabit and, where appropriate, the divine.

How different forms of myths convey meaning

Creation myths

Creation myths have existed for as long as humans have told and recorded their stories. Many consider the account of creation, as described in the Judeo-Christian traditions, an account rich in mythical language. It is one that, in common with other creation myths from the ancient Near East, proposes a creation that came about *ex nihilo*: that is, 'out of nothing'.

> **Specification content**
>
> Supportive evidence – different forms of myths to convey meaning: creation myths

The Judeo-Christian creation account: 'In the beginning …'

The account as recorded in the first chapter of Genesis runs thus:

> In the beginning God created the heavens and the earth. Now the earth was formless and empty, darkness was over the surface of the deep, and the Spirit of God was hovering over the waters.
>
> And God said, 'Let there be light', and there was light. God saw that the light was good, and he separated the light from the darkness. God called the light 'day', and the darkness he called 'night'. And there was evening, and there was morning – the first day. (Genesis 1:1–5)

The mythical language used here is particularly notable. The beginning of the account describes a vast emptiness (void) yet populated by primordial waters – these would traditionally be signifying chaos.

Water as a mythical symbol

Water, particularly the waters of the oceans, would have presented a great mystery to the ancients. The ability to traverse these oceans was initially unavailable to ancient societies, who originally formulated these myths. The seas and oceans were also uncontrollable and seemingly unpredictable, and therefore became a natural symbol for chaos.

This is what we have here at the beginning of the Judeo-Christian creation myth: the chaos of primordial water being brought under the control of the God-figure. This signifies that, in the most ancient of mythical themes, order is brought out of chaos. The God of the myth is a God who possesses the ability to conquer chaos – to impose his will upon it.

This God goes on not only to calm the waters, but to divide them – bringing forth land (which would have signified, among other things, stability and order). He further demonstrates his power over the chaotic waters by filling them with differentiated life, and widens this even further by also populating the remaining spheres – for example, the skies and the land – with life. All this demonstrates his power and control over his creation.

Order and chaos as mythical themes in Judeo-Christianity

Furthermore, the great theme of order versus chaos is symbolised again in light versus darkness. In the beginning, light (which is universally a symbol for knowledge, understanding and righteous power) has no place in the chaos. It does not exist. As the myth progresses, light floods creation, initially in the great separation of night and day and then, later, by the heavenly bodies of the Sun, Moon and stars, whose function it is to bring light to the world during these two times. Even the night – the time of darkness – has not returned to the primordial chaos because, this time, there are lights within it. The creator God has exerted influence for all creation, shining a light in the darkness and causing order in which created life-forms can flourish.

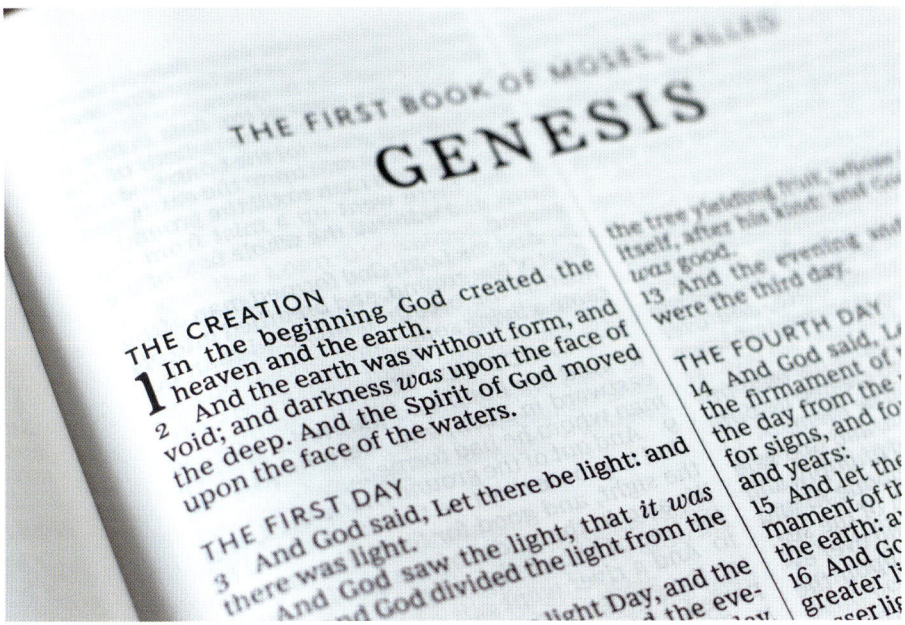

The mythical language found in the Genesis creation account shows how order was brought out of chaos

Water as a mythical symbol in other religious cultures

The mythical image of water is particularly significant in creation myths

In his 1964 work *Myths of Creation*, Philip Freund notes the similarity between the Judeo-Christian creation myth and other myths that start in the waters and bring about creation through the actions of an agent of order:

- In Egyptian myths, the Morning Sun God, Khepri, lifts himself from the waters to bring about creation.
- The Zuni tribe of America has a creation myth that tells how the Sun-Father brings about creation from the waters through his divine actions, before eventually creating humankind.
- The nineteenth-century epic Finnish poem, based on the myths of the country, speaks of primordial waters where the virgin daughter of the air descends to become the water-mother. Through her interaction with these chaotic waters, she ends up giving birth to the first man, Väinämöinen, after an immaculate conception.
- New Zealand's Māori creation myth recounts how the demigod Maui pulled up the islands of New Zealand from the depths of the ocean, beginning the history of life on those islands.
- Similar stories are told in British Columbia, Japan, South America and Ireland, to name but a few. What is fascinating about all this is the commonality of order being brought out of chaos – with water being the symbol of chaos and land/life being the symbol of order.

Paul Tillich notes that it is inescapable that the language of myth is found within religion. He states:

> Myths are always present in every act of faith, because the language of faith is the symbol … It puts the stories of the gods into the framework of time and space although it belongs to the nature of the ultimate to be beyond time and space.
> (Tillich, *Dynamics of Faith*)

The significance of water as a theme within the creation myths is therefore evident.

The primacy and divine purpose of humanity as a mythical theme

Another key feature of most creation myths is to recognise the primacy of human beings within creation. The divine being responsible for creation usually directly bestows on them that particular role.

The Judeo-Christian myth concludes with the following information:

> Then God said, 'Let us make humankind in our image, according to our likeness, and let them have dominion over the fish of the sea and over the birds of the air and over the cattle and over all the wild animals of the earth and over every creeping thing that creeps upon the earth.'
>
> So God created humans in his image, in the image of God he created them; male and female he created them.
>
> God blessed them, and God said to them, 'Be fruitful and multiply and fill the earth and subdue it and have dominion over the fish of the sea and over the birds of the air and over every living thing that moves upon the earth.' God said, 'See, I have given you every plant yielding seed that is upon the face of all the earth and every tree with seed in its fruit; you shall have them for food. And to every beast of the earth and to every bird of the air and to everything that creeps on the earth, everything that has the breath of life, I have given every green plant for

food.' And it was so. God saw everything that he had made, and indeed, it was very good. And there was evening and there was morning, the sixth day. (Genesis 1:26–1:31, NRSV)

The role of human beings, communicated through the mythical language, is quite straightforward: to take on the role of stewardship for the creator; to look after the created order; to preserve it. Not just that: humankind is given pre-eminence within creation, as the only part of creation made in the image of the creator.

According to Irenaeus of Lyons' interpretation, humanity is endowed with the qualities of the uncreated God, even if only initially in potential. Irenaeus saw this myth as demonstrating that human beings had the ability to transform into God's likeness, having been created in his image – but only through fulfilling the divine commands, and by developing God-like qualities, would this be possible.

It is this complex form of mythical language that communicates humankind's purpose directly – and, as such, provides insight into the purpose of existence.

The purpose of humanity as expressed in symbolic and mythical language

The meaning that is derived from this mythical account may not be cognitive in nature, but it reveals information about the world and the role of human beings in it. This information is meaningful because it provides both context and purpose. The language of myth, albeit a non-cognitive form of language, provides meaning in a deeper way possible than any other form of language could hope to do.

As Tillich states:

> Symbols of faith cannot be replaced by other symbols, such as artistic ones, and they cannot be removed by scientific criticism. They have a genuine standing in the human mind, just as science and art have. Their symbolic character is their truth and their power. Nothing less than symbols and myths can express our ultimate concern. (Tillich, *Dynamics of Faith*)

Humans are often given a specific role in creation myths

Heroic myths and myths of good against evil

> **Key quote**
>
> At least with superhero characters, we know … they do fill the gap in a secular culture, because they open up dimensions of the cosmic and transcendent, which is stuff legends usually have to deal with. It's not so much that they are new versions of the gods, because the gods were always just our eternal qualities. Superman possesses the qualities of the very best man we can imagine at any given time. In that sense, he's divine. Batman is representative of our dark subconscious, who nevertheless works for the good of humanity. They embody the same ideals.
>
> (G. Morrison, 'In Supergods, Grant Morrison Probes Superhero Myths', *Wired*)

Specification content

Supportive evidence – different forms of myths to convey meaning: myths of good against evil; heroic myths. Myths help to overcome fears of the unknown; myths' effective way of transmitting religious, social and ethical values.

While creation myths are able to give meaningful insight into the purpose of humanity and its relationship with the rest of the universe (created order), other types of myths can reveal different insights. One such example is the category of myths described as 'heroic'.

Inevitably, these tend to focus on either one or a small number of individuals, and recount stories of how the individual conquers great adversity and is triumphant as a result. The themes of these myths are often rooted in the struggle of good versus evil. Such myths provide insight into the daily struggle of human existence and provide inspiration.

These types of myths have existed throughout human history, and exist even today in retellings found in the world of cinema, comic-book heroes and videogames. Their persistence speaks to the deep and often emotional responses that they provoke in all those who encounter them. They usually involve archetypal character themes, such as those of the hero, the villain, the companion and the wise counsellor, and they engage their audiences in the timeless language of symbol and myth. Moojen Momen notes that there are many ways to interpret myths, but a particularly useful method of interpretation:

> ... is the mythological approach employed by such scholars as Carl Jung, Mircea Eliade and Joseph Campbell. This is based on the understanding that, if one studies the common themes in the different mythologies of the world, one can find the basic rhythms by which all human beings live. Myth explores the deeper inner questions and problems that have troubled humankind. Among the commonest themes uncovered by such studies are those which relate closely to religion: for example, the themes of creation, transformation, death and resurrection. (Momen, *The Phenomenon of Religion*)

The heroic myth is often retold in cinema, comics and videogames in the twenty-first century

One of the most commonly recurring forms of the heroic myth is the myth of the solar hero. Sun worship was common in many ancient societies. The Sun, in purely scientific terms, is the source of all life on Earth – being the prime requisite for the process of photosynthesis. However, long before the scientific age, the Sun's life-giving properties were well known, and their importance became enshrined in the myths of a myriad different cultures and religions.

The solar hero: Ancient Egypt – Ra

Perhaps one of the best-known 'sun gods' is the Ancient Egyptian sun god Ra. In some creation myths associated with Ra, he rises from the primordial waters and is responsible for creating air and moisture. His role as a life- and light-giver is what he is best known for, travelling across the sky during the day, bringing warmth to the whole world. Then, at night, he travels through the underworld to do the same for those who dwell there. Ra is therefore both a sun god and a sky god. His heroic deeds are centred around his ability to provide the life-giving properties of the Sun and to battle the forces of chaos and darkness that threaten to overrun the ordered world.

The solar hero: Ancient Canaanite religion – Baal

The theme of the battle between order/light and chaos/darkness is echoed in the ancient Canaanite religion where the god Baal, another key god, is the promoter of life and fertility, and is worshipped for these attributes. Although more properly considered to be a storm god, the theme of solar hero also runs through the mythological accounts associated with Baal.

The Judeo-Christian literature casts Baal in an unfavourable light, putting his followers in direct opposition to the early Israelites, as Baal and Yahweh battled for supremacy – with Yahweh triumphing each time. Evidence from ancient manuscripts suggests that Yahweh was initially regarded as a sky god, before taking on a role more closely associated with another Canaanite deity, El, who was regarded as the father of the gods.

The myths of the Canaanite and Egyptian gods were often rooted in an account that detailed the cycle of the seasons and the associated fertility of the agricultural year. In both cases, the key figures give life, are killed by a dark force opposed to life (the agent of chaos) but, usually through the intervention of a female deity, are restored to life to start the cycle of fertility over again. The mythical language here is a clear parallel for the passage of the seasons, as we have already seen. However, it is also the precursor for another form of myth – the resurrection myth.

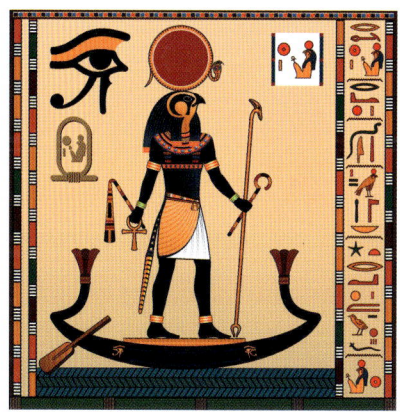

Ra, the Ancient Egyptian sun god

The solar hero and resurrection myth

Resurrection myth is most often associated with the notion of the solar hero as an **archetype** (a direct evolution of the prominence of the sun god). It exists in many cultures and details how the agent of order is destroyed by the agents of chaos, only to be brought back to life again in a victory against its enemies:

> The myth of the solar hero typically begins with a Golden Age. Then the affairs of the solar hero and his family or nation go into decline; he appears to be defeated and even to die (as does the sun and the fertility of the earth in winter). At this point, the hero is separated from his people. In some versions, he descends into an underworld where he struggles against the forces of darkness. He wins a great victory and acquires the means for saving humanity. And so, just when everything seems hopeless and the world is full of darkness and the earth barren, the hero returns to 'save' the world. He brings a new era of justice and hope, a new order; a new Golden Age dawns (as the sun returns in spring and revives the fertility of the earth). (Momen, *The Phenomenon of Religion*)

> **Key term**
>
> **archetype:** according to Jung, a primitive concept inherited from the earliest human ancestors and found in the collective unconscious

The solar hero: variations in other cultures

Not only does this mythical account exist in the cultures of Ancient Egypt and Canaan, but it is also found in the religions of the present day. The Ramayana in Hinduism tells how Rama is banished to the forest by his evil stepmother and how his wife Sita is kidnapped by the demon Ravana. The forces of darkness seem to overwhelm Rama until, with the help of his allies, he battles the forces of darkness, rescues his wife from the clutches of the evil demon and is restored to his rightful throne.

Furthermore, the story in the New Testament of Jesus of Nazareth is seen by some as myth. He is taken prisoner as a result of wicked authorities, has his friends abandon him in his hour of need and is subsequently killed.

Eventually, he rises from the dead and heralds the dawn of a new age with the promise of eternal reward for those who follow him.

The story of Siddhartha becoming Buddha echoes these themes, as he becomes separated from the rest of the world and is accosted by the demon Mara before eventually finding enlightenment. He is then able to teach his message of hope to his followers.

The solar hero and the triumph of good over evil

These heroic triumphs, through mythical language, not only teach the ability of the hero to overcome insurmountable odds, but also show how good will always triumph over evil – no matter how much it seems that evil has won. These myths provide inspiration for all those exposed to them. The meaningfulness of the message is found within the myth – the archetypal themes exist throughout history, providing a unique insight into the human condition.

The solar hero always embodies the virtues associated with moral purity and goodness. These serve not only as a counter to the destructive and selfish vices associated with evil within these mythical accounts, but also as inspiration for the cultures that promoted them. Living up to the standards of the hero, as shown through myth, has also been traditionally reinforced in many cultures in the rituals observed throughout the year that are associated with these heroes, such as in the rituals observed during festivals.

The aspirational figure of the solar hero, in promoting the qualities of goodness, would have also served to promote and protect the values of the culture from which he or she came. Demonstrating through myth that good always triumphs over evil – no matter what temporary setbacks may be experienced – would serve as inspiration for listeners, and help provide hope in the challenges that they faced in their everyday existence. The significance of this symbolic struggle, as told through myth, provided a stability for social order. The repetition of the myths through ritual observances would reinforce these ideals. Whether it was Rama achieving victory over Ravana, Baal defeating Mot or Siddhartha overcoming Mara, the triumph of good over evil was assured.

Rama's victory over the demon-king Ravana symbolises the triumph of good over evil – an important theme in heroic myths

Myths help to overcome fears of the unknown

The fear of the unknown is one humankind's oldest known fears. The lack of certainty over what the future holds, what happens to a person when their life ends, or why unpredictable natural events occur, are fears that gripped our ancestors and to some extent, still present a concern to many in the world today. Humankind strives to bring areas of lived experiences under control – to put things into a framework that can help provide certainties – or at least reasonable predictabilities. We order the passage of time into days and seasons; we structure our societies so that there is order between people, and we provide reasons in the mythological fabric of our culture that helps make sense of those things that are unknown. Our ancient myths provided comfort to our ancestors in explaining why the world is the way that it is. The myths of creation explained where the world had come from and often explained the purpose of humankind too; the myths of nature explained why unpredictable events, such as floods, occurred; the myths of the hero demonstrated that evil and suffering would eventually always be overcome and that even death was nothing to be feared for their was reward after this life for those who obeyed the will of the gods. Thus, myths provided explanations and helped our ancestors (and still help many today) overcome their fears of the unknown.

Effectiveness of myths in transmitting religious, social and ethical values

Many myths provide accounts of interactions between beings – both divine and human. These interactions often exist in a framework or context which serves to illustrate a point (moral) about desired behaviours and the consequences of these. They showed that humankind had a purpose, and, for many cultures, there was also a hope of an existence after this one where the gods would reward (or punish) humans for their actions – giving hope of justice where perhaps people felt there was none. The creation accounts of Genesis provide, for the Judeo-Christian context, guidance on social and ethical values such as stewardship, companionship, obedience and authority. These themes are echoed in myths from other cultures too. Understanding the values that underpinned the particular culture, were essential for successful participation in that culture and as such, it was very often that the retelling of these myths was a feature of the education of the young. This is still the case in many cultures today – creation myths, nature myths and myths of the hero and good and evil, all serve the purpose of explaining the importance of religious, social and ethical values for the society from which they derive. Heroes represent and personify the values and ideals that people are encouraged to emulate in their own lives; the powerful symbolism within many of these myths means they are often psychologically significant for the believer and provide intrinsic motivation for them to aspire to do good and avoid evil.

Challenges to myths and problems associated with them

For many, mythical language can be a powerful way to convey meaning at its deepest level. It invokes a response from the human psyche. For Jung, it was an integral part of the collective unconscious and allowed us to gain insights into what it means to be human. However, like all forms of non-cognitive language, mythical language can be challenged with regards to its meaningfulness.

> **Specification content**
>
> Challenges: problem of competing myths; meanings of myths change over time as they reflect the values of society as societal constructs; demythologisation of myths results in varying interpretations, myths often incompatible with scientific understanding of the world

Problems of competing myths

Firstly, if we consider that any particular myth is meaningful, then that would presume that the integrity of the myth is preserved. By this, we mean that, if we are to consider that the myth reveals insights and truths, then we would rightly expect those insights and truths to have a validity worth preserving and even sharing. Such mythical accounts are often the foundation for societies and their key beliefs and values. Their integrity is often paramount.

However, what then happens when another myth stakes a claim to competing truths or competing values? Does this challenge the meaningfulness of the original myth, or is it that the competing myth should be disregarded?

A particular example of this, it could be argued, is the idea that creation and evolution are competing myths. Since the publication of Darwin's *Origin of the Species* in 1859, a fiercely contested debate has been held as to who has the claim of truth with regard to the question 'Where did humankind come from?' Of course, others would not consider these to be competing myths, assuming that science is based on empirically verifiable data, while religion is not. Controversially, that assumption itself may be part of the myth!

Less controversial, perhaps, is that the Genesis myth of creation (an event told as a direct action of the Judeo-Christian God) is the starting point for God's relationship with humankind and a necessary part of the theology for both religions. What happens then, when a very similar account can be found in a culture that predates the Judeo-Christian tradition by several hundred years? If the myth is not unique, does that therefore mean that the faith-based truth claims from the myth are likewise not unique? Does this therefore weaken them?

Similarly, the central claim of Christianity that Jesus' resurrection was a unique event in history, if treated as mythical literature, seems to have several parallels in other cultures, suggesting it may not be as unique an event as is claimed within the Christian tradition. Of course, this assumes that the resurrection of Jesus of Nazareth is a mythical event, which it may not have been.

Meanings of myths change over time as they reflect the values of society as societal constructs

Much like the value of symbolic language, as addressed earlier in this book, the value of mythical language, and therefore its meaning, will inevitably change with the values of societies. The meaning of a myth may alter to fit the prevailing intellectual mood of the day, or it may change as we better understand the ancient cultures from where the myth originated. Either way, this would seem to destabilise the ability of myths to communicate meaningful information, if such information is subject to change over time.

Demythologisation of myths results in varying interpretations

No study of mythical language within religious studies would be complete without reference to the German theologian Rudolf Bultmann. His work on the text of the New Testament had a significant effect on all biblical scholarship that followed, and on the treatment of the person of Jesus of Nazareth in particular.

Bultmann considered that much of the literature in the New Testament, particularly the literature of the four canonical gospels, should be reinterpreted, as it was primarily mythical language. He then set about deconstructing or 'demythologising' these texts to make sense of them. Ian Barbour describes Bultmann's approach thus:

> [Bultmann] objects to myth because it tries to represent the divine in the objective categories of the physical world. In the New Testament these misleading categories include space (e.g. Christ as 'coming down' and 'ascending'), time (eschatology as temporal finality), and causality (miracles and supernatural forces).
>
> These first-century thought-forms must be rejected, according to Bultmann, both because they are scientifically untenable in a world of lawful cause-and-effect and because they are theologically inadequate: the transcendent cannot be represented in the categories of the objective world.
>
> Moreover, he insists, the true meaning of scriptural myth always did involve man's self-understanding. The gospel was concerned about man's hopes, fears, decisions and commitments in the present, not about miraculous occurrences in the past.
> (Barbour, *Myths, Models and Paradigms*)

Myths are often incompatible with scientific understanding of the world

In essence, Bultmann rejected the mythological language of the New Testament as unhelpful to the modern mind. He believed it actually obstructed a modern faith, and his work on demythologisation set out to present a gospel message that was free from the unscientific descriptions found in the mythical language of the New Testament. In summary, Bultmann believed that the world of the New Testament was mythical in character.

The mythical world of the New Testament

There were three levels in the physical world: Heaven above, Earth in the middle and an underworld beneath (this is based on the cosmological beliefs of Judaism as presented in this period of history).

Bultmann says:

> Heaven is the abode of God and of celestial beings – the angels. The underworld is hell, the place of torment. Even the earth is more than the scene of natural, everyday events, of the trivial round and common task. It is the scene of the supernatural activity of God and his angels on the one hand, and of Satan and his demons on the other.
> (Bultmann, 'The New Testament and Mythology')

Bultmann believed that the writers of the New Testament wanted to show that the everyday existence of human beings occurred in a world where supernatural forces were commonplace. They would intervene in human affairs, influence human thinking and even directly impact on human health and wellbeing.

The significance of all this was to show that human beings were not in control of their own lives. They could be physically possessed by evil spirits or inspired with evil thoughts by Satan; they could be the subject of miracles or visions from God; they could even take on fantastic or supernatural abilities after being inspired by the spirit of God.

> **Key quote**
>
> Can Christian preaching expect modern man to accept the mythical view of the world as true? To do so would be both senseless and impossible. It would be senseless, because there is nothing specifically Christian in the mythical view of the world as such. It is simply the cosmology of a pre-scientific age ... Modern thought as we have inherited it brings with it criticism of the New Testament view of the world.
>
> (Bultmann, 'The New Testament and Mythology')

Human history is both set in motion by and ultimately controlled by these supernatural forces – humankind is completely at their whim. These events are also set against the backdrop of a prophesised end of days where, as Bultmann says, there will be:

> ... a cosmic catastrophe. It will be inaugurated by the 'woes' of the last time. Then the Judge will come from heaven, the dead will rise, the last judgment will take place, and men will enter into eternal salvation or damnation.
> (Bultmann, *Kerygma and Myth*)

Summary

- As a specialised form of language, myth holds a unique place in all human cultures and religions.
- In the twentieth century, there was a tendency to try to deconstruct myths using empirical methodologies, but this has been criticised more recently as a reductionist approach and one that therefore misunderstands and even misrepresents the purpose of these accounts.
- There are a variety of different myths with common themes; these include myths of creation, myths of heroes and myths of good against evil.
- Challenges to myths and mythical language have considered issues relating to competing myths and the associated issues of their interpretation. A key thinker in this field was Rudolf Bultmann who, in the twentieth century, applied a process of demythologisation to the accounts in the New Testament.

AO1 Activity

a Examine key challenges to the meaningfulness of mythical language. Include reference to problems of competing myths; how time and culture can impact the meaning of myths; the concept of demythologisation; and the incompatibility of myths with science.

This helps with presenting a thorough and extensive knowledge and understanding of the topic area.

b Draw a two-column table. In the left-hand column, name a creation myth. In the right-hand column, identify common features of creation myths that appear in that particular myth. Find four or five examples from different cultures.

This helps with prioritising and selecting relevant material and with providing an excellent use of evidence and examples. It also means that you are able to make accurate reference to sacred texts and sources of wisdom, where appropriate.

> **Specification content**
> The effectiveness of the terms *non-cognitive*, *analogical* and *mythical* as solutions to the problems of religious language

> **This section covers AO2 content and skills**

Issues for analysis and evaluation

The effectiveness of the terms *non-cognitive*, *analogical* and *mythical* as solutions to the problems of religious language

Possible line of argument	Critical analysis and evaluation
Cognitive language does not reflect the whole of human experience	Treating language as if it can be directly provable, verified or falsified was the domain of those who wished to see language as being open to empirical enquiry. However, while certain aspects of language can indeed be open to such things, not all language is used in this way. In fact, to treat language purely cognitively (i.e. to view language as something that can be empirically tested) is to have a very narrow view of the function of language within the human experience.
Non-cognitive language is not empirically verifiable, yet is still meaningful	When language is non-cognitive, it is not used to express empirically knowable facts about the external world. It is not something that can be held up to objective scrutiny. This is because non-cognitive language is language that expresses opinions, attitudes, feelings and/or emotions. It is language that relates to a person's view of what reality may mean to him or her – and this may differ from the view of another, even though they may be experiencing the same reality. Both views are valid – but in a non-cognitive sense.
Non-cognitive language is necessary to reflect the richness of human existence	The effectiveness of such a way of viewing language is powerful because it is these forms of language that give human existence its richness and depth. Beliefs, ideals and relationships can only be expressed passionately in non-cognitive ways – a purely cognitive use of language would remove these things from human existence; an idea almost unimaginable.
Religious language reflects part of the human experience and should be valued as such	Why, then, should we consider religious language to have value only in a cognitive sense? The reaction to this would be that it is entirely unfair, inappropriate even, to expect of religious language something that would not be fairly expected of human language as a whole. Meaningfulness can come from more than one form of expression and, while objective agreement on what is being said may not always be possible, this should not undermine the effectiveness of meaning that can be transmitted in this way.
Religious believers often use religious language in a cognitive way when they express beliefs	However, some philosophers have identified a particular difficulty with the non-cognitive approach. Religious believers are not making statements about any kind of reality that could be described as 'objective'. This poses an issue for the religious believers who might state that 'God exists' or 'sacred writings are the word of God' or 'I believe in a life after death'. These are not just expressions of attitude for the religious believer. They are, in fact, and in the context appropriate to the particular religion, assertions about how reality actually is.
Such use of language cannot be open to verification and is therefore meaningless	In a very real sense, the religious believer considers these to be statements about the external world – in other words, is using them in a cognitive, not non-cognitive, sense. This brings us back to the original challenge from Logical Positivism, that such statements are neither analytic nor synthetic – they cannot be verified. Therefore, perhaps non-cognitive language is not an effective solution to the problems of religious language.

Possible line of argument	Critical analysis and evaluation
Analogies can be effective language tools	Analogies can be powerful language tools for communicating complex ideas in a far less complex way. They can make the unknowable knowable, albeit in a relational way. When talking about God, analogies – as Aquinas envisioned – allow us insights into God's character and being that would otherwise be impossible for us.
Analogies depend on knowing how far the objects being compared are similar	However, as Hume recognised, an analogy is only as good as the point at which the two things being compared are similar. The issue for religious language is: Do we know what we mean when we use the word 'God'? How do we 'know' (in the sense of being able empirically to quantify what we are talking about) what constitutes 'God'? Unless we are able, in some measure, to do this, then our point of comparison fails. If this fails, then so does the analogy, rendering analogical language not only meaningless but, in a very real sense, useless – as far as talking about God is concerned. This shows that analogical language is an ineffective solution to the problem of religious language.
Mythical language provides insight into the purpose of human existence	By rejecting the claims that religious language must make only empirically verifiable claims, mythical language offers a type of language use that permits insight into universal truths about existence and humankind's relationship with the universe. The myths of creation, the heroic myths and the myths concerning good versus evil do not have to be taken in a literal cognitive sense to provide meaning. It is the very fact that they are symbolic and highly imaginable, and make extensive use of metaphor, that permits myths to convey meaning in a unique way. This is how the meaning of life is revealed – not in an empirical way, but rather in an inspirational way. Myths, in this sense, are therefore an effective solution to the problem of religious language.
Mythical language is too open to interpretation	The counterargument is that myths can be interpreted in a myriad of different ways – and this can result in their meaning being unclear. The issue of competing myths can lead to undermining the understanding of the purpose of human existence.
Non-cognitive language does not solve the problems of religious language but still has value	From considering the various approaches of non-cognitive language to the problems of religious language, it would seem that it has not provided an effective solution. The challenges of meaningfulness, in the sense of a meaningfulness that can be universally accepted and agreed upon, seem too overwhelming to solve easily. However, that is not to say that the non-cognitive use of language has no value. It may not be an effective solution to the problems of religious language, but it does provide some partial solutions to these issues and should therefore be treated with a measure of respect.

AO2 Activity

a   Select three lines of argument from the critical analysis and evaluation of the effectiveness of the terms *non-cognitive*, *analogical* and *mythical* as solutions to the problems of religious language. Find three references from scholars, schools of thought or religious and philosophical texts that would support those arguments.

b   Using the strongest line of argument, try to identify three key quotations that might be used – they could be from scholars, religious texts or schools of thought.

Exam practice

Sample question
Evaluate the relevance of religious language issues in the twenty-first century.

Sample answer
The work of the Logical Positivists, which came to the fore in the early part of the twentieth century, ignited the debate about the meaningfulness of metaphysics and, in our sphere of study, religious language, in particular. The philosophical propositions that affirmed the importance of those tools that gave prominence and support to the field of scientific enquiry were the same as those used to undermine the meaningfulness of those things that belonged to the realm of metaphysics.

Therefore, religious language came under fire – essentially because its propositions and terminology could be neither verified nor falsified, belonged neither to the analytic nor synthetic forms of language that the scientific community were so fond of and, of course, religious language was neither tautological nor was it mathematical. It was therefore considered essentially meaningless. However, those who took a less narrow view of the meaningfulness within the world realised that the Logical Positivists had missed the point. Even their own verification principle fell foul of its own criteria – somewhat undermining its validity.

Philosophers such as Popper, Randall, Tillich and even, later, Wittgenstein were able to demonstrate that meaningfulness in language comes not from the words themselves but rather from the way they are used or the way we can interpret the context they come from. Meaningfulness can be understood in a myriad of ways that Logical Positivism had not given credit for and, therefore, the debates and credibility of Logical Positivism soon lost their force as the twentieth century, and the philosophical movements associated with it, developed. By the beginning of the twenty-first century, the debate about the meaningfulness of religious language had moved on considerably and the old criticisms just didn't seem to be effective any more.

So are these issues no longer relevant in the twenty-first century? Quite simply, the answer is yes – although the debate has matured somewhat. The issues regarding religious language, when we consider the issue of the inherent problems of religious language, have not disappeared. Religious language can, at its face value, often seem to be saying things that are difficult to understand or difficult to root in any meaningful way, once taken out of the context immediate to religious believers and their dialogue. In some instances, even religious believers can find it difficult to articulate the meaning of some of their own propositions – even though they claim that understanding is a matter of faith, not logic, and therefore not open to objective verification.

> **Specification content**
> The relevance of religious language issues in the twenty-first century

This is a clear introduction that provides a helpful overview of historical background to the issue being considered.

This paragraph brings the issue into focus by presenting relevant evidence relating to the specific challenges to religious language, along with an immediate counterpoint regarding a flaw in one of those.

This paragraph develops the previous line of reasoning by presenting relevant evidence.

The candidate raises a question that directly relates to the issue under debate, and provides a response that explores why it is still relevant.

> **Philosopher**
>
> The candidate raises a series of questions to demonstrate that the issues surrounding the initial debate have not been fully resolved.

The wider scope of the philosophy of language (as opposed to purely religious language) takes several things into consideration when reflecting on the purpose of language. For instance, what does our language reveal about reality? How does it do this and is it meaningful? What constitutes meaningfulness? Is it related to the ideas of empiricists such as Hume who proposed meanings were nothing more than mental contents brought about by specific signs; or is meaningfulness derived, as Wittgenstein said, through the way in which language is used? Or perhaps the Logical Positivists had it right when they suggested that meaning comes from what can be proven when linked to our knowledge of the physical world? We can relate each of these back to the debate about how religious language is used, and therefore demonstrate the relevance of religious language issues in the twenty-first century.

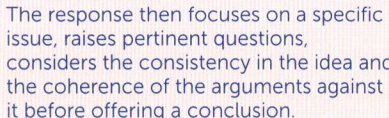

> The response then focuses on a specific issue, raises pertinent questions, considers the consistency in the idea and the coherence of the arguments against it before offering a conclusion.

In some senses, the debate has also narrowed. For instance, much discussion has been held about specific religious terms, such as the word *God*. For centuries, the word has been used as either a title, a descriptive noun or a name. In many religions, the word *God* is used as the respectful proper noun, whereas there is sometimes a more personal utterance that can be used to address the same being – especially in acts of devotion, worship and prayer. Such 'personal' names can be found in the Jewish and Hindu traditions – both of which would use the word *God* in its generic sense as well. A similar idea can be found in the mystical traditions of Christianity (e.g. in the works of Teresa of Avila) and Islam (e.g. in the works of Rumi), where the term *God* is replaced with a far more intimate form of address. In such cases, do they provide meaningfulness for the word that would otherwise not be available to those outside of the traditions? When atheists reject belief in God, they are not dismissing the term as one of nonsense or as something non-verifiable. They reject the term because of its associations with the reality it proposes. In many ways, we can liken the New Atheists to St Anselm's Fool, in the way in which they reject the word. Again, the relevance of religious language in the twenty-first century is evident.

Evaluation

This is an effective response. It considers the key issue and presents evidence to support its reasoning. The candidate makes accurate use both of terminology and of the views of different schools of thought.

Over to you

Your task is to write a response, under timed conditions, to a question requiring an evaluation of whether religious language still has meaning today. Do this exercise either as a group or independently.

A suggested approach is given on the next page.

Question
Evaluate whether religious language still has meaning today.

Suggested approach
1. Begin with a list of indicative arguments or lines of reasoning, as you may have done previously. This does not need to be in any particular order at first, although as you practise this you will see more order in your lists, particularly by way of links and connections between arguments.
2. Develop the list by using one or two relevant quotations. Now add some references to scholars and/or religious writings.
3. Write out your plan, under timed conditions, remembering the principles of explaining with evidence and/or examples.
4. Collaborative marking will help you appreciate alternative perspectives and possibly draw your attention to things you may have missed or the strengths of other arguments. With this in mind, it is a good idea to swap and compare answers.

When you have completed the task, refer to the band descriptors for A2 (WJEC) or A Level (Eduqas) and, in particular, look at the demands described in the higher band descriptors, which you should be aspiring towards. Ask yourself:

- Is my answer a confident, critical analysis and perceptive evaluation of the issue?
- Is my answer a response that successfully identifies and thoroughly addresses the issues the question raises?
- Does my work show an excellent standard of coherence, clarity and organisation?
- Will my work, when developed, contain thorough, sustained and clear views that I have supported with extensive, detailed reasoning and/or evidence?
- Have I used the views of scholars/schools of thought extensively, appropriately and in context?
- Does my answer convey a confident and perceptive analysis of the nature of any possible connections with other elements of my course?
- When used, is specialist language and vocabulary both thorough and accurate?

This section covers AO1 content and skills

Specification content

Meaningful to people who participate in same language game (Ludwig Wittgenstein); supportive evidence – non-cognitive form of language provides meaning to participants within language game; consider use of language not meaning; language games fit with coherence theory of truth; religious language as expressions of belief

F: Religious language as a language game

> **Key quote**
>
> One can mistrust one's own senses, but not one's own belief.
>
> Every word has a meaning. This meaning is correlated with the word. It is the object for which the word stands.
>
> (Wittgenstein, *Philosophical Investigations*)

Language games: an introduction

Imagine that a person comes to your home. She is there with the express purpose of helping to make some kind of home improvements. She talks about two-by-fours, noggins, risers, renders, second fixes and stocks. These words are interspersed by other words that you would understand from a standard conversation. You may feel justifiably confused by the person's conversation with you. However, you may find yourself agreeing with what she is asking of you just because you don't want to seem ignorant of words that, to all intents and purposes, are part of a standard English-language conversation, although the words themselves seem as if they form part of a different language.

In many ways, this is precisely what they are. It is understanding how language is used in this way (and, more significantly, how language is understood when it is used it in this way) that led Wittgenstein to develop his earlier philosophy of language. In his earlier philosophy, he discussed language as a kind of picture-based system of communication; he developed this into a philosophy of language that described language, and its use, in terms of **language games**.

Language games: meaningful to people who participate in the same language game

For Wittgenstein, it was imperative that we understand which game we are playing when we use particular forms of language. If we are unable to understand, then we will inevitably misunderstand how that particular language game is played. Equally, once all participants understand the language game they are playing, that language game becomes meaningful to them.

So, to borrow the example from above, if you trained as a person who undertook home improvements, then those phrases would become part of your language game and you would be able to use them and understand them; you would finally understand the 'rules' of the language game that you are playing. Language is a facility people use to communicate ideas that are specific to their particular form of life – their 'game'. Language is a social and public activity – it is through this that language is understood and its meaning is established.

There are many ways to use language, in the same way that there are many different ways to play games. This 'family resemblance' is an idea that permeated Wittgenstein's language games philosophy.

Ludwig Wittgenstein

Key term

language games: Wittgenstein's analogy that states that language is meaningful to those who use it within their own form of life/language game

As Wittgenstein states:

> What is common to all these activities, and what makes them into language or parts of language? ... I am saying that these phenomena have no one thing in common which makes us use the same word for all – but that they are related to one another in many different ways. And it is because of this relationship, or these relationships, that we call them all 'language'. (Wittgenstein, *Philosophical Investigations*)

The concepts of game and family resemblance

To appreciate that using language is analogous to playing a game, and that understanding this is key to understanding how language functions as a public activity, Wittgenstein first asks us to reflect on the concept of a game.

He lists a number of different games, such as 'boardgames, card-games, ball-games, Olympic games, and so on'. He then invites us to try and understand what it is that links them together; why it is that we regard them all as games.

In his examination of the different types of games that people may have experienced, Wittgenstein points out that the games have many elements in common. He also notes that these elements will change according to the types of game being played. He notes similarities between certain sorts of games that do not exist when those games are compared with other types of games, even though all are regarded as games.

For Wittgenstein, this ebb and flow of shared characteristics seemed to be particularly pertinent when he made the analogy between games and the use of language. The uses of language by empiricists and Logical Positivists share a very close relationship.

The relationship between these two uses of language and the use of religious language could also be established. Both uses of language include words, phrases and speech patterns to communicate particular information to their specific audiences. In this sense, they bear the same sort of resemblance as the games of chess and cricket.

Both are games, yet both have significant differences. These family resemblances 'overlap and criss-cross', which is what gives them their resemblances. Yet they are not the same. It would be a mistake to treat them in the same way, as they are clearly different – even though they share commonalities. The same can be said for the way in which language is used.

These relationships may exist in some games and not in others. When we look across all games, we can see these relationships in the same way as we might see the resemblance between people of the same family. Family members often share similar features but, other than in the case of identical twins, they never look exactly the same.

Evidence supporting Wittgenstein's theory of language games

Language games fit with the coherence theory of truth

In philosophical terms, there are two main understandings of the concept of truth. These are *correspondence* and *coherence*.

Correspondence

The **correspondence understanding of truth** is often referred to by certain philosophers as the **realist** position. In this understanding of truth, something is held to be true (or 'meaningful') by virtue of its relationship to the external

> **Key terms**
>
> **correspondence understanding of truth:** belief that something is true because it relates (corresponds) to an objective external reality
>
> **realist:** the philosophical position that adopts the correspondence understanding of truth

and knowable world. It is very much an empiricist position and is a view of truth that is sympathetic to the philosophical position of the Logical Positivists.

For instance, if I assert that 'the grass is green', then the truth of that statement can be verified by determining what is meant by the noun *grass* and then identifying whether that noun was *green* in the sense of the colour green as agreed by the standard interpretation of the light spectrum. If the colour of the grass corresponds to the statement (i.e. the grass is green), then the truth of that statement is established. If the grass is any other colour, then the statement is considered to be 'false' in the sense that it is not meaningful to say that the grass is green because it is some other colour.

Another way to appreciate the correspondence understanding of truth is to cite an example from history: the belief that the planet that we live on is approximately spherical in shape. This belief is true because we know that it corresponds to the actual reality of the shape of the planet – as verified by photographic, geophysical and mathematical evidence.

Coherence

The coherence understanding of truth is somewhat different. In this instance (sometimes referred to as the **anti-realist** position), the truth of a matter is determined, not by its correspondence to an external reality, but rather by its interpretation within a specific group of people. For instance, with reference to the previous example of the colour of the grass, if, for whatever reason, a group of people decided that the use of the adjective *red* was the correct adjective for the colour of the grass, then the statement 'the grass is green' would not, in their view, be true. That is because the 'grass is green' does not *cohere* (or fit with) their understanding of what it means for the grass to be a specific colour. For them, the statement 'the grass is red' would be meaningful and therefore true, in their view of the world. Truth is determined not by an external reality, but rather by an interpretation of that reality that may (or may not) be true.

> **Key term**
>
> **anti-realist:** a philosophical position that adopts the coherence understanding of truth

Again, an example from history is useful here. Prior to the seventeenth century, the shape of the Earth was not widely accepted as spherical. Many people believed that the Earth was flat, and their world-view was determined as 'true' because it fitted with how they believed reality actually was. That this was scientifically inaccurate did not matter – for them, it was 'true' because it helped them make sense of the world in which they lived. It *cohered* with their understanding of the physical world and therefore represented a truth of the shape of the world.

Flat versus round Earth: coherence versus correspondence theories of truth

In simple terms, we can argue that the use of language games to determine how language is meaningful to the people who participate in that particular language game is an anti-realist or coherence theory of truth position.

Non-cognitive form of language provides meaning to participants within language game

Language in this context is understood to be non-cognitive, rather than cognitive. The meaningfulness comes from the context within which the form of language is used. It therefore provides meaning to those who participate in the game, even if it is not always clear what the meaning is to those outside the game.

Wittgenstein does not conclude that each language game is entirely exclusive, as each game can be 'learned' as long as the rules can be explained and understood. This is because, in common with games, language use has common features – a 'family resemblance', as already stated. As language is always a public activity – Wittgenstein strongly denied that language could ever be considered as a private activity – it was an activity that was potentially open to all. To restate this point: each language game could be learned.

Consider use of language not meaning

Once the individual understands the rules of the language game, he or she will understand the meaning of the language. Or – to put it in the way that Wittgenstein did – the meaningfulness of the language comes, not from the words themselves, but rather from the way in which those words are used.

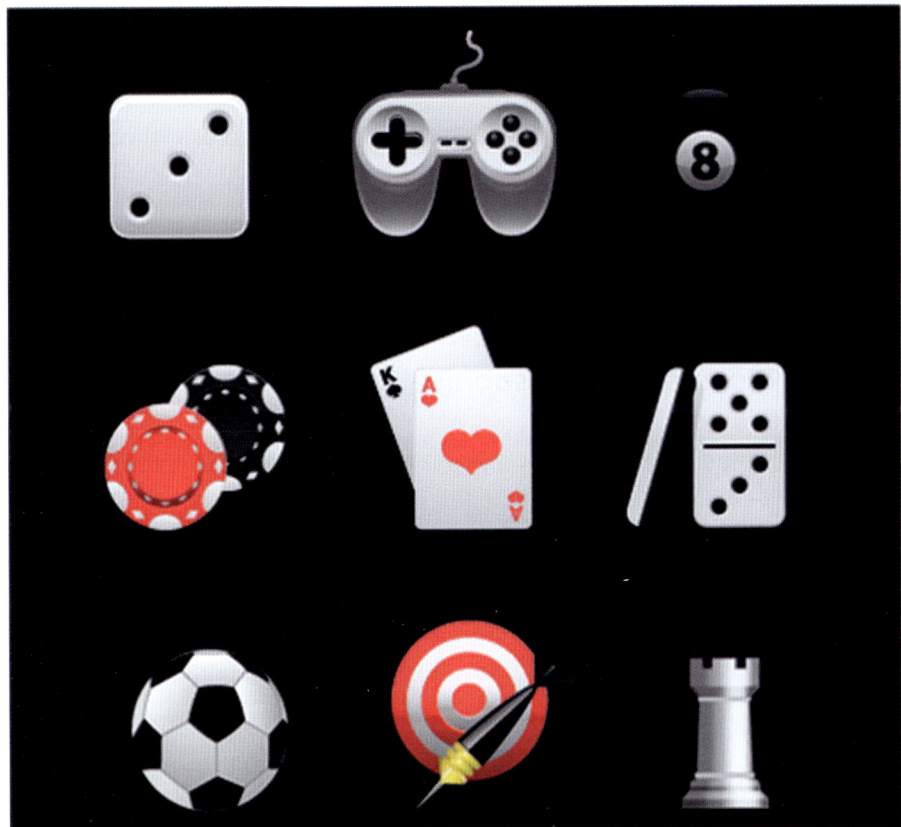

The concept of different ways to play games allows us to understand how we can use language in different ways too

> ## " Key quote "
>
> For a *large* class of cases – though not for all – in which we employ the word 'meaning' it can be defined thus: the meaning of a word is its use in the language.
>
> **(Wittgenstein,** *Philosophical Investigations*)

Wittgenstein further noted that understanding language is not always a straightforward task. He draws a parallel with what it means to understand a picture. When we listen to words and sounds, ultimately they mean nothing unless placed into context. Wittgenstein said the same was true of a picture or painting. A painting is actually nothing more than the arrangement of colours – 'patches of colour on the canvas' – and should not make any sense at all. However, because we appreciate what the picture relates to, we are able to make sense of it. The arrangement of colours takes on relatable shapes and images and means something to us – so that the picture becomes a picture of something.

When we understand what the colours and shapes represent, we can understand the picture; in the same way, when we understand the sounds that are being made or the shapes on the page, we can understand the language

The same is true with language: the random sounds become sounds that mean something because they are relatable; we understand them because we have learned to understand them; and we associate them with their respective meanings according to the way in which we have learned them.

To put it another way, in learning the rules of the particular language game that we are involved in, we are able to understand the sounds that we hear or the words that we read because we are able to understand the rules of the language game.

Religious language as expressions of belief

Understanding that religious language, as a particular language game, has its own rules is significant when we consider how meaningful it is. Expressing beliefs such as 'God exists', 'there is life after death', 'I have an immortal soul' and 'my actions in this life will affect what happens to me in the next' may not be meaningful to those outside religious traditions but, as Wittgenstein observed, this is because they are not part of the language game that is religious language. The beliefs are meaningful within the language game – it is irrelevant whether others accept them as meaningful because weighing the meaningfulness of a statement by this criterion is a complete misunderstanding of Wittgenstein's argument.

Language games: a philosophical tool to understand how language is used

Ultimately, Wittgenstein recognised that the scope of his investigations into the use of language was to present a philosophical view of how language is used – not to influence its use or to change how we use language, but purely to recognise, through the tools of the philosopher, the function of language in the human sphere of existence:

> Philosophy may in no way interfere with the actual use of language; it can in the end only describe it. For it cannot give it any foundation either. It leaves everything as it is.
> (Wittgenstein, *Philosophical Investigations*)

Challenges to Wittgenstein's theory of language games

Rejection of any true proposition in religion that can be empirically verified

First and foremost, Wittgenstein's theory of language games is a theory that treats language in a non-cognitive rather than a cognitive way. As such, many of the criticisms or challenges that can be levelled against non-cognitivism also apply to language games.

So, for example, where a statement is regarded as cognitive, we know that it is providing us information about the external world that we can verify, by applying empirical methods. This means that some things that we speak about can be objectively verified or proven as true. In this instance, the statement 'God exists', which many theists contend as being a statement that is knowable through experience, is true.

> **Specification content**
>
> Challenges, including rejection of any true propositions in religion that can be empirically verified; does not allow for meaningful conversations between different groups of language users; does not provide adequate meaning for the word 'God'

However, as soon as we treat language as being non-cognitive, we are recognising that language is not being used in a way that can be held up to objective scrutiny. Therefore, we are implying that any religious language statement cannot be held up to be objectively true. At least, we cannot prove it as such.

Many theists would find this position at best distasteful and at worst abhorrent. The statement 'God exists' for them is objectively true. Similarly, any faith claim, used cognitively, is open to empirical verification. When it is treated as being non-cognitive, it is not open to such verification.

Is there a cognitive way to talk about God?

Wittgenstein's theory does not allow for meaningful conversations between different groups of language users

One of the other general critiques of Wittgenstein's theory is that each language game has its own rules that are pertinent to it; they do not extend, in their entirety, to any other game (although other language games may share similarities with it).

If so, this suggests that it would not be possible for two users of different language games to communicate in an entirely meaningful way between them – for they would each be using language in a way that was unique to them.

The anti-realist position, while defending the 'truth' within each group, is unable to objectify that truth between groups, and so could lead to both misunderstanding and confusion. If neither group can lay claim to an objective truth (as would be the case with the realist position), then how can they find a middle ground where they are able to communicate meaningfully with each other? The inclusivity of meaningfulness within each language game would seem inevitably to lead to an exclusivity of meaningfulness when the two (or more) groups attempt to communicate with each other.

Wittgenstein's theory does not provide adequate meaning for the word *God*

Finally, if the word *God* has no objective meaning, then how can we talk meaningfully about God? An anti-realist approach to the word *God* would undermine attempts to define God, such as those offered by St Anselm ('God is that than which nothing greater can be conceived'), Descartes ('God is the supremely perfect Being') and Malcolm ('God as unlimited being').

If the word *God* becomes subject to a language game, then that would imply that there is no definitive, objective, cognitive way to use the word, and it could therefore lead to uncertainty about what is meant when the word is used in any given context. For instance, would the word *God* mean the same to the theist and atheist?

Wittgenstein would regard them as playing different language games, so how, therefore, can we know that what the atheist is denying is actually the same thing that the theist is affirming? Many religious believers would assert that the word *God* has a definitive, cognitive meaning and would struggle to accept anything else. This suggests that perhaps Wittgenstein's language games seem not to allow for an adequate meaning of the word *God*.

Summary

- Ludwig Wittgenstein, in his *Philosophical Investigations*, proposed the idea that language derives its meaning from its use, rather than any other factor. To explain this idea, he developed his analogy of language games.

- He recognised that language, like games, has common factors, but considered these to be more of a 'family resemblance' than actual identical features.

- Wittgenstein stated that, unless individuals understand the rules of the game they are playing, they will not be able to participate successfully in it and certainly won't understand it. He proposed that the way that we access language is the same.

- Challenges to Wittgenstein's ideas include the accusation that he treats language in a purely non-cognitive way and this has the consequence of reducing religious language to something that cannot be objectively true; if the word *God* has no objective meaning, then how can religious believers talk meaningfully about God?

AO1 Activity

a Explain how Wittgenstein uses the analogy of games to demonstrate how language is understood.

This helps with presenting a thorough and extensive knowledge and understanding of the topic area.

b Construct an information diagram or mind map that separates Wittgenstein's ideas about language games into key areas for focus.

This helps with prioritising and selecting a core set of points to develop an answer and with making accurate use of specialist language and showing an excellent standard of coherence, clarity and organisation.

> **Specification content**
> The extent to which language games provide a suitable way of resolving the problems of religious language

> **This section covers AO2 content and skills**

Issues for analysis and evaluation

The extent to which language games provide a suitable way of resolving the problems of religious language

Possible line of argument	Critical analysis and evaluation
Effective communication depends upon language being understood	Language is the vehicle that we use for most of our communication. It allows us to articulate our wishes, our feelings, our knowledge, our beliefs. As language functions in this way for us to articulate, it also functions in a way where all those things are potentially decipherable for the receivers of these communications. Language, then, is a two-way process involving both transmitters and receivers – relying on the assumption that what is being transmitted can be received and understood. When a person first learns a language, it is something he or she does in infancy, and it is intimately bound to the cultural and societal conventions where the language is being learned.
Problems of religious language can arise because it is not understood	The problems of religious language arise when someone from outside the tradition (comparable to someone attempting to understand a language that he or she has not been taught) attempts to understand what is being said. If people are not schooled in the form of language being used, then it is highly unlikely that they will be able to appreciate what the religious person is trying to communicate. To explain religious concepts to a person with no appreciation of the religion being discussed is like two individuals attempting to communicate using two different languages.
Religious language is often not understood because it is treated the same as language about the empirical world	This has inevitably led to some regarding religious language as a 'nonsense', suggesting that the propositions within it have no place in the 'real' world. In many of these cases, the language of religion is interpreted through an empirically focused lens. The words and phrases of the religious person are held up to the scrutiny of objects relating to the external physical world and, again inevitably, are unable to be understood in such a way. Meaningful dialogue can therefore not be established and the task of the non-religious believers to understand the religious believer is doomed to failure. This then leads to a dismissal of religious beliefs and the language that expresses them as being ultimately meaningless – but is this fair?
Wittgenstein's theory of language says that forms of languages should be given their own categories, much like what happens with games	The work of Wittgenstein with language games leads to a resounding denial of the last claim. Wittgenstein's assertion that we should be looking, not for the meaning of words, but for how they are used is an essential gateway into understanding the world of religious language. Equally, the idea that language can be categorised into a series of 'games' according to the form of life that they are representing (in this case, the religious form of life) is particularly useful in helping us to realise that it is inappropriate to try and understand the rules of the religious language game by applying the rules of another language game (in the case of the Logical Positivists, the empirical game).

Possible line of argument	Critical analysis and evaluation
If religious language is understood as its own 'game', then the problems around it no longer exist	Therefore, recognising religious language as a specific game means that there is an appreciation that it has certain rules that apply to it. By engaging with those rules and coming to an understanding of them, we are able at least to appreciate what is being communicated within the 'game'. Therefore, we can largely resolve the challenges to religious language that come from the Logical Positivists.
Meaningfulness comes through participation	Finally, the problems of religious language can be resolved by the use of Wittgenstein's language games because understanding that something has validity for those within the game – even if it doesn't for those external to it – is to adopt a coherence theory of truth. Meaningfulness is established through participation. What is meaningful for those within the group may be nonsense to those outside, but that view should not detract from the point that there is a very real sense of meaning attached to the use of that particular language within the group.
A lack of understanding from one should not detract from the meaningfulness of another	I may not understand the language that those working within the building trades employ, but I recognise that it has meaning for them, and that the structure and integrity of the house that I live in depends on their language having a very real meaning for all those associated in the work that they do. My understanding of their language should not detract from the meaningfulness that it has for them.
Language games successfully solve the problems of religious language	The same can be applied to the Logical Positivists and others who claim that religious language is problematic and ultimately meaningless. Religious language may not be meaningful to them or to others outside of the sphere of religious activity but, as long as it serves the purpose of bringing meaning and cohesion to the community that uses it, then religious language is a valid and meaningful form of language. Adopting such a view shows that using Wittgenstein's language games resolves the problems of religious language.

AO2 Activity

a Analyse three possible conclusions that could be drawn from the critical analysis and evaluation of the extent to which language games provide a suitable way of resolving the problems of religious language. What are their strengths and weaknesses? Which conclusion is strongest?

b Using the strongest conclusion, select three lines of argument that you would use to support this conclusion. Try to explain why you have selected these.

Exam practice

Sample question
Evaluate whether the strengths of language games outweigh the weaknesses.

Sample answer
Wittgenstein's contribution to the religious language debate is significant. The initial challenge from the Logical Positivists, in asserting that religious language as essentially metaphysical was meaningless, was a particularly bold assertion. Nevertheless, it caused reaction from those who wished to defend the integrity of language use in religion, and the language debate widened. The Logical Positivists had treated language as entirely cognitive – something that could be held up to objective scrutiny. This meant that it could be proven either true or false and, consequently, meaningful or meaningless. As religious language, understood in this sense, could not be verified or falsified, it was condemned as meaningless and consigned to Hume's flames as being little more than sophistry.

Wittgenstein, who was initially associated with the Logical Positivists, developed his earlier philosophy and ended up refuting much of his early work. He recognised that language use was what made it meaningful; not purely its definition and application to empirical testing. In this interpretation, Wittgenstein saw language as non-cognitive – it held meaning for those who used it: deep meaning; meaning associated with passionate statements, significant emotional attachments and life-changing commitments. This then was one of language game theory's initial strengths: namely, that it recognised that religious language was made meaningful through its use by the religious believer. The way the religious believer accessed and utilised the language gave the words meaning. Those words had clear transformational effects on the lives of religious believers; how then could they not be regarded as meaningful? By establishing religious language as a particular language game, Wittgenstein recognised that it related to a form of life that was unique; a way of living that defined itself through religious activity. By adopting Wittgenstein's analogy as accurate, the meaningfulness of religious language was unquestioned.

Religious language, as a language game, had its own rules, in common with all other language games. It was therefore possible for religious believers to teach other believers about these rules, to share them and thereby demonstrate the meaningfulness of the language. The strength of language games was evident as it showed not only how the meaningfulness of religious language could be shared among the community, but also that the rules could be taught to those who wished to learn, permitting religious language to be a self-sustaining system.

One of the criticisms sometimes levelled against language games is that they do not permit those outside the game to understand the way the language is true. This would suggest that the language game analogy is weak. However, this critique is only partially accurate. If there is willingness to learn, and a willingness to participate in the activity, then it is possible to learn the rules of the language game and to gain

> **Specification content**
> Whether the strengths of language games outweigh the weaknesses

News reporter
This is a good introduction that provides a helpful background to the debate. It uses terminology accurately.

Detective
The candidate presents evidence, via a line of reasoning, showing how Wittgenstein's language games gave legitimacy to the meaningfulness of religious language.

News reporter
This paragraph further consolidates the previous point with a specific overview of religious language and how it functioned as a language game.

This paragraph explores an alternative line of reasoning, looking at the coherence of the argument.

The response provides counterarguments and critiques and gives an appropriate explanation of these, in relation to the information presented so far.

This paragraph further develops the previous point via a different line of reasoning, examining the challenges to language games with a focus on non-cognitive language.

The response then considers the evidence presented so far and draws the conclusion, following two pertinent questions, that the persuasiveness of each form of argument may be an entirely subjective matter, based on preference.

an understanding of the meaning of the language. While Wittgenstein recognised that those outside of particular games, with no experience of them, may find them strange in terms of understanding what is going on, he never claimed that such games were entirely exclusive; only that those who had not had the experience or opportunity to learn the rules of the game would not be able to understand them.

While there are several strengths to the language games analogy, it is not without its weaknesses. The first weakness is within the analogy itself. If we reject the similarities between games and language, then Wittgenstein's language games analogy is severely weakened. As with any analogy, the strength of it is entirely determined by how far the two things being compared are similar. While there may be a passing resemblance between the two, we could argue that Wittgenstein stretches the similarity too far. It is possible to explain a game to someone who has never experienced a game before; however, it is not possible to explain the concept of language to someone who has never accessed language before. This is because an explanation of language has to be given in language, whereas this does not apply to an explanation of games.

A further weakness in the analogy is that, to know what it means to play a game, you need to know what people are doing when they play games. However, when a person uses language, it is not enough just to know what that person is doing; you also need to be able to understand him or her.

Another weakness in the language game theory comes from its non-cognitive stance. If language in religion cannot be treated cognitively, then does that mean that statements such as 'God exists' are not an expression of an external reality, but are instead nothing more than an opinion or expression of emotion? This would significantly undermine any rational basis that religion may lay claim to. Following this, how would religious believers know what they meant by using the word *God* if it meant something different in every religious language game that was played? Also, while the religious language game could be learned, it would be initially unclear, and this is something that could alienate rather than attract those from outside the game. Such an attitude would certainly seem contrary to the mission of some of the world religions, which seek to spread their faith beyond their existing membership.

It would seem that the weaknesses of language games are significant and cannot be easily dismissed. Are these weaknesses 'fatal flaws' in Wittgenstein's analogy? Is this just a matter of personal opinion, rather than academic debate? Wittgenstein's work is based on certain assumptions (that language is non-cognitive and that the rules of a game and the use of language are similar), which can either be accepted or rejected. It depends on which view is chosen whether the strengths of his language games analogy outweigh the weaknesses.

Evaluation

This is an effective and balanced response. It considers both sides of the argument and raises questions before putting forward a conclusion. The candidate makes accurate use both of terminology and of the views of different schools of thought.

Over to you

Given limitations of time, it is impossible for you to write full responses to all the possible examination questions you might be asked. However, it is a good exercise to develop detailed plans that you can use under timed conditions.

As a final exercise:
1. Create some ideal plans by using what we have done so far in the Theme 4 'Over to you' sections.
2. This time, stop at the planning stage and exchange plans with a study partner.
3. Check each other's plans carefully. Talk through any omissions or extras that could be included, not forgetting to challenge any irrelevant materials.
4. Remember, collaborative learning is very important for revision. It will not only help to consolidate your understanding of the course and your appreciation of the skills involved, but also increase your motivation and confidence. Although you will sit the examination alone, revising in a pair or small group is invaluable.

When you have completed the task, refer to the band descriptors for A2 (WJEC) or A Level (Eduqas) and, in particular, look at the demands described in the higher band descriptors, which you should be aspiring towards. Ask yourself:

- Is my answer a confident, critical analysis and perceptive evaluation of the issue?
- Is my answer a response that successfully identifies and thoroughly addresses the issues the question raises?
- Does my work show an excellent standard of coherence, clarity and organisation?
- Will my work, when developed, contain thorough, sustained and clear views that I have supported with extensive, detailed reasoning and/or evidence?
- Have I used the views of scholars/schools of thought extensively, appropriately and in context?
- Does my answer convey a confident and perceptive analysis of the nature of any possible connections with other elements of my course?
- When used, is specialist language and vocabulary both thorough and accurate?

Glossary

a posteriori: a statement that is based on actual observation, evidence, experimental data or experience – relates to *inductive reasoning*

a priori: without or prior to evidence or experience

actual infinite: a concept that suggests things can exist in time and space yet be never ending; this idea was classically rejected by Aristotle and is also rejected by Craig in his Kalam argument

actuality: when something is in its fully realised state

aesthetic: related to the concept and appreciation of beauty

Age of Enlightenment: an intellectual and philosophical movement in Europe in the eighteenth century

alpha-male: the dominant male in a community or group

Amrit: literally meaning 'immortality'; the name of the holy water that the Khalsa drink in the baptism ceremony in Sikhism

analogy: where something (that is known) is compared with something else (usually something unknown) to explain or clarify

anthropic: related to being human

anthropology: the study of human beings, their culture and social development

anti-realist: a philosophical position that adopts the coherence understanding of truth

apologist: a person who promotes and explains a specific point of view or cause, often in the context of responding to opposition to that view or cause

archetype: according to Jung, a primitive concept inherited from the earliest human ancestors and found in the collective unconscious

archetypes: literally meaning 'original pattern', these refer to symbolic forms that all people share in their collective unconscious; the archetypes give rise to images in the conscious mind and account for the recurring themes – these mould and influence human behaviour

atonement: making up for wrongdoing; the reconciliation of human beings with God through life, suffering and the sacrificial death of Christ

attributes: descriptive characteristics that someone or something possesses

attribution: relating to the attribute or characteristic an object possesses

blik: a term used by R.M. Hare to describe the point of view that someone may hold that influences the way he or she lives

charismatic worship: exuberant and expressive forms of worship, often involving ecstatic religious experiences (e.g. speaking in 'tongues' and healing miracles)

cognitive: language that is empirically verifiable and makes assertions about objective reality

coherence understanding of truth: belief that something is true when it fits in (coheres) with the views of those within the community

collective neurosis: a neurotic illness that afflicts all people

collective unconscious: elements of unconsciousness that are shared with all other people

contingency miracle: a remarkable and beneficial coincidence that is interpreted in a religious fashion

contingent: anything that depends on something else; in the case of a contingent being, it is contingent upon another being for its existence (e.g. a child is contingent upon its parent)

conversion: in a religious context, the change of state from one form of life to another

corporeal: of a material nature, physical

correspondence understanding of truth: belief that something is true because it relates (corresponds) to an objective external reality

deconstruct: analyse a text by taking it apart to work out what it means

deductive proof: a proof where, if the premises are true, then the conclusion must be true

disclosure: where something is made known that previously was hidden or unknown

dream-based: in terms of visions, the unconscious state where knowledge or understanding is gained through a series of images or a dream-narrative, which would not normally be available to the individual in the conscious state

ecstatic: an overwhelming feeling of bliss or peace

efficient cause: the 'third party' that moves potentiality to actuality

ego: the part of the psyche that resides largely in the conscious and is reality-orientated; it mediates between the desires of the id and the superego

empirical evidence: knowledge received by means of the senses, particularly by observation and experimentation

empirical knowledge: knowledge that is acquired (or acquirable) through the five senses; it is knowledge that provides information about the external, physical world

empirically: using knowledge gained through the experiences of any of the five senses

empiricist: a person who believes that all knowledge is based on sense experience

Enlightenment: in Buddhism, the experience of awakening to insight into the true nature of things

epistemic distance: a distance measured in terms of knowledge rather than space or time

equivocally: where there is more than one meaning, usually in relation to a word or phrase

eschatological verification: John Hick's assertion that certain religious statements may be verifiable at a future point (i.e. after death); in this sense, they are 'verifiable in principle' and should therefore be regarded as meaningful

evil: anything that causes pain or suffering

evolutionary theory: scientific theory, originally proposed in the nineteenth century, that posits that life developed from simpler to more complex life-forms via a process of natural selection and genetic mutation

ex nihilo: literally 'out of nothing'; a Latin term often associated with creation myths

faith: a strong belief or trust in something or someone

fallacy of composition: philosophical notion that what is true of the parts is not necessarily true of the whole (i.e. atoms are colourless but this does not mean that a cat, which is made of atoms, is colourless)

falsification: proving something false by using evidence that counts against it

free will: the theological and philosophical concept that states that humans have the ability to choose freely between good and evil

geological: the science relating to how the Earth was formed

God of classical theism: God as defined in religions such as Christianity, Islam and Judaism — a God who is held to possess certain attributes such as omnipotence, omniscience and omnibenevolence

id: the part of the psyche that resides in the unconscious and relates to basic needs and desires

incarnation: the Christian belief in the embodiment of God the Son in human flesh as Jesus Christ

individuation: the process of attaining wholeness and balance

inductive proof: argument constructed on evidence and/or experience that puts forward a possible conclusion based on these

ineffable: something that a person cannot speak of as no words can describe the experience

instinctual impulse: an instinct that is in the unconscious but active in the psyche

intellectual: in terms of visions, what brings the recipient(s) knowledge and understanding

Khalsa: literally meaning 'pure'; the name for those who have undergone the Amrit ceremony in Sikhism

language games: Wittgenstein's analogy that states that language is meaningful to those who use it within their own form of life/language game

laws of nature: the scientifically agreed physical laws by which the universe usually operates

Lent: in Christianity, a season of 40 days of prayer and fasting before Easter

literalist: interpreting the text of the Bible in a literal sense — that is, every word should be taken at face value; interpretation is not required

Logical Positivists: philosophers who supported the claim that language could be meaningful only if it could be verified by empirical means

mandala: a geometric design symbolic of the universe, often used in Buddhism as an aid to meditation; they are usually circular in form, with one identifiable centre point

metaphysical: something that is beyond, or not found in, the physical world

moral evil: evil caused as a result of the actions of a free-will agent

mysticism: a religious experience where union with God or the absolute reality is sought or experienced

natural evil: evil caused by the means of a force outside the control of free-will agents — usually referred to as 'nature'

natural theology: philosophical reasoning based on information that can be rationally gained about the physical world and that leads to revelation about the divine

natural world: the world of nature, comprising all objects (organic and inorganic)

naturalism: something that arises from real life or the world of nature

necessary being: Aquinas' contention that a non-contingent being is necessary for contingent beings to exist; it is this necessary being that is the source of all existence for all other contingent beings

New Atheism: also known as *antitheism*; the belief that religion is a threat to the survival of the human race

noetic: knowledge gained through mystical experience that would otherwise not be available to the recipient through ordinary means

non-cognitive: language that is not empirically verifiable or falsifiable, but instead expresses an attitude towards something

obsessional neurosis: sometimes called *compulsive neurosis*; uncontrollable obsessions that can create certain daily rituals

Oedipus complex: the theory that young boys are sexually attracted to their mothers but resent their fathers; the feelings are repressed as they fear the father — *Oedipus* refers to a character in a Greek legend that unwittingly killed his father and married his own mother

omnibenevolent: all-loving

omnipotent: all-powerful

ontological argument: argument for the existence of God based on the concept of the nature of being

partisan: person who holds a particular political view, usually someone who holds an opposing point of view from the ruling political powers; Basil Mitchell probably uses 'partisan' to refer to members of the resistance movement in the Second World War

passive: in the context of mysticism, where the mystical experience is 'done to' the recipient — it is not instigated by the individual or group, but is instead due to some kind of external force or influence

perfection: the complete absence of flaws; also the ultimate state of a positive trait

personal unconscious: memories that have been forgotten or repressed

potential infinite: the potential infinite is something that could continue, were effort to be applied (e.g. it would be possible always to continue a number line if we wanted to, as we could always come up with a bigger number)

potentiality: the ability to become something else

prayer: in simple terms, communication with the divine

predicate: a defining characteristic or attribute

premises: statements or propositions used to construct an argument

primordial: existing from the beginning

privation: the absence or loss of something that is normally present (e.g. *a privation of health* means that a person is ill and not healthy)

proportion: relating to the relative value of something according to its nature

Proslogion: a work written by St Anselm's, used as a meditation, but including within it the classical form of the ontological argument

psyche: the mental or psychological structure of a person

psychoanalysis: a method of studying the mind and treating mental and emotional disorders based on revealing and investigating the role of the unconscious mind

psychology: the study of the mind and behaviour

psychotherapy: treatment of mental or emotional illness by talking about problems rather than by using medicine or drugs

qualifier: a term used by Ramsey to mean a word or phrase used to give a deeper meaning to the model that the qualifier precedes

realist: the philosophical position that adopts the correspondence understanding of truth

reason: the use of logic in thought processes or in an argument

redemption: the act of saving something or someone; in the Christian context, it refers to Jesus saving humanity from evil and sin

reductio ad absurdum: an argument that shows a statement to be false or absurd if its logical conclusions were to be accepted

Reformation: the religious movement in Europe in the sixteenth century that led to the creation and rise of Protestantism

Renaissance: period of European history between the fourteenth and seventeenth centuries that was a time of great revival of art, literature and learning

revelation: a supernatural disclosure to human beings

Rosh Hashanah: the Jewish New Year

Sacrament: one of the Christian rites considered to have been instituted by Christ to confer or symbolise grace

sensory: a vision where external objects, sounds or figures convey knowledge and understanding to the recipient

Sitz im Leben: a German phrase meaning 'situation in life'; used as a theological term to refer to the context where an account is written usually influencing the writer because of the particular circumstances of the context

sophists: Greek teachers and writers particularly skilled in rhetoric and reasoning

soul-making: a process where the soul is developing towards spiritual perfection by gaining the wisdom always to make the correct moral choices when faced with the ambiguities of life as a human being

superego: part of the unconscious mind

symposium: a meeting, often academic or legal in nature, where a particular topic or subject is discussed

tabernacle: in Roman Catholicism, a box-like vessel for the exclusive reservation of the consecrated Eucharist

tautological: a self-explanatory statement in which something is repeated in different words (e.g. 'the evening sunset')

telos: this term can have a number of meanings, but it generally refers to the 'end' (as in the final destination), 'goal' or 'purpose' of something – the term is frequently found in Aristotle's philosophy

tenets: key beliefs or principles

thaler: currency used in eighteenth-century Prussia

the fall: the events of Genesis, Chapter 3, where Adam and Eve face God's punishment for disobeying his divine command not to eat of the fruit from the tree of knowledge of Good and Evil

theological propositions: beliefs or ideas put forward in the context of religious doctrines or philosophies

Theravada Buddhism: a school of Buddhism that draws its scriptural inspiration from the Pali canon

totem: something (e.g. an animal or plant) that is the symbol for a family or tribe

totemism: a system of belief where human beings are said to have some kinship or mystical relationship with a spirit-being (e.g. an animal or plant)

transcendent: everything that lies beyond the everyday realm of the physical senses

transient: an experience that is short-lived yet has far-reaching and/or long-lasting consequences

transubstantiation: the Roman Catholic doctrine that, in the Eucharist, the whole substance of the bread and wine changes into the substance of the body and blood of Christ

unitive: the feeling of complete oneness with the divine

univocally: where something has one universal and unambiguous meaning

verification: proving something true by using evidence that counts towards it

vision: the ability to 'see' something beyond normal experiences (e.g. the vision of an angel); such visions usually convey information or insight concerning a specific religious tradition

Yom Kippur: in Judaism, the day of Atonement and the holiest day of the year

Index

a posteriori 8–9, 14, 21
a priori 30, 34
Acts 113, 114–15
actual infinite 12
actuality 9
aesthetic argument 19
Age of Enlightenment 100
agnosticism 102–3
Allah 117–18
Allport, Gordon 93
alpha-male 75
Amrit 146–7
analogy 196–200, 236
Angels of Mons 113
anima/animus 89
anthropic principle 18–19
anthropology 128
antitheism 101, 103–12
apparent design 25
Aquinas, Thomas
  cosmological argument 9–11
  on language 178, 196–200
  on miracles 153, 160
  teleological argument 16
archetypes 87–90, 92, 229
Aristotle 9–10
Arnold, Matthew 101
atheism 99–112
atonement 76
Augustine of Hippo 58, 115, 122, 153
Augustine's theodicy 58–64
Ayer, Alfred J. 182–3
Baal 228
Becker, Carl 157
Big Bang theory 23, 26, 106
bliks 188
Buddha 90, 141
Buddhism 80, 92, 94, 99, 141–3, 157
Bultmann, Rudolf 232–3
Canaanite sun gods 228
Caravaggio 115
castration complex 77

cause and effect 10
celebrations 143
charismatic worship 144
Christian fundamentalism 107
Christianity 141–4, 147, 157, 223–6, 231–2
cognitive language 176–7, 235
collective neurosis 74–5
collective unconscious 86–7, 91
commitment, renewal of 146
complex design analogy 17–18
contingency 11
contingency miracle 154–5
conversion experiences 114–16, 149
cosmological argument 9–13, 21–3, 42–3
Craid, William Lane 11–13
creation myths 223–6
credulity 134
Cupitt, Don 101
Darwin, Charles 26, 74–5, 79
Dawkins, Richard 101–5, 109
deductive arguments 30–43, 34, 44–9
deductive proofs 30–1
Dennett, Daniel 103–4
Descartes, René 37–9, 41, 45, 47–8
Diagoras of Melos 99
Dostoyevsky, Fyodor 102
dream analysis 78–9, 83, 85, 91–2
dreams 114
   see also visions
Eckhart, Meister 116, 119
Edwards, Paul 213
efficient cause 10
ego 73, 86
Egypt, sun gods 227–8
empirical evidence 93, 96–7
empirical knowledge 8, 209
empiricism 164
Enlightenment 141
Ephesians 99
Epicurus
  Epicurean hypothesis 25

  Epicurean paradox 55
  logical problem of evil 51, 55
epistemic distance 66–7
equivocal language 195
eschatological verification 187
Everitt, Nicholas 103
evil 50–1
  Augustine's theodicy 58–64
  evidential problem of 53–4
  inconsistent triad 52–3
  Irenaean theodicy 66–71
  logical problem of 51, 55
  soul-deciding theodicy 59–60
  soul-making theodicy 66–7
  and suffering 50–5, 59, 68, 169
evolution 18–19, 26, 60–1, 79, 87, 106
ex nihilo 222
experience-based language 172–4
Ezekiel 113
faith 31, 141, 144–5
fall, the 60
fallacy of composition 23
falsification 176, 185–90
fasting 147
felix culpa 59
festivals 143, 147, 149
Flew, Antony 102, 166, 178, 185–6, 188
Franks Davis, Caroline 132, 137–8
free will 60–2, 68
Freud, Sigmund 73–86, 91, 95
Freund, Philip 225
fundamentalism 107
Gaunilo 41, 44, 47–9
gender identity 88
Genesis 60, 66, 196, 223–6, 231
God
  of classical theism 186
  defining 37–9, 245–6
  within 91
Grunbaum, Adolf 80
guilt 59, 74–9, 83, 84
Hardy, Alister 140

Hare, Richard 178, 187–8
Harris, Sam 103–4
healing 158–9
Hebrews 158
heroic myths 226–30
Hick, John 66–7, 186–7
Hinduism 80, 89, 115–16, 229
Hitchens, Christopher 101, 103–4
Holland, R.F. 154–5, 160
holy places 148, 158–9
Holy Spirit 114–15
Holyoake, George 100
Homer 99
Hume, David
   on evil 51
   on the existence of God 23–5, 27
   on language 173, 200
   on miracles 133, 153–4, 160, 164–5, 167–71
Huxley, Thomas 102
ichthus 214
id 73
incarnation 141
inconsistent triad 52–3, 56
individuation 90–1, 92
inductive arguments 8, 14–15
   challenges to 23–9
   cosmological 9–13, 21–3, 42–3
   teleological 16–20, 24, 42–3
inductive proofs 8
infinity 12
instinctual impulses 74
Irenaean theodicy 66–71
Irenaeus of Lyons 66, 226
Islam 114, 117–18, 141, 143, 157
Islamic fundamentalism 107
Jainism 99
James, William 115, 117, 122, 125–7, 129–30, 149
Jesus Christ 141, 143–4, 229
   resurrection 157–8, 232
   as saviour 60
   self archetype 90
John the Baptist 141
Judaism 142–3, 147, 157, 223–6, 231–2
Julian of Norwich 116
Jung, Carl 86–97, 229
Kalam cosmological argument 11–13

Kant, Immanuel 41, 45, 47–9
Keats, John 66
Khalsa 145–6
language
   analogy 196–200, 236
   cognitive/non-cognitive 176–7, 235–6, 242
   equivocal/univocal 195
   experience-based 172–4
   falsification 176, 185–90
   games 240–50
   metaphysical 173, 182
   mythical 221, 236
   qualifiers 199–200
   religious 174–6, 178–80, 191–2, 195–204, 235–8
   symbolic 206–18
   verification 176, 182–4, 186–7
   see also Logical Positivism
laws of nature 153–5, 165–6
Lent 147
libido 76, 78
literalists 60
Little Hans 78
Logical Positivism 173, 178, 182–3, 191–4, 201–2, 213, 218–19
Lord's Prayer 149
Lourdes 158–9
Mackie, J.L. 52–3, 56
Malcolm, Norman 39–40
Malinowski, Bronislaw 80
mandala 90
Martyr, Justyn 99
Maslow, Abraham 210
Matt, D.C. 221
McGrath, Alister 102, 106–8
McKinnon, Alistair 160
mediation 92, 146
metaphysical language 173, 182
Miller, Ed 116
miracles 153–71
Mitchell, Basil 134, 188–9
Momen, Moojen 227
Mool Mantra 142, 149
moral evil 50–1
Morrison, Grant 226
Moses 143, 157
mysterium tremendum 128

mysticism 116–21, 125–30
mythical language 221–33, 236
myths 221–33
natural evil 50–1
natural laws 153–5, 165–6
natural selection 26
natural theology 208
natural world 18
naturalism 128
necessary being 11, 39
neurosis 74, 77, 79–82, 85, 91–2
New Testament 142, 221–2, 229, 232–3
Niebuhr, Reinhold 206
non-cognitive language 176–7, 235–6, 242
numinous experience 127–8, 130–1
obsessional neurosis 74
Oedipus complex 76–7, 80, 84
Oedipus Rex 76
omnibenevolence 37, 52–3, 60–1, 68
omnipotence 37, 45, 52
omnipresence 45
omniscience 37
ontological argument 31–5, 37–43, 47–9
opposition 145–6
Otto, Rudolf 91, 127–8, 130–1
Paley, William 17–18, 20, 196
Paley's watchmaker 196
Pankejeff, Sergei 78–9
Paul, Gregory S. 54, 56
Paul the Apostle 142
perfections 37
persona archetype 87–8
personal growth 86–7
personal unconscious 86
personality 73
pilgrimage 145, 148–9
Plato 20
Polkinghorne, John 106
Popper, Karl 185
potential infinite 12
potentiality 9
prayer 119–21, 146, 149
   see also worship
predicates 45
premature deaths 54

primal horde 74–6, 79
primordial themes 87
privation 59, 62
Proslogion 31–2, 39
psyche 73, 86–7
psychoanalysis 73, 79
psychology 73, 92
psychoneurosis 91–2
    see also neurosis
psychosexual development 76
psychotherapy 79
qualifiers 199–200
Ra 227–8
Ramsey, Ian 199–201
Randall, John 206–10, 214–19
reason 31
redemption 60
reductio ad absurdum 44
reductionist view 93
Reformation 100
religious experience 91, 122–4, 140, 150–1
    as affirmation 141–2
    challenges to 132–8
    community cohesion 143
    conversion 114–16
    holy places 148, 158–9
    impact of 141–9
    miracles 153
    mysticism 116–21, 125–30
    visions 113–16
religious language see language
Renaissance 100
resurrection myths 229
revelation 141, 210
Revelation (Book of) 113
rituals 141, 144
Robinson, John 100
Rosh Hashanah 147
Rowe, William 53–4, 56
Rumi 117–18

Sacrament 167
salvation 68
Schlick, Moritz 182
Schreber, Daniel 78
science
    and language 177, 207
    and religion 20–2, 27, 80, 91, 105–7, 207–8
second-order goods 67
self archetype 89–91, 92
self-realisation 90
sexual identity 76, 89
shadow archetype 88–9
Shakti 89
signs versus symbols 209
    see also symbols
Sikhism 115, 142, 145–7
sin 58–9, 88
Singh, Sundar 115
Sitz im Leben 221–2
Smart, Ninian 140, 155
Socrates 99
sophists 99
Sophocles 76
soul-deciding theodicy 59–60
soul-making theodicy 66–7
Spencer, Herbert 26
St Anselm 31–2, 39, 41, 44, 47–9
St Augustine see Augustine of Hippo
St Bernadette 113
St Bernard of Clairvaux 118–19
St Teresa of Avila 114
St Thomas Aquinas see Aquinas, Thomas
Stevens, Cat 114
stewardship 226
suffering 50–5, 59, 68
Sufism 117
sun gods 227–30
superego 73, 77
Suso, Henry 119

swastika 214
Swinburne, Richard 134, 155–7, 160, 165–8, 170–1, 189–90
symbolic language 206–18
symbols 206, 209–14
synthetic statements 182
tabernacle 167
Taoism 99
tautological statements 182
teleological argument 24, 42–3
teleological arguments 16–20
telos 16
Ten Commandments 143
Tennant, F.R. 18–20
Teresa of Avila 118, 119–21
thalers example 45
Theravada Buddhism 94
Tillich, Paul 206, 210–14, 215–19, 225–6
totemism 75
transcendence 116
transubstantiation 167
universal salvation 68
univocal language 195
unlimited being 39
verification 176, 182–4, 186–7
Vienna Circle 182, 213
Virgin Mary 89
visions 113–16
water, as symbol 223–5
Werleman, C.J. 109
Wesley, John 115
Whirling Dervishes 118
Wisdom, John 185–6
wish fulfilment 77
Wittgenstein, Ludwig 240–50
Wolf Man 78–9
worship 144
   see also prayer
Yahweh 228
Yom Kippur 147

Photo credits

Photos reproduced by permission of: p.8 © Antonbrand/stock.adobe.com; **p.11** © Artem Shadrin/stock.adobe.com; **p.16** © Joe Gough/stock.adobe.com; **p.17** © Mikecarduk/stock.adobe.com; **p.19** © Mick-j/stock.adobe.com; **p.23** © Marina Sun/stock.adobe.com; **p.25** © Debbie Ann Powell/stock.adobe.com; **p.26** © Justin Hobson/Royal Geographical Society/Alamy Stock Photo; **p.30** © Fieldwork/stock.adobe.com; **p.31** Wikimedia Commons; **p.37** *t* © North Wind Picture Archives/Alamy Stock Photo, *b* © SAMYA/stock.adobe.com; **p.38** © Francesco/stock.adobe.com; **p.44** © Alma_sacra/stock.adobe.com; **p.45** © Georgios Kollidas/stock.adobe.com; **p.50** *cl* © Markobe/stock.adobe.com, *cr* © Kasto/stock.adobe.com, *bl* © Oleksandr Pokusai/stock.adobe.com, *br* © AungMyo/stock.adobe.com; **p.58** © Petrik/stock.adobe.com; **p.59** © Vladischern/stock.adobe.com; **p.67** © Dolphfyn/stock.adobe.com; **p.68** © Stillfx/stock.adobe.com; **p.74** © LIGHTFIELD STUDIOS/stock.adobe.com; **p.75** © Kennytong/stock.adobe.com; **p.76** © Erik Cornelius/Nationalmuseum; **p.80** *tl* Malinowski/3/18/2. Malinowski archive/LSE Library, *bl* © Louise Batalla Duran/Alamy Stock Photo; **p.86** Photo from Clark University; **p.88** *t* © Carlos_bcn/stock.adobe.com, *b* © Siphosethu Fanti/Peopleimages.comf/stock.adobe.com; **p.89** *tr* © Vadim Cebaniuc/stock.adobe.com, *b* © atiger/stock.adobe.com; **p.90** © Stnazkul/stock.adobe.com; **p.99** © The Picture Art Collection/Alamy Stock Photo; **p.101** © Anthony Devlin/PA Images/Alamy Stock Photo; **p.102** © Pictorial Press Ltd/Alamy Stock Photo; **p.104** *cl* © Jeff Gilbert/Alamy Stock Photo, *cr* © GL Portrait/Alamy Stock Photo, *bl* © D Legakis/ATHENA PICTURE AGENCY ZING LIMITED/Alamy Stock Photo, *br* © EPA/Epa european pressphoto agency b.v./Alamy Stock Photo; **p.106** © Photo Researchers/Science History Images/Alamy Stock Photo; **p.115** © Rudall30/stock.adobe.com; **p.116** © AndreusK/stock.adobe.com; **p.118** © Fahrettin/stock.adobe.com; **p.119** © Bill Perry/stock.adobe.com; **p.120** © Georgy/stock.adobe.com; **p.125** © Kues1/stock.adobe.com; **p.126** © Prostock-studio/stock.adobe.com; **p.127** *c* © PX Media/stock.adobe.com, *br* © Choat/stock.adobe.com; **p.133** © Art Alex/stock.adobe.com; **p.135** © Slonme/stock.adobe.com; **p.140** *cl* © Pressmaster/stock.adobe.com, *c* © Godong Photo/stock.adobe.com, *cr* © WESTOCK/stock.adobe.com; **p.142** © Taras/stock.adobe.com; **p.143** Wikimedia Commons; **p.144** © Thew/stock.adobe.com; **p.146** © Dinodia Photos/Alamy Stock Photo; **p.148** © Vector Tradition/stock.adobe.com; **p.153** © GRANGER - Historical Picture Archive/Alamy Stock Photo; **p.154** *tl* © Godong Photo/stock.adobe.com, *tc* © North Wind Picture Archives/Alamy Stock Photo; **p.156** © Pixel-Shot/stock.adobe.com; **p.158** © PhotoGranary/stock.adobe.com; **p.159** © Epa european pressphoto agency b.v./Alamy Stock Photo; **p.172** © Mintra/stock.adobe.com; **p.174** © Vovan/stock.adobe.com; **p.175** © Artisticco/stock.adobe.com; **p.176** © Igor kisselev/Shutterstock.com; **p.183** *cl* © Racksuz/stock.adobe.com, *c* © DG-Studio/stock.adobe.com; **p.186** © Andreaobzerova/stock.adobe.com; **p.187** © ABCDstock/stock.adobe.com; **p.189** © Mashikomo/stock.adobe.com; **p.190** © Moviestore Collection Ltd/Alamy Stock Photo; **p.195** *bl* © Jonathan Werner/stock.adobe.com, *b* © Pituk/stock.adobe.com, *br* © Sasiko kaan/stock.adobe.com; **p.196** © Bigmen/stock.adobe.com; **p.197** *tl* © Coetzee/Peopleimages.com/stock.adobe.com, *tr* © Menno Schaefer/stock.adobe.com; **p.198** © Missty/stock.adobe.com; **p.206** © Chekman/stock.adobe.com; **p.207** © EtiAmmos/stock.adobe.com; **p.209** © Sangkatang Jungpang/stock.adobe.com; **p.211** © MicroOne/stock.adobe.com; **p.213** © Ribah/stock.adobe.com; **p.214** *t* © Magann/stock.adobe.com, *c* © All themes/Shutterstock.com; **p.215** *tl* © Terri/stock.adobe.com, *t* © James Steidl/stock.adobe.com, *tr* © Xiaotong Ge/stock.adobe.com; **p.221** © TungCheung/stock.adobe.com; **p.224** *c* © Marinela/stock.adobe.com, *b* © Andrej pol/stock.adobe.com; **p.226** © Elenarts/Shutterstock.com; **p.227** *cl* © Deyan G. Georgiev/Shutterstock.com, *c* © Willrow Hood/stock.adobe.com, *cr* © Vividflowstudio/stock.adobe.com; **p.228** © Vladimir Zadvinskii/stock.adobe.com; **p.230** © Stockillustrator/stock.adobe.com; **p.240** © GRANGER - Historical Picture Archive/Alamy Stock Photo; **p.242** © Dulya/stock.adobe.com; **p.243** © Laenz/Shutterstock.com; **p.244** © Fine Art Images/Heritage Image Partnership Ltd/Alamy Stock Photo; **p.245** © Peter Barritt/Alamy Stock Photo.